New Perspectives on

Microsoft®
Visual Basic® 5.0
for Windows®

INTRODUCTORY

The New Perspectives Series

The New Perspectives Series consists of texts and technology that teach computer concepts and microcomputer applications (listed below). You can order these New Perspectives texts in many different lengths, software releases, custom-bound combinations, CourseKits™ and Custom Editions®. Contact your Course Technology sales representative or customer service representative for the most up-to-date details.

New Perspectives on
Microsoft®
Visual Basic® 5.0
for Windows®

Michael V. Ekedahl

William A. Newman
University of Nevada—Las Vegas

COURSE
TECHNOLOGY

ONE MAIN STREET, CAMBRIDGE, MA 02142

an International Thomson Publishing company I T P®

Cambridge • Albany • Bonn • Boston • Cincinnati • London • Madrid • Melbourne • Mexico City
New York • Paris • San Francisco • Singapore • Tokyo • Toronto • Washington

New Perspectives on Microsoft Visual Basic 5.0 for Windows®—Introductory is published by Course Technology.

Associate Publisher	Mac Mendelsohn
Series Consulting Editor	Susan Solomon
Product Manager	Cindy Johnson
Developmental Editor	Kathleen Habib
Production Editor	Nancy Ray, Nancy Shea
Text and Cover Designer	Ella Hanna
Cover Illustrator	Douglas Goodman

© 1998 by Course Technology.
A Division of International Thomson Publishing Inc —I(T)P®

For more information contact:

Course Technology
One Main Street
Cambridge, MA 02142

International Thomson Publishing Europe
Berkshire House 168-173
High Holborn
London WCIV 7AA
England

Thomas Nelson Australia
102 Dodds Street
South Melbourne, 3205
Victoria, Australia

Nelson Canada
1120 Birchmount Road
Scarborough, Ontario
Canada M1K 5G4

International Thomson Editores
Campos Eliseos 385, Piso 7
Col. Polanco
11560 Mexico D.F. Mexico

International Thomson Publishing GmbH
Königswinterer Strasse 418
53227 Bonn
Germany

International Thomson Publishing Asia
211 Henderson Road
#05-10 Henderson Building
Singapore 0315

International Thomson Publishing Japan
Hirakawacho Kyowa Building, 3F
2-2-1 Hirakawacho
Chiyoda-ku, Tokyo 102
Japan

Trademarks
Course Technology and the Open Book logo are registered trademarks and CourseKits is a trademark of Course Technology. Custom Editions and the ITP logo are registered trademarks of International Thomson Publishing.

Microsoft, Visual Basic, and Windows are registered trademarks of Microsoft Corporation.

Some of the product names and company names used in this book have been used for identification purposes only and may be trademarks or registered trademarks of their respective manufacturers and sellers.

Disclaimer
Course Technology reserves the right to revise this publication and make changes from time to time in its content without notice.

ISBN 0-7600-5380-4

Printed in the United States of America

10 9 8 7 6 5 4 3 2 1

At Course Technology we have one foot in education and the other in technology. We believe that technology is transforming the way people teach and learn, and we are excited about providing instructors and students with materials that use technology to teach about technology.

Our development process is unparalleled in the higher education publishing industry. Every product we create goes through an exacting process of design, development, review, and testing.

Reviewers give us direction and insight that shape our manuscripts and bring them up to the latest standards. Every manuscript is quality tested. Students whose backgrounds match the intended audience work through every keystroke, carefully checking for clarity and pointing out errors in logic and sequence. Together with our own technical reviewers, these testers help us ensure that everything that carries our name is error-free and easy to use.

We show both how and why technology is critical to solving problems in college and in whatever field you choose to teach or pursue. Our time-tested, step-by-step instructions provide unparalleled clarity. Examples and applications are chosen and crafted to motivate students.

As the New Perspectives Series team at Course Technology, our goal is to produce the most timely, accurate, creative, and technologically sound product in the entire college publishing industry. We strive for consistent high quality. This takes a lot of communication, coordination, and hard work. But we love what we do. We are determined to be the best. Write us and let us know what you think. You can also e-mail us at *New Perspectives @course.com.*

The New Perspectives Series Team

Joseph J. Adamski	Jessica Evans	Mac Mendelsohn
Judy Adamski	Marilyn Freedman	William Newman
Roy Ageloff	Kathy Finnegan	Dan Oja
Tim Ashe	Robin Geller	David Paradice
David Auer	Donna Gridley	June Parsons
Daphne Barbas	Kate Habib	Harry Phillips
Dirk Baldwin	Roger Hayen	Sandra Poindexter
Rachel Bunin	Charles Hommel	Mark Reimold
Joan Carey	Cindy Johnson	Ann Shaffer
Patrick Carey	Janice Jutras	Karen Shortill
Sharon Caswell	Chris Kelly	Susan Solomon
Barbara Clemens	Mary Kemper	Susanne Walker
Rachel Crapser	Stacy Klein	John Zeanchock
Kim Crowley	Terry Ann Kremer	Beverly Zimmerman
Michael Ekedahl	John Leschke	Scott Zimmerman

NEW PERSPECTIVES SERIES

What is the New Perspectives Series?

Course Technology's **New Perspectives Series** is an integrated system of instruction that combines text and technology products to teach computer concepts and microcomputer applications. Users consistently praise this series for innovative pedagogy, creativity, supportive and engaging style, accuracy, and use of interactive technology. The first New Perspectives text was published in January of 1993. Since then, the series has grown to more than 100 titles and has become the best-selling series on computer concepts and microcomputer applications. Others have imitated the New Perspectives features, design, and technologies, but none have replicated its quality and its ability to consistently anticipate and meet the needs of instructors and students.

What is the Integrated System of Instruction?

New Perspectives textbooks are part of a truly Integrated System of Instruction: text, graphics, video, sound, animation, and simulations that are linked and that provide a flexible, unified, and interactive system to help you teach and help your students learn. Specifically, the *New Perspectives Integrated System of Instruction* includes a Course Technology textbook in addition to some or all of the following items: Course Labs, Course Test Manager, Online Companions, and Course Presenter. These components—shown in the graphic on the back cover of this book—have been developed to work together to provide a complete, integrative teaching and learning experience.

How is the New Perspectives Series different from other microcomputer concepts and applications series?

The **New Perspectives Series** distinguishes itself from other series in at least four substantial ways: sound instructional design, consistent quality, innovative technology, and proven pedagogy. The applications texts in this series consist of two or more tutorials, which are based on sound instructional design. Each tutorial is motivated by a realistic case that is meaningful to students. Rather than learn a laundry list of features, students learn the features in the context of solving a problem. This process motivates all concepts and skills by demonstrating to students *why* they would want to know them.

Instructors and students have come to rely on the high quality of the **New Perspectives Series** and to consistently praise its accuracy. This accuracy is a result of Course Technology's unique multi-step quality assurance process that incorporates student testing at at least two stages of development, using hardware and software configurations appropriate to the product. All solutions, test questions, and other supplements are tested using similar procedures. Instructors who adopt this series report that students can work through the tutorials independently with minimum intervention or "damage control" by instructors or staff. This consistent quality has meant that if instructors are pleased with one product from the series, they can rely on the same quality with any other New Perspectives product.

The **New Perspectives Series** also distinguishes itself by its innovative technology. This series innovated Course Labs, truly *interactive* learning applications. These have set the standard for interactive learning.

How do I know that the New Perspectives Series will work?

Some instructors who use this series report a significant difference between how much their students learn and retain with this series as compared to other series. With other series, instructors often find that students can work through the book and do well on homework and tests, but still not demonstrate competency when asked to perform particular tasks outside the context of the text's sample case or project. With the **New Perspectives Series**, however, instructors report that students have a complete, integrative learning experience that stays with them. They credit this high retention and competency to the fact that this series incorporates critical thinking and problem-solving with computer skills mastery.

How does this book I'm holding fit into the New Perspectives Series?

New Perspectives applications books are available in the following categories:

Brief books are typically about 150 pages long and are intended to teach the basics of an application.

Introductory books are about 300 pages long and consist of four to seven chapters or tutorials that go beyond the basics. These books often build out of the Brief editions by providing two or three additional tutorials. The book you are holding is an Introductory book.

Comprehensive books are typically about 600 pages long and consist of all of the chapters or tutorials in the Introductory book, plus a few more chapters or tutorials covering higher-level topics. Comprehensive books also typically include two Windows tutorials, and three or four Additional Cases.

Advanced books cover topics similar to those in the Comprehensive books, but into more depth. Advanced books present the most high-level coverage in the series.

Custom Books The New Perspectives Series offers you two ways to customize a New Perspectives text to fit your course exactly: *CourseKits* ™ two or more texts packaged together in a box, and *Custom Editions*®, your choice of books bound together. Custom Editions offer you unparalleled flexibility in designing your concepts and applications courses. You can build your own book by ordering a combination of titles bound together to cover only the topics you want. Your students save because they buy only the materials they need. There is no minimum order, and books are spiral bound. Both CourseKits and Custom Editions offer significant price discounts. Contact your Course Technology sales representative for more information.

New Perspectives Series Concepts and Applications

■ Brief Titles or Modules	■ Introductory Titles or Modules	■ Intermediate Modules	■ Advanced Titles or Modules	■ Other Modules	☐ Individual Concepts Chapters

Brief	Introductory	Comprehensive	Advanced Applications	Custom Editions
Concepts and Applications				
2 to 4 tutorials or chapters	Brief + 4 or 5 more tutorials or chapters	1 Introductory + 3 or 4 Intermediate tutorials or chapters. Applications have Brief Windows, Additional Cases and Reference section.	Quick Review of basics + in-depth, high-level coverage	Choose from any of the above to build your own Custom Editions® or CourseKits®

In what kind of course could I use this book?

This book can be used in any course in which you want students to learn all the most important topics of Visual Basic 5.0 for Windows, including working with data from another file or database. Students learn how to plan, program, and debug the Visual Basic applications using modern programming techniques and practicing good graphical user interface design. This text is suited for a three-credit introductory Visual Basic course for students with little or no programming background. It assumes that students have learned basic Windows 95 navigation and file management skills from Course Technology's *New Perspectives on Microsoft Windows 95—Brief* or an equivalent book.

How do the Windows 95 editions differ from the Windows 3.1 editions?

Sessions   We've divided the tutorials into sessions. Each session is designed to be completed in about 45 minutes to an hour (depending, of course, upon student needs and the speed of your lab equipment). With sessions, learning is broken up into more easily-assimilated portions. You can more accurately allocate time in your syllabus, and students can better manage the available lab time. Each session begins with a "session box," which quickly describes the skills students will learn in the session. Furthermore, each session is numbered, which makes it easier for you and your students to navigate and communicate about the tutorial. Look on page VB 1.5 for the session box that opens Session 1.1.

Quick Checks   Each session concludes with meaningful, conceptual Quick Check questions that test students' understanding of what they learned in the session. Answers to all of the Quick Check questions in this book are provided on pages VB 6.45 through VB 6.52.

New Design   We have retained the best of the old design to help students differentiate between what they are to *do* and what they are to *read*. The steps are clearly identified by their shaded background and numbered steps. Furthermore, this new design presents steps and screen shots in a larger, easier to read format. Some good examples of our new design are pages VB 2.31 and VB 2.32.

What features are retained in the Windows 95 editions of the New Perspectives Series?

"Read This Before You Begin" Page   This page is consistent with Course Technology's unequaled commitment to helping instructors introduce technology into the classroom. Technical considerations and assumptions about software are listed to help instructors save time and eliminate unnecessary aggravation. The "Read This Before You Begin" page for this book is on page VB 1.2.

Tutorial Case   Each tutorial begins with a problem presented in a case that is meaningful to students. The problem turns the task of learning how to use an application into a problem-solving process. The problems increase in complexity with each tutorial. These cases touch on multicultural, international, and ethical issues—so important to today's business curriculum. See page VB 1.3 for the case that begins Tutorial 1.

Step-by-Step Methodology   This unique Course Technology methodology keeps students on track. They enter data, click buttons, or press keys always within the context of solving the problem posed in the tutorial case. The text constantly guides students, letting them know where they are in the course of solving the problem. In addition, the numerous screen shots include labels that direct students' attention to what they should look at on the screen. On almost every page in this book, you can find an example of how steps, screen shots, and labels work together.

TROUBLE?

TROUBLE? Paragraphs   These paragraphs anticipate the mistakes or problems that students are likely to have and help them recover and continue with the tutorial. By putting these paragraphs in the book, rather than in the Instructor's Manual, we facilitate independent learning and free the instructor to focus on substantive conceptual issues rather than on common procedural errors. Two representative examples of TROUBLE? are on pages VB 1.17 and VB 2.19.

Reference Windows   Reference Windows appear throughout the text. They are succinct summaries of the most important tasks covered in the tutorials. Reference Windows are specially designed and written so students can refer to them when doing the Tutorial Assignments and Case Problems, and after completing the course. Page VB 1.37 contains the Reference Window for setting the size and position of a form.

Tip:

Tips   Tips appear throughout the text. They provide user interface, performance, and general suggestions to make writing programs easier and to make the programs you write better.

Task Reference   The Task Reference contains a summary of how to perform common tasks using the most efficient method, as well as references to pages where the task is discussed in more detail. It appears as a table at the end of the book.

Tutorial Assignments, Case Problems, and Lab Assignments   Each tutorial concludes with Tutorial Assignments, which provide students with additional hands-on practice of the skills they learned in the tutorial. See page VB 1.44 for examples of Tutorial Assignments. The Tutorial Assignments are followed by four Case Problems that have approximately the same scope as the tutorial case. In the Windows 95 applications texts, the last Case Problem of each tutorial typically requires students to solve the problem independently, either "from scratch" or with minimum guidance. See page VB 1.45 for examples of Case Problems. Finally, if a Course Lab accompanies a tutorial, Lab Assignments are included after the Case Problems. See page VB 1.49 for examples of Lab Assignments.

Exploration Exercises   The Windows environment allows students to learn by exploring and discovering what they can do. Exploration Exercises can be Tutorial Assignments or Case Problems that challenge students, encourage them to explore the capabilities of the program they are using, and extend their knowledge using the online Help facility and other reference materials. Page VB 1.45 contains Exploration Exercises for Tutorial 1.

What supplements are available with this textbook?

Student Developer's Kit   Students can discover more about Visual Basic's capabilities with New Perspectives Student Developer's Kit CD-ROM. The disc contains a sampling of hundreds of additional controls produced by third party vendors that can be used in Visual Basic programs. Students can also print a complete listing of the standard Visual Basic object naming conventions and access design documentation templates for use in planning their programs. See the page facing the back cover for more about the Student's Developer's Kit.

Course Labs: Now, Concepts Come to Life   Computer skills and concepts come to life with the New Perspectives Course Labs—highly interactive tutorials that combine illustrations, animation, digital images, and simulations. The Labs guide students step-by-step, present them with Quick Check questions, let them explore on their own, test their comprehension, and provide printed feedback. Lab icons at the beginning of the tutorial or chapter and in the tutorial margins indicate when a topic has a corresponding Lab. Lab Assignments are included at the end of each relevant chapter or tutorial. The Lab available with this book and the tutorial in which it appears is:

Visual Programming
Tutorial 1

Course Test Manager: Testing and Practice at the Computer or on Paper
Course Test Manager is cutting-edge Windows-based testing software that helps instructors design and administer practice tests and actual examinations. This full-featured program allows students to randomly generate practice tests that provide immediate on-screen feedback and detailed study guides for questions incorrectly answered. Instructors can also use Course Test Manager to produce printed tests. Course Test Manager can automatically grade the tests students take at the computer and can generate statistical information on students' individual and group performance.

Online Companions: Dedicated to Keeping You and Your Students Up-To-Date   When you use a New Perspectives product, you can access Course Technology's faculty and student sites on the World Wide Web. You can browse the password-protected Faculty Online Companion to obtain all the materials you need to prepare for class, including online Instructors Manuals, Solutions Files, and Student Files. Please see your Instructor's Manual or call your Course Technology customer service representative for more information. Students may access their Online Companion in the Student Center using the URL **http://www.course.com.**

Instructor's Manual New Perspectives Series Instructor's Manuals contain instructor's notes and printed solutions for each tutorial. Instructor's notes provide tutorial overviews and outlines, technical notes, lecture notes, and extra Case Problems. Printed solutions include solutions to Tutorial Assignments, Case Problems, and Lab Assignments.

Student Files Student Files contain all of the data that students will use to complete the tutorials, Tutorial Assignments, Case Problems. A Readme file includes technical tips for lab management. See the inside covers of this book and the "Read This Before You Begin" pages for more information on Student Files.

Solution Files Solution Files contain every file students are asked to create or modify in the tutorials, Tutorial Assignments, and Case Problems.

The following supplements are included in the Instructor's Resource Kit that accompanies this textbook:

- Instructor's Manual
- Solution Files
- Student Files
- Visual Programming Course Lab
- Course Test Manager Test Bank
- Course Test Manager Engine

Some of the supplements listed above are also available over the World Wide Web through Course Technology's password-protected Faculty Online Companions. Please see your Instructor's Manual or call your Course Technology customer service representative for more information.

Acknowledgments

Our appreciation goes to each of the reviewers whose suggestions and comments helped to create this book. We would also like to thank Mac Mendelsohn for giving us flexibility in creating this book. We would like to thank all the members of the New Perspectives team who helped guide the book's development and production. We would also like to thank the staff at GEX for their fine work.

Special thanks to Kate Habib for her valuable suggestions and efforts as developmental editor, and to Cindy Johnson for her efforts. We would also like to thank the members of the New Perspectives Team for their help in making the book possible.

Michael V. Ekedahl thanks his wife Katrina for her patience while he completed his work. He would also like to thank his dogs Rio and KC for their constant companionship

William A. Newman thanks his wife Anthea, mother Irene, and mother-in-law Annette Karnas, for their encourgement and support. Special thanks to his two dogs Sasha and Sabrina for their companionship.

Michael V. Ekedahl
William A. Newman

Table of **Contents**

Microsoft®
Visual Basic® 5.0
for Windows®

LEVEL I

TUTORIALS

Read This **Before You Begin**

STUDENT DISKS
To complete the tutorials and end–of–tutorial assignments in this book, you need 3 Student Disks. Your instructor will either provide you with Student Disks or ask you to make your own.

If you are supposed to make your own Student Disks, you will need 3 blank, formatted high-density disks. You will need to copy a set of folders from a file server or the *Student Developer's Kit* CD-ROM onto your disks. Your instructor will tell you which computer, drive letter, and folders contain the files you need. The following table shows you which folders go on each of your disks, so that you will have enough disk space to complete all the tutorials, Tutorial Assignments, and Case Problems:

Student Disk	Write this on the disk label	Put these folders on the disk
1	Introductory Tutorials 1-4	Tutorial.01, Tutorial.02, Tutorial.03, Tutorial.04
2	Introductory Tutorial 5	Tutorial.05
3	Introductory Tutorial 6, Appendix A, Appendix C	Tutorial.06, Appendix.A, Appendix.C

When you begin each tutorial, be sure you are using the correct Student Disk. See the inside front or inside back cover of this book for more information on Student Disk files, or ask your instructor or technical support person for assistance.

COURSE LAB
This book features one interactive Course Lab to help you understand visual programming concepts. There are Lab Assignments at the end of Tutorial 1 that relate to this Lab. To start a Lab, click the **Start** button on the Windows 95 Taskbar, point to **Programs**, point to **Course Labs**, point to **New Perspectives Applications**, and click **Visual Programming**. (This path may have changed by the time you read this, please refer to the README file for the lab or consult your instructor if you encounter difficulties.)

USING YOUR OWN COMPUTER
If you are going to work through this book using your own computer, you need:

- **Computer System** Microsoft Windows 95 or Microsoft Windows NT 4.0 (or later), move and either Microsoft Visual Basic 5.0 Enterprise Edition, Visual Basic 5.0 Professional Edition or Microsoft Visual Basic 5.0 Learning Edition, must be installed on your computer. This book assumes a complete installation of Visual Basic. The screens captured for this text show Microsoft Visual Basic 5.0 Professional Edition.

- **Student Disks** You can make student disks from the files on the *Student Developer's Kit* CD-ROM. You will not be able to complete the tutorials or end–of–tutorial assignments in this book using your own computer until you have Student Disks. The Student Files may also be obtained electronically over the Internet or from your instructor. See the inside front or inside back cover of this book for more details.

- **Course Lab** Install the Course Lab software by following the Readme file on the *Student Developer's Kit* CD-ROM. If you don't have a CD-ROM drive, see your instructor or technical support person to obtain the Course Lab software for use on your own computer.

VISIT OUR WORLD WIDE WEB SITE
Additional materials designed especially for you are available on the World Wide Web. Go to **http://www.course.com**.

To complete the tutorials in this book, your students must use a set of files on 3 Student Disks. These files are included in the Instructor's Resource Kit and the *Student Developer's Kit*. They may also be obtained electronically over the Internet. See the inside front or inside back cover of this book for more details. Follow the instructions in the Readme file to copy the files to your server or standalone computer. You can view the Readme file using WordPad.

Once the files are copied, you can make Student Disks for the students yourself, or tell students where to find the files so they can make their own Student Disks. Make sure the files get correctly copied onto the Student Disks by following the instructions in the Student Disks section above, which will ensure that students have enough disk space to complete all the tutorials and end–of–tutorial assignments.

COURSE LAB SOFTWARE
Tutorial 1 features an online, interactive Course Lab that introduces basic visual programming concepts. This software is distributed on a CD-ROM included in the Instructor's Resource Kit and on the *Student Developer's Kit* CD-ROM. To install the Course Lab software, follow the setup instructions in the Readme file on the CD-ROM. Once you have installed the Course Lab software, your students can start the Lab from the Windows 95 desktop by clicking **Start**, pointing to **Programs/Course Labs/New Perspectives Applications**, and then clicking **Visual Programming**.

COURSE TECHNOLOGY STUDENT FILES AND COURSE LAB SOFTWARE
You are granted a license to copy the Student Files and Course Lab to any computer or computer network used by students who have purchased this book.

Getting Started with Visual Basic

Creating and Running a Program for Southern Properties Group

LABS
Visual Programming

CASE

Southern Properties Group

Southern Properties Group, located in Boca Raton, Florida, has been leasing and selling commercial real estate in southern Florida for more than five years. The company was started by Gerrold Campbell, who retired from a large real estate firm in New York City. This year he decided to computerize many of the company's operations so Southern Properties Group could be more responsive to the needs of its clients.

Mark Fisk is the chief computer programmer/analyst for Southern Properties Group. Based on Mark's recommendations, the company is beginning to use Visual Basic 5 for Windows 95 as its standard programming language. Mark believes that Southern Properties Group should use Visual Basic for its programs for several reasons:

■ The company uses many other Windows 95 programs, and Visual Basic programs can include buttons, menus, and other Windows 95 features that users are accustomed to already.

■ Visual Basic has an Integrated Development Environment (IDE). That is, you write your Visual Basic statements and test your programs in the same windows the user sees when the program is running.

■ Programs can be written quickly in Visual Basic because of the many other tools available to the programmer.

■ Visual Basic can work effectively with business data because it can interact with databases like Microsoft Access.

The first program Gerrold asked Mark to create was one that will display pictures of the various pieces of real estate that Southern Properties Group has available for sale or lease. Before you create this program, Mark suggests you create a sample program so you can identify the different Visual Basic windows and how they are used to create, run, and save a program. This way you can become familiar with the Visual Basic user interface and the different parts of a program. In this tutorial, you will create a sample program and then create another program that will allow sales agents to view and show clients the pictures.

Using the Tutorials Effectively

These tutorials will help you learn about Visual Basic 5 for Windows 95. The tutorials are designed to be used at a computer. Each tutorial is divided into sessions. Watch for the session headings, such as Session 1.1 and Session 1.2. Each session is designed to be completed in about 45 minutes, but take as much time as you need. It's also a good idea to take a break between sessions.

Before you begin, read the following questions and answers. They are designed to help you use the tutorials effectively.

Where do I start?

Each tutorial begins with a case, which sets the scene for the tutorial and provides background information to help you understand what you will be doing in the tutorial. Read the case before you go to the lab. In the lab, begin with the first session of a tutorial.

How do I know what to do on the computer?

Each session contains steps that you will perform on the computer to learn how to use Visual Basic 5 for Windows 95. Read the text that introduces each series of steps. The steps you need to do at a computer are numbered and set against a colored background. Read each step carefully and completely before you try it.

How do I know if I did the step correctly?

As you work, compare your computer screen with the corresponding figure in the tutorial. Don't worry if your screen display is somewhat different from the figure. The important parts of the screen display are labeled in each figure. Check to make sure these parts are on your screen.

What if I make a mistake?

Don't worry about making mistakes—they are part of the learning process. Paragraphs labeled "TROUBLE?" identify common problems and explain how to get back on track. Follow the steps in a TROUBLE? paragraph *only* if you are having the problem described. If you run into other problems:

- Carefully consider the current state of your system, the position of the pointer, and any messages on the screen.

- Complete the sentence, "Now I want to…" Be specific, because you are identifying your goal.

- Develop a plan for accomplishing your goal, and put your plan into action.

How do I use the Reference Windows?

Reference Windows summarize the procedures you learn in the tutorial steps. Do not complete the actions in the Reference Windows when you are working through the tutorial. Instead, refer to the Reference Windows while you are working on the assignments at the end of the tutorial.

How can I test my understanding of the material I learned in the tutorial?

At the end of each session, you can answer the Quick Check questions. The answers for the Quick Checks are at the end of the book.

After you have completed the entire tutorial, you should complete the Tutorial Assignments and Case Problems. They are structured carefully so you will review what you have learned and then apply your knowledge to new situations.

What if I can't remember how to do something?

You should refer to the Task Reference at the end of the book; it summarizes how to accomplish tasks using the most efficient method. The Notes column includes shortcuts or additional information.

Before you begin the tutorials, you should know how to use the menus, dialog boxes, Help system, and My Computer in Windows 95. Course Technology publishes two excellent texts for learning Windows 95: *New Perspectives on Microsoft Windows 95—Brief* and *New Perspectives on Microsoft Windows 95—Introductory*.

Now that you have seen how to use the tutorials effectively, you are ready to begin.

SESSION

1.1

In this session you will learn about the different windows and components of the Visual Basic system, and how to use them. You will learn how to start Visual Basic, use the online Help, create and save a Visual Basic project, run and stop a program, and exit Visual Basic.

What Is Visual Basic?

Visual Basic is a computer programming language. **Computer programming** is the process of writing a set of organized statements that accomplish a specific task using a programming language. A **programming language**, like the English language, uses words with a specific meaning, connected together in a specific order, to form a statement. A **statement** is much like a sentence in English. Just like English, the spelling of words and rules about how those words are connected together to form statements are clearly defined. A reader usually can understand the meaning of a sentence written in English even when words are misspelled or punctuation is not correct. When programming a computer, however, the statements you type must be exactly correct. The rules describing the valid statements of a programming language are known as **syntax**. When you assemble several statements together to accomplish a task, you create a program. A **program** is a set of statements written in a computer language to accomplish a specific task. Some tasks may be simple, like adding a list of numbers together. Other tasks may be extremely complex, like navigating a satellite. In this tutorial you will use the Visual Basic programming language to create a program that will display different graphical images on the screen as selected by the sales agents. The program will contain words used to form statements. All the statements together form the computer program. In this book you will learn how to use the Visual Basic 5 programming language.

When you write a computer program in Visual Basic, you use various tools to design the user interface. The **user interface** is what a user of the program sees on the screen and how the user interacts with the program. The screen that the user sees is called a form. A **form** is a window just like any other window you see in Windows 95. It can contain tools like buttons, and boxes that contain text. These buttons also are considered windows. A **window** is any rectangular area on the screen and can exist inside another window.

Visual Basic also has a user interface, just as programs like Microsoft Word and Excel have a user interface. When you create programs with Visual Basic, you use an **Integrated Development Environment (IDE)**. That is, all of the tools necessary to create and run a program have been combined into a single user interface, rather than operating as separate programs. In other words you can create the user interface for your program, write the necessary statements and run your program inside of the IDE.

Visual Basic is an **event-driven** programming language, which means that different pictures, boxes, and buttons on the screen can respond to events. An **event** is an action that occurs as a result of some user activity. One event is generated when the user clicks a button while a different event is generated when the user types characters into a text box or places the cursor in the text box. These events result in the program's statements being executed to perform a specified task.

Visual Basic also is an **object-oriented** programming language. That is, you use objects like buttons to perform tasks. Think of an **object** as a real-world item that you use every day. A telephone, for example, can be thought of as an object. As such, you can clearly define the actions a telephone can perform. When you pick up a telephone, it responds to the event by providing a dial tone. As numbers are dialed on the phone, it responds to different events by sending audible tones to the telephone system to dial the number. A telephone also has certain behaviors or settings. That is, it can be off the hook or on the hook. Also, it can be connected to another phone or not. The actions performed by an object and the behavior of an object are similar to the nouns and verbs of a sentence. Each object has a predefined set of behaviors called **properties** (nouns), and can perform a predefined set of actions called **methods** (verbs).

You use different tools to create objects on a form, such as buttons the user can click and boxes that can display text or pictures. Some tools are designed to reflect how you might fill out a paper form. For example, there are tools that allow the user to check a box or choose one item from a list of items.

In Visual Basic, these tools are called **controls**. Each kind of control has a different appearance (properties), responds to events which can vary for different controls, and can perform a unique set of actions (methods). In this tutorial you will learn how to use four different controls.

- A **Label** control consists of a box that displays text to describe the purpose of another control.

- A user will enter characters into a **TextBox** control to specify the name of a picture stored on the disk.

- The **Image** control consists of a box that can display pictures saved in certain graphic formats. The Image control in your program will display the file typed by the user into the text box.

- The **CommandButton** control allows the user to click a command button to display the picture specified by the file name, which is stored in the text box, into the Image control.

You add a control to a form by drawing a copy of the control on the form. Each control you place on a form is considered an object. Figure 1-1 shows a sample of Visual Basic controls drawn on a form, and their purpose.

Figure 1-1 ◀
Sample of
Visual Basic
controls

enter letters and
numbers into a
TextBox control

display a graphical
image into an Image
control

display descriptive
text for another object
such as a TextBox
control

click a command
button to cause some
action to occur

A control is considered a class. A **class** is just a template for an object that defines the supported properties, methods, and events. When you draw a control on a form, you are creating an object, or an **instance** of a class.

Each form is stored as a separate file on the disk. In Visual Basic, the specifications for all the forms used by a program are stored in another file called a project file. A **project file** lists each file used in the program along with information about the controls used. It acts as a container for all the program components. Each part of your program stored as a file on the disk is called a **module**. A **standard module** contains Visual Basic statements that can be used by several forms. Each program has a single project file that lists the components of the program. One of these components is the form module. The **form module** contains all the objects on the form and all the code for those objects. **Code** is the statements written for a program to perform a specific action. The sample project you are creating for Mark will contain two forms and one standard module. The project manages all the different components of your program. Figure 1-2 shows the relationship between a project file, its forms, and standard modules.

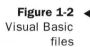

Figure 1-2
Visual Basic
files

Project File

Identifies each form and
other files used in the
program.

frmDocument
frmMain
Module1

Form File (frmDocument)
Contains a box to edit text.

Objects drawn on the form. Text box	Visual Basic code executed when the form is displayed on the screen.

Form File (frmMain)
Contains a menu bar, toolbar, an object to display
images and another to display text.

Objects drawn on the form. Menus Toolbars	Visual Basic code executed in response to events like clicking a tool or menu.

Module File (Module1)

Visual Basic code executed when explicitly called by a
statement in a form file, or module file.

With Visual Basic, programming is a three-step process. First, you create the user interface, then you write the statements to perform each of the tasks required by the program. The third step is a loop; you test the program, correct any errors, and test the program again. Figure 1-3 shows the steps you take to write a program.

Figure 1-3 ◄
Steps for
writing a
program

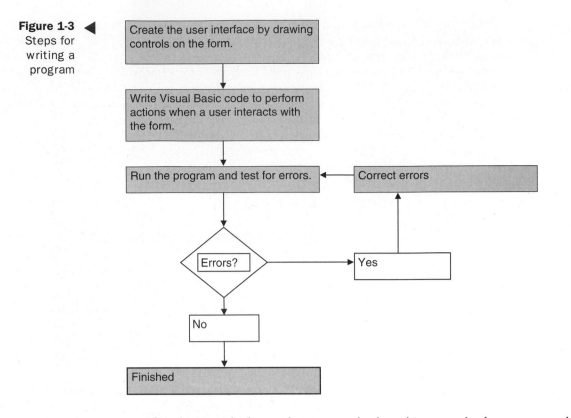

After drawing the boxes, buttons, and other objects on the form, you need to write the Visual Basic statements that are executed when a user enters text or clicks a button. These statements will perform the tasks needed to solve the problem. For example, Southern Properties Group needs a program to display graphical images stored as individual files on the computer's disk. Therefore, you will write a program that contains statements to display an image when a user types a file name into a text box, and clicks a command button to display the picture. As you write code to accomplish specific tasks, you will want to test the code to make sure it works correctly.

Starting Visual Basic

To create the program for Mark, you first need to start Visual Basic. You can start Visual Basic using the Start button on the taskbar or a shortcut icon on the Windows 95 desktop, if an icon has been defined for Visual Basic on the computer you are using. Your instructor will tell you how to start Visual Basic in your particular environment.

To start Visual Basic using the Start button:

1. Make sure your computer is on and the Windows 95 desktop is displayed on your screen.

2. Find the Start button, which usually is located at the bottom-left corner of the screen on the taskbar.

3. Click the **Start** button to display the Start menu, then point to the **Programs** command.

   When the Programs command is highlighted, a submenu appears listing the programs available on your computer.

4. Move the mouse pointer to the item labeled **Microsoft Visual Basic 5.0**. Another submenu appears, listing the options available in the Visual Basic system. See Figure 1-4.

Figure 1-4 ◀
Starting Visual
Basic

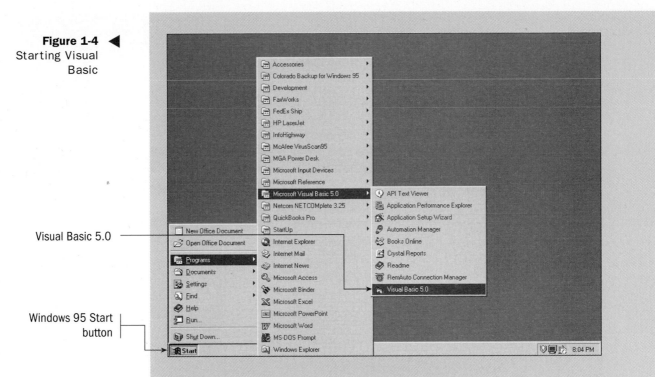

Visual Basic 5.0

Windows 95 Start
button

The Start menu options on your screen might be different from those in Figure 1-4, depending on the software you have on your computer.

TROUBLE? If the Microsoft Visual Basic 5.0 option is not listed on your Programs menu, check to see if a shortcut icon for Visual Basic appears on the desktop, then double-click the icon to start Visual Basic. If you cannot locate Visual Basic anywhere on your computer, ask your instructor or lab staff for assistance.

5. Click **Visual Basic 5.0**.

The introductory Visual Basic screen appears while the rest of the Visual Basic system is loaded into the computer's memory. This introductory screen commonly is called a splash screen. It provides a visual clue to the user that the desired program is being loaded. Once Visual Basic is loaded, the New Project window will appear and your screen should look similar to Figure 1-5.

Figure 1-5 ◀
New Project
window

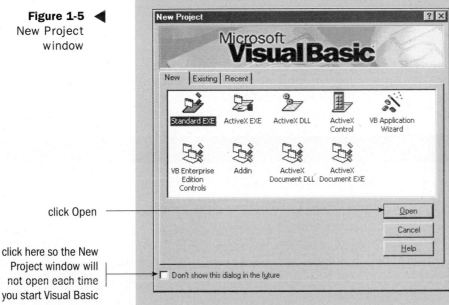

click Open

click here so the New
Project window will
not open each time
you start Visual Basic

TROUBLE? If the New Project window shown in Figure 1-5 does not appear, your computer may be configured differently. Depending on how you or the lab manager set up your computer, some windows might be open or closed initially, or might be a different size. Skip Step 6.

6. Click the **Don't show this dialog in the future** check box to prevent the New Project window from opening every time Visual Basic is started. Click the **Open** button. When you start Visual Basic from now on, your screen will look similar to Figure 1-6, and Visual Basic will create a default project for you.

Figure 1-6 ◀
Visual Basic
windows

menu bar

toolbar

toolbox

Project window
Properties window

Form
window

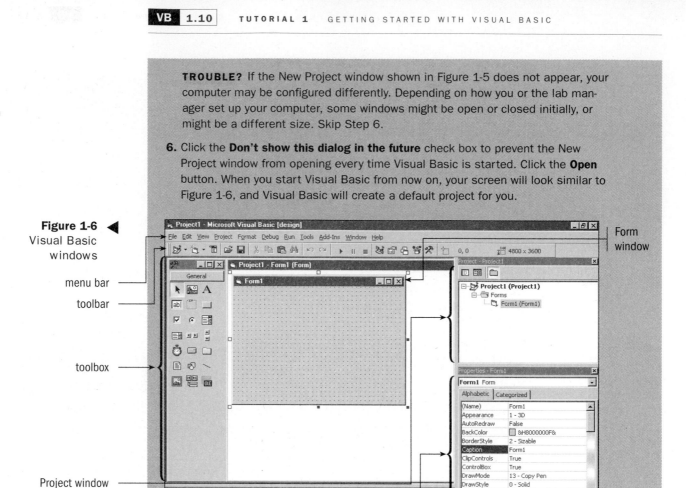

When you start Visual Basic and open different project files, the size and location of the windows on the screen will vary. You can change the size and position of most Visual Basic windows to suit your own preferences, just as you can resize or move other windows in Windows 95. Some of the windows in Figure 1-6 may not be visible on your screen, depending on the current settings of your application.

When you start Visual Basic, be sure the Visual Basic startup screen contains the text Visual Basic Learning Edition 5.0, Visual Basic Professional Edition 5.0, or Visual Basic Enterprise Edition 5.0. There are several operating differences between Version 5.0 and older versions. You must be using Version 5.0 of Visual Basic to complete these tutorials.

Notice the IDE contains several components common to many other Windows 95 programs. It has a menu bar and toolbar. It also has a toolbox that allows you to create the buttons and other visual objects that make up the user interface.

The Menu Bar and Toolbar

The menu bar provides the commands you use to create and run Visual Basic programs. The menu bar functions like the menu bar in any other Windows 95 program.

The toolbar provides buttons for many of the commands available from the menu bar. Clicking a toolbar button is a faster way of choosing a command than using the menu bar. As in other Windows 95 applications, you can display a ToolTip for a button on the Visual Basic toolbar by positioning the mouse pointer on the button. The ToolTip that appears shows the name of the button.

To practice displaying a ToolTip for a toolbar button:

1. Position the mouse pointer over the **Add Standard EXE Project** button 🖳 at the far left of the toolbar.

   After a few seconds, the ToolTip appears and displays the button name, Add Standard EXE Project.

2. Move the mouse pointer off the button. The ToolTip disappears.

The Visual Basic toolbars can be customized depending on your personal preferences or the specific actions you are performing. This is accomplished by adding or removing different groups of tools from the toolbar. Mark suggests you verify that only the Standard toolbar is showing.

To configure the toolbars:

1. Click **View** on the menu bar, then point to **Toolbars** then click **Customize**.

   The Customize dialog box appears on your screen.

2. Click the **Toolbars** tab if necessary.

3. Be sure the Menu Bar and Standard check boxes are checked. Clear any other check boxes. Notice that you cannot disable the Menu Bar check box. Your dialog box should look like Figure 1-7.

Figure 1-7 ◄
Customize window

Toolbars tab is active ——

Menu Bar cannot be deactivated |

displays the Standard toolbar |

click Close to accept the toolbar settings

4. Click the **Close** button.

Planning a Program

You always should consider carefully the problem you are trying to solve and the best solution to the problem before you begin writing the program. Part of planning a program consists of deciding on the placement and purpose of the buttons, boxes, and other components seen by the user. You should consider carefully the layout and organization of the different visual elements, and the specific tasks they will perform, before sitting down and creating the program on the computer. This will make the programming process easier and less error prone. Mark has created the main form's screen layout as shown in Figure 1-8. It lists the controls on the form and their placement.

Figure 1-8 ◀
Form design for
image viewer

| Label prompt |
| Text box to enter file name |
| Image box to display pictures |
| Command button |

Creating a Project

When you want to create a Visual Basic program, you begin by either creating an empty project file with no visible objects or statements, or using a Wizard to create a project for you. A Wizard can help you create a template for the different parts of the project, which you can then expand on to make the program perform the specific tasks you desire.

The **Application Wizard** creates a project that is a template for a completed program. That is, it will create the forms, menus, toolbars, and other items for you to perform tasks like opening and closing files. You as the programmer must modify this template to accomplish specific tasks like displaying the graphical files you open. The Application Wizard only can create new programs. It is not possible to use the Application Wizard to modify programs that already have been created.

Creating a project in Visual Basic with the Application Wizard is much like creating a document in Microsoft Word using a template. You select an item from the Visual Basic menu bar or toolbar to create a new project, then specify the characteristics of the project. Mark suggests you create a new project file using the Application Wizard to identify the different parts of a Visual Basic program.

To start the Application Wizard:

1. Click **File** then **New Project** on the menu bar. The New Project window appears as shown in Figure 1-9.

Figure 1-9 ◀
Creating a new
project

click VB Application
Wizard

New Project	
Standard EXE	ActiveX EXE	ActiveX DLL	ActiveX Control
VB Application Wizard	VB Enterprise Edition Controls	Addin	ActiveX Document DLL
ActiveX Document EXE			

OK
Cancel
Help

click OK to start
the Wizard

2. Click the **VB Application Wizard** icon, then click **OK**.

3. The Application Wizard - Introduction dialog box opens as shown in Figure 1-10.

Figure 1-10 ◀
Using the
Application
Wizard

click Finish to
create the project

TROUBLE? If you do not see this dialog box, but see a dialog box titled Application Wizard - Interface Type, do not worry. Click the Finish button on the dialog box and the Application Wizard will create the same application.

4. Click **Finish**.

When clicked, Visual Basic will begin to create the program template for you. You will see several windows opening and closing as Visual Basic creates each of the different parts of the program. The template contains the foundation for a more complete Visual Basic program.

5. If you see the dialog box shown in Figure 1-11, click **OK**.

Figure 1-11 ◀
Application
Created dialog
box

click OK to close
the dialog box

6. If you see the dialog box shown in Figure 1-12, click **Close**.

Figure 1-12 ◀
Application
Wizard
Summary
Report

click Close to close
the report

Now that you have created your first project, Mark suggests you look at the Help system about projects so you can begin to understand the system's components and how they work.

Getting Help

Visual Basic has an extensive Help system that provides on-screen information about Visual Basic components, features, commands, and so on. For example, you can look up how to write Visual Basic statements or how to use any of the financial and mathematical functions built into Visual Basic. The Help system is based on the idea of hypertext, which means that you can navigate through the Help system by looking at definitions of terms you do not understand or related topics without having to search for the information. Most of the Help screens contain examples you can copy and paste into actual Visual Basic code.

You can get help at any time by pressing the F1 key or by selecting an option from the Help menu. Figure 1-13 describes the options available on the Help menu.

Figure 1-13 ◄
Help menu
options

Microsoft Visual Basic Help Topics	Displays the Help window that provides a list of available Help Topics on the Contents tab or searches for a particular topic from the Index tab.
Books Online	Activates Visual Basic Books Online containing complete reference information about Visual Basic. Depending on your system configuration, the CD-ROM containing the Visual Basic software must be inserted into the CD-ROM drive.
Obtaining Technical Support	Displays the Contents tab of the Help window where you can search for different ways to get support for Visual Basic.
Microsoft on the Web	Allows you to access the Internet, if your computer is set up correctly, for information about Visual Basic
About Microsoft Visual Basic	Displays a dialog box telling you the version number, a copyright notice, and the amount of available memory.

Depending on whether you are running the Visual Basic Learning, Professional, or Enterprise edition, your Help menu options might differ from those shown in Figure 1-13.

Using the Index Tab

The Index tab of the Help window displays an alphabetical list of topics, just like a typical index in the back of a book. You either can scroll through the list and select a topic or type a topic to find information about it.

Mark suggests you use the Index tab to find Help information about projects.

To use the Index tab to find information about projects:

1. Click **Help** on the menu bar, then click **Microsoft Visual Basic Help Topics**.

2. Make sure the Index tab is selected in the Help window, as shown in Figure 1-14.

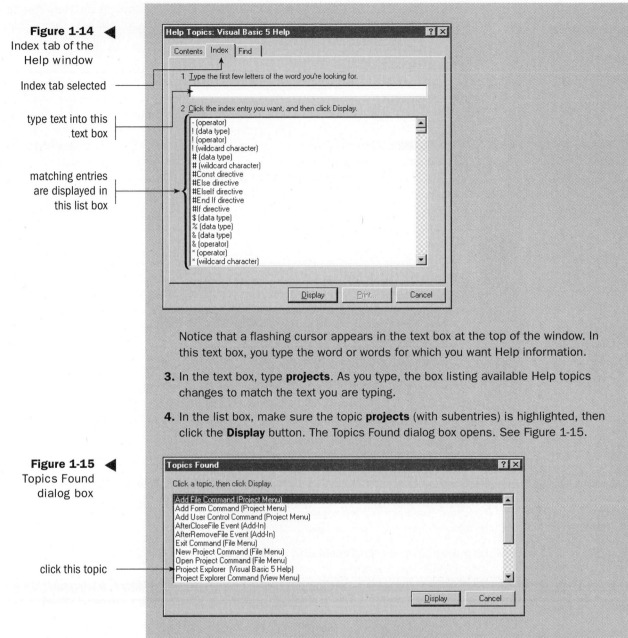

Figure 1-14
Index tab of the
Help window

Index tab selected

type text into this
text box

matching entries
are displayed in
this list box

Notice that a flashing cursor appears in the text box at the top of the window. In this text box, you type the word or words for which you want Help information.

3. In the text box, type **projects**. As you type, the box listing available Help topics changes to match the text you are typing.

4. In the list box, make sure the topic **projects** (with subentries) is highlighted, then click the **Display** button. The Topics Found dialog box opens. See Figure 1-15.

Figure 1-15
Topics Found
dialog box

click this topic

5. Click the topic **Project Explorer (Visual Basic 5 Help)**, then click the **Display** button. The Help system displays information about the Project Explorer. See Figure 1-16.

Figure 1-16 ◀
Help
information
about the
Project
Explorer

scroll up arrow ──

scroll box ──

scroll down arrow ──

Depending on the settings of your system, the size and shape of your Help window might differ from the window in Figure 1-16. Just like most windows, you can move the mouse pointer over a window's border and drag the border to increase or decrease its size depending on your personal preference.

6. Read the displayed information, using the up and down scroll arrows or the scroll box to move through the screen.

7. When you are finished reading the information, scroll to the top of the screen. Note that some terms are displayed in a different color and underlined with dashes. You can click these terms to display additional Help information.

8. Click the highlighted text **Forms**, read the displayed definition of this term, then click anywhere on the screen to close the definition window. You may need to scroll down through the Help screen to locate the highlighted text depending on the size of the Help window and the resolution of your computer's monitor.

Note the text "See Also" at the top of the screen. You can click this text to display a list of related Help topics.

9. Click **See Also**, look at the displayed list of related topics, then click the **Cancel** button on the Topics Found window to close it.

10. Click the **Close** button ⊠ on the Help window title bar to close the window and exit the Help system.

Now that you have learned how to use the Help system and viewed information on a project, you are ready to work on the project for Mark. Before you look at the different parts of a project, you should save your work to your Student Disk. As you make changes to a program, they are not saved to your Student Disk until you explicitly do so. Saving your work frequently will prevent accidental loss due to a power outage, or other computer malfunction.

Saving the Project

You now need to use the Save File As and Save Project As dialog boxes to save the different files that make up the project. When a project is saved for the first time, each of the form files is saved first, then the project file is saved. Thus, you will be asked to save the two form files, the standard module file, and the project itself.

As you create and work on programs, it is a good idea to save your work to the Student Disk regularly so it will not be lost as a result of a power outage or system failure. Although the forms and the project are stored in separate files, you can save them using one Visual Basic command.

Mark would like you to save this project using the default name "Project1", and the form files also with the default names. Visual Basic creates standardized names for each form it created, so you do not need to change any of the form names. The standardized names for forms begin with the prefix "frm" followed by descriptive words for the form.

To save the Southern Properties Group project:

1. Place your Student Disk in drive A.

   TROUBLE? If you don't have a Student Disk, you need to get one before you can proceed. Your instructor either will give you one or ask you to make your own.

   If your floppy disk drive is not drive A, substitute the appropriate name of your floppy disk drive throughout these tutorials.

2. Click **File** on the menu bar, then click **Save Project** to activate the Save File As dialog box as shown in Figure 1-17. Because you have not yet saved any of the files associated with the project, Visual Basic first will ask you to save each of the files that make up the project, then save the project file itself.

Figure 1-17 ◀
Saving the form

save in the Tutorial.01 folder on your Student Disk

file name for the form

saves the form file on disk

3. Click the Save in list arrow, click **3½ Floppy (A:)**, then double-click the folder named **Tutorial.01**

4. Because you will use the default file name supplied by Visual Basic, you do not need to type in the file name. Click the **Save** button in the dialog box to save the first form.

5. The Save File As dialog box will appear again asking you to save the form named **frmMain**. Click **Save** to save the form. Because you already specified the folder in the previous step, you do not need to change the Save in list box entry.

6. The Save File As dialog box appears again asking you to save the basic module named Module1. Click **Save** again to save the module named **Module1** using the default name.

7. Finally the Save Project As dialog box appears as shown in Figure 1-18. Click **Save** to save the project file.

Figure 1-18 ◀
Saving the
project

file name for the
project

> **Save Project As**
>
> Save in: ☐ Tutorial.01 ◀ ──   save in the Tutorial.01 folder on your Student Disk
>
> ☐ Cases
> ☐ TAssign
>
> File name: Project1.vbp   Save ◀── saves the project file on disk
> Save as type: Project Files (*.vbp)   Cancel
>   Help

Now that you have saved the project, you can open it at any time using the Open Project command on the File menu. The project file then will locate all the forms and other Visual Basic components and load them.

The Visual Basic Environment

The Visual Basic Integrated Development Environment (IDE) can be used in two modes. You can select the mode by clicking Tools then Options on the menu bar to open the Options dialog box. The Advanced tab contains a check box named SDI Development Environment. If this box is checked, Visual Basic will operate in SDI mode. Otherwise it will operate in MDI mode.

- Using the single document interface (SDI) mode, the different windows used by Visual Basic can appear anywhere on the screen.

- Using the multiple document interface (MDI) mode, the region of each Visual Basic window appears inside another window called an **MDI parent window**. This is much like working with multiple documents in Microsoft Word or multiple spreadsheets and charts in Microsoft Excel. Each Word document or Excel spreadsheet appears inside the region of another window.

Which mode to use is a matter of personal preference but this book will use the MDI mode so it is easy to determine which windows are applicable to Visual Basic. The main Visual Basic screen (MDI parent window) contains common Windows 95 components, such as the menu bar and toolbar, plus application-specific components such as the Project Explorer, Form window, Properties window, and toolbox. Together, these windows allow you to design, create, edit, run, and test programs. Which windows are open and their position on the screen also is a matter of personal preference.

Another feature of the Visual Basic IDE is called docking. When docking is turned on, different windows can be displayed and moved relative to the other windows and the edge of the MDI parent window. When turned off, windows are positioned anywhere inside the MDI parent window. In this tutorial you will not use docking. Mark suggests you begin by verifying that Visual Basic is running in MDI mode and that docking is turned off.

To do this you will use the Options dialog box. This dialog box is used to configure Visual Basic's user interface to fit your particular needs.

To configure the Visual Basic environment:

1. Click **Tools** then **Options** on the menu bar to open the Options dialog box.

2. Click the **Advanced** tab in the dialog box.

3. Be sure the **SDI Development Environment** check box is not checked.

4. Click the **Docking** tab in the dialog box.

5. Be sure only the **Toolbox** check box is checked.

6. Click **OK** to close the Options dialog box.

As you develop the programs throughout this book, you should open, close, and resize the windows as you see fit. There is neither a right number of windows to keep open or closed nor a proper size for those windows. Mark suggests you now look at the different windows that make up the IDE so you can develop your own program in the next session.

Interactive Development Environment Windows

In addition to the toolbar and menu bar, Visual Basic uses several windows in which you design the user interface, the appearance of the objects you create, and write Visual Basic statements.

Project Explorer

The **Project Explorer** shows all the program components. You use the Project Explorer to manage the program components. (The project is the same as the program.) A project usually consists of at least one form, which is referred to as a form module. Other types of modules, including standard modules and class modules, also can be a part of a project. Visual Basic also can work with several projects at a time.

To open the Project Explorer:

1. Click the **Project Explorer** button [icon] on the toolbar if necessary to activate the Project Explorer as shown in Figure 1-19.

Figure 1-19 ◄
Project
Explorer

Toggle Folders button ——

View Code button ——

View Object button ——

Forms
folder
open

Modules
folder
open

Project
Explorer

2. Move or resize the window as necessary so the position and shape of the window is similar to Figure 1-19.

3. Display, move, and resize the other windows as necessary so your window resembles Figure 1-19.

The Project Explorer displays a hierarchical list of all the forms and modules used in a project. Forms and modules appear in different folders much like they do in the Windows Explorer program. Each line in the Project Explorer has the following components.

- A box containing a plus or a minus sign. Clicking the plus sign will open the folder and display its contents. Clicking the minus sign will close the folder such that its contents will not be displayed.

- An icon describing the type of object or file.

- The name of the object used inside of Visual Basic.

- The file name of the object saved on the disk.

The Project Explorer also contains three buttons.

- The **View Code** button opens a window to display the Visual Basic statements that apply to the selected module.

- The **View Object** button displays a form or other object in a window called the Object window.

- The **Toggle Folders** buttons is used to hide and show the object folders.

Mark suggests you list the complete hierarchy so you can identify all the files used in the project, then look at the main form created by the Application Wizard.

To identify the project components and view a form:

1. If any of the folders are closed, click the **plus** button ⊞ next to the folder in the Project Explorer to open the folder.

2. Click the form named **frmMain**.

   TROUBLE? If you cannot see frmMain in the Project Explorer, the Forms folder may be closed. Click the "+" sign next to Forms to open it. Then repeat Step 2.

3. Click the **View Object** button 🖹 in the Project Explorer to display the Form window. Your screen should look like Figure 1-20.

Figure 1-20 ◀
Displaying
a form

form's menu bar

form's toolbar

frmMain displayed

The Form Window

The **Form window** is the window in which you design the user interface for the program. When a user runs the program, the user communicates with the program by clicking buttons or typing characters into the objects on the form. As shown in Figure 1-20, the Form window shows the main form that was created by the Application Wizard. The Wizard created several objects on the form. It created a menu bar and toolbar to execute commands. It also set the caption of the form on the title bar.

Properties Window

The **Properties window** provides options you use to manage the appearance of each object on a form. A **property** is a characteristic of an object, such as the object's color, caption, screen location, or size.

To display the Properties window for the form:

1. Click the **Properties Window** button 🖾 on the toolbar to activate the Properties window if necessary.

2. Use the scroll bar to locate the Caption property. Note that the value for this property is the same as the caption shown on the form. By setting properties in this way, you can change the appearance of the form or other object. See Figure 1-21.

Figure 1-21 ◀
Properties
window
components

title bar

object box

property names

list arrow for selecting
other objects

scroll bar

property values

You will use the Properties window in the next session when you create the program to display graphical images.

Toolbox

The **toolbox** contains all the visual tools necessary to create a program. You use the icons in the toolbox to place controls on a form. As noted earlier, a control is a class, such as a box, button, or label. When you draw an instance of a control on a form it becomes an object. You can create objects that users interact with, and objects to enhance the visual appeal of a form.

Mark suggests you run the program to see the different objects he created. To help you identify the different controls in the toolbox, a ToolTip is displayed whenever the mouse is positioned over a control for about one second.

Running a Program

Now you can run the program and begin to interact with its objects. By using some of the different Visual Basic controls, you will begin to see how they function before creating the program for Mark to display images.

Operating Modes

Visual Basic always operates in either run mode, design mode, or break mode. The title bar at the top of the Visual Basic menu bar indicates the current mode. When you are in the process of running a program, the Visual Basic title bar contains the text "run," meaning that your program is being executed, or is in **run mode**. In another mode called **design mode** you perform activities like creating and saving projects, designing forms, setting properties, and writing code. You will learn more about design time in Session 1.2 when you create the program to display graphical images. **Break mode** is similar to run time, but your program temporarily is suspended allowing you to examine the program statements as they are being executed. You will learn more about break mode in later tutorials.

When you run a program, Visual Basic loads the startup, or first form, and displays all the objects drawn on the form. The Application Wizard sets the main form as the startup form for you. After the main form is displayed, the document form is displayed inside the region of the main form. Then the program waits for you to interact with it. When you click an item on the menu or a toolbar button, you generate an event, and Visual Basic executes the code written in response to the event.

Mark suggests you test the program to see how a Visual Basic program looks when it runs.

To run the Southern Properties Group project:

1. Click the **Start** button ▶ on the toolbar. A document form appears inside of the main form, and the Visual Basic title bar displays [run]. Figure 1-22 shows the running form.

Figure 1-22 ◀
Running a
program

title bar

menu bar

toolbar

document form
(frmDocument)

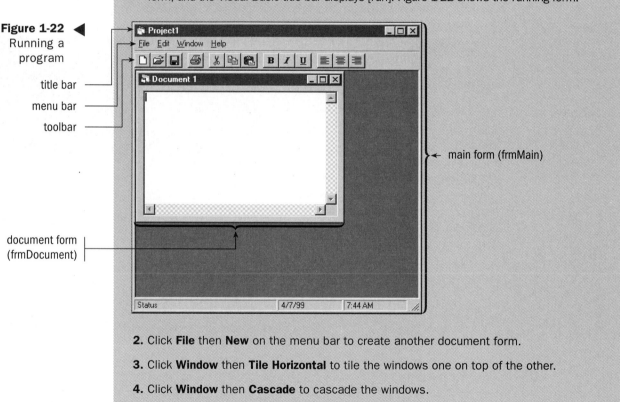

main form (frmMain)

2. Click **File** then **New** on the menu bar to create another document form.

3. Click **Window** then **Tile Horizontal** to tile the windows one on top of the other.

4. Click **Window** then **Cascade** to cascade the windows.

The Application Wizard wrote the necessary statements to manage the windows for you and to create new windows. It did not, however, complete all the code. For example, most of the buttons will display a message indicating that the code goes here, telling you that the procedure is not complete. The next step is to stop running the program.

Stopping a Program

You have finished looking at the Southern Properties Group program, so you now can stop running it. When you stop a program from running, you change the operating mode from run mode to design mode. There are two ways to stop running a program—using the End button on the toolbar or the End command on the Run menu.

To stop running the Southern Properties program:

1. Click the **End** button ▪ on the toolbar. Visual Basic stops running the program and returns to design mode. Note that the form no longer contains information and the title bar displays the text "[design]".

Exiting Visual Basic

Now that you have created the Southern Properties Group demo program, and saved the project and other files, you can exit Visual Basic. Because you have not made any changes to the program since last saving it, you do not have to save it again before exiting.

You can exit Visual Basic either by clicking the Close button on the Visual Basic title bar or choosing the Exit command from the File menu. When you exit Visual Basic, it checks to see if you have made any changes to your program that need to be saved. If there are unsaved changes to the project or any of the forms, Visual Basic displays a message asking if you want to save the file that was changed. Before exiting, Visual Basic closes all open forms and the project file.

To exit Visual Basic:

1. Click the **Close** button ⊠ on the Visual Basic title bar.

TROUBLE? If you resized the form or made any other changes to it, Visual Basic will ask if you want to save the changes to the files that have been modified. Click the No button.

Visual Basic closes any open forms, then closes the project file and exits Visual Basic.

Quick Check

1. Describe the steps to create a program.

2. What is the Application Wizard?

3. What is a project?

4. What is a form?

5. What is the difference between using the Index tab and the Contents tab on the Help window to locate specific information?

6. How do you run and stop a program?

SESSION

1.2

In this session, you will learn how to create a new project without a Wizard, how to create instances of controls on a form, and how to set properties for the form and its objects. You will add Visual Basic statements to the program so it can open and display graphical images. Finally, you will test the completed program.

Creating a New Project

The project you created in Session 1.1 contained the structure of a program so you could identify the parts of a Visual Basic program and how to run it. Mark now would like you to create a new project without a Wizard, and then create the user interface so the new program can display graphical images. When you start Visual Basic, it automatically will create a new project for you.

To create the new project for Southern Properties Group:

1. Start Visual Basic if you have not already done so. Visual Basic creates a new project with a single form for you as shown in Figure 1-23.

Figure 1-23 ◀
New project
created by
Visual Basic

toolbox contains
controls for project

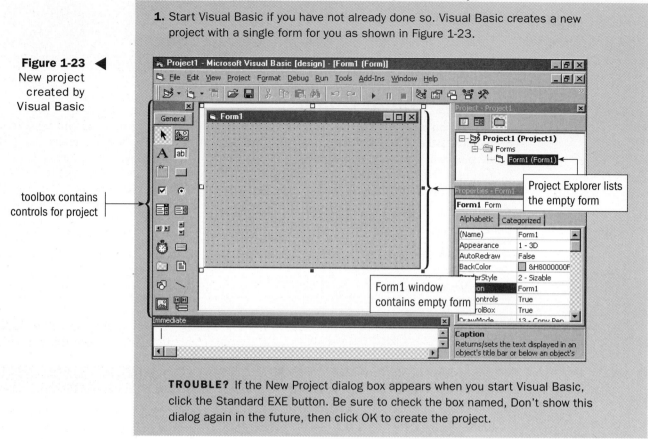

TROUBLE? If the New Project dialog box appears when you start Visual Basic, click the Standard EXE button. Be sure to check the box named, Don't show this dialog again in the future, then click OK to create the project.

As shown in Figure 1-23, the new project contains a single form named Form1. Also, the toolbox contains the different controls that you can use to create objects on the form. Finally, both the Project Explorer and Properties window contain information about the current project and object, respectively.

You need to create four objects on the form. You need an Image object that will display the pictures Southern Properties Group has stored on the computer. A text box needs to be created in which the user can type a file name to display. A command button needs to be created that, when clicked, will cause the image to be displayed. Finally, a label needs to be created that will describe the purpose of the text box. Mark suggests you use the Help system to learn more about the specific controls you will be adding to your form. The fastest way to get help on a control is to open a window called the toolbox that contains all the available controls, activate the control by clicking it, then press the F1 key to display the Help window.

To learn more about the Label control:

1. Click the **Toolbox** button 🛠 on the toolbar to open the toolbox if necessary.

2. Click the **Label** control Ⓐ on the toolbox. Remember, if you leave the mouse over a control for a few seconds the ToolTip will appear.

3. Press the **F1** key to display Help information about the control.

    The Visual Basic Help window opens to the page describing the Label control.

Because you will be using both the Label and CommandButton controls when you create your program, you will print a copy of the Help Topic for reference later on. Like most programs, Visual Basic supports shortcut menus. A **shortcut menu** is a menu that appears when the right mouse button is clicked. The list of menu items depends on the active window or active control. Shortcut menus provide a quick way to execute frequently used commands.

To print the Help Topics for the Label and CommandButton controls:

1. Read the text in the displayed Help window, using the scroll arrows and scroll box to move through the text.

2. Click the **right mouse** button while the cursor is positioned in the Help window to activate the shortcut menu, then click **Print Topic** on the shortcut menu.

   The Print dialog box will appear on your screen.

3. Click the **OK** button in the Print dialog box.

4. Click the **Help Topics** button at the upper-left corner of the Help window.

5. Click the **Index** tab if necessary.

6. Enter the text **CommandButton control** in the text box, then click **Display**.

7. Click the **right mouse** button while the cursor is positioned in the Help window to activate the shortcut menu, then click **Print Topic** on the shortcut menu.

   The Print dialog box will appear on your screen.

8. Click the **OK** button in the Print dialog box.

In addition to the Label and CommandButton controls, your program also will include an Image control. So, you also will display and print Help information about this control.

Using the Table of Contents

The Contents tab of the Help system displays a set of books, each of which contains a particular category of information. You click a book icon to open it and display the topics in that category; then you can choose a particular topic to view. You will use the Contents tab to view information about the Image control.

To use the Contents tab to find information about the Image control:

1. Click the **Help Topics** button in the upper-left corner of the Help window.

   Your screen should look like Figure 1-24. If necessary, click the Contents tab to make it the active tab.

Figure 1-24 ◀
Contents
tab of the
Help window

Contents tab active ——

open this book icon ——

Depending on whether you are running the Visual Basic Learning, Professional, or Enterprise edition, the items listed in the Contents tab might differ from those shown in Figure 1-24.

2. Click the book icon labeled **Controls Reference**, then click the **Open** button. The icon changes from a closed book to an open book and several other options appear.

3. Click the book icon labeled **Intrinsic Controls**, then click **Open** again, as shown in Figure 1-25.

Figure 1-25 ◀
Contents tab
with an
open book

closed book icon

open book icon

click to display help
for the Image Control

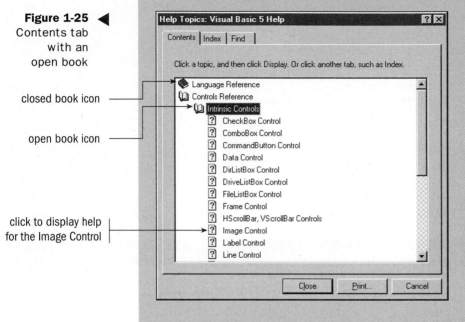

4. Click the **Image control** Help Topic, then click the **Display** button to open it. Read the text in the Help Topic that explains the Image control.

5. Use the shortcut menu to print the Help Topic.

6. Click the **Close** button ☒ on the Help window title bar to close the window and exit the Help system.

Now you are ready to begin creating the buttons and boxes on the blank form. First, you need to set the properties of the form itself and then you can create the necessary control instances. When Visual Basic was started, a new project was created with a single form. Now you are ready to modify the form so it is useful to Southern Properties Group. In this case, you need to change the size of the main form so the images Mark wants to display will fit inside the region of the form, and set the form's Caption property to display a more meaningful title in the form's title bar.

To set or change any property, you first need to display the Properties window for the selected object (in this case, the form).

To display the Properties window for the main form using the shortcut menu:

1. Click **Form1 (Form 1)** in the Project Explorer.

TROUBLE? If necessary, open the Project Explorer by clicking the Project Explorer button.

If the forms are not displayed under the Forms folder click the "+" sign to display them.

2. Click the **View Object** button ⊞ at the top of the Project Explorer. The Form1 window becomes the active window.

3. Click the **right mouse** button while the cursor is positioned over the Form1 window to activate the shortcut menu.

4. Click **Properties** to activate the Properties window, then click the **Categorized** tab if necessary. See Figure 1-26.

Figure 1-26 ◀
Properties
window
components

title bar

object box

Height property

property names

property values

list arrow for selecting other objects

scroll bar

The Properties window title bar identifies the current object, in this case Form1, which is the value of the Name property assigned to the form. The object box identifies the selected object, which also is Form1, followed by the type of the object, which is a form. The list arrow at the right side of the object box allows you to select another object and display its properties. The left column in the window lists the properties available for the selected object, and the right column lists the current value for each property. If all the properties will not fit in the window, you can use the displayed scroll bar to scroll through the Properties window. Note that properties either can be displayed in alphabetical order or in a categorized order by clicking the Alphabetic or Categorized tab. The Categorized tab divides properties into categories based on their purpose. For example, the Position category lists the properties that control the size and position of the form on the screen.

To view properties in the Properties window:

1. Use the scroll bar to move through the list of properties to see which properties you can set for a form.

2. Click the **Categorized** tab in the Properties window to view the properties applicable to a form organized by category.

You now can use the Properties window to set properties for the form.

Setting the Size and Position of a Form

The needs of a particular program determine the size of each form. The program you are creating will display a 3-by-3-inch picture or smaller. In addition, you will be adding a Label object to the form that will display the name of the currently loaded file. This information will occupy the top 1 inch of the form. Thus, the form should be about 4 inches tall and 4½ inches wide. The dimensions of a form are set using the Height and Width properties. All Visual Basic dimensions are measured in twips. A **twip** is a unit of screen measurement specifying about 1440 twips per inch. So, to create a 4-by-4½-inch form, you would set the Height and Width properties to 4335 and 5025 twips, respectively. The size indicator on the far right of the toolbar tells you the height and width in twips of the current object.

You also can specify where on the screen the form should be displayed by setting the Left and Top properties. If you set both the Left and Top properties of a form to zero (0), the form would be displayed in the upper-left corner of the screen. The position indicator on the right of the toolbar tells you the position of the current object. If the object is a form, the position is relative to the upper-left corner of the screen. If the object is an instance of a control you drew on the form, the position is relative to the upper-left corner of the form.

REFERENCE window

SETTING THE SIZE AND POSITION OF A FORM

- If the Properties window is not displayed, place the pointer in an empty area of the form, click the right mouse button to display the shortcut menu, then click Properties.
- Click the value for the Height property, then type in the new value for the height.
- Click the value for the Width property, then type the new value for the width.
- Click the values for the Left and Top properties, then type the new value for each.

To change the size and location of the form relative to the screen, you need to change four properties: Height, Width, Left, and Top. Mark has asked that you create a 4-by-4½-inch form, located about 1 inch from the upper-left corner of the screen. Remember that 1 inch equals approximately 1440 twips, so the height of the form will be 4335, the width of the form will be 5025, and the left and top dimensions will be 1440 each.

To set the size and position of the form:

1. Be sure the Properties window is active and set to the form named **Form1**. Click the **Categorized** tab.

2. Scroll down the Properties window to locate the **Position** section.

3. Locate the **Height** property, then highlight its default property value. The text you type next will replace the highlighted default value.

4. Type **4335**.

5. Press the **Enter** key.

   The form changes size on your screen.

6. Locate the **Width** property, highlight the property value, then type **5025**.

7. Locate the **Left** property, highlight the property value, then type **1440**.

   The size and location of the form changes as you enter each value.

8. Locate the **Top** property, highlight the property value, then type **1440**.

   The form repositions itself to the new Top property value on your screen.

Setting the Caption for a Form

Like any window in Windows 95, a Visual Basic form contains text in the title bar to identify the purpose of the form. You specify this text by setting the form's Caption property. Unlike a name, a caption can include spaces and punctuation characters. Although the caption can contain any number of characters, it should fit in the title bar of the form.

Mark suggests you use the caption "Southern Properties Group - Image Viewer" for the form you are editing. This will communicate the purpose of the form to the user.

To set the caption for the form:

1. Locate the **Caption** property in the Appearance section of the Properties window, then highlight its property value **Form1**.

2. Type **Southern Properties Group - Image Viewer**. The caption in the form's title bar changes to the new value. See Figure 1-27.

Figure 1-27 ◀
Setting the
form's caption

caption in the
form's title bar

Now that you have set the properties for the form, you are ready to create instances of the necessary controls on the form. Then you can set the properties for each control.

Setting the Name of the Form

In addition to the Caption property, each object you create has an associated name, which is stored in the Name property of the object. When Visual Basic created the form for you, it assigned a default name (Form1) for the form. Mark suggests, however, you assign a more meaningful name to the form. Note that the Caption and Name properties are different. You use the Caption property to display informational text inside the title bar of the form; and you use the Name property to identify the object and to refer to it when writing Visual Basic statements. You should set the Name property for most objects so the code in your program is easier to understand. There are several rules for naming objects like forms:

- The first character of the name must be a letter.

- The following characters can be letters, numbers, or the underscore character.

- The name must be fewer than 255 characters in length.

- A name cannot include special characters such as symbols or spaces.

- A name should begin with a standard prefix describing the type of the object.

Mark suggests you set the name of the form so the name describes its purpose. Because the standard prefix of the form is frm and the program is an image viewer for Southern Properties Group, he suggests you use the name frmSouthernImageViewer.

To set the name for the form:

1. Locate the **Name** property in the Misc section of the Properties window, then highlight its property value **Form1**.

2. Enter the name **frmSouthernImageViewer**.

Before continuing to create the objects on the form, Mark suggests you first save both the form and the project. If you make a mistake, you will be able to open the files you already saved and continue.

To save the form and project files:

1. Be sure your Student Disk is in the drive then click **File** on the menu bar, then click **Save Project** to activate the Save File As dialog box. Remember that any unsaved forms are saved, then the project is saved.

2. Click the **Save in** list arrow, click **3½ Floppy (A:)**, then click the folder named **Tutorial.01.**

3. Accept the default file name **frmSouthernImageViewer.frm**, then click **Save**.

4. After saving the form, the Save Project As dialog box will appear. Enter the project name **Southern Image Viewer.vbp**, then click **Save**.

You now have saved the form and project files to your Student Disk. If you make a mistake, you can start by loading the project file named Southern Image Viewer.vbp and begin again from this point. By saving your work frequently, you will be able to start again from that point and continue. Mark suggests you continue by creating the necessary objects on the form to display pictures of the properties they sell.

Adding Controls to a Form

When you place a control on a form, you are creating an instance of the control that also is known as an object. The form itself also is an object. You can have multiple occurrences or instances of the same type of object on a form. That is, you can have three buttons on the same form that perform different actions like an OK button, a Cancel button, and a Help button. The controls available on the toolbox depend on both the version of Visual Basic you are using and whether or not any third-party add-in controls have been added to the toolbox. A **third-party add-in control** is a control created by another vendor and sold for use with the standard Visual Basic controls. Such add-in controls can provide added functionality, such as spell checking, or they might simply provide ways to make your programs more visually appealing.

In this session you need to use four different controls to create the program as shown in Figure 1-28; a text box for the user to type in the name of a file, a label to describe the purpose of the text box, an image to display the picture stored in the file, and a command button that, when clicked, will cause the picture to be displayed.

Figure 1-28 ◀
Controls
created on
the form

label

text box

image

command button

You will begin by adding a Label control that will describe to the user the purpose of the text box in which they will enter a file name. You then will create the text box. Remember, you use the controls on the toolbox to add objects to a form. After you place an object on the form, you can manipulate it; for example, you can reposition, resize, or delete any object you create.

Adding a Label Control

The Label control allows you to display text on your form. For example, you might want a label to include text that identifies another object. Another use of the label is to display the results of some computation. For example, you might have a program that adds sales numbers and displays a number representing total sales. You can display such a value in a label. Remember, labels are for display purposes only; a user cannot interact with a label. Like a form, labels too have properties. In addition to having Caption, Height, Left, Top, and Width properties, a label has properties that describe the font and color of the foreground and background.

REFERENCE window	**ADDING A LABEL CONTROL TO A FORM**
	■ Click the Label control on the toolbox.
	■ Click and drag the mouse to draw and position a label on the form.
	■ Set the Caption property to the desired text.
	■ Set the Height, Left, Top, and Width properties to change the label's position on the form.

In this case, the label you will add to your form will display a prompt that will describe the purpose of the control it identifies, the text box. The prompt will not change while the program is running. (You will create the TextBox control later in this session.)

To add the Label control to your form:

1. Click the **Label** control ⌐A⌐ on the toolbox.

   Move the pointer to the left side of the Form window, which is where you want the upper-left corner of the Label object to be located. See Figure 1-28 for the location of the Label control. The pointer changes to $+$.

2. Click and hold down the **left mouse** button, then drag the pointer down and to the right to create an outline of the Label object.

   Notice that while you are in design time the form includes a grid of dots. When you draw objects on the form, the object is aligned with the dots on the grid.

3. When the size of the object is similar to the size of the Label object shown in Figure 1-29, release the left mouse button. The object appears on the form.

Figure 1-29 ◄
Creating a label

default caption for object

sizing handles

TROUBLE? Do not worry if the Label object on your screen is not exactly in the same location or is not the same size as the object shown in the figure. You will reposition and resize objects later.

Note that Visual Basic assigns a name to the object; in this case, Label1. Each object on a form must have a unique name. Therefore, if you place a second instance of the Label control on the form without changing the name of the first label, Visual Basic would assign the name Label2 to the second Label object. Also, notice the eight small, colored boxes that appear around the border of the label. These boxes are called **sizing handles** and they identify the active object. You can use the handles to resize the object, as you will learn later in this session. Because the label is the active object, the Properties window shows the properties for this object.

Setting a Label's Properties

Just as a form has properties, each object on a form has properties. The properties of an object can determine the appearance of the object (for example, its color), the font of the object's text (if any), the position of the object on the screen, and whether or not the object is visible on the screen. Some properties, such as color and screen location, are common to most types of objects. Other properties are unique, however, and define the specific attributes of a particular object type. As an analogy, consider two objects—an automobile and an airplane. Both an automobile and an airplane have similar properties, such as color, weight, and engine size. This does not necessarily mean that they have the same color, just that each has a color. Some properties, however, are meaningful only to the airplane; for example, only an airplane has a wing size. Visual Basic objects are similar. For example, both a label and an image have properties like Left and Top that determine where the object appears on the form. Because the label is used to display text, however, it has a Caption property to describe text, while the image has a Picture property to describe the picture to be displayed.

Next, you need to set the properties for the Label object. Although you can set properties at any time while you are developing the program, it is best to set them immediately after creating the object so you do not forget to set the necessary properties. Here you need to set the Caption property for the label to describe the purpose of the text box you will create in a moment.

Naming the Label Object

The initial name of the Label object you created is Label1, just as the initial name of the form object was Form1. Like the form, you should change the name to a more meaningful one by setting the Name property.

The label you just created contains a prompt to describe the contents of the text box you will create in a moment so lblPrompt is an appropriate name.

To set the Caption and Name properties of the Label object:

1. Make sure the Label object still is selected (that is, handles appear on the object).

2. Click the **Alphabetic** tab in the Properties window if necessary, then highlight the default **Caption** property value **Label1**.

3. Enter **Enter file name:** as the caption.

4. Highlight the default value for the **Name** property. Enter the text **lblPrompt** for the property's value. The Label object now contains the text you just entered. See Figure 1-30.

Figure 1-30 ◄
Setting
the label's
properties

Name property set

Caption property set

Moving an Object

When you create an object on the form, you often will need to change the location of the object—perhaps because a design specification has changed or because the objects on the form are not visually balanced. You can move any object on a form by first clicking the object to select it then using the pointer to drag the object to a new location. You will practice moving the Label object on your form.

To move the Label object:

1. Make sure the Label object still is selected. (The sizing handles should be visible.)

2. Place the pointer anywhere within the Label object, but not on a handle.

3. Click and hold down the **left mouse** button, then move the mouse to drag the object to a different location. An outline of the object appears on the form and moves to show the new object position as you move the mouse. See Figure 1-31.

Figure 1-31 ◄
Moving the
label

outline of object ────

position ToolTip ────

Note that the position indicator ToolTip shows the position of the active object, the label.

4. Release the left mouse button when the object is in the location you want.

5. Use the mouse to move the Label object back to the original location shown in Figure 1-31.

6. To deselect the Label object, click anywhere in a blank area of the Form window. The form now becomes the selected object, and its properties are displayed in the Properties window.

Resizing an Object

In addition to moving an object, you also can change an object's size by modifying the object's width or height. Again, this might be necessary because of changes in design specifications or to improve or correct the appearance of objects on the form. For example, if you create a Label object that is too small to hold the label's Caption property value, you would need to increase the size of the object.

To resize the Label object:

1. Click the Label object to select it and display the sizing handles.

   TROUBLE? If you accidentally double-click the object, the Code window will be activated. (You will learn more about the Code window later in this session.) Click the Close button ☒ on the Code window title bar to close the window, then repeat Step 1.

2. Position the pointer on the handle in the lower-right corner of the object. The pointer changes to ↘ . When you use one of the four corner sizing handles to resize an object, the object will be resized both horizontally and vertically. When you use one of the center sizing handles, the object will be resized in one direction only, depending on the handle you are using.

3. Click and hold down the **left mouse** button, then move the pointer down and to the right to increase the size of the object, as shown in Figure 1-32.

Figure 1-32 ◀
Resizing
the label

outline shows the
resized object

ToolTip shows new
width and height

Note that the ToolTip reflects the width and height of the active object, the label.

4. Release the left mouse button when the object is the size you want.

Just as you set the size and position of the form by setting the Height, Left, Top, and Width properties of the form, you can set the properties of an object in the same way. The only difference is that the Left and Top properties of an object are relative to the form, not the entire screen.

To set the size and position of the label using the Properties window:

1. Click the label to activate it. The Properties window displays the properties for the Label object.

2. Set the following properties for the Label object in the Properties window: Height = **255**; Left = **120**; Top = **120**; Width = **1215**.

Deleting an Object

Occasionally, you will need to delete an object from a form, perhaps because you created the object by mistake or the object is no longer used in the program. To delete an object you simply click the object then press the Delete key. Because you will be using the Label object in your program, there is no need to delete it.

Now that you have created the label and set its properties, you can create the next object on the form—the TextBox object.

Adding a TextBox Control to a Form

There is another control similar to a label that works with text called a TextBox control. In addition to just displaying textual information, however, the user can enter text into a text box. Like the label, it has a Name property. It also has the same properties as the label to describe the position of the label on the form. The information displayed in a text box, however, is controlled by the Text property rather than the Caption property. A text box also has a three-character prefix like a label. The standard three-character prefix for a text box is "txt".

Because the text box you are creating will be used to get the file name of a picture from the user, Mark suggests you set the Name property for the object to txtFileName. Also, because the user will enter the text into this object when the program is running, the Text property should be blank when the program starts.

To create the text box:

1. Click the **TextBox** control 🔲 on the toolbox.

2. Move the pointer to the left side of the Form window just below the label you created, which is where you want the upper-left corner of the TextBox object to be located. See Figure 1-33 for the location of the TextBox control.

Figure 1-33 ◀
Creating the
text box

new TextBox object ——

3. Click and hold down the **left mouse** button, then drag the pointer down and to the right to create an outline of the TextBox object.

Notice that while you are in design time the form includes a grid of dots. When you draw objects on the form, the object is aligned with the dots on the grid.

4. Set the Name property to **txtFileName.**

5. Remove the text from the Text property.

6. Set the Height property to **285**, the Left to **120**, the Top to **480**, and the Width to **3255**.

Adding a CommandButton Control to a Form

After the user enters the file name containing a picture into the text box, you need a way to tell the program that it should use the file name to display the picture in an image. There is a control called a command button that when clicked will perform some type of action, like displaying a picture. You probably have used command buttons before, as they are used throughout most Windows 95 programs. When you used the Options dialog box in the first session to customize Visual Basic settings, the dialog box had three command buttons across the bottom of the form with the captions OK, Cancel, and Help. In this session you need to create a command button that, when clicked, will display a picture in an Image object. You will create the Image object later in the session.

Like the Label and TextBox objects you just created, the command button uses the same properties to define the size of the button and its position on the form. Inside a command button you usually create a descriptive prompt to describe the button's purpose. The prompt, like the label, is stored in the Caption property. Like the other objects you have created, you should set the name of a command button using a standard prefix followed by a name that describes the button's purpose. The standard prefix for a command button is "cmd". Because the command button will be used to display an image, you will name the button cmdDisplayImage.

Mark suggests you now create the command button and set the necessary properties.

To create the command button and set its properties:

1. Click the **CommandButton** control ⬚ on the toolbox.

2. Draw a command button on the form.

3. In the Properties window, click the **value** column for the Name property.

4. Enter the name **cmdDisplayImage**.

5. Click the **Caption** property. You may need to use the scroll bars to locate the property.

6. Enter the caption **Display Image**. Note that as you edit the value of the Caption property, the caption in the command button changes.

7. Set the Height property to **375**, the Left to **3480**, the Top to **3480**, and the Width to **1335**.

Adding an Image Control to a Form

The program you are creating for Southern Properties Group must display different graphical images as selected by the user. You also can include graphic images or pictures on a form to add visual interest to your program. Graphic images are stored in many different formats. In this case the images Southern Properties Group is using are Windows bitmap files. Bitmap files have the extension .bmp.

The Image control allows you to display graphic images on a form. If you display too many large images in your program at the same time, the program may run slowly.

By default, the picture you insert into an Image object has a fixed size and may differ from the size and shape of the Image object. So, if you create a 1-by-1-inch Image object on your form and insert a 2-by-2-inch picture, the picture will appear cropped. Setting the Image object's Stretch property to True causes the picture to be the size of the Image object.

Whether or not you should set the Stretch property to True depends on the particular picture you are placing on the form. For example, if the shape of the picture is significantly different from the shape of the Image object and the Stretch property is set to True, the picture will be scaled to fill the Image object and could appear distorted. Like the Label control, the Image control should have a standard prefix for the Name property so you can identify the type of object easily as you write Visual Basic code. The standard prefix for an Image object is "img".

REFERENCE window

ADDING AN IMAGE CONTROL TO A FORM

- Click the Image button on the toolbox.
- Click and drag the mouse to draw the Image object on the form.
- Set the Name property to the prefix img followed by a meaningful description.
- Set the Stretch property to True to cause the picture to be stretched to fill the Image object, or leave it set to False to include the picture in your form at its original size.
- Set any other necessary properties for the selected Image object in the Properties window.

Mark suggests you create the Image object now and set its properties so it can display different images when the program is running. Because all the images will be of the same size, you do not need to set the Stretch property to True.

To create the Image object:

1. Click the **Image** control 🖻 on the toolbox.

2. Position the pointer in the upper-left corner of the form.

3. Hold down the **left mouse** button and move the mouse down and to the right. An outline of the Image object is displayed.

4. In the Properties window, set the Height property to **2895**, the Left property to **120**, the Top property to **960**, and the Width property to **3255**.

5. Set the Name property to **imgCurrent**. Your form should look like Figure 1-34.

Figure 1-34 ◀
Creating the
Image object

You have created the necessary objects to display the file name and an image. The next step in the program's development is to write the necessary statements to accomplish these tasks.

The Code Window

To create the Visual Basic code that will display a graphical image, and its corresponding file name, you must define the actions taken when the event (clicking an item on the menu) occurs. These actions consist of Visual Basic code contained in event procedures. An **event procedure** is a set of Visual Basic statements that are executed when a user performs an action on an object, such as clicking a command button. An object can have several different event procedures. For example, some objects can execute one series of statements when the user clicks the mouse button and another series of statements when the user double-clicks the mouse button. This is because these are two different events, and an object can execute different event procedures in response to different events.

You write all Visual Basic statements using a text editor called the **Code window**. After you type a line of code and press the Enter key, Visual Basic will format the line and check the syntax of the statement to make sure it is correct. If you enter a statement that Visual Basic cannot understand, it will display a dialog box describing the error.

The code you write will perform one task. It will load a picture into the Image object you created. This code needs to be executed when the user clicks the command button on the form.

Entering the Code for the Command Button

To create the code for the command button, you need to open the Code window and enter the necessary statement. Before you can write the code for the cmdDisplayImage object's Click event procedure, you need to learn how to use the Code window to select an object and the appropriate event procedure.

The Code window contains two list boxes. The Object list box shows all the objects in your program, which consist of the form itself and all the different controls you have drawn on the form. The Procedure list box lists all the different events to which the object can respond. Each object can respond to events like a command button being clicked. The events shown in the Procedure list box depend on the type of object you selected, because different objects respond to different events.

There are two ways to locate a specific event procedure for an object. If you double-click an object like a command button, the Code window will be opened to the most frequently used event for the object. In the case of the command button, this is the Click event. You also can select an event procedure manually by first selecting the desired object using the Object list arrow, then selecting the desired event procedure using the Procedure list arrow.

To select the object and event in the Code window:

1. Be sure the Form window is the active object.

2. Click the **right mouse** button while the cursor is positioned inside of the Form window to activate the shortcut menu.

3. Click **View Code** on the shortcut menu. The Code window opens.

4. Click the **Object** list arrow, then click **cmdDisplayImage**, as shown in Figure 1-35.

Figure 1-35 ◄
The Code window

Object list box

Object list arrow

Procedure list box

TROUBLE? The size and shape of the Code window might differ from the window in Figure 1-35. You can resize the Code window to suit your preferences. The initial entries in the Object and Procedure list boxes also might differ from those in the figure, depending on the object selected when the Code window opened.

You need to write the code to display the file in the Image object and the file name in the Label object. Now that you have selected the object and the event procedure, you can complete the code necessary to open a graphical image and display it in an Image object.

You need to type the statements shown in bold:

```
Private Sub cmdDisplayImage_Click( )
    'Load the image using the file name stored in
    'the TextBox control.
    imgCurrent.Picture = LoadPicture(txtFileName.Text)
End Sub
```

Before you enter the code in the Code window, take a moment to first examine each statement separately and see what it does.

```
Private Sub cmdDisplayImage_Click( )
```

The line begins with the words Private Sub. The Private and Sub keywords tell Visual Basic that this is the beginning of an event procedure that can contain Visual Basic code. The word Private tells Visual Basic that this event procedure only can be used inside this form. The word Sub tells Visual Basic that the procedure will not send information back to other procedures. Visual Basic created the Private Sub statement automatically.

```
End Sub
```

The End Sub statement tells Visual Basic where the event procedure stops. When this statement is reached, the program will stop executing the event procedure and wait for the user to do something that causes another event. Visual Basic created the End Sub statement automatically.

The procedure named cmdDisplayImage_Click( ) will be executed when a user clicks the Display Image command button. Notice that the name of the event procedure consists of the name of the object (stored in the Name property) followed by an underscore, followed by the name of the event. It is by using this procedure name that Visual Basic can determine which event procedure to execute. If you accidentally change the name of the procedure, Visual Basic will not be able to locate the event procedure and execute the code it contains in response to an event.

```
'Load the image using the file name stored in
    'the TextBox control.
```

These two statements are known as program comments. You include **program comments** in code to explain the purpose of the program and describe what it accomplishes. A program comment always begins with the apostrophe character ('). Visual Basic ignores all program comments and does not execute them.

```
imgCurrent.Picture = LoadPicture(txtFileName.Text)
```

This line in the program contains a statement that is executed by Visual Basic. This statement is made up of two parts; a leftmost side and a rightmost side separated by an equal sign (=). This is called an **assignment statement**. In other words, the task on the rightmost side is performed and assigned to the leftmost side. The rightmost side contains a **function** named LoadPicture. A function is a way of executing a set of statements that perform a common task. Visual Basic supplies you with several **intrinsic functions** to perform mathematical tasks like computing the square root of a number or loading a graphical image into an Image object. To send information to a function, you use arguments. **Arguments** contain information like numbers, in the case of the function to compute a square root, or a string of characters representing a file name, in the case of the LoadPicture function. When you use a function in a Visual Basic statement, you call the function. When you call a function, the code in the function is executed using the supplied arguments. After the code has been executed, intrinsic functions return a value like the square root of a number, or an object like a graphical image.

This statement also sets a property a run time. Until now, you have set an object's properties by changing values in the Properties window when you created the objects. You also can write Visual Basic statements that allow you to view and change properties while a program is running. You can perform many tasks, such as changing the font of text in a text box for emphasis while a user is entering text.

As you have seen, you can use the Properties window to set the Caption property of a label. You also can set many properties at run time using Visual Basic code. When to set properties depends on the needs of your program. Properties that do not change, or the initial value for a property, such as a label's caption, should be set at design time using the Properties window. When the appearance of an object needs to change while the program is running, you must change the property by writing Visual Basic code. In fact, you cannot use the Properties window while the program is running. For example, you might set the initial font and type style of a label using the Properties window. Then, when the object is active while the program is running, the font can change to emphasize the object to the user.

To set the properties of an object while the program is running, you use the following syntax for the code you enter in the Code window:

ObjectName.PropertyName = value

- *ObjectName* is the name you assigned to the object's Name property when you created it. Remember, Visual Basic always assigns a name to an object. You should set the Name property to change the name to something meaningful to your program.

- *PropertyName* is the name of the object's property you want to change while the program is running.

- The *value* is the new value for the property. You must be careful to assign only valid values to properties. For example, properties such as Caption can contain any text value, whereas properties such as Picture, which you use to control the graphical image displayed in an Image object, can contain only pictures.

The LoadPicture function is used to load a graphical image into the Picture property of an Image object at run time. The LoadPicture function accepts one argument—a string of characters containing the name of the file to be loaded into the picture—and returns the picture that can be stored in the Picture property of an Image object.

This statement is shown indented in the code. Statements between the Private Sub and End Sub statements usually are indented so the start and end of a procedure can be recognized easily. Indenting statements is solely for the benefit of the programmer. Visual Basic ignores all leading spaces and tab characters that you use to indent statements.

Now that you understand the code you need to write, you're ready to enter the code in the Code window.

To enter the code for the Display Image command button:

1. Enter the code as shown in Figure 1-36.

Figure 1-36 ◀
Entering
statements in
the Code
window

cmdDisplayImage
object selected

enter these three
statements

Click event selected

```
Private Sub cmdDisplayImage_Click()
    'Load the image using the file name stored in
    'the TextBox control.
    imgCurrent.Picture = LoadPicture(txtFileName.Text)
End Sub
```

2. Click the **Close** button ☒ on the Code window title bar to close the window.

Now that your program is complete, Mark suggests you run it, verify it is working correctly, and save the form and project files.

Running the Completed Program

To run a program, you simply click the Start button on the toolbar. Remember, any time you run a program, Visual Basic switches from design mode to run mode, activates the startup form, and waits for user input. You can stop a program at any time by clicking the End button on the toolbar.

To run and test the program:

1. Click the **Save Project** button 🖫 on the toolbar to save your work.

2. Click the **Start** button ▶ on the toolbar.

Your form appears on the screen; Visual Basic has loaded all the form's objects and their associated code.

3. Test the program by entering the file named **A:\Tutorial.01\Item1.bmp**.

4. Click the **Display Image** command button to load the image stored in the file named **Item1.bmp**.

5. The graphical image and file name should appear in the main form as shown in Figure 1-37.

Figure 1-37 ◀
Running the
completed
program

image displayed

enter the file name
to display

click the command
button to display
the image

6. Click the **End** button ▣ on the toolbar.

7. Click the **File** menu, then click **Exit** to exit Visual Basic.

When you clicked the command button, the Click event procedure corresponding to the button was executed. That is, Visual Basic located the event procedure named cmdDisplayImage_Click and executed the statement you wrote. Then it located the End Sub statement and waited for the user to click the button again.

Congratulations, you have completed the task of writing your first Visual Basic program. Mark is pleased with the results and is certain you are ready to create more challenging programs.

Quick Check

1 What is the Properties window used for?

2 What is the purpose of the Label and TextBox controls?

3 How do you resize, move, and delete objects?

4 What is the purpose of the Image control?

5 What is the purpose of the Code window?

Figure 1-38 lists and defines the new terms presented in this tutorial.

Figure 1-38 ◀
New terms

Term	Definition
Application Wizard	The Application Wizard is a tool that creates a template for a program that you then can modify to perform the different tasks you desire.
Arguments	An argument is how information is passed to a function. Arguments contain information like numbers or text.
Assignment statements	An assignment statement is a type statement containing a leftmost side, an equal sign, and a rightmost side. The value of the leftmost side is stored in the rightmost side.
Basic module	A type of module containing statements that can be used by other modules.
Break mode	Break mode is an operating mode of Visual Basic where the execution of the program temporarily is suspended.
Class	A class is a template for an object that defines the supported properties, methods, and events.
Code	A Visual Basic statement or statements to accomplish a particular task.
Code window	The Code window is a text editor where you enter Visual Basic statements. You can select an object and event procedure, then type statements into the window.
Computer programming	Computer programming is the process of writing a set of organized statements that accomplish a specific task.
Control	A control is a tool used to perform some task in Visual Basic. Every control has a set of characteristics known as properties. A control can recognize different events, such as a mouse click or a keystroke.
Design time	Design time is an operating mode of Visual Basic where you create an object on the form, and write the Visual Basic statements to perform the tasks in your program.

Figure 1-38 ◀
New terms
(continued)

Term	Definition
Event	An event is an action that occurs because of some user or program activity. A program can respond to events, such as clicking a mouse button or typing a keystroke.
Event-driven	An event-driven program is a program that performs actions in response to some user activity like clicking a button.
Event procedure	A set of Visual Basic statements that are executed in response to a user action like clicking the mouse.
Form	When a user runs a program, the user communicates with the program using the objects on the form. Forms are stored on the disk with the extension .frm. Form names are stored in the program's project file.
Form module	A form module contains all the objects on the form, and the code for those objects
Form window	A form window is a window in which you design a user interface.
Function	A function is a way of executing a set of statements to perform a common task.
Instance	An instance is a control drawn on a form. An instance of a control also is considered an object.
Integrated Development Environment (IDE)	The Integrated Development Environment (IDE) contains all the tools necessary to create, run, and test a Visual Basic computer program.
Intrinsic functions	An intrinsic function is a function supplied by Visual Basic to perform a common task like loading a picture.
MDI parent window	An MDI parent window is a window that contains other windows. The Visual Basic IDE has an MDI parent window that displays all the other Visual Basic windows.
Method	A method describes the different actions you can perform on an object. For example, many objects support a Move method that allows you to reposition the object on the form while the program is running.
Module	A module is a part of your program stored as a file on the disk. All the parts of a form are stored in a single file, which is called a form module.
Object	An object is an instance (occurrence) of a control drawn on a form. An object might be a label or an image.
Object-oriented	An object-oriented programming language uses objects like buttons and boxes to perform tasks.
Program	A program is a set of statements written in a computer language to accomplish a specific task. The task may be as simple as adding two numbers together or as complex as computing the payroll for a large corporation.
Programming language	A programming language uses words with a specific meaning connected together in a specific order to form statements. All the different words with a specific meaning make up a programming language.
Program comments	A program comment is a line that begins with the apostrophe character ('). These comments are used to describe the task that is being performed. Visual Basic ignores program comments and does not execute them.
Project Explorer	The Project Explorer shows all the program components. It is used to manage the program components.
Project file	A project file is the collection of files that make up a Visual Basic program. A project file is stored on the disk with the extension .vbp. A project file contains a list of the forms and other parts of a program.

Figure 1-38 ◀
New terms
(continued)

Term	Definition
Properties window	The Properties window provides options you use to manage the appearance of each object on a form.
Property	A property is a characteristic of an object, such as the object's color, caption, screen location, or size. Properties also determine whether an object is visible or not.
Run time	Run time is one of the operating modes of Visual Basic. When in run time, the user can interact with the objects on the form.
Sizing handles	Sizing handles are boxes that surround the active object. You can use the handles to resize the object by clicking and dragging the mouse over the handle.
Shortcut menu	A shortcut menu is a menu that appears when the right mouse button is clicked. A shortcut menu provides a quick way to execute frequently used commands.
Statements	A statement is like a sentence in English. It is made up of different words entered in a defined order to accomplish a specific task.
Syntax	Syntax is the rules describing the valid statements for a programming language.
Third-party add-in control	A third-partyadd-incontrol is a control that is not part of Visual Basic. Instead, it is written by another software vendor for use in Visual Basic. The control adds additional functionality to Visual Basic.
Toolbox	The toolbox is a window containing all the different controls available for use in your program.
Twip	A twip is a device, independent unit of measurement used to position objects on the screen. There are about 1440 twips per inch.
User interface	The user interface is what the user of the program sees on the screen and how the user interacts with the program.
Window	A window is any rectangular area on the screen.

Tutorial Assignments

Amy DuBrava, an account manager at Southern Properties Group, reviewed the program you created that displayed graphical images. Amy would like you to create another program to display a stop light that can be green, yellow, or red, depending on which command button is clicked. To do this you will need to create an Image object to display three similar pictures. You also will need three command buttons that, when clicked, will display the correct image. Each object should have an appropriate name and caption. When you finish creating the program, you will run and test it. When complete, your form should look like Figure 1-39.

Figure 1-39 ◀

Southern Properties Group - Stop Sign

| Stop | Caution | Go |

1. Make sure your Student Disk is in the appropriate disk drive, then start Visual Basic.

2. Set the appropriate property so the title bar of the form contains the text **Southern Properties Group - Stop Sign.**
3. Set the Name property of the form to **frmSouthernStopSign.**
4. Resize the form so it is similar to Figure 1-39.
5. Draw an Image control on the form. Refer to Figure 1-39 for placement and sizing.
6. Set the name of the image to **imgStopSign.**

7. Set the Stretch property so the picture will fill in the region of the Image object.
8. Create three command buttons. Set the Caption property of the buttons to **Stop, Caution,** and **Go.** Set the Name property for each command button using the correct prefix and be sure the name conveys the purpose of the object.

9. The images are stored in three different files, **Stop.ico, Caution.ico,** and **Go.ico.** When the command button is clicked, you need to display the image corresponding to the button. In addition to using the Text property of a text box as an argument in the LoadPicture function, you can specify a file name explicitly by enclosing the file name in quotes. Thus, to display the image named **Stop.ico** stored in the folder named **A:\Tutorial.01\TAssign** into the object name **imgStopSign,** you would use the following statement.

```
imgStopSign.Picture = LoadPicture("A:\Tutorial.01\TAssign\StopSign.ico")
```

10. Write the necessary statements in the Click event procedure for each command button to display the corresponding bitmap file into the image object. Add a program comment to the event procedure to describe its purpose.
11. Save the form and project in the **TAssign** folder of the **Tutorial.01** folder on your Student Disk. Use the form name **frmSouthernStopSign** and the project name **Southern Stop Sign.vbp.**
12. Run the program.
13. Click each of the command buttons to be sure that a stop sign appears with the green, yellow, and red light appearing.
14. Correct any mistakes you have made and save your work again if necessary.
15. Exit Visual Basic.

Case Problems

1. Advance Computer Graphics Advance Computer Graphics uses a large number of graphic images in the Visual Basic programs created throughout the company. The owners of Advanced Computer Graphics know that Windows 95 contains a large number of bitmap (bmp) graphics files and they would like to use the Image control to display them on their forms. But they are unsure about how the Stretch property works. You will create a program with a text box for the user to enter the name of a bitmap image and a command button that when clicked will display the selected bitmaps into two Image objects. One of these Image objects will have the Stretch property set to True, and one will have the Stretch property set to False. This will illustrate to the owners how the Stretch property controls the size of Image objects. When complete, your screen should look like Figure 1-40.

Figure 1-40 ◀

1. Make sure your Student Disk is in the appropriate disk drive, then start Visual Basic.
2. Resize the form as shown in Figure 1-40.
3. Set the form name to **frmAdvanceImage**.
4. Set the title bar on the form so it contains the text **Advance Computer Graphics - Stretch**.
5. Draw a text box on the form and set the Name property using the correct prefix.
6. Remove the initial text from the text box.
7. Draw a label to describe the purpose of the text box. The text in the label should read **Enter File Name:**.
8. Draw two Image objects on the form, one on the right side of the form and one on the left. Make both objects fairly large, but leave room for the CommandButton object.

9. Change the Stretch property of the right Image object to **True** so the bitmap will fill in the region of the object.
10. Create a command button and set the caption as shown in Figure 1-40.
11. Set the Name of the command button to **cmdDisplayImages**.
12. Write two statements that will execute when the button is clicked; one to display the selected bitmap into the first image object, and the second statement to load the selected bitmap into the other image.
13. Save the form and project using the names **frmAdvanceImage.frm** and **Advance Image.vbp**. Be sure to save the project in the folder named **Tutorial.01\Cases** on your Student Disk.
14. Run the program using the bitmap images named **Advance1.bmp** and **Advance2.wmf**. These files are stored in the **Cases** folder of the **Tutorial.01** folder on your Student Disk.
15. Correct any mistakes you have made and save your work again if necessary.
16. Exit Visual Basic.

2. Atlantic Beverages Atlantic Beverages is a wholesale supplier of soft drinks specializing in the hotel industry. The delivery manager, Sam Levinson, would like a program to produce a list that will be used by the company's drivers. The program you create will move a variety of standard text items to different parts of the completed shipping document. You'll create a sample form to demonstrate how text can be moved to different parts of the form. The form you need to create will include three labels and three command buttons. Figure 1-41 shows the completed form.

Figure 1-41 ◀

Atlantic Beverages - Move Text	_ □ ×

Caption 1	Caption 2	Caption 3
Caption 1	Caption 2	Caption 3
Caption 1	Caption 2	Caption 3

1. Make sure your Student Disk is in the appropriate disk drive, then start Visual Basic.
2. Set the name of the form to **frmAtlanticMoveText**.
3. Set the title bar so it contains the text shown in Figure 1-41.
4. Draw three Label objects of approximately the same size in the upper half of the form. Be sure to set the Name property appropriately.
5. Set the BorderStyle property to **1 - Fixed Single** so a border appears around the labels.
6. Remove the text from each of the labels.
7. Draw three text boxes of approximately the same size just below the labels. Be sure to set the Name property appropriately.
8. Remove the text from each of the text boxes.
9. Draw three CommandButton objects of approximately the same size in the lower half of the form. Set the caption of each command button to **Caption 1**, **Caption 2**, and **Caption 3**, respectively, and set the Name property appropriately.

10. Open the Code window for the first command button's Click event.
11. Write the two statements that will display the command button's caption in the corresponding label and text box.
12. Save the form and project in the **Cases** folder of the **Tutorial.01** folder on your Student Disk. Use the names **frmAtlanticMoveText.frm** and **Atlantic Move Text.vbp**.
13. Run the program and click each command button. The caption of the command button should appear in the corresponding label and text box as shown in Figure 1-41.
14. Correct any mistakes you have made and save your work again if necessary.
15. Exit Visual Basic.

3. Kate's Printing Kate's Printing prints unique greeting cards for the general public. When customers come into the shop they typically see a variety of fonts, styles, colors, etc. to help them choose their cards. Kate Liu, the owner of the shop, wants to know if a Visual Basic program could be used to demonstrate the various printing options to customers by changing different properties of a label, command button, line, and image. You will look at a number of properties for each of these controls. Consult the Visual Basic Help system for additional information about the different properties.

1. Start Visual Basic.
2. Starting from the top middle of the form and working down, draw a Label object, a TextBox object, and a CommandButton object.
3. Select the Label object, then select at least five properties that you have not seen before and use them to modify the characteristics of the Label object. Make sure the Properties window does not obscure the Label object. In particular, change the various Font properties, and observe the results. Write down what occurs when you change each property. The following is a list of some commonly used label properties:

   BackColor (choose a variety of colors from the palette)

   BorderStyle (cycle through the options)

   ForeColor (choose a variety of colors from the palette)

   Font (choose a variety of sizes and types)

   Height (choose various sizes)

   Left (choose various sizes)

   Width (choose various sizes)

4. Repeat Step 3 for each of the other objects. If you do not see an obvious change to make to the object, consult the Help system for that property.
5. Save the form and project using the names **frmKateFonts.frm** and **Kate Fonts.vbp**. Be sure to save the projects in the **Cases** folder of the **Tutorial.01** folder on your Student Disk.
6. Exit Visual Basic.

4. Mountaintop College Mountaintop College is a small, private two-year college in the Sierra Nevada. The chairperson of the computer department, Mary Gorden, would like an organization chart of the department, but she does not have a computer application specifically designed for drawing organization charts. You will use Visual Basic to create the organization chart. The top box of the chart will contain the name of the department chairperson (Mary Gorden). Two middle-level boxes will contain the names of the two computer instructors, Judie Kindschi and Tom Galvez. One bottom-level box will contain your name. You will use labels as the boxes that hold the names. After the form for the organization chart is created, it will look like Figure 1-42. You will run the program to test it.

Figure 1-42 ◀

1. Start Visual Basic.
2. Starting from the top and working down, draw four labels that resemble the boxes shown in Figure 1-42.
3. Change the BorderStyle property of all four labels to **1 - Fixed Single**.
4. Look up "Line control" in online Help and read the Help information. Then, using the Line control, draw lines showing the departmental relationship between the labels.
5. Draw a CommandButton object on the bottom-right side of the form.
6. Specify the caption **Click Here To Insert Names** for the CommandButton object. If the entire caption does not fit in the command button, increase the size of the button.
7. Open the Code window for the CommandButton object and type the following program comment as the first two lines of code:

   ```
   'This code will place each department member's name in the
   'appropriate label.
   ```
8. Type the following lines of Visual Basic code between the Private Sub and End Sub lines. Substitute your name for the reference Your Name.

   ```
   Label1.Caption = "Mary Gorden"
   Label2.Caption = "Judie Kindschi"
   Label3.Caption = "Tom Galvez"
   Label4.Caption = "Your Name"
   ```
9. Close the Code window.
10. Run the program.
11. Click the command button to insert the names. Your screen looks like Figure 1-42. If any names do not fit correctly in the label, click the End button on the toolbar and resize the label. Repeat this step as necessary until all names are fully displayed in the labels.
12. End the program.
13. Save the form and project using the names **frmMountaintopOrgChart.frm** and **Mountaintop Org Chart.vbp**. Be sure to save the projects in the **Cases** folder of the **Tutorial.01** folder on your Student Disk.
14. Exit Visual Basic.

Visual Programming Lab

Visual Programming

This Lab Assignment is designed to accompany the interactive Course Lab called Visual Programming. To start the Visual Programming Lab, click the Start button on the Windows 95 taskbar, point to Programs, point to Course Labs, point to New Perspectives Applications, and click Visual Programming. If you do not see Course Labs on your Programs menu, see your instructor or lab manager.

In the Visual Programming Lab, you use an event-driven, object-oriented programming environment to create simple programs. This lab provides a "taste" of what it would be like to program in a visual language such as Visual Basic.

1. Click the Steps button to learn how to create a graphical user interface containing buttons, labels, and text boxes. As you work through the steps, answer all the Quick Check questions. After you complete the steps, you will see a Summary Report of your answers. Follow the directions on the screen to print this report.

2. In Explore, create a program to calculate the total cost of carpeting a room. Test your program, then print it showing the cost of $12.99/square yard carpeting for a 10 x 14-foot room.

   Assume the room is rectangular. The known information is the length and width of the room, and the price of a square yard of carpet. You must calculate:

   ■ the square feet of carpet needed (length * width of room)

   ■ the square yard of carpet needed (square feet/9)

   ■ the total price of carpet (price per square yard * the square yards needed)

   Your user interface should look like Figure 1-43.

Figure 1-43 ◀

| Visual Programming - EDIT |

File   Run   Help

| Button | **AB** Label | **abl** Text Box | **Current Program** SOL2.VPG | 🗑 | **Please dispose of objects properly!** |

Carpeting Calculator

This program calculates the cost of carpeting a rectangular room.

Instructions: Enter the dimensions of the room and the price per square yard of the carpet, then click the Calculate Cost button.

Length: _____
Width: _____
Price Per Yard: _____

[Calculate Cost]

The square footage of the room is _____
Yards of carpet needed is _____
The total price of carpeting will be $ _____

3. Suppose you like to shop from catalogs. Your favorite catalog is having a sale—selected merchandise is discounted 10%, 20%, 30%, or 40%. You want to know how much you'll save if you buy some of the merchandise you want. In Explore, create a program to calculate savings. Test your program, then print it showing the savings for an $863 item at a 30% discount.

   Assume the items you purchase will be discounted, and there is no additional charge for shipping. The known information is the original price of the item and its discount—10%, 20%, 30%, or 40%. Calculate how much you will save. (For example, for a 10% discount, multiply the original cost by .10.) Your user interface should look like Figure 1-44.

Figure 1-44 ◄

```
┌──────────────────────────────────────────────────────────────────────┐
│ ─            Visual Programming - EDIT                        ▼ ▲      │
│ File  Run  Help                                                        │
│ ┌─────────────────────────────────────────────────────────────────┐  │
│ │ ┌────┐   ┌──────┐  ┌──────┐   Current Program   🗑  Please dispose of│
│ │ │    │   │ AB   │  │ abl  │       SOL3.VPG          objects properly!│
│ │ └────┘   └──────┘  └──────┘                                        │
│ │  Button    Label    Text Box                                        │
│ ├─────────────────────────────────────────────────────────────────┤  │
│ │                                                                     │
│ │ DISCOUNT SHOPPER                      Product price:                │
│ │                                       ┌───────────┐                 │
│ │ This program helps you                │           │                 │
│ │ calculate how much money              └───────────┘                 │
│ │ you save when you shop!                                             │
│ │                                                                     │
│ │ Instructions:  Enter the price                                      │
│ │ of the product, then click                                          │
│ │ the appropriate discount     ┌────┐┌────┐┌────┐┌────┐               │
│ │ button.                      │10% ││20% ││30% ││40% │               │
│ │                              └────┘└────┘└────┘└────┘               │
│ │                              You save $ ┌───────────┐               │
│ │                                         └───────────┘               │
│ │                                                                     │
│ └─────────────────────────────────────────────────────────────────┘  │
└──────────────────────────────────────────────────────────────────────┘
```

4. In your recording studio, studio musicians are paid by the hour, but your sound technicians are salaried. You started to make a program to calculate weekly paychecks, but it doesn't seem to work. Your assumption is that some employees are salaried and some are hourly. You know the salaries for the salaried employees. You know the hourly wage and the hours worked each pay period for the hourly employees. You want to calculate the weekly pay for salaried employees (wages/52) and the weekly pay for hourly employees (wages * hours).

   In Explore, open the program **pay.vpg** and test it.

   Enter **32240** in the Wages box, then click the Salaried button. The output should be 620. Next enter **8** in the Wages box and **40** in the Hours box. Click the Hourly button. The output should be 320. Find what's wrong with this program and correct it. Print your solution.

Understanding Code and Variables

Designing and Writing a Financial Calculator Program
for the Island Financial Company

OBJECTIVES

In this tutorial you will:

- Become familiar with the elements of program design

- Create multiple instances of labels, text boxes, and command buttons

- Use properties to change font sizes, font color, and the alignment of characters

- Modify the tab order of objects on a form

- Use graphical objects on a form to create a visually appealing user interface

- Declare and use variables to store information

- Create expressions to perform computations like multiplication and division

- Write code inside a form module to compute the future value of an investment and format the results

- Use Visual Basic functions to convert data, format data, and compute financial values

- Identify syntax and run-time errors

CASE   Island Financial Company

The Island Financial Company maintains its headquarters in Honolulu, Hawaii, and has branch offices on each of the neighboring Hawaiian Islands. The company has been managing the investments of the wealthy retired population of the Hawaiian Islands for over five years. Island Financial was started by Kaiopo Iniki and his wife, Selena. Selena has a background in computer programming and experience in Visual Basic.

As part of the Island Financial Company's everyday business practices, analysts forecast their clients' investment growth over time. The analysts use this information to estimate cash flow and income, and to prepare the necessary financial statements. Often, clients use these statements to consider the effects of different interest rates on their income. To streamline the forecasting process, Kaiopo and Selena have asked you to help Selena create a Visual Basic program that will compute the necessary information.

Before creating the program, Selena spent time designing it so it would meet the needs of the financial analysts using it. Once her design was complete, she began to create many of the objects on the form. She still needs to create the remaining objects, write the statements to compute the future value of an investment, and then run and test the program to make sure it works properly. After reviewing Selena's design specifications, you will help her complete the program to calculate the future value of investments made by Island Financial's clients.

In this session you will learn the basic elements of good design and how to design a form for a program, create multiple instances of objects that make up the user interface and set their properties, and set the tab order of objects on a form.

Designing a Computer Program

Selena has been a programmer for many years, and she realizes that creating programs involves more than simply sitting down at a computer, designing the interface, and writing the code. In fact, to ensure a quality product, Selena has established strict guidelines specifying that an adequate amount of time be spent understanding the problem and finding the best solution before writing the actual program. You would not think of starting to build a house without a set of plans and some thought given to the materials and time involved. The same is true for programming. A little time spent in planning will save you many hours of work debugging a program or correcting design flaws. Computer programs look and work better with some forethought to the final product and where that product will fit into other programs. The company has a standard set of steps, known as a **methodology**, for designing programs. The methodology requires that each step be completed in sequence before moving on to the next step. The steps in designing a computer program are as follows:

1. Completely understand the problem and what data you need to solve it.

2. Analyze and break down the problem into simple, nontechnical terms using English sentences.

3. Sketch a picture of the user interface design for each computer screen in the program.

4. Identify the tasks that are to be performed and where those tasks will be performed.

After these steps are accomplished, you can begin creating the actual user interface and writing program code. Selena uses a methodology or design tool called the Newman-Ekedahl Application Development Tool (**NEADT**). For complete information about this design tool refer to the Design Appendix. Selena already completed the design specifications and the user interface for the program.

To view and print the NEADT chart for the calculator program:

1. Using Microsoft Word, open the file named **Island.doc** that is located in the Tutorial.02 folder on your Student Disk. If you do not have Word, open the file named **Island.txt** using WordPad.

2. Print the file.

3. Exit the word processing program.

The five forms that make up the NEADT chart describe what the program should do and how it will do it. The first form simply defines the general goal of the program in English terms called **pseudocode**. The second form shows the design of the user interface.

Moving from the general to the specific, the third form (level 3) provides the detail about the specific tasks that need to be performed, and where and when. For the calculator program, certain tasks need to be performed when the user clicks one of the two buttons, and as each text box gets and loses focus. Figure 2-1 shows the user interface design (level 2).

Figure 2-1
User interface design for the calculator program

input section

output section

descriptive labels

command button to clear input and output objects

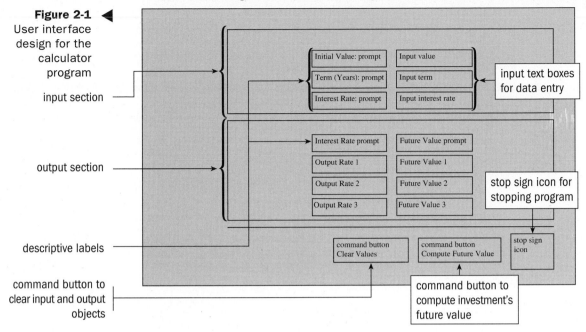

As shown in Figure 2-1, the interface will provide three text boxes for the user to input the necessary data—the initial value of the investment, the term, and the interest rate. Note that the design includes descriptive labels (prompts) to the left of these three text boxes so that the user will know what data to enter in them. The interface also contains labels for the three different interest rates and the corresponding future values of the investment. The form also will include two command buttons—one to compute the future values of an investment using the three interest rates, and the other to clear both the input and output values in preparation for another calculation. Finally, a stop sign image will be used to stop the program. Level 4 contains a more detailed breakdown of where the tasks are performed and the properties that are set.

Designing a user interface requires a bit of an artistic eye and adherence to several design principles. Figure 2-2 describes the principles that will help you create a good user interface.

Figure 2-2 ◀
Principles
of a good
user inter-
face

Control	The user always should control the program, not the other way around.
User-friendliness	The interface should help the user accomplish tasks and not call attention to itself. In other words, too many different fonts, lines, or images tend to distract the user from the task at hand.
Intuitiveness	The interface should follow a direct style that proceeds logically. So, if a user needs to complete different steps to accomplish an activity, the steps should be grouped together.
Consistency	The interface should be conceptually, linguistically, visually, and functionally consistent. Also, the font style used should be consistent throughout the interface. Avoid using more than two or three different fonts on a form. Too many fonts can cause the user interface to appear cluttered and unbalanced.
Clarity	Visual elements should be readily comprehensible.
Feedback	The interface should provide immediate and clear feedback to the user. For example, if a user adds a record to a file, the interface should inform the user that the record was added. Likewise, if a user makes an error when entering data, the interface should communicate the cause of the error and possible solutions to the user.
Graphics	The interface should not be cluttered with graphics that serve no useful purpose. Graphics can cause your program to run more slowly and they can detract from the form objects that are most important to complete the task. Logos, icons, and pictures frequently are used to guide the user. For example, an icon of a stop sign is an intuitive metaphor to use as a button to end the program.
Input	The interface should minimize instances in which the user needs to switch input modes from the mouse to the keyboard and back. This will allow the user to complete tasks more efficiently.

Creating the Calculator Program

According to Selena's design specifications for the calculator program, a user will supply input values representing an initial value, term, and beginning interest rate. When the user clicks the Compute Future Value button, the program will process and display the three future value results along with the interest rates, based on the input values. The finished form for the calculator program will look like Figure 2-3.

Figure 2-3 ◀
Completed
calculator
form

labels identifying
input

labels identifying
output

line

command button
to clear input
and output

shape surrounding
input section

shape surrounding
output section

image to stop running
program

command button to
compute future value

You will begin by opening the project file that contains the partially completed calculator form and saving it with a different name. Saving files to a new name will keep the original files intact, allowing you to start over if you make a serious mistake.

To start Visual Basic and open the project file containing the calculator form:

1. Be sure your Student Disk is in the appropriate disk drive.

2. Start Visual Basic then open the project file named **Island.vbp** located in the Tutorial.02 folder on your Student Disk.

Selena already created the form for the program and added some objects to it.

3. Highlight **frmIslandCalculator** in the Project Explorer if the form does not appear on the screen.

TROUBLE? If the Project Explorer is not open on your screen, click the Project Explorer button on the toolbar to open the window.

4. Click the **View Object** button [⊞] in the Project Explorer, if necessary. The Form window opens and displays the partially completed form. See Figure 2-4.

Figure 2-4 ◄
Calculator form
with some
objects created

labels to describe
output

labels to hold output

caption for form

Before working on the form, you will save it with a different name, then save the project file with a different name. Doing so will keep the original files intact, allowing you to start over if you make a serious mistake.

5. Click **File** on the menu bar, then click **Save frmIsland.frm As**.

6. Select the **Tutorial.02** folder on your Student Disk, change the entry in the File name text box to **frmIslandCalculator.frm**, then click the **Save** button to save the form with the new name.

7. Click **File** on the menu bar, then click **Save Project As**.

8. Select the **Tutorial.02** folder on your Student Disk, change the entry in the File name text box to **Island Calculator.vbp**, then click the **Save** button to save the project file with the new name.

As you perform the steps to write the program, you frequently will save your work. If you make an error you cannot correct, you can load the most recently saved copies of the form and project files and continue your work from that point.

Note the objects that Selena already has created. The two labels containing the text, Interest Rate and Future Value, identify the output areas for the program. The labels below the two prompts display the output data after the program processes it. Finally, Selena set the form's Caption property to "Island Financial - Time Value of Money Calculator" that appears in the title bar of the form.

Fundamentals of Visual Basic Project Files

Every Visual Basic program is composed of a number of files called modules. Whether or not a program uses all the types of modules depends on the needs of the program. When you create and save a form, all its information is stored in a Form module. This module is stored on the disk as a file with the extension ".frm".

Every Visual Basic program contains one project file with the extension ".vbp". The project file lists all the other files that make up the program. Project files usually are stored on the disk in the same folder as the other module files related to a program. One of the elements in a project file is a form. Most projects generally contain many forms.

If the project file cannot locate all the form files in the program, you might need to add the form file back into the project. The instructions in this text ask you to save all your project and form files to your Student Disk. You inadvertently might save a project or form to the hard disk on your computer instead of to your Student Disk. The most common instance of this is when your form file is on the hard disk while your project file is on your Student Disk. The project file contains a number of items related to your program including where to find and load the form or forms for the project. If you open a saved project from your Student Disk, and Visual Basic displays the message "File not found: Continue Loading Project?," the project file cannot locate one or more of its form files.

To fix the problem, you need to continue loading the project, then find the missing form file and copy it to your Student Disk in the same folder as the project file, using a program like Explorer. Then you can click Project, then Add Form. The Add Form dialog box will appear. Click the Existing tab, locate the folder containing the form, then click the Open button. Finally, you will need to set the startup object to the correct form. You can do this by clicking Project, then Project Properties. Then select the General tab, click the Startup Object list arrow, then select the desired form.

Creating the Label Objects

As you learned in Tutorial 1, you add objects to a form and then set their properties. You will use the Label control to add labels that will display both descriptive text and the results of the calculations on the screen. The user will not change the text in the labels or interact with them in any way. You can refer to Selena's plan of the user interface (Figure 2-1) to help you determine where to place the labels on the form.

To place the Initial Value label on the form:

1. Click the **Label** control $\boxed{\text{A}}$ on the toolbox.

2. Move the **pointer** to the upper-left part of the form.

3. Click and hold down the **left mouse** button, then move the mouse down and to the right. An outline of the object is displayed as you move the pointer. Also a ToolTip is displayed containing the width and height of the object.

4. When the width of the label is set to **1335** and the height is **255**, release the left mouse button.

5. To ensure an exact placement, set the Left property to **1200** and the Top property to **240**. Be sure the Height property of the label is set to **255** and the Width property is set to **1335**. The Form window should look like Figure 2-5.

Figure 2-5
Creating the
Label object

Label object

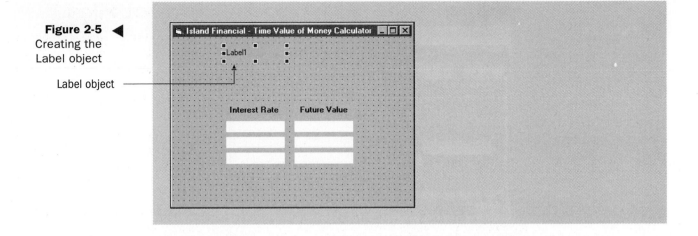

Setting the Properties for the Label Object

Now you need to change the appearance of the label you just created. Selena wants the text in each of the labels to be bold so it will stand out from the rest of the form, and she wants the labels to be right-justified so the prompts appear next to the corresponding TextBox objects. Also, she asks you to give each label a meaningful caption. Because you will not be writing any Visual Basic code to change the contents of these labels, however, there is no need to change the name of the objects.

To set the properties for the Label object:

1. Be sure the label you just created is selected, that is, the handles appear around the label.

   If the object is not selected, click the label so the handles appear.

2. Click the **Properties Window** button ⊞, if necessary, to open the Properties window.

3. Be sure the Categorized tab is active. In the Properties window for the label, click the value for the **Alignment** property.

4. Click the **Properties** button ▾ for the Alignment property in the Misc section, then click **1 - Right Justify**. This selection will cause the text of the label to be aligned on the right of the Label object.

5. Set the Caption property to **Initial Value:**.

   Note that as you type text in the Properties window, the same text appears in the Label object in the Form window, and the text is right-justified. See Figure 2-6 to see the setting for the Caption property in the Properties window.

Figure 2-6 ◀
Setting the
label's
properties

Categorized tab
active

text displayed inside
the Label object

Selena wants the prompts on a form to stand out. Next, you need to set the font
for the label to bold.

6. Click the value for the **Font** property to display the Properties button [···], then
click the **Properties** button. The Font dialog box opens.

7. Click **Bold** in the Font style list box, then click the **OK** button. See Figure 2-7. The
text in the label now appears in the bold font.

Figure 2-7 ◀
Font dialog box

font set to Bold

sample of selected
font

Creating Multiple Instances of Objects

So far, you have created only one instance of an object on your form. You could create
additional instances of the Label object by following the same steps you just completed.
Each new object you create, however, would assume the default (standard) properties of
the control, and you would have to change each individually. To save time and effort,
Selena suggests you use the copy and paste features to make copies of the Label object
already on the form and preserve the properties you set in the Initial Value object.

As you create additional instances of an object, Visual Basic assigns them unique
names. For example, if you create two labels, they will be named Label1 and Label2,
respectively.

Tip: When you will be writing statements that set the properties of an object, you should change the name so it conforms to the Naming Conventions Appendix. This will make your program more readable. When an object like a label is being used as a prompt, however, there is no need to change the object name because you will never write statements to operate on the object.

You now are ready to create the labels to prompt the user for the term of the investment in years and the interest rate.

To create the additional Label objects:

1. If necessary, click the **Initial Value:** label to select it.

2. Click the **Copy** button 🖹 on the toolbar to copy the object on the Windows Clipboard.

3. Click the **Paste** button 🖺 on the toolbar to paste a copy of the object from the Clipboard onto the form.

   Visual Basic displays a message box asking if you want to create a control array. See Figure 2-8. Control arrays are used to manipulate objects as a group and are discussed in later tutorials. For now, you do not want to create a control array.

Figure 2-8 ◀
Control array
message box

click No ——

4. Click the **No** button to close the message box. The copy of the Label object appears in the upper-left corner of the form.

   TROUBLE? If you clicked the Yes button by mistake, a control array was created. To delete the control array, delete both the object you just pasted and the original object you copied on the Clipboard. Then re-create the original label, set its properties, and repeat Steps 1 through 4.

5. Click and hold the mouse button on the object, then move the object by dragging it below the first label you created. Your screen should look like Figure 2-9.

Figure 2-9 ◀
Copying and
pasting the
Label object

original label ——

copied label ——

Note that the copied label already has the correct property values for right-justified alignment and bold font. The only property you need to set is the Caption property.

6. Set the Caption property in the Appearance section for the copied label to **Term (Years):**.

7. Activate the Form window by clicking its title bar, click the **Paste** button [icon] on the toolbar to make another copy of the label from the Clipboard. Respond "No" to the message box asking if you want to create a control array.

TROUBLE? If a new copy of the object did not appear in the upper-left corner of the form, either the Form window was not active or the contents of the Clipboard were cleared. Make sure the Form window is active; if it is, then the Clipboard was cleared. Click one of the labels you created, click the Copy button on the toolbar. Then repeat Step 7.

8. Move the new label below the second label you created.

9. Set the Caption property for the third label to **Interest Rate:**. Your form should look like Figure 2-10.

Figure 2-10 ◀
Descriptive
labels on the
form

Next, you need to create text boxes for user input to the right of each label prompt. Unlike the labels you just created, you will need to write Visual Basic code that will use the information in these objects to compute the future value of an investment. Thus, you will set the Name property of each object to make the program more readable.

Creating a TextBox Object

A **TextBox** object displays textual information and allows a user to type in values so those values can be used in the program. A text box is similar to a label. Only Visual Basic code, however, can change the contents of a label while the program is running; a user cannot type information into it.

> *Tip:* Use the Label control for text that will not change, like prompts, or when only output will be displayed. Use the TextBox control when the object must both receive input and display output.

Like a label, a TextBox object has properties, such as Alignment and Font, that you can set so the text a user enters in the text box appears as you desire. The text displayed in a label is controlled by the Caption property, whereas the text displayed in a text box is controlled by the Text property. The text box has some properties that allow it to behave differently than a label. If you want the text to appear on multiple lines you can set the MultiLine property to True. Sometimes, the text may not fit in the region of the text box. If the MultiLine property is set to True, you can set the ScrollBars property to True, allowing the user to scroll through the contents that are not visible on the screen.

CREATING A TEXTBOX OBJECT

- Click the TextBox control on the toolbox, then use the mouse to draw a TextBox object on the form.
- Set the necessary properties for the TextBox object, such as Alignment, BorderStyle, and Font, in the Properties window.
- If you want the text to appear on multiple lines, set the MultiLine property to True.
- If you want scroll bars to appear, set the ScrollBars property to True. The ScrollBars property is meaningful only if the MultiLine property is set to True.
- If you want the text to be right-justified, then set the Alignment property to 1 - Right Justify. You also must set the MultiLine property to True.
- If you want the text box to appear blank when the program is first started, delete the default Text property.
- If you want to set the Text property to blank with Visual Basic code, use the statement *TextBoxName*.Text = "".
- Set the prefix for the Name property to "txt", followed by a descriptive name.

Now you will create the three text boxes in which a user will enter the necessary input data for the initial value, term, and interest rate. These boxes will appear to the right of the labels that you created to identify the text boxes. The first text box is used to enter the initial value for the investment. Because the prefix for a TextBox object is "txt", Selena suggests you name the object txtInitialValue.

To create the first TextBox object for the calculator program:

1. Click the **TextBox** control [abl] on the toolbox, then use the mouse to draw a text box on the form to the right of the Initial Value: label.

2. The text box should be the same size as the adjacent label, and aligned to the right of it. In the Position section, set the Height property of the label to **285**, the Left property to **2760**, the Top property to **240**, and the Width property to **1335**.

3. For the text box, set the Name property in the Misc section to **txtInitialValue**.

   Next, you need to set the Text property, which determines what text, if any, is initially displayed in the text box when a user runs the program. Selena wants the text boxes to be empty so a user can immediately type the input data into them. So, you need to delete the default Text property value.

4. Select the default value **Text1** for the Text property in the Misc section, then press the **Delete** key.

You now can create the remaining TextBox objects by copying and pasting the text box you just created.

To copy and paste the other two TextBox objects:

1. Make sure the text box you just created is selected and the Form window is active.

2. Click the **Copy** button on the toolbar. A copy of the TextBox object is placed on the Clipboard, overwriting the current contents of the Clipboard, if any.

3. Click the **Paste** button 📋 on the toolbar. When the message box appears for creating a control array, click the **No** button. A copy of the text box is pasted on the form.

4. Move the new text box to the right of the Term (Years): label.

5. For the new text box, set the Name property in the Misc section to **txtTermYears**.

6. Activate the Form window, then click the **Paste** button 📋 on the toolbar to paste another copy of the text box on the form. Be sure not to create a control array.

7. Move the new text box to the right of the Interest Rate: label.

8. For the new text box, set the Name property in the Misc section to **txtInterestRate**. Your form should look like Figure 2-11.

Figure 2-11 ◀
Form after
creating the
TextBox objects

TROUBLE? If the position or the size of any label or text box is not correct, click and drag the object to reposition it, or use the sizing handles to resize the object as necessary.

Next, you need to create the two CommandButton objects on the form. The first command button allows a user to click a button to calculate the future values for the three different interest rates. The second command button allows a user to clear the values in preparation for another calculation.

Creating a CommandButton Object

The **CommandButton** control on the toolbox allows you to create a button that a user clicks to carry out an action. This is much like the buttons you have used in dialog boxes; buttons like OK and Print. When a user clicks a command button, Visual Basic executes the code written for the button's Click event. You will write these statements in the next session. A command button usually appears as a three-dimensional raised object. Inside the object you can place text to describe the button's function or display a picture to metaphorically describe the button's purpose. In this session you will learn how to display text in the command button. Because most physical buttons are raised off of some surface, command buttons almost always should appear raised.

Tip: Most windows, like the Print and Options dialog boxes in Visual Basic, place all the buttons horizontally across the bottom of the form or vertically along the rightmost side. Notice that the buttons are of the same size and positioned the same distance from each other. You should include these design standards in the programs you create to present the most consistent and easy-to-use user interface.

Like a label, a command button has a Caption property and a Name property. It has additional properties, however, to control its appearance.

- You can create your own ToolTips by setting the **ToolTipText** property. Whenever the mouse pointer is positioned over the button for about one second, the message stored in this property will appear just below the button.

- The CommandButton control has a **Default** property that, when set to True, allows a user to press the Enter key as an alternative to clicking the button to activate the button's Click event procedure. Only one CommandButton object on a form can be the default object, that is, have its Default property set to True. It would not make sense to try to have two default objects that would both try to respond to the Enter key being pressed.

- You also can create a hot key for a command button. A **hot key** is a set of keystrokes like Alt+C that, when typed, will act just like clicking the command button. You create a hot key by inserting an ampersand character (&) in the Caption property just before the character you want to act as the hot key. Each hot key on a form must be unique.

- Like other objects, you should use a standard prefix for the name. The standard prefix for the command button is "cmd".

Setting the Default property of a command button can improve the form's user interface, because it allows the user to press the Enter key to execute the most commonly used button rather than having to move their hand from the keyboard to the mouse and back. It is important to minimize the transitions between the keyboard and mouse whenever possible in the user interface. Using hot keys also allows the user a quick way to click a command button.

REFERENCE
window

CREATING A COMMANDBUTTON OBJECT

- Click the CommandButton control on the toolbox, then use the mouse to draw a CommandButton object on the form.
- Set the Caption property to describe the purpose of the button. If you want to include a hot key, precede the hot key character by an ampersand.
- Set the Default property to True to allow the user to press the Enter key rather than clicking the button. Only one button per form may have the Default property set to True.
- Set the ToolTipText property to display a message that will be helpful to the user.
- Set the prefix for the Name property to "cmd", followed by a descriptive name.

Now you need to create the command buttons for the calculator program. When a user runs the calculator program and clicks the Compute Future Value command button, the program will calculate the different future values based on information the user has entered. When the Clear Values button is clicked, the contents of the input text boxes and output labels will be cleared.

According to Selena's design, each button will include a meaningful caption to identify its function and a ToolTip to assist the user. Like the other objects you just created, the command button should have a descriptive name identifying the purpose of the object. Because the prefix of a command button is "cmd", and the button's purpose is to compute a future value, Selena suggests you name the first object "cmdComputeFutureValue".

To create the CommandButton object and set its properties:

1. Click the **Save Project** button 💾 to save the form and project.

2. Click the **CommandButton** control ▭ on the toolbox, then use the mouse to draw the CommandButton object on the form, below the rightmost column at the bottom of the form.

3. Set the Height property of the button to **375**, the Left property to **2760**, the Top property to **3240**, and the Width property to **1935**.

4. Set the Caption property of the command button to **Compute &Future Value**. Alt+F is the hot key combination for the command button.

5. Set the Name property of the command button to **cmdComputeFutureValue**.

   Next, you need to set the Default property for the command button to True so that a user can press the **Enter** key to activate the button. This will make it easier for a user to complete the form by typing the input data, then pressing the **Enter** key to calculate the results.

6. Click the value for the **Default** property, click the **Properties** button ▾ then click **True**. See Figure 2-12. With this setting, a user either can press the **Enter** key or click the command button to activate it.

Figure 2-12 ◀
Setting the command button properties

Alphabetic tab shown ———

Default property set to True

Name property set

Caption property appears in command button

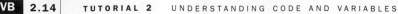

7. Click the value for the **ToolTipText** property, then type **Click to compute the investment's future value.**

Next, you need to create the command button to clear the values of the input text boxes and the output labels. Like the command button you just created, this button also will have a meaningful caption, a hot key, and a ToolTip.

To create the Clear Values command button:

1. Click the **Compute Future Value** command button to activate it.

2. Click the **Copy** button 📋 on the toolbar. A copy of the CommandButton object is placed on the Clipboard, overwriting the current contents of the Clipboard, if any.

3. Click the **Paste** button 📋 on the toolbar. When the message box appears for creating a control array, click the **No** button. A copy of the command button is pasted on the form.

4. Move the object to the left of the Compute Future Value button and set the Caption property to **&Clear Values**, the Name property to **cmdClearValues**, and the ToolTipText property to **Reset the calculator**.

Because you copied and pasted the object, the new command button inherited the properties of the original, including the Default property. This is not the desired default button.

5. Activate the Properties window for the **cmdComputeFutureValue** command button and reset the Default property to **True**.

The next object you need to create is an Image object that will contain a stop sign icon. Selena wants a user to be able to click the icon to stop the program from running.

Creating an Image Object

In Tutorial 1 you used the Image control to create an Image object that contained different graphical images. You also can create an Image object that will respond to an event when clicked. Because the standard prefix for an Image object is "img", and most menus use the word Exit to exit a program, a good name for the object is imgExit. As you saw in Tutorial 1, part of creating an image is to load a picture into the Image object by setting its Picture property. The image chosen by Selena is a stop sign that is stored as an icon file on your Student Disk. Icons and images can significantly improve the user interface of your program by providing a metaphorical clue to the button or object's purpose. In addition, icons add interest to your program. Because the size of the Image object is the same size as the image file stored on the disk, you do not need to set the Stretch property.

To create the Image object and set its properties:

1. Click the **Image** control 🖼 on the toolbox, then use the mouse to draw the Image object to the right of the command button on the form.

2. Set the Height property to **480**, the Left property to **4800**, the Top property to **3240**, and the Width property to **480**.

3. Click the value for the **Picture** property to display the **Properties** button ▾, then click it. The Load Picture dialog box opens.

4. Make sure Tutorial.02 is the displayed folder, click **Stop.ico**, then click the **Open** button. The stop sign icon appears in the Image object. See Figure 2-13.

Figure 2-13 ◄
Creating the
Image object

Compute Future Value
command button

Clear Values
command button

image with Picture
property set at
design time

5. Set the Name property for the image to **imgExit**.

6. Set the ToolTipText property to **Stop running the program**.

Setting the Tab Order

Every form has only one active object at a time. When you type text into a TextBox object, for example, you are using the active object that is said to have the **focus**. When using a program, you generally change the focus between one object and another by pressing the Tab key or clicking an object.

The TabIndex property for an object determines the order in which the object receives the focus when a user presses the Tab key. This order, called the **tab order**, is determined initially by the order in which you created objects on the form, but you can change the tab order by changing the value of the TabIndex property. When you change the TabIndex property of an object, the TabIndex properties of the other objects are adjusted accordingly. The TabIndex property begins by counting from 0 and incrementing each object by 1. So, the first object has a TabIndex property of 0, the second a TabIndex property of 1, the third a TabIndex property of 2, and so on. You do not have to set the tab order for objects such as labels, because they never receive the focus.

> *Tip:* Setting the tab order logically for the objects on the form is impor-
> tant; you want to make sure it follows a vertical or horizontal
> sequence each time the user presses the Tab key. When a user
> types information into the objects on a form, the information should
> be completed from top to bottom or left to right, depending on the
> program.

The analysts at Island Financial will type information into the three text boxes you created on the form. The objects are arranged in a column, so the tab order should move from top to bottom. Initially, the tab order will be the order in which the objects were created on the form. The order should be set so the first text box in the column (txtInitialValue) receives the focus first, then the next text box, and so on. So, the first text box needs a TabIndex property setting of 0, the second a TabIndex property setting of 1, and the third a TabIndex property setting of 2. After typing information in all the TextBox objects the user usually will want to activate the Compute Future Value button, so its TabIndex property setting will be 3. After calculating the present value, it is likely that the user will want to clear the values to prepare for another calculation, so the Clear Values button will have a TabIndex property setting of 4.

To set the TabIndex property of the objects used for input:

1. Click the **TextBox** object to the right of the Initial Value: label to select it.

2. Change the TabIndex property value for the text box to **0**. A TabIndex property of 0 indicates that this object will be the active object (first object to receive the focus) when a user runs the program.

3. Click the **TextBox** object to the right of the Term(Years): label, then set its TabIndex property to **1**.

   When a user presses the **Tab** key after entering the initial value of the investment, this text box will receive the focus and the user can enter the term.

4. Click the **TextBox** object to the right of the Interest Rate: label, then set its TabIndex property to **2**.

   After a user enters the term and presses the **Tab** key, the text box for Interest Rate will have the focus and the user can enter the interest rate.

5. Click the **Compute Future Value** command button, then set its TabIndex property to **3**.

   After a user enters the interest rate and presses the **Tab** key, the command button will have the focus.

6. Click the **Clear Values** command button, then set its TabIndex property to **4**.

You only need to set the tab order for those objects that can receive focus, like command buttons and text boxes, so you do not have to change the TabIndex property for any other objects on the form. Even though an image can respond to a Click event, it cannot actually receive focus so that TabIndex property is not applicable.

Next, you need to add the visual objects to the form—a line to separate the command button and stop sign image from the rest of the form, and two dark gray areas to identify the input and output sections.

Improving the User Interface with Graphical Controls

You have seen that the organization and position of different controls can have an effect on the user interface, and the consistency between these visual elements will improve the user interface. Sometimes you want the user to perceive several controls as belonging to a group. For example, the calculator can be viewed as three sections: a section for input, a section to display the output, and a section containing the buttons to perform processing. To communicate this to the user, you can change the shading of these sections by using another control called the **Shape** control. In addition to drawing shapes on a form, you also can draw lines to separate groups of objects.

Color also is an important part of the user interface. When selecting colors for your program, keep them simple and consistent. While different applications may have different color requirements, the following guidelines should help you with color selection.

- Use bright colors like red, orange, and yellow to attract the user's attention to something important or extraordinary. As such, use of these colors should be restricted to unusual conditions.

- For the objects the user regularly interacts with, choose neutral soft colors. Generally, form backgrounds should be light gray, for example.

- Similar objects should have similar colors. That is, all the labels on a form describing text boxes should have the same color and font.

- Make sure there is adequate contrast between foreground and background colors. Text boxes, for example, should have a white background and a dark-colored or black text foreground.

- Remember, the user of your program may be color-blind.

Adding a Shape Object to the Form

Selena suggests that you separate the input and output sections of the program by enclosing them in a dark gray region. To do this, you need to learn how to use the Shape object.

The Shape object will identify visually the input and output sections of the form.

A Shape object has several properties to define its size, pattern, color, border, and shape.

- The **BackColor** and **BackStyle** properties work together to define the shape's background. When the BackStyle property is set to its default, 0-Transparent, the BackColor setting is ignored.

- The **BorderStyle** property defines the appearance of the border surrounding the shape. This property can assume any of the values listed in the Properties window for the shape or on the BorderStyle property Help screen.

- The thickness of the shape's border is set using the **BorderWidth** property. A BorderWidth setting of 0 indicates that no border will be drawn around the shape.

- The **FillColor** property works with the FillStyle property to set the color of the shape. When the FillStyle property is set to its default, 1-Transparent, the FillColor setting is ignored.

- The **FillStyle** property lets you draw a pattern on the shape's background. You can identify the valid values for the different patterns in the Properties window for the shape.

- The appearance of the Shape control is set using the **Shape** property (not to be confused with the Shape control). This is the Shape property of the Shape control. The valid values for the Shape property are Rectangle, Square, Oval, Circle, Rounded Rectangle, and Rounded Square.

- The **Visible** property of a shape can be set to True or False. A shape can be seen at run time only when its Visible property is set to True.

For more information about the properties for a Shape object, or how to set them by writing code that will be executed at run time, look at online Help for the specific property.

The calculator program will include a rectangular shape drawn around the input and output sections of the program to visually identify the two sections to the user.

REFERENCE **window**

ADDING A SHAPE OBJECT TO A FORM

- Click the Shape control on the toolbox.
- Click and drag the mouse to draw a shape on the form.
- Set the BackColor and BackStyle properties to define the shape's background appearance.
- Set the BorderStyle property to create a solid, dashed, or dotted border.
- Set the BorderWidth property to increase or decrease the thickness of the border. To remove the border set the BorderStyle to 0 - Transparent.
- Set the Shape property to make the object a rectangle, oval, circle, or other shape.
- The standard prefix for a Shape object is "shp".

Selena suggests that you now create the Shape object for both the input and output sections of the form and change their appearance so they appear dark gray with a solid black border. Because you will not write any code to reference properties of the shapes, there is no need to change the Name property.

To add the Shape objects to the calculator program:

1. Click the **Shape** control on the toolbox.

2. Move the pointer to the form and draw an outline of the shape so it looks like the shape shown in Figure 2-14. By default, the Shape control draws a rectangle.

Figure 2-14 ◄
Creating the
Shape object

rectangular shape to
group input section

3. Activate the **Properties** window for the Shape object.

4. Set the BackStyle property to **1 - Opaque**. This setting will fill the region inside the shape with the default BackColor.

5. Click the value column for the BorderColor property, then click the **Properties** button to activate the color palette.

6. Click the **Palette** tab to display the color palette, if necessary.

7. Set the BackColor property to **dark gray** and the BorderColor property to **black**, to emphasize the region against the background of the form.

   TROUBLE? If the color of the shape does not change to dark gray, the BackStyle property is probably set to 0 - Transparent. Repeat Step 4.

   Note that the Shape has obscured the Label objects. You need to put the Shape object behind the Label objects.

8. While the Shape object is the active object and the cursor is positioned over the shape, click the **right mouse** button to activate the shortcut menu, then click **Send to Back**.

9. Repeat Steps 1 through 8 to create the second shape so your form looks like Figure 2-15.

Figure 2-15 ◄
Shape objects
with properties
set

shaded shape
surrounding input
section

shaded shape
surrounding output
section

Creating a Line Object

You also can draw lines to identify different sections of the form or to draw attention to a particular form area by using the Line control on the toolbox. You can draw lines in any direction and choose different thicknesses and colors for lines.

- The color of the line can be changed by setting the **BorderColor** property.
- You also can create dashed and dotted lines by setting the **BorderStyle** property.
- The thickness is set using the **BorderWidth** property.

REFERENCE window

CREATING A LINE OBJECT

- Click the Line control on the toolbox, then use the mouse to draw a line on the form.
- To define the color of the line, change the BorderColor property.
- To change the type of line, set the BorderStyle property. For example, the style could be dashed or solid.
- To change the thickness of the line, set the BorderWidth property.
- The standard prefix for a Line object is "lin".

In the calculator program, Selena suggests you draw a horizontal line to separate the input and output sections from the buttons.

To create a horizontal line on the form:

1. Click the **Line** control ⬚ on the toolbox, then use the mouse to draw a horizontal line between the output section (labels and text boxes) and the processing section (command buttons and stop sign). Release the mouse button when the line is the same width as the shape above it. See Figure 2-16.

Figure 2-16 ◀
Creating the
Line object

line begins here ⟶

line ends here

Island Financial - Time Value of Money Calculator

Initial Value:

Term (Years):

Interest Rate:

Interest Rate   Future Value

Clear Values   Compute Future Value   STOP

2. Set the BorderWidth property to **2**.

3. Click the value column of the BorderColor property.

4. Click the **Properties** button ⬚ to open the color palette. Set the BorderColor property to **light blue**.

Your line should look like the one shown in Figure 2-17.

Figure 2-17 ◀
Setting the
line's color and
thickness

Line object
with thickness
and color set

Island Financial - Time Value of Money Calculator

Initial Value:

Term (Years):

Interest Rate:

Interest Rate   Future Value

Clear Values   Compute Future Value   STOP

TROUBLE? If the line is in the wrong place or is not horizontal, click the object to select it. Use the mouse to reposition the line, or use the mouse on one of the sizing handles to resize the line, as necessary.

The form now contains all the necessary objects as shown in Selena's plan. This is a good time to save the form and project files.

To save the form and project files:

1. Make sure the Form window is active.
2. Click the **Save Project** button on the toolbar.

Quick Check

1. Describe the differences between a Label control and a TextBox control.
2. How do you change the font of a text box's or label's contents?
3. What is the benefit of using the Windows Clipboard to create new instances of a control?
4. What is the purpose of the CommandButton control?
5. What is focus and how do you change the order in which objects receive focus?
6. What is the purpose of the Shape and Line controls?
7. Describe the effects of using different colors in a user interface.

Now that you have completed Session 2.1, you can exit Visual Basic or you can continue to the next session.

SESSION 2.2

In this session, you will set properties using Visual Basic code, declare form-level and local variables, use the Val, Format, and Future Value functions. You also will understand the types of errors that can prevent your program from running correctly.

Setting Properties Using Visual Basic Code

To improve the user interface, Selena wants to emphasize the active text box by displaying the text in blue bold while the user is entering the text (has focus). When the user presses the Tab key to move to a different object, the text in the newly selected object should appear in a blue bold type and the text in the previously selected object should no longer be bold. To accomplish this task, you need to learn about two events applicable to the text box.

As you have seen, objects can respond to events like being clicked. Different objects can respond to different events. A TextBox object can respond to several events, including GotFocus and LostFocus.

- The **GotFocus** event occurs when a text box receives the focus.
- The **LostFocus** event occurs when a text box loses focus.

You can write code for these events to provide visual help to the user, such as displaying a message in a status bar, changing the type style of text, or performing other tasks. In your program, you need to use the GotFocus and LostFocus events to change the type style of text in the active object to bold and change the color of the text.

Before you can write the code for the GotFocus and LostFocus events, you need to learn how to use the Code window to select an object and the appropriate event procedure. The Code window contains two list boxes. The Object list box shows all the objects on the form. After you select an object, you can select an event procedure from the Procedure list box. The events shown in the Procedure list box depend on the type of object you selected, because different objects respond to different events. When you select an object, Visual Basic sets the Procedure list box to the most commonly used event for that object. The Code window can display a single procedure or multiple procedures depending on which view (located at the lower-left corner of the Code window) is selected. If the Procedure View button is active, the Code window will display one procedure at a time, as shown in Figure 2-18. If the Full Module View button to the right of it is active, multiple procedures are displayed separated by a horizontal line.

You will begin by opening the Code window to the first object you need to program, txtInitialValue.

To select the Code window for frmIslandCalculator:

1. Click the **Project Explorer** button 🖳 on the toolbar, if necessary, to open the Project Explorer.

2. Highlight the form named **frmIslandCalculator,** then display the form.

   TROUBLE? If frmIslandCalculator is not visible, the Forms folder probably is not open; click the Open Folder button ⊞ next to the Forms folder.

3. Double-click the object named txtInitialValue to activate it and open the Code window. The Code window opens as shown in Figure 2-18.

Figure 2-18 ◀
Selecting an object in the Code window

view one procedure (active)

view many procedures

Code window showing:
```
Project1 - frmIslandCalculator (Code)

txtInitialValue          Change

    Private Sub txtInitialValue_Change()

    End Sub
```
Procedure list box arrow

Object list box arrow

4. Click the **Procedure View** button ▤ to view a single procedure.

   TROUBLE? The size and shape of your Code window might differ from the window in Figure 2-18. You can resize your Code window to suit your preferences.

Well-Written Comments

While a few small programs are self-explanatory, most are not. Comprehensive standardized program comments will help you and other programmers understand what your program is doing and how. Comments should be written as you develop a program. As you modify what a program does, the comments should be changed to reflect the program's new behavior.

All procedures you write should begin with a comment block if the procedure is not self-explanatory. This comment block should contain the following elements.

- The purpose of the procedure.
- Information that the procedure needs (inputs) to operate properly. These usually are variables that are declared outside the procedure or variables in other forms.
- A description of what the procedure produces (outputs).

These guidelines are a foundation for good comments. As you develop more and larger programs, you may find it useful to add more information like a history of revisions. This is especially important when multiple programmers develop and modify a program. Comments in many programs may comprise 50 percent or more of the program's statements. Increasing the number of comments will not affect the speed of your program, because when you create an executable file of your program, all the comments are removed. They are used only by the developers as they look at the code.

You must observe the following syntax rules when writing comments:

■ Any line beginning with an apostrophe is considered a comment line and is ignored by Visual Basic.

■ Any characters following an apostrophe after a statement on one line are considered a comment and are ignored by Visual Basic.

You will continue to work on Selena's program by selecting the first text box, txtInitialValue, and its GotFocus event.

To select the GotFocus event procedure for the txtInitialValue object in the Code window:

1. Click the **Procedure View** button ▤, if necessary.

Next, you need to specify the correct desired object and event procedure. Selena wants the text typed into the text boxes to be bold and dark blue when each TextBox object has the focus. So, you need to select the GotFocus event for the first text box named txtInitialValue.

2. Click the **Object** list arrow, then click **txtInitialValue**, if necessary.

3. Click the **Procedure** list arrow, then click **GotFocus**. The code you will enter for the event will be executed when the TextBox object gets the focus. See Figure 2-19.

Figure 2-19 ◀
Select an object and event procedure

TROUBLE? If the object or event procedure does not appear in the list box, use the scroll bars to search for them.

The TextBox object supports 23 different events. In addition to getting and losing focus, a Change event occurs each time the contents of a text box change. This is useful if you want to verify that the user entered valid information in the text box. Each time a user types a character into a text box, a KeyPress event also is generated, allowing you to find out exactly what key the user typed into the box. Even though Visual Basic generates these events while your program is running, you do not need to write code to respond to them. Thus, if you do not want to validate keystrokes, you would not write any code for the KeyPress event. Understanding the different events supported by an object and when they occur is an important part of Visual Basic programming. You will learn more about events in the next tutorial.

Visual Basic makes the process of writing code easier by helping you complete statements. This feature, called automatic code completion, displays list boxes with applicable properties and their values as you write statements.

Now that you have selected the object and the event procedure, you can write the code for the event so that text typed in the object will be bold and dark blue while the user is typing it. The FontBold property, when set to True, causes the text to appear in bold type.

To change the font when the text box receives focus:

1. First enter the comment as shown in Figure 2-20.

2. In the blank line between the beginning and ending lines of code, enter the code shown in Figure 2-20. Note that when the period (.) is typed, Visual Basic displays a list of the applicable properties that you can set.

Figure 2-20 ◀
Writing a
statement

Procedure comment

characters you typed

Auto List Member
list box displays
possible options

3. Use the scroll bars to locate the **FontBold** property. Click the **FontBold** property to highlight it, then press the spacebar. Note that the text is placed on the line you are typing.

4. Type an **equal sign** (=). Another list box appears listing the possible values for the property as shown in Figure 2-21. In this case the FontBold property can have the values True or False. Click the value **True** and press the **Enter** key to finish entering the line. Note that Visual Basic inserts a space between the equal sign and the word True.

Figure 2-21 ◀
Completing a
statement

select True

you type the
equal sign

Auto List Member
list box displays
possible options

Now you need to write the code to change the color of the text when the object receives focus. As with other properties, the color of an object can be set at design time using the Properties window or at run time using Visual Basic code. The easiest way to specify a color at run time is to use a constant.

Looking Up Intrinsic Constants with the Object Browser

Constants have values that do not change while the program is running. There are two types of constants: intrinsic constants and user-defined constants. **Intrinsic constants** are defined by Visual Basic. **User-defined constants** are defined by you, the programmer, with a Visual Basic statement. You will learn about user-defined constants in later tutorials.

Using a Visual Basic tool called the Object Browser, you will see how to express color values as intrinsic constants. Visual Basic has defined several intrinsic constants you can use in a program to make it more readable and intuitive.

The **Object Browser**, which is available only at design time, allows you to look at the intrinsic constants defined by Visual Basic that relate to the properties of all the objects you create, as well as the modules and procedures you have defined for your project. Many of these constants also are listed in the Help system.

To make your program more readable, you will use intrinsic constants to change the color of the foreground text in each text box when it has focus. Before you can use these constants, you need to find out their names. You can look up intrinsic constants using the Object Browser. The names of all Visual Basic intrinsic constants begin with the prefix "vb".

To use the Object Browser to examine the intrinsic constants applicable color:

1. Click the **Object Browser** button [icon] on the toolbar. The Object Browser dialog box opens.

2. Click **ColorConstants** in the Classes section of the Object Browser dialog box. Use the scroll bars if needed to locate the correct list item.

   The Members of 'ColorConstants' section of the dialog box contains the different color constants, as shown in Figure 2-22.

Figure 2-22 ◄
Object Browser
dialog box

vbBlack will return the
color to its original
setting

Click vbBlue to view
its value

Visual Basic color
constants

3. Click **vbBlue**. Notice that the value of the constant, 16711680, is displayed at the bottom of the dialog box. You could use either the number 16711680 or the constant vbBlue to set the color. As you can see, the constant name is much more meaningful when you are programming or reading code.

4. Click the **Close** button [X] on the Object Browser title bar to close the Object Browser.

When you use intrinsic constant names in a program, Visual Basic converts the names into their respective values when the program is run, which makes the program more readable and reliable. For example, if you needed to set the ForeColor property to blue, the following two statements would accomplish this; however, the statement containing the constant makes it easier for the programmer to understand that the foreground color is set to blue:

```
txtInitialValue.ForeColor = 16711680
txtInitialValue.ForeColor = vbBlue
```

You will use intrinsic constants to write the code to change the foreground color of the text box to blue.

To change the color of the text box:

1. Enter the line of code shown in Figure 2-23 in the GotFocus event procedure for the txtInitialValue text box on the line following the code that sets the FontBold property. Remember that the automatic code completion feature will help you type the statement.

Figure 2-23 ◀
Setting the
color with code

```
Project1 - frmIslandCalculator (Code)                    _ □ ×
txtInitialValue              ▼    GotFocus              ▼
' ****************************************************
' Purpose:  Set the font to bold and the foreground
'           color to blue to emphasize the object
'           with focus.
' ****************************************************
Private Sub txtInitialValue_GotFocus()
    txtInitialValue.FontBold = True
    txtInitialValue.ForeColor = vbBlue ◀
End Sub
```

enter this statement
to set foreground
color to blue

Now that the code is written for the object's GotFocus event, you can proceed to change the font to normal and the color to black when the object loses focus.

To write code for the LostFocus event:

1. Click the **Procedure** list arrow, then click **LostFocus**. When you select the new event, the Code window displays the beginning and ending lines of code for the new event procedure, and the code you wrote for the previous event procedure is no longer displayed in the Code window.

2. Enter the following code (displayed in bold) for the txtInitialValue_LostFocus event procedure:

```
' ****************************************************
' Purpose:  Set the font to normal and the foreground
'           color to black when the object loses
'           focus.
' ****************************************************'
Private Sub txtInitialValue_LostFocus()
    txtInitialValue.FontBold = False
    txtInitialValue.ForeColor = vbBlack
End Sub
```

The code you entered for the Initial Value text box will change the text to normal when the text box is no longer active, that is, when the LostFocus event occurs for the object. You now need to enter the same code for the other two text boxes. To do so, you first need to select the txtTermYears object using the Object list arrow in the Code window. Then you can write the code for the object's GotFocus and LostFocus events.

To write the code for the other two TextBox objects:

1. Click the **Object** list arrow, then click **txtTermYears**.

2. Click the **Procedure** list arrow, then click **GotFocus**.

3. Enter the following code for the txtTermYears_GotFocus event procedure:

```
Private Sub txtTermYears_GotFocus( )
    txtTermYears.FontBold = True
    txtTermYears.ForeColor = vbBlue
End Sub
```

4. Enter a comment like you did in the previous steps.

5. Select the **LostFocus** event procedure, then enter the following code for the txtTermYears_LostFocus event procedure:

```
Private Sub txtTermYears_LostFocus
    txtTermYears.FontBold = False
    txtTermYears.ForeColor = vbBlack
End Sub
```

6. Enter a comment like you did in the previous steps.

7. Repeat Steps 1 through 6 for the **txtInterestRate** object. Remember to change "txtTermYears" in each statement to "txtInterestRate".

Before you continue, Selena suggests you run the program to determine if the code you just entered is correct, then save your work. As you develop programs, it is a good idea to test your work frequently so you can discover and correct mistakes as you make them. Before testing, you should save your work in case you make an error, the computer crashes, or the power goes out.

To test the code for the GotFocus and LostFocus event procedures:

1. Click the **Close** button ☒ on the Code window title bar to close the window.

2. Click the **Save Project** button 🖫 on the toolbar.

3. Run the program by clicking the **Start** button ▶ on the toolbar. Notice that the cursor (a flashing vertical line) appears in the text box to the right of the Initial Value label, because you set its TabIndex property to 0, making it the first active object in the form when the program is running.

4. Type any number in each of the three text boxes, pressing the **Tab** key to move from one text box to the next. Check to see that the text you type is displayed in blue and bold when a text box has the focus and a regular black font when the text box loses focus.

TROUBLE? If the text in any of the text boxes did not appear bold when you were typing in them, open the Code window and select the GotFocus event for the appropriate text box. Make sure that your code is correct by checking it against the code shown earlier in the steps. If the text does not return to a normal type style when you leave the object, check the code for the appropriate LostFocus event. Make any necessary corrections, then repeat Steps 1 through 4.

5. Check that the Compute Future Value button is the fourth object to receive focus. Nothing will happen if you press **Enter** when this button is active because you have not entered statements into its Click event yet. Because you have not yet written the code for the stop sign icon, you cannot use it to stop running the program.

6. Move the mouse over the Compute Future Value button and leave it there for a moment. Be sure the ToolTip appears. Repeat the process for the stop sign.

7. Click the **End** button ■ on the toolbar to stop running the program.

When you want to stop running a program, you always can click the End button on the toolbar, as you did in the preceding steps. Most programs, however, are saved as "exe" files and are run outside of the Visual Basic environment. Thus, the user will not see the End button on the toolbar. Therefore, the program should include a button or image that the user can click to stop the program from running. This button or image should respond to the Click event that executes the End statement, which works in the same way as the End button on the toolbar. To include the End statement in a procedure, you simply type the word "End" before the End Sub statement in the Code window.

In your program, Selena wants a user to be able to click the stop sign image to stop the program from running. So, you need to write the code for the Image object's Click event procedure.

To write the code for the Image object:

1. Open the Code window and select the **imgExit** object.

2. Click the **Procedure** list arrow, and select the **Click** event, if necessary.

3. Type the word **End** on the line above the End Sub statement. Because this procedure is very intuitive, there is no need to include a comment.

4. Click the **Close** button ⊠ on the Code window title bar to close the window.

Variables

In addition to receiving user input with text boxes and displaying information with labels, a program generally needs to perform computations on the input to produce the output. The calculator program you are writing for Selena needs to compute two interest rates based on the annual interest rate entered into the Interest Rate text box. The program then must compute the future value of an investment based on the different interest rates. To store the results of the computations while the program is running, you use variables. A **variable** is a programming element used to store a value in the program. Like an object, every variable you create has a name. A variable is much like a box where you can store and retrieve information.

Every variable also has a data type that determines the kind of output the variable can store. A variable can store either textual information or numbers, but not both. There are specific data types to store whole numbers, numbers containing decimal points, and dates. Other data types store values like True or False. Unlike objects, a variable does not have properties nor does it respond to events. It simply stores information while the program is running.

Just like object names, variable names should adhere to certain standards. Figure 2-24 presents some basic requirements and recommendations for naming variables. When you create a variable, you should assign it a name that adheres to the naming conventions in the Naming Conventions Appendix.

Figure 2-24 ◀
Variable
naming
conventions

Variable names must	Variable names should
begin with a letter.	begin with a four-character prefix indicating the scope and type of data stored in the variable, followed by a descriptive name.
not contain periods or spaces.	always capitalize the first character of each word in the descriptive name.
not exceed 255 characters in length.	
be unique.	

Figure 2-25 contains examples of valid and invalid variable names.

Figure 2-25 ◀
Variable
names

Valid Variable Name	Invalid Variable Name
strValidStringName	1InvalidStringName
intValid_Integer	intInvalid.Integer

Declaring a Variable

The process of creating a variable is known as declaring a variable. To declare a variable, you use either the Visual Basic **Private** statement or **Dim** statement, which have the following syntax:

[**Private|Dim**] *Varname* **As** *Type*

- The **Private** keyword causes the variable to be created. The variable can be used only in the form in which it is declared, but by all the procedures in the form. Another keyword, **Public**, is used to create variables that can be used by different forms and modules and is discussed in later tutorials.

- The **Dim** keyword, depending on where it is used, creates variables that can be used only in the procedure in which they are declared or may be used by other procedures.

- *Varname* is the name you want to assign to the variable.

- *Type* is the data type of the variable. The data type can be any valid Visual Basic data types. Figure 2-26 lists the data types you will use in this tutorial. A programmer can create additional data types as well.

Every declared variable consumes physical space in computer memory. Variables of different types consume a different amount of space and store different kinds of values. Also, variables should have a prefix that identifies the data type of the variable.

Figure 2-26 lists some of the Visual Basic data types, their storage sizes in bytes, standard prefixes, and some possible values for each type. You will learn about other Visual Basic data types in other tutorials.

Figure 2-26 ◀
Partial
list of
Visual Basic
data types

Data Type	Storage Size	Prefix	Possible Values
Integer	2 bytes	int	Positive and negative whole numbers between -32768 and 32767. A number such as 84 or -1715 can be stored as an integer.
Single	4 bytes	sng	A number with a decimal point, such as 3.14, -10034.388, or 0.113.
String	1 byte per character	str	You can store up to about 2 billion characters for variable-length strings. Text entries such as "John Doe" or "Pacific Ocean" are stored as strings.

Choosing the correct data type for a variable is important. For example, if a variable will contain only whole numbers (numbers without a decimal point), you should choose the Integer data type instead of Single. Although a program usually works with either data type, operations on floating point values (numbers with a decimal point) take considerably longer to perform. Also the Single type variable consumes more memory than an Integer type variable. Although you will not declare any String variables in this program, the information stored in the Text property of a TextBox object always is considered a String in Visual Basic. When you want to perform a calculation on a String, you must convert it to a number.

When you use the Private or Dim statement to declare a variable, you are *explicitly* declaring the variable, but there is another way to create variables. If you use a variable name in any Visual Basic statement without first explicitly declaring the variable with the Private or Dim statement, Visual Basic will create the variable for you. This is referred to as implicit declaration, and is strongly discouraged. For example, if you intended to use a variable named InterestRate in a statement but you made a typographical error, Visual Basic would assume you wanted to create a new variable. Although the program would run, the variable would not contain the correct information. So, the results would be wrong when you use the variable in a computation.

You can prohibit Visual Basic from implicitly creating variables by using the Option Explicit statement, which has the following syntax:

Option Explicit

- This statement forces variable names to be explicitly defined with the Dim or Private statement. If you try to use a variable that was not declared with the Dim or Private statement, Visual Basic will display a dialog box telling you the variable is not defined. The Option Explicit statement also helps you identify incorrectly spelled variables that would create other errors, called logic errors, which are more difficult to detect. All programs you create in this book will contain the Option Explicit statement.

- The Option Explicit statement should be the first statement in the general declarations section of the form.

> *Tip:* To include the Option Explicit statement in all your programs click Tools then Options on the menu bar. Be sure the Require Variable Declarations check box on the Editor tab is checked. Any new project or module then will include the Option Explicit statement.

Local and Form-Level Variables

Now that you know how to declare variables, you need to know where to declare them. If you declare variables inside a procedure (between the Private Sub and End Sub statements), you can use the variable inside that procedure only. A variable declared inside a procedure exists only while the procedure is running, and is called a **local variable**. If you declare a variable outside a procedure, the variable can be used by all the different procedures in your form. The variable and its value exist whenever the program is running; this type of variable is called a **form-level variable.**

If (General) is displayed in the Object list box and (Declarations) is displayed in the Procedure list box, this is known as the general declarations section, and you use it to declare form-level variables.

Now you need to open the Code window and select the general declarations section so that you can enter the form-level variables for your program.

To open the general declarations section of the Code window:

1. Click the **View Code** button ▣ in the Project Explorer to open the Code window.

2. Click the **Object** list arrow then click **(General)**.

3. Click the **Procedure** list arrow then click **(Declarations),** if necessary.

In the general declarations section of each form, you should include a series of comments called a comment block containing a brief description of the form's purpose. This description should describe what the form does.

Declaring Form-Level Variables

Some of the variables in the calculator program need to be used by different event procedures, so you must declare them as form-level variables. In addition to a prefix to identify the type of a variable, you should precede form-level variables with the character "m" to indicate that they can be used by the entire form module. Selena suggests you use msngMonthRate1, msngMonthRate2, and msngMonthRate3 as the names for the three variables to hold the monthly interest rates. Also, because interest rates are expressed with a decimal point (i.e., 7% is expressed as 0.07), you will use the Single data type for the variables.

REFERENCE window	**DECLARING A FORM-LEVEL VARIABLE**
	▪ In the general declarations section in the Code window, enter the keyword Private.
	▪ Following the Private keyword, enter the name of the variable.
	▪ Following the variable name, enter the keyword As followed by the data type.

Now you are ready to declare the three form-level variables for your program.

To declare the variables for the three monthly interest rates:

1. Make sure the Code window shows **(General)** as the selected object and **(Declarations)** as the selected procedure.

2. Enter the comments and variable declarations as shown in Figure 2-27. As you write the statements notice that the automatic code completion feature of Visual Basic will open list boxes containing possible options.

Figure 2-27
Declaring form-level variables

each comment line starts with the ' character

three form-level variables

The first statement (Option Explicit) tells Visual Basic you must declare all variables in the module before using them. The next lines are comment lines, so they each must start with the apostrophe (') character.

> *Tip:* You can include blank lines between comments or statements, known as whitespace, which is ignored by Visual Basic. Inserting whitespace in your code between the declaration of groups of related variables or between other related statements can improve the readability of the code. Including the apostrophe on a blank line is optional.

The last three lines declare three different form-level variables of the Single data type to store the three monthly interest rates. Because they are form-level variables of the Single data type their names begin with the prefix "msng".

When you type the statements into the Code window, Visual Basic automatically capitalizes the first character of all reserved words, even if you type in lowercase letters. **Reserved words** are words that are part of the Visual Basic language. Option Explicit, Private, Dim, As, and Single are all reserved words.

Declaring Local Variables

In addition to declaring form-level variables, you need to declare local variables that will be used only inside the Click event procedure for the Compute Future Value command button. These variables will hold the three future values of the investment and the input data entered by the user. There is a significant difference between local variables, declared inside a procedure, and form-level variables, declared in the general declarations section. The storage space in computer memory is allocated for form-level variables when the program starts and remains allocated whenever the form is open. Storage space for local variables is allocated only when a procedure is executed, and the space is deallocated when the procedure finishes. So, by declaring local variables you can reduce the total amount of memory used by variables. By decreasing the amount of memory your program uses, it generally will run faster and leave more memory for other Windows 95 programs to run.

REFERENCE window

DECLARING A LOCAL VARIABLE

- Inside of a procedure, enter the keyword Dim.
- Following the Dim keyword enter the name of the variable.
- Following the variable name, enter the keyword As followed by the data type.

You now can declare the variables that will hold the results of the future value computations and the variables that will hold the input data entered by the user. These local variables will exist only while the Compute Future Value command button's Click event procedure is running.

To declare the local variables for the Compute Future Value command button's Click event:

1. Make sure the **Code** window is active.

2. Click the **Object** list arrow, then click **cmdComputeFutureValue**.

3. Be sure that the **Procedure** list box is set to the **Click** event.

4. Enter the comments and variable declarations shown in Figure 2-28.

Figure 2-28 ◀
Declaring local
variables for the
command
button

Comment block
to describe
procedure's purpose

statements indented
to improve readability

```
Project1 - frmIslandCalculator (Code)
cmdComputeFutureValue            Click

' **************************************************
' Purpose:    From the information contained in the text
'             boxes, compute three future values using
'             computed interest rates.
'
' Inputs:     txtInitialValue, txtInterestRate,
'             txtTermYears, msngMonthRate1, msngMonthRate2,
'             msngMonthRate3
'
' Returns:    lblFutureValue1, lblFutureValue2, lblFutureValue3
' **************************************************
Private Sub cmdComputeFutureValue_Click()
    Dim psngFutureValue1 As Single
    Dim psngFutureValue2 As Single
    Dim psngFutureValue3 As Single

    Dim psngInterestRate As Single   ' Interest rate (monthly)
    Dim psngInitialValue As Single   ' Initial amount of investment
    Dim psngMonthTerm As Single      ' Term of investment in months
```

Notice the comment block at the beginning of the event procedure. It contains a brief description of the procedure's purpose, the inputs, and the outputs. The variable names psngFutureValue1, psngFutureValue2, and psngFutureValue3 indicate that the Single data type variables will be used to store the results of the three future value computations while the procedure is executing. When the procedure finishes (the End Sub statement is reached), these variables no longer exist and thus cannot be used by other procedures in the program. Because they are local variables, the "m" prefix is replaced with the prefix "p" indicating a procedure level (local) variable. When you perform arithmetic computations on variables that contain a decimal point, you must use a numeric data type like Single.

All the statements inside a procedure should be indented evenly so the beginning and end of the procedure are clearly identifiable. Four spaces (a tab) is considered the standard. Notice that the comment describing the three future value variables is indented the same number of spaces as the statements the comment describes. Proper indentation will be especially important as your procedures become large enough that they cannot be completely displayed in the Code window.

Using Expressions and Operators to Manipulate Variables

Now that all the variables for your program have been declared, you can store information in them and use them to compute the output for your program. For example, you need to take the annual interest rate entered by the user and divide it by 12 to get the monthly interest rate. The result of this computation will be stored in the form-level variable msngMonthRate1, which you declared earlier.

You use **expressions**, which consist of variables, **operators** (+, − , and so on), and constants, in statements to perform calculations and store the results in other variables. Operators fall into three categories: arithmetic, comparison, and logical. The simple expressions in Figure 2-30 through Figure 2-32 later in this section use the addition (arithmetic) operator and the division (arithmetic) operator to perform computations and store the results in other variables.

When you write expressions using operators and variables, you need to understand the concept of precedence. **Precedence** is a term used to explain the standard order of execution in which arithmetic operations are performed with operators like + − / ^ and *. The concept of precedence was formulated to allow an expression to be written as one continuous statement to a computer. To do this, the computer scans the formula from left to right, looking for an operation that has the highest level of precedence. The highest level of precedence is to raise a number to a power. If the computer does not find any operations at that level, it goes to the beginning of the expression and starts at the next level, multiplication and division, and looks for those operations. If the computer finds an operator at the proper level, the computer executes that operation. If the computer finds more than one operator at the same level, it performs the leftmost operation first.

Figure 2-29 lists the Visual Basic operators that work with numeric data in the order of their precedence and gives an example of each.

Figure 2-29 ◀
Arithmetic
operators

Operators in Order of Precedence	Description	Example
^	Raises a number to the power of an exponent	2 ^ 3 is equal to 8
*, /	Multiplication and division	2 * 3 is equal to 6 8 / 4 is equal to 2
\	Integer division	10 \ 3 is equal to 3 5 \ 2 is equal to 2
Mod	Modulo Arithmetic; returns the integer remainder of a division operation	10 mod 3 is equal to 1
+, −	Addition and subtraction	2 + 3 is equal to 5 2 − 3 is equal to −1

Often, you need to change the standard order of operations to ensure that the correct sequence of operations is performed. You can do so by using one or more matched pairs of parentheses. By enclosing an operation within parentheses, that operation takes precedence over the levels in the standard order. For example, in the formula $(Var1 + Var2)^{Var3}$, the addition would take place first rather than the exponentiation, because the addition operator is enclosed in parentheses. In the formula $((Var1 + Var2) - (Var3 + Var4))^{Var5}$, the parentheses are **nested**, which means that the innermost and leftmost operation Var1 + Var2 would occur first, (Var3 + Var4) would occur second, the result of ((Var1 + Var2) − (Var3 + Var4)) would occur next, and finally the result would be raised to the power Var5. Consider the formula shown in Figure 2-30.

Figure 2-30 ◀
Algebraic
formula

$$\left(\frac{Var1+Var2}{Var3+Var4}\right) * Var5^{Var6}$$

In Figure 2-30, the order of operations clearly is shown by the way the formula is presented. If you transformed this formula directly into a computer-readable expression, it would look like the formula in Figure 2-31.

Figure 2-31 ◀
Computer-
readable
expression

Var1 + Var2 / Var3 - Var4 * Var5 ^ Var6

Without using parentheses, the order of operations would follow the standard order of evaluation, but adding parentheses will change the results. Figure 2-32 shows the different order evaluation with and without parentheses.

Figure 2-32 ◀
Evaluating
expressions

Standard order of evaluation

Order of evaluation with parentheses

$$((\text{Var1} + \text{Var2}) / (\text{Var3} + \text{Var4})) * (\text{Var5} \wedge \text{Var6})$$

Additional parentheses also can improve the readability of your program, so you should use them liberally. Including parentheses around the sub-expression (Var5 $^{\text{Var6}}$) in Figure 2-32 does not change the order of the expression, but it does enhance the readability by clarifying the order in which you want the computer to evaluate the expression.

In addition to writing expressions containing arithmetic operators, you also can write expressions that use operators to perform comparisons. Comparisons are useful to evaluate such situations as whether or not two numbers are equal or two text strings are the same. Furthermore, you also can use logical operators to connect expressions together. You will learn about comparison and logical operators later in this text.

Using Visual Basic Functions

Visual Basic includes financial and mathematical functions, which are **intrinsic functions** built into the programming language. Functions are procedures that have been written by the language designers. Like an event procedure, a function procedure contains one or more Visual Basic statements that are executed when a user performs an action. Function procedures differ from event procedures in that you have to explicitly write a Visual Basic statement to call them. Function procedures also return a value like a number string or other data type that you can store into a variable or a compatible object property. This is referred to as calling a function. In your program, you will use three intrinsic function procedures: the Val function, the Format function, and the Future Value (FV) function. You can look up how to use other intrinsic functions in Visual Basic online Help.

Converting Data Using the Val Function

Although the values entered by the user in the three TextBox objects will contain only digits (0 - 9) and possibly a decimal point, Visual Basic stores each of these values in a text box as a string of characters rather than a number. Visual Basic does not know how you intend to use the information stored in a TextBox object, so it always stores the value as a string of characters. When the program tries to perform an arithmetic operation on the text in the text box, Visual Basic tries to convert the value from a string of characters to a number. If the user entered a letter instead of a number in one of the TextBox objects, however, Visual Basic cannot properly convert the value into a number, and a run-time error will occur. You will learn about run-time errors later in this session.

The **Val** function converts a string of characters (a value assigned the String data type) to a number, which is necessary if you want the data to be used in a calculation. To use a number in a calculation, you need to convert the information into a numeric value and store the result in a variable specifically created as a numeric value. The Val function performs this task automatically. If the string contains letters, the Val function stops scanning the string and returns the value of the digits already scanned. When you use a function like Val, you provide information to it using an **argument**. Variables in your program, constants, or literal values can be used as arguments.

You use the following syntax for the Val function:

result = **Val**(*string*)

- The Val function accepts one argument, a *string*, and attempts to convert the string into a numeric value. The converted value is stored in *result*, a variable or object property.

- If *string* contains no digits, the value 0 is stored in *result*.

Figure 2-33 shows how the Val function would convert several different strings.

Figure 2-33 ◀
Results
of the Val
function

Expression	Result
Val(123.4a)	123.4
Val("")	0
Val(aaa)	0
Val(23aa34)	23

Notice the string named "" in Figure 2-33. This is known as an empty string or **Null string**. If you want to delete the text from the Caption property of a label or the Text property of a text box, you must assign an empty string to the property.

The next step in creating your program is to write the code for the event procedure to update the three labels containing interest rate values whenever the interest rate text box looses focus. Just as you wrote code to change the type style when an object became active (GotFocus) or became inactive (LostFocus), you now need to add code to display the different interest rates in the output section, whenever the value of the Interest Rate text box loses focus.

The future value of the investment should compound interest monthly, so you need to compute the value of the variables for the three monthly interest rates. The future value is computed using the variables msngMonthRate1, msngMonthRate2, and msngMonthRate3 when the user clicks the Compute Future Value command button.

To write the code for the Interest Rate TextBox object's LostFocus event:

1. Select the **txtInterestRate** object and the **LostFocus** procedure in the Code window.

2. Enter the code shown in bold at the beginning of the event procedure:

```
Private Sub txtInterestRate_LostFocus()
    Dim psngInterestRate As Single     'Interest rate (monthly)
    psngInterestRate = Val(txtInterestRate.Text)
    msngMonthRate1 = psngInterestRate / 12
    msngMonthRate2 = (psngInterestRate + 0.01) / 12
    msngMonthRate3 = (psngInterestRate + 0.02) / 12
End Sub
```

Before you proceed, you need to examine the code in more detail. First, notice that the procedure is named "txtInterestRate_LostFocus( )." This name indicates that the program will respond to a LostFocus event generated by the object named txtInterestRate. Whenever a user changes the focus from txtInterestRate to another object, the statements in this LostFocus event procedure will be executed.

```
Dim psngInterestRate As Single     'Interest rate (monthly)
```

This statement creates a local variable named psngInterestRate. The variable is local because you declared it inside the event procedure txtInterestRate_LostFocus and, therefore, it can be used inside this procedure only. This variable will store the numeric representation of the annual interest rate contained in the TextBox object named txtInterestRate.

```
psngInterestRate = Val(txtInterestRate.Text)
```

This statement uses the Val function to convert the text a user enters (stored in the Text property of the txtInterestRate text box), into a numeric value and stores the result in the variable psngInterestRate so it can be used in the subsequent calculations. Even though a user will enter a number into this text box, Visual Basic will store the entry as a string of characters rather than a numeric value.

```
msngMonthRate1 = psngInterestRate / 12
msngMonthRate2 = (psngInterestRate + 0.01) / 12
msngMonthRate3 = (psngInterestRate + 0.02) / 12
```

Recall that you declared the variables msngMonthRate1, msngMonthRate2, and msngMonthRate3 in the general declarations section, so they are form-level variables and can be used by this or any procedure in the form module. The user will enter an annual interest rate value. Because the interest on an investment is compounded every month, however, these statements divide the annual rate by 12; the number of months in a year. Then the statements compute different interest rates by adding 1% to the annual rate. Note that parentheses are needed to override the default precedence rules, so that the addition is completed before the division.

Formatting a Numeric Value

The code you just wrote computes the monthly interest rate for the three form-level variables. These variables will be used in the Click event procedure for the command button to compute the future value of the investment. So, now you have all the information needed to display the three interest rates in the output labels. Remember from Tutorial 1 that you displayed text in a label by setting its Caption property. You will use the Caption property again to display information. This time, however, you will display numbers instead of text. Selena wants interest rate values to appear with a leading zero (0) and two decimal places. You can change the way numbers are displayed using the Format function, which has the following syntax:

Format(*expression*[,*format*])

- The **Format** function reads the numeric value contained in the *expression* and converts it to a string. The function allows you to control the appearance of the string by placing information in the *format* argument. Unlike the Val function, the Format function requires two arguments.

- You can specify an optional *format* argument in one of two ways. You can select from a list of named formats that already have been defined for you, or you can use special symbols to control, in more detail, the appearance of the text. One of the more common named formats, the **Fixed** format, displays information with two decimal places and a leading zero (0) if the value is less than one (1). Another format, **Currency**, displays information with a leading dollar sign and two decimal places. Use Help on the Format function to look at all the options for named formats.

When you use the Format function, or write other more complicated statements, the statement might not fit on a single line in the Code window. You can break up a line using the underscore (_) character at the end of a line to tell Visual Basic that the next line is a continuation of the statement on the current line. When used in this way, the underscore character is called a **continuation character**. You always must precede the continuation character with a space. You cannot put a trailing comment at the end of a line with a continuation character. You can insert a continuation character only between words, but you cannot break up a word. You can break up an expression into multiple lines but you cannot split a variable name over multiple lines. If a statement still will not fit within the displayed region of the Code window, you should include the continuation character at the end of the multiple lines. Generally you indent **continuation lines** — lines that follow the continuation character in a statement — so they stand out in the code.

Next, you will enter the statements that format the different interest rates; these statements are split over two lines to improve the readability of the code.

To display the formatted values in the interest rate Label objects:

1. Add the following code to the end of the LostFocus event procedure for the Interest Rate text box so the different rates will be formatted correctly whenever the user moves the cursor to another object. Be sure to enter the code just after the statements you just wrote to calculate the monthly interest rates. Note that after the word Format is typed, Visual Basic will display a ToolTip to help you fill in the arguments.

```
lblInterestRate1.Caption = Format(psngInterestRate, _
    "Fixed")
lblInterestRate2.Caption = Format(psngInterestRate + _
    0.01, "Fixed")
lblInterestRate3.Caption = Format(psngInterestRate + _
    0.02, "Fixed")
```

The statements appear after the variable declarations and calculations, and place the results in the label captions with the Format function, so each numeric value will appear with a leading zero (0) and two decimal places, as specified by the named format, Fixed.

There are many different formats supported by the Format function. For more information start Help and select Format function.

Next, you need to write the code for the CommandButton object that will compute the future value of the initial investment at different interest rates.

Using the Future Value Function

The **Future Value (FV)** function returns the future value of a fixed amount of money based on a constant interest rate. The FV function has the following syntax:

FV (*rate,periods,payment*[,*present-value*][,*type*]])

- The *rate* represents the interest rate per period, and *periods* represents the number of time periods.

- If regular payments are made, they are identified in *payment*. So, if you are computing the future value of a fixed amount, which does not involve regular payments, the value of *payment* would be 0. You can think of a regular payment as making a deposit into the investment account each period.

- The next two arguments are optional, which is why they are enclosed in brackets. When computing the future value of an amount, the *present* or (*current*) *value* of the sum is listed. The *type* argument is used to describe when payments are made. If payments are made at the end of the period, the value for *type* is 0. If payments are made at the beginning of a period, the value for *type* is 1.

Your program will use the FV function to compute the three future values of an investment made by an Island Financial client. Because the statements containing the FV function are too long to fit on a line, you will use the continuation character to break the statement across two lines.

To create the code necessary to compute the future values:

1. Select the **cmdComputeFutureValue** object and the **Click** event procedure in the Code window.

2. Enter the following code after the Dim statements, which you entered earlier:

```
psngMonthTerm = Val(txtTermYears.Text) * 12
psngInitialValue = Val(txtInitialValue.Text)

psngFutureValue1 = FV(msngMonthRate1, psngMonthTerm, 0, _
    -psngInitialValue)
psngFutureValue2 = FV(msngMonthRate2, psngMonthTerm, 0, _
    -psngInitialValue)
psngFutureValue3 = FV(msngMonthRate3, psngMonthTerm, 0, _
    -psngInitialValue)

lblFutureValue1.Caption = Format(psngFutureValue1, _
    "Currency")
lblFutureValue2.Caption = Format(psngFutureValue2, _
    "Currency")
lblFutureValue3.Caption = Format(psngFutureValue3, _
    "Currency")
```

Before proceeding, take a minute to examine in more detail the code you just entered.

```
psngMonthTerm = Val(txtTermYears.Text) * 12
```

Earlier, when writing the LostFocus event procedure for the txtInterestRate object, you set the variables for the three monthly interest rates, which you will use to compute the future value of the investment. But, you need to compute the term of the investment expressed in months. To do so, this statement multiplies the term of the investment expressed in years by 12 and stores the result in the variable psngMonthTerm. Because the information in the text box is a string of characters, the statement includes the Val function to convert the string to a number before performing the multiplication.

```
psngInitialValue = Val(txtInitialValue.Text)
```

This statement calls the Val function to convert the initial value of the investment, which is stored as a string of characters in the Initial Value text box, into a numeric value.

```
psngFutureValue1 = FV(msngMonthRate1, psngMonthTerm, 0, _
    -psngInitialValue)
psngFutureValue2 = FV(msngMonthRate2, psngMonthTerm, 0, _
    -psngInitialValue)
psngFutureValue3 = FV(msngMonthRate3, psngMonthTerm, 0, _
    -psngInitialValue)
```

These three statements call the FV function to compute the future value of the investment using three different interest rates. You already set the value for the first argument, msngMonthRate1, when you defined the LostFocus event procedure for the txtInterestRate object. Remember the three monthly rate variables are form-level variables declared in the general declarations section, so they can be used by any procedure in your program. The second argument, psngMonthTerm, is the term of the investment, which you defined at the beginning of this event procedure. Both the rate and term are expressed in months. Because there are no additional deposits for the investment, the third argument representing the payment is 0. Because the statements were too long to fit on a line, you use the continuation character. Also the continuation line was indented for readability.

For all arguments, payments are represented by negative numbers. Because the variable psngInitialValue represents the initial payment, the number should be negative.

```
lblFutureValue1.Caption = Format(psngFutureValue1, _
    "Currency")
lblFutureValue2.Caption = Format(psngFutureValue2, _
    "Currency")
lblFutureValue3.Caption = Format(psngFutureValue3, _
    "Currency")
```

These three statements display the results in the appropriate Label objects by storing the formatted number in the Caption property of the appropriate label. The statements use the Currency format so numbers will be displayed with a leading dollar sign and two decimal places. Again, this will improve the appearance of the information for the user.

You now have completed all the code to compute the future values of the investment, format the future values with a leading dollar sign, and display the output in the appropriate labels. You now are ready to test your program and run the code you just have written. Selena suggests you use an initial investment amount of $1500.00, an interest rate of .05, and a term of 10 years.

To run the program and enter the test values:

1. Close the **Code** window.

2. Click the **Save Project** button 🖫 on the toolbar to save your work.

3. Click the **Start** button ▶ on the toolbar to run the program. Your form should look like Figure 2-34.

Figure 2-34 ◀
Running the
completed
calculator
program

4. Enter the values shown in the text boxes in Figure 2-35, pressing the **Tab** key to move from one text box to the next.

5. Press the **Tab** key to move to the Compute Future Value button.

Because you set the Default property of the command button to True, you can press the **Enter** key to activate the command button, and execute its Click event procedure.

6. Press the **Enter** key to activate the Compute Future Value button. The program calculates the results for the three interest rates and the corresponding future values. See Figure 2-35.

Figure 2-35 ◀
Testing the
calculator
program

TROUBLE? If your results differ from those in Figure 2-35, there is probably an error in the code for either the cmdComputeFutureValue object's Click event procedure or the txtInterestRate object's LostFocus event procedure. Stop the program then check the event procedures in your program first for code accuracy against the code shown in the tutorial figures. Also, refer to the next section, "Handling Errors," for help in identifying and correcting errors. Make any necessary corrections, then repeat Steps 2 through 6.

7. Click the **stop sign** image to stop the program from running.

Pressing the Enter key to activate the Click event for the Compute Future Value command button causes the code you wrote to multiply the annual term of the investment by 12 to derive the term expressed in months. The monthly interest rates were computed in the LostFocus event procedure for the txtInterestRate object. This information was supplied as arguments to the FV function to compute the future value. You did not have to worry about exactly how Visual Basic computed the future value. The intrinsic function did this for you. The output then was displayed according to the settings specified by the Format function.

Explicitly Setting the Focus

The final step in the program is to program the Clear Values command button. This button when clicked must clear the values from the text boxes used for input, the label to hold the output, then finally make the text box that holds the initial value get focus. You can explicitly set the focus to an object by calling a method called set focus. Methods are like procedures built into an object. The following statement will set the focus to the object named txtInitialValue.

```
txtInitialValue.SetFocus
```

You now can write the code for the Clear Values command button.

To program the Clear Values command button:

1. Activate the Code window to the **Click** event procedure for the object named **cmdClearValues.**

2. Enter the following statements, shown in bold, into the Code window.

```
Private Sub cmdClearValues_Click()
    txtInitialValue.Text = ""
    txtTermYears.Text = ""
    txtInterestRate.Text = ""
    lblInterestRate1.Caption = ""
    lblInterestRate2.Caption = ""
    lblInterestRate3.Caption = ""
    lblFutureValue1.Caption = ""
    lblFutureValue2.Caption = ""
    lblFutureValue3.Caption = ""
    txtInitialValue.SetFocus
End Sub
```

These statements clear the text from the object on the form and set the focus to the text box named txtIntialValue. You now should test to be sure the code for the button is working correctly.

To test the Clear Values command button:

1. Save the program.

2. Start the program.

3. Enter the values shown in Figure 2-35 and click the **Compute Future Value** button.

4. Click the **Clear Values** button. The values in the text boxes, the output interest rates, and the output future values should be blank, and the cursor should be located in the Initial Value text box.

5. End the program.

You now have written all the code for the calculator. If you made mistakes writing statements, or entered invalid data in any of the text boxes, however, you may have received an error. There are several causes for errors and types of errors.

Handling Errors

Errors are divided into three types: syntax errors, run-time errors, and logic errors. **Syntax errors** occur when a statement you have written violates the rules of the Visual Basic language. Typographical errors, mismatched parentheses, omitting the comment character as the first character on a comment line, are all examples of syntax errors. Visual Basic identifies some syntax errors while you are writing code in the Code window. After you type each line, Visual Basic scans the line for correctness.

Many errors are not discovered until you run a program. These are **run-time errors**, and they occur when you enter a valid statement that is impossible to carry out for some reason.

Logic errors occur when your program contains a design problem that causes the program to produce incorrect results. For example, you might have added two variables together rather than multiplied them. Logic errors are not found by Visual Basic; you must identify and correct them.

Fixing Syntax Errors

When a syntax error occurs, Visual Basic displays a message box like the one shown in Figure 2-36.

Figure 2-36 ◀
Syntax error
message box

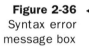

To correct a syntax error, click the OK button in the message box. Visual Basic activates the Code window and highlights the statement containing the error. Analyze the statement and make the necessary corrections. Continue running the program by clicking the Start button on the toolbar.

Fixing Run-time Errors

A common run-time error occurs when the program tries to store too large a number in a variable. This is called **numeric overflow**. For example, if you try to enter too large a number in your calculator program's text boxes, a numeric overflow error will occur. Run-time errors also occur when you try to store the wrong kind of information in a variable, and when you try to perform arithmetic operations, such as multiplication, on variables that do not contain numbers. The latter is called a **type mismatch** error, because when you perform the arithmetic operation, Visual Basic expects the variables to contain numbers, not text.

To practice fixing a run-time error, you purposely will generate an error by entering values that are too large for the text boxes in the input section.

To purposely generate a run-time error:

1. Click the **Start** button 🔘 on the toolbar to run the program.

2. Enter the value **1000000** for the Initial Value, **100000** for the Term (Years), and **100000** for the Interest Rate, then press the **Enter** key to activate the Compute Future Value button. Remember to use the **Tab** key to move around in the form. Visual Basic displays the run-time error message box indicating numeric overflow. See Figure 2-37.

Figure 2-37 ◄
Run-time error
message

error description ──────

> **Microsoft Visual Basic**
>
> Run-time error '6':
>
> Overflow
>
> [Continue]   [End]   [Debug]   [Help]

3. Click the **End** button in the message box to stop the program. Your program returns to design time.

Locating and correcting errors in your program is an important part of the programming process. For more information about locating and correcting errors refer to the Debugging Appendix. After you have corrected any errors you have made, it is a good idea to print the program code.

Printing Your Program

As you develop a program, it often is helpful to print the code you have written, the object properties you changed using the Properties window, or an Image of the form itself. Furthermore, as your programs become larger and more complex, it is helpful to have a printed copy of all the code available for reference.

Now that your program is complete, Selena asks you to print the entire program so she can keep it for later reference.

To print the elements of the calculator program:

1. Click **File** on the menu bar, then click **Print**. The Print dialog box opens. See Figure 2-38.

Figure 2-38 ◄
Print dialog box

> **Print - Island Calculator.vbp**   [X]
>
> Printer: HP LaserJet 5/5M - Enhanced   [OK]
>
> ┌Range──────────┐ ┌Print What──────┐   [Cancel]
> ○ Selection   ☐ Form Image
> ○ Current Module   ☑ Code   [Setup...]
> ● Current Project   ☐ Form As Text
>
> Print Quality: [High   ▼] ☐ Print to File   [Help]

2. Click the **Current Module** option in the Range section of the Print dialog box, because there is only one module in your program.

3. Select the **Form Image**, **Code**, and **Form As Text** options in the Print What section of the dialog box, then click the **OK** button.

   Visual Basic will print the Code for your Island Calculator project first, the Form As Text next, and finally the Form Image.

4. Exit Visual Basic.

The Code option prints the contents of the general declarations section and then each of the procedures you have written for the form. The Form As Text option prints all the objects you created on the form and the properties you changed. For each object, all the properties you set using the Properties window are displayed. If you did not change a property, it will not be printed. As you learned in Tutorial 1, the Form Image option prints an Image of the form as it appears on the screen.

Now examine the information you just printed. The Code contains all the code in your program. First, the statements in the general declarations section are printed. Then each of the event procedures is printed in alphabetical order of the object's name.

Look at the selected output from the Form As Text section, the second part you printed.

```
VERSION 5.00
```

The first line lists the version of Visual Basic.

```
Begin VB.Form frmIslandCalculator
BackColor       = &H00C0C0C0&
Caption         = "Island Financial - Time Value of Money
                  Calculator"
ClientHeight = 3840
ClientLeft   = 3330
ClientTop    = 2970
...
```

These lines define the form itself, identifying the name of the form and the properties set for the form, including all the nondefault values on the form, such as the background color. Remember, the Caption property was set for you already. The ClientHeight, ClientLeft, and ClientTop properties determine the form's position on the screen. You did not set these properties explicitly—Visual Basic set them when you created the form. Depending on the location of your form on your screen, these property values might differ from those in your printout.

```
Begin VB.CommandButton cmdComputeFutureValue
Caption     = "Compute Future Value"
Default     = -1 'True
Height      = 375
Left        = 2760
TabIndex    = 3
ToolTipText = "Click to compute the investment's future value."
Top         = 3360
Width       = 1935
End
```

These lines identify the properties you set for the CommandButton object. As with the form, the Caption and position of the object are defined, but two new properties—Default and TabIndex—also are listed. You set the Default property so the Click event occurs when a user presses the Enter key. You also set the TabIndex property, which determines the order in which objects are selected when a user presses the Tab key. Finally, the definition is terminated by the End statement.

The output includes a final End statement that signifies the end of the form definition.

Your calculator now is complete. Selena plans on showing the analysts how to use the program so they can begin testing it. After they are confident that it is producing correct results, Selena plans on making the program available to the analysts so they can use it to forecast investments.

Quick Check

1. What is the purpose of the Dim and Private statements?

2. Describe the difference between the GotFocus, LostFocus, and Click events and when they occur.

3. Put the following operators in their correct order of precedence: MOD, +, −, \, ^, *, /.

4. What is the difference between syntax errors, run-time errors, and logic errors?

5. List the three options for printing a program and describe the output that each option produces.

Figure 2-39 lists and defines the new terms presented in this tutorial.

Figure 2-39 ◀
New terms

Term	Definition
Argument	An argument is the way you send information to a function. Arguments can be variables, literal values, constants, object properties, or expressions.
Continuation character	The continuation character (an underscore in Visual Basic) allows you to write a statement that spans multiple lines.
Continuation lines	Lines that follow the continuation character in a statement.
Expression	An expression consists of operators that perform tasks, such as addition, on operands, which are variables, constants, or literal numbers.
Focus	Only one object on a form is active at one time. For example, if a TextBox object is active, the user can type information into it. The active object is said to have the focus.
Form-level variables	Form-level variables are declared in the general declarations section of a form with the Private keyword. They exist whenever the form is loaded and can be used by all the procedures in the form.
Hot key	A set of keystrokes that when typed will act just like clicking the command button (i.e., Alt+C).
Intrinsic constants	Constants defined by Visual Basic to make a program more readable.
Intrinsic function	Intrinsic functions perform many mathematical, financial, or other operations using code already written and built into the Visual Basic system.
Local variable	A variable declared with the Dim statement that only exists while the procedure is executing. Local variables can be referenced only inside the procedure in which they were declared.
Logic error	A logic error occurs whey your program contains a design problem that causes the program to produce incorrect results. For example, you might have added two variables together, rather than multiplying them
Methodology	A well-defined standardized set of steps to design a computer program.
NEADT	A design methodology that helps you identify the components of your program and break them down.
Nested	Parentheses are used to change the order of operations (performed according to precedence within the parentheses). Parentheses also enhance the readability by clarifying the order of evaluation.
Null string	A Null string is a string that contains no data. In other words the string is empty.
Numeric overflow	A common run-time error that occurs when the program tries to store too large a number in a variable.
Object Browser	Available only at design time. Allows you to look at the intrinsic constants defined by Visual Basic that relate to the properties of all the objects you create, as well as the modules and procedures you defined for your project.
Operators	Operators are used in expressions to perform computations and comparisons. Examples of operators are +,−,*, /, and ^.
Precedence	Precedence is the predetermined order in which arithmetic operators are evaluated.

Figure 2-39 ◀
New terms
(continued)

Term	Definition
Pseudocode	Pseudocode is a way to express the actions of a program in general, nontechnical terms. An example of pseudocode is "Get the input data."
Reserved words	Words that are part of the Visual Basic language, such as Option Explicit, Private, Dim, As, and Single.
Run-time error	A run-time error occurs while the program is running because you entered a valid statement that, for some reason, is impossible to carry out.
Syntax error	A syntax error is an error that occurs when you write a statement that violates the rules of the Visual Basic language.
Tab order	The order in which the objects drawn on the form receive focus.
Type mismatch	A common run-time error that tries to store the wrong kind of information in a variable, and when you try to perform arithmetic operations, such as multiplication, on variables that do not contain numbers.
User-defined constants	Constants defined by you, the programmer, with a Visual Basic statement that will make your program more readable.
Variables	Variables are named locations in the computer's random access memory used to store information temporarily, such as numbers or textual data.

Tutorial Assignments

In addition to investment services, the Island Financial Group provides tax preparation services for its clients. Selena has asked you to create a program that will compute the straight-line depreciation of an asset for a period. The program should provide an interface that allows the user to input the initial cost of an asset, the value of an asset at the end of its useful life, and the life of the asset. Because the program has a similar function as the future value calculator you just created, its user interface should be very similar. To create the program, you will use the SLN function, which is an intrinsic financial function like the FV function. When complete, your user interface should look like Figure 2-40.

Figure 2-40 ◀

1. Make sure your Student Disk is in the appropriate disk drive, then start Visual Basic.

2. Create a new project if necessary.

3. Change the Caption property of the form to **Island Financial - Straight Line Depreciation**. Change the Name property to **frmIslandDepreciation**.

4. Draw four Label objects in a column on the form.

5. Change the Caption property of these labels to **Cost:, Salvage:, Life:**, and **Depreciation:** starting from the top label.

6. Check the Font and Alignment property values for the Island Calculator project. Change the Font and Alignment properties of the labels to use the same settings as the Island Calculator.

7. Draw four TextBox objects next to the labels. Change the Name property of the text boxes to **txtCost**, **txtSalvage**, **txtLife**, and **txtDepreciation**, starting from the top text box. Change the Text property for each text box to blank.

8. Draw a Shape object behind the Cost:, Salvage:, and Life: labels and text boxes. The shape should be a dark gray rectangle to resemble the shapes in the Island Calculator project.

9. Draw two CommandButton objects on the bottom of the form.

10. Change the Name property of the leftmost button to **cmdCalculateDepreciation**; change its Caption property to **Calculate Depreciation**. Set it as the default button and use the character **D** as the hot key. Adjust the width of the command button to accommodate its caption as needed. Create a ToolTip for the command button.

11. Change the Name property of the rightmost button to **cmdClearValues**; change its Caption property to **Clear Values**. Use the character **C** as the hot key. Create a ToolTip for the command button.

12. Draw an Image object in the bottom-right corner of the form. Change its Name property to **imgExit**. Set its Picture property to the **stop.ico** file in the **TAssign** folder of the **Tutorial.02** folder on your Student Disk.

13. Draw a Line object between the Depreciation: label and text box and the command buttons. The line should be light blue to resemble the line in the Island Calculator project.

14. Open the Code window for the imgExit object's Click event procedure, then enter the code that will end the running program when this button is clicked. Remember to include comments about what the procedure does in all your code.

15. Open the Code window for the cmdClearValues object's Click event procedure and enter code that will set to blank the Text property of the four TextBox objects and set the focus to the text box named txtCost.

16. Use the Index tab in the Help window to consult Visual Basic online Help for information on financial functions. Open the Help window for the SLN function. Print the Help topic to guide you through creating the rest of this program.

17. Open the Code window for the cmdCalculateDepreciation object's Click event procedure. Type the code that will set the txtDepreciation object's Text property to the straight-line depreciation of txtCost, txtSalvage, and txtLife. Format the result as Currency. Enter a comment to describe what this procedure does.

18. Test your program by entering **100000** as the asset cost, **50000** as the salvage value, and **5** for the asset life in years. Click the Calculate Depreciation button to cause the depreciation function to execute. The result should be $10,000.00 as the depreciation amount for each year.

19. Test the Clear Values button.

20. Continue to run and test the program with numbers of your choice in the Cost, Salvage, and Life text boxes.

21. Test the stop sign.

22. Print the form image.

23. Save the project as **Island Depreciation.vbp** in the **TAssign** folder of the **Tutorial.02** folder on your Student Disk. Accept the default form name, **frmIslandDepreciation.frm**.

24. Exit Visual Basic.

Case Problems

1. Perfect Printing Perfect Printing is a business that specializes in unique printing products for industrial applications. The owner, Roger Kringle, would like to have a program that can display a variety of fonts, sizes, and colors on a computer screen after a user types in some text. Roger asks you to write a program for Perfect Printing that tests different fonts in an output label using a text box for input. Your finished form should look similar to Figure 2-41.

Figure 2-41 ◀

![Perfect Printing - Label Testing form with a text box at the top, a horizontal line, an "Empty Label" in bold italic text, and an "Exit" button in the lower right corner]

1. Make sure your Student Disk is in the appropriate disk drive, then start Visual Basic.

2. Create a new project if necessary.

3. Change the Name property of the form to **frmPerfectLabelTesting**. Change the Caption property of the form to **Perfect Printing - Label Testing**.

4. Draw a TextBox object on the form. Change its Name property to **txtInput**. Delete the value of the Text property to clear it.

5. Draw a Label object on the form below the TextBox object. It should be about the same size as the text box. Change its Name property to **lblOutput**. Change its Caption property to **Empty Label**. Change the formatting of the label so that it resembles Figure 2-41.

6. Draw a line that separates the text box from the label.

7. Draw a CommandButton object on the form. Change its Name property to **cmdExit**. Change its Caption property to **Exit**. Use the character **x** as the hot key for the button.

8. Create a ToolTip for the command button.

9. Open the Code window for the cmdExit object's Click event procedure, then type the code that will exit the running program when this button is clicked. Remember to include a comment that describes what this procedure does.

10. Open the Code window for the txtInput object and select its Change event procedure. Type the code that will set the Caption property of the lblOutput object to anything typed in the text box (that is, the Text property of the text box). Consult Visual Basic online Help for more information on the Label object's Caption property and the TextBox object's Change event and Text property. Remember to include a comment that describes what this procedure does.

11. Run the program.

12. Type anything you want in the text box, and note the results displayed in the label.

13. Test the Exit button.

14. Open the Properties window for the lblOutput object and change the Font, Font Style, and Size properties to any setting you choose. Change the BackColor and ForeColor to any combination that you think looks the best.

15. Run and test the program.

16. Repeat Steps 12 and 13, changing the properties until you are satisfied with the results.

EXPLORE

17. Change the MultiLine property of the text box to **True.** Then run the program again and type multiple lines in the text box. How does the label react?

18. Print the form image and code.

19. Save the project as **Perfect Label Testing.vbp** in the **Cases** folder of the **Tutorial.02** folder on your Student Disk. Accept the default form name, **frmPerfectLabelTesting.frm.**

20. Exit Visual Basic.

2. Timberline Ltd. Timberline Ltd. is an engineering firm that constructs planning models in Visual Basic of various ecosystems around the world. Because so much of the work at Timberline Ltd. is based on using proper formulas in their calculations, it is important for the model formulas to be correct. You will work on one of these models to test your ability to convert algebraic formulas to their proper computational form. Specifically, you will build a program to convert and test the formulas shown in Figure 2-42:

Figure 2-42 ◀

1    $$\frac{(mintVar1 + mintVar2)}{(mintVar3)}$$

2    $$\frac{(mintVar1)^{mintVar5}}{(mintVar2)(mintVar4)}$$

3    $$\frac{(mintVar1 - mintVar2)^{mintVar3}}{(mintVar4)}$$

4    $$\frac{(mintVar4 - mintVar2)(mintVar3)}{(mintVar5)^{mintVar2}}$$

5    $$\left(\frac{\frac{mintVar2}{mintVar1}}{\frac{mintVar4}{mintVar5}}\right)^{mintVar2}$$

6    $$\frac{\left(\frac{mintVar1}{mintVar2}\right)\left(\frac{mintVar3}{mintVar4}\right)}{(mintVar5)^{mintVar1}}$$

When complete, your form should look like Figure 2-43.

Figure 2-43 ◀

Timberline Ltd. - Testing Formulas

Click for Answer 1

Click for Answer 2

Click for Answer 3

Click for Answer 4

Click for Answer 5

Click for Answer 6   Exit

1. Make sure your Student Disk is in the appropriate disk drive, then start Visual Basic.

2. Create a new project if necessary.

3. Change the Name property of the form to **frmTimberlineTesting.** Change the Caption property of the form to **Timberline Ltd. – Testing Formulas.**

EXPLORE

4. Open the general declarations section in the Code window and type the code that requires variables to be declared in the program and declare five Integer type variables—**mintVar1**, **mintVar2**, **mintVar3**, **mintVar4**, and **mintVar5**. Consult Visual Basic online Help for more information on declaring Integer-type variables.

5. In the Code window for the frmTimberlineFormulas object's Load event procedure, assign numerical values to each of the variables as follows: **mintVar1 = 1**, **mintVar2 = 2**, **mintVar3 = 3**, **mintVar4 = 4**, and **mintVar5 = 5**. Consult the Visual Basic online Help for more information on assigning a value to a variable. Close the Code window for the form.

6. Draw a CommandButton object on the lower-right corner of the form. Change its Caption property to **Exit.** Change its Name property to **cmdExit**.

7. Open the Code window for the cmdExit object's Click event procedure, then type the code that will exit the running program when this button is clicked.

8. Draw six Label objects in one column on the form. Change the Name property for the objects to **lblAnswer1**, **lblAnswer2**, **lblAnswer3**, **lblAnswer4**, **lblAnswer5**, and **lblAnswer6**, starting from the top label. Set the background color to white so the labels stand out from the rest of the form. Change the Caption property for the Label objects to **Click for Answer 1**, **Click for Answer 2**, etc.

   Hint: The Copy and Paste commands also work within the Properties window.

9. Open the Code window for the lblAnswer1 object's Click event procedure, then enter the expression that will set the caption of lblAnswer1 to the converted algebraic form of Formula 1 in Figure 2-42. Consult Visual Basic online Help for more information on setting the Caption property of the label with Visual Basic code.

10. Create a ToolTip for each of the labels and the command button.

11. In the remaining five Label objects, enter the proper formula conversion for the formulas 2 through 6 in Figure 2-42. Close the Code window.

12. Save the project as **Timberline Testing Formulas.vbp** in the **Cases** folder of the **Tutorial.02** folder on your Student Disk and accept the default form name, **frmTimberlineTesting.frm**.

13. Run the program and test each label. The following answers should be displayed in the labels:

   lblAnswer1.Caption = 1

   lblAnswer2.Caption = 0.125

   lblAnswer3.Caption = –0.25

   lblAnswer4.Caption = 0.24

   lblAnswer5.Caption = 6.25

   lblAnswer6.Caption = 0.075

If any of your answers do not match the answers shown, you have made a mistake converting a formula. Click the Exit button. Fix each incorrect expression by changing the code in the Code window for the appropriate label. Repeat this step until your answers are correct.

14. Test the Exit button.

15. Print the Form Image and the Code.

16. Save the project again if you made any corrections after you last saved, then exit Visual Basic.

3. Summit Bank Summit Bank has asked you to modify some of its customer reports. The bank purchased a set of add-on financial controls from a vendor and installed them in your copy of Visual Basic. These controls have no errors but they all seem to require that data, having the type Single, be formatted differently. Refer to Visual Basic online Help for more information about the Format function.

When finished, your user interface should look like Figure 2-44.

Figure 2-44 ◄

1. Create the NEADT documentation and a test program according to Steps 2 through 12.

2. Start Visual Basic and create a new project.

3. Set the Name property of the form to **frmSummitFormatTesting**.

4. Draw the shape, line, and title label, and set the properties as shown in Figure 2-44.

5. Draw the top text box. Name the text box with a valid name. Clear the Text property. Change its background color and font if you like.

6. Draw four empty labels. Name the labels with valid names of your choice. Clear their captions. Change their background colors and fonts if you like.

7. Draw a working Exit command button.

8. Draw a command button with a valid name and the caption **Move Number**.

9. Create a ToolTip for each of the command buttons.

10. Declare a Single data type variable in the general declarations section in the Code window with a valid name.

11. Write a statement in the Move Number command button's Click event procedure to move: the Text property value of the top text box to the Single data type variable you declared using the Val function; and the Single data type variable to the first label with no formatting, to the second label formatted as Currency, to the third label formatted as Fixed, and to the fourth label formatted as $#,###,###.##. Refer to Visual Basic online Help for more information about the Format function. Draw descriptive labels for the text box and output labels and set the appropriate properties.

12. Save the project as **Summit Format Testing.vbp** in the **Cases** folder of the **Tutorial.02** folder on your Student Disk. Accept the default form name.

13. Test your program with a variety of numbers, both integer and decimal. Use the text box to enter a number, and then click the Move Number button.

    Hint: Do not use any special characters such as dollar signs or commas when you type the number or the Val function will not be able to perform the conversion operation.

14. When you are finished, save the form and project again, if you have made any changes since your last save.

15. Print the Form Image, the Code, and the Form As Text.

16. Exit Visual Basic.

4. Ms. Phillips Grading Program One of your former instructors at school, Ms. Phillips, would like you to design and build a Visual Basic program that will take the name of a student and the student's three test grades for the term, then compute the average for the tests and display a letter grade. To build a good program for Ms. Phillips, you first need to start with a good design. Refer to the Design Appendix, then create the necessary NEADT documentation for the grading program.

Objects and the Events They Generate

Developing an Event-Driven Cash Register Program for Master Burger

In this tutorial you will:

- Create instances of several new controls including scroll bars, check boxes, frames, and option buttons

- Create a control array

- Write code for event procedures that will generate other events

- Execute code conditionally using the If and Select Case statements

- Create Function and Sub procedures

- Display a message box by calling the MsgBox function

- Perform operations on text strings

CASE

Master Burger Company

Master Burger Company is a fast-food franchise business with headquarters in Lemming, California. Currently, it operates more than 270 stores in the United States and Europe, and is planning to expand into New Zealand and Australia. The company's mission always has been to provide fresh food and exceptionally fast service, so it maintains a very simple menu of food items to avoid any spoiled or stale food. Gill Clark, the information services manager, wants you to use Visual Basic to develop a prototype for a point-of-sale cash register program to be used in each Master Burger restaurant. Ultimately, the company will use this cash register program to perform additional tasks, such as tracking inventory and using a touch screen for input.

For the prototype program, the mouse will be the only input device. The program will eventually be used, however, on a computer with a touch screen for all user input. So, the program must only use Visual Basic controls that do not require keyboard input. You can use a box for each menu item that, when checked, indicates the item has been ordered. The program will use scroll bars to change the quantity ordered for each menu item. Each store delivers orders and charges for delivery based on distance. To simplify the delivery charges, they divide the delivery area into three zones and charge a different amount for each zone.

When an item is selected or the quantity ordered for an item changes, the program must compute the extended price of the item (unit price × quantity ordered), the sales tax for the order, any delivery charges, and the order total.

Master Burger has been experimenting recently with 24-hour operation. To attract more business during these hours, they offer a 10% discount for purchases made between 1 A.M. and 8 A.M. The cash register must be able to compute this discount and deduct it from the order total.

In this session you will learn how to use the ScrollBar, CheckBox, Frame, and OptionButton controls to create the user interface for a cash register program that will receive input only from a mouse. You also will create event procedures that change the values of other objects, which in turn will generate other events.

Designing the Program

The program you will create is a prototype of the complete cash register program that Gill will show to senior management before putting the final program in the company's 270 stores. The following are some of the significant design criteria for the program:

- The clerk must be able to select menu items and specify the quantity ordered for each menu item by clicking objects. No keyboard input can be used.

- The program must update extended prices (unit price × quantity ordered) for each item when the quantity ordered changes.

- Whenever the extended price for an item changes, the sales tax and order total must be recomputed and displayed.

- The delivery amount, if any, must be computed and displayed when one of the delivery buttons is clicked. The order total also must be recomputed and displayed.

- The discount, if any, must be calculated depending on the time the order is placed. The order total also must be recomputed and displayed.

Gill already has completed the NEADT documentation for the program. You can look at this design documentation to help you create the program.

To view and print the NEADT charts for the cash register program:

1. Using Microsoft Word, open the file **Master.doc,** which is located in the **Tutorial.03** folder of your Student Disk. If you do not have Word, open the file **Master.txt** using WordPad.

2. Print the file and then exit the word processing program.

It is helpful to keep the NEADT charts next to you as you create the program. Gill already has designed the user interface screen, as shown in Figure 3-1.

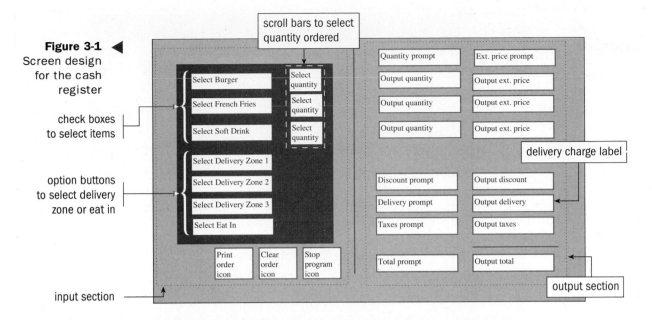

Figure 3-1 ◄
Screen design
for the cash
register

check boxes
to select items

option buttons
to select delivery
zone or eat in

input section

The user interface design visually identifies the objects used for input by enclosing them in a different colored box. These input objects will be used to select a menu item and the quantity ordered. The Stop program icon will be used to exit the program. The output section contains several Label objects that display and describe the output.

Adding a CheckBox Object to the Form

The cash register program needs three objects to represent the menu items for a burger, french fries, and soft drink, so a clerk can click the items as the customer orders them. Visual Basic provides several ways to indicate an item has been ordered. You could add a TextBox object and have the clerk type in a number, but that would require input from the keyboard, which would violate the design specifications. In this case a **CheckBox** control is the best control for the task, because a clerk can click a check box to mark an item that has been ordered.

To create the order menu check list, you will create multiple instances of the CheckBox control—one for each menu item. This is the task object on the NEADT chart—to create three check boxes representing the three different products sold by Master Burger.

A check box, like a command button, can respond to the Click event. When a check box becomes checked or cleared in this cash register, you want to execute code that will perform one action or another action if the check box is cleared. A CheckBox object has three valid values. If it is not checked (default) the Value property is 0 - Unchecked. When a check box is checked, the Value property is 1 - Checked. Finally, if a check box is dimmed, the Value property is 2 - Grayed. A CheckBox object that is dimmed has a gray check mark in it; it neither is checked nor unchecked. If you click a dimmed check box once, it becomes unchecked; if you click it twice, it becomes checked. You can use a dimmed check box so the user can tell that the box neither is checked nor unchecked and that input needs to be provided. When the user clicks the check box, Visual Basic sets the Value property for the check box and generates a Click event. Like many other controls, the check box supports the Caption property to describe the object's purpose. The standard prefix for a check box is "chk".

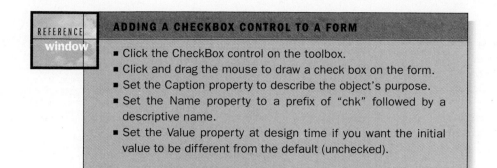

REFERENCE window

ADDING A CHECKBOX CONTROL TO A FORM

- Click the CheckBox control on the toolbox.
- Click and drag the mouse to draw a check box on the form.
- Set the Caption property to describe the object's purpose.
- Set the Name property to a prefix of "chk" followed by a descriptive name.
- Set the Value property at design time if you want the initial value to be different from the default (unchecked).

In the cash register program, different check boxes will indicate whether a customer ordered a burger, french fries, and/or a soft drink.

To create the CheckBox objects for the menu items:

1. Make sure your Student Disk is in the appropriate disk drive and start Visual Basic.

2. Open the project file named **Master.vbp** in the **Tutorial.03** folder on your Student Disk.

3. View the form named **frmMaster**. Your form should look like Figure 3-2.

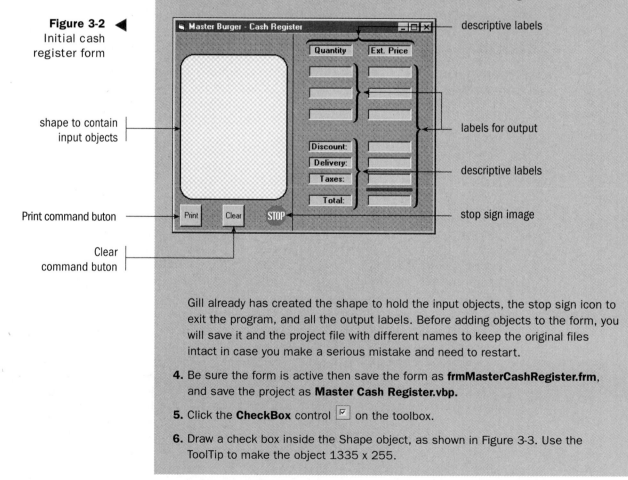

Figure 3-2 ◀
Initial cash register form

descriptive labels

shape to contain input objects

labels for output

descriptive labels

Print command button

stop sign image

Clear command buton

Gill already has created the shape to hold the input objects, the stop sign icon to exit the program, and all the output labels. Before adding objects to the form, you will save it and the project file with different names to keep the original files intact in case you make a serious mistake and need to restart.

4. Be sure the form is active then save the form as **frmMasterCashRegister.frm**, and save the project as **Master Cash Register.vbp.**

5. Click the **CheckBox** control ☑ on the toolbox.

6. Draw a check box inside the Shape object, as shown in Figure 3-3. Use the ToolTip to make the object 1335 x 255.

Figure 3-3 ◀
Creating a
CheckBox
object

new check box

7. Set the Caption property for the check box to **Burger** and the Name property to **chkBurger.**

8. Create the second check box and position it directly below the first check box.

9. Set the Caption property for the second check box to **French Fries** and the Name property to **chkFrenchFries**.

10. Repeat Steps 8 and 9 setting the Caption to **Soft Drink** and the Name property to **chkSoftDrink**. Your form should look like Figure 3-4.

Figure 3-4 ◀
Completed
CheckBox
objects

new check boxes

Now you can create the objects that will specify the order quantity of a specific item.

Adding Scroll Bars to the Form

The user interface for the cash register program must permit a clerk to use only a mouse or touch screen to enter the quantity. For example, if a customer orders three burgers, the clerk will click the Burger check box to indicate the item has been ordered, but the clerk also needs to indicate that the customer wants three burgers. Because the mouse or touch screen is the only means of input, the clerk cannot type in the number of burgers ordered using a control such as a text box.

You could create two command buttons for each item—one that would contain the code to increment a variable representing the quantity ordered, and one that would contain the code to decrement the variable. Although this approach would work, you would have to write several lines of code, so it is not the most efficient or easiest solution. Visual Basic supports a **ScrollBar** control that will increment and decrement the quantity ordered of an item without requiring you to write any code. Determining the correct control for a particular task makes the programming job more efficient and the program easier to use.

Visual Basic provides vertical and horizontal scroll bars, which work in the same way as the scroll bars in most Windows 95 programs. The two types of scroll bars share the same properties. The choice of which one to use depends on the requirements of the user interface. Horizontal scroll bars are well-suited for measures of distance, such as inches, because the metaphor of a ruler on a map tends to be a left-to-right sliding scale. Because you would think of an order quantity going up or down rather than left to right, the vertical scroll bar is the better choice for the cash register program. In circumstances where the type of scroll bar is irrelevant, consider using the one that will balance the layout of the screen. In this session you will use the following ScrollBar properties:

- The **Value** property of a scroll bar is an integer that contains the current value of the scroll bar. When a user clicks on the scroll bar, a Change event is generated and Visual Basic sets the Value property.

- The range of valid values is controlled by the **Max** and **Min** properties. A scroll bar is divided into two regions. When a user clicks the arrows, the Value property increases or decreases by the value contained in the **SmallChange** property. The default value of the SmallChange property is 1. When a user clicks the region between the arrows, the Value property changes by the value of the **LargeChange** property. The default value of the LargeChange property is 1. Figure 3-5 shows the two regions of a vertical scroll bar.

- The prefix for a vertical scroll bar (VScrollBar) control is "vsb" and the prefix for a horizontal scroll bar (HScrollBar) control is "hsb".

Figure 3-5 ◀
Changing
the value
of a vertical
scroll bar

click here to change
Value property
by LargeChange

click here to change
Value property by
SmallChange

scroll box is a relative
indicator of Value
property

By default, the value of a vertical scroll bar grows as the bar moves downward. If you set the Min property to 0 and the Max property to 25, clicking the up arrow would cause the value to decrease, and clicking the down arrow would cause the value to increase. Think of using a scroll bar to scroll down through a document; the down arrow moves you from line 1 of the document to the next line. The line number continues to grow as you move down the document, as illustrated in Figure 3-6.

Figure 3-6 ◀
Setting the
Max and Min
properties

Min=0, Max=25

Smaller

Larger

Min=25, Max=0

Larger

Smaller

REFERENCE
window

ADDING A SCROLLBAR CONTROL TO A FORM

- Click the VScrollBar or HScrollBar control on the toolbox.
- Click and drag the mouse to draw a scroll bar on the form.
- In the Properties window set the LargeChange property for the scroll bar to the value by which the scroll bar will change when any gray area of the scroll bar is clicked. Set the SmallChange property for the scroll bar to the value by which the scroll bar will change when either arrow is clicked.
- Set the Min and Max property values for the scroll bar to define the range for the scroll bar.
- Set the Name property to a prefix of "vsb" or "hsb" followed by a descriptive name.

For the cash register program, you will create three vertical scroll bars that can be used to specify the quantity ordered for each of the three products on the menu. This is the second task in the NEADT chart—to change the quantity of each menu item using a scroll bar. When a clerk clicks the vertical scroll bar's up arrow, the order quantity for the specific item must increase by 1. When a clerk clicks the scroll bar's down arrow, the order quantity must decrease by 1.

By setting the Max property to 0 and the Min property to the expected value of the largest order, the value of a scroll bar will increase when its up arrow is clicked. Gill thinks it is reasonable to set 25 as the expected value of the largest order.

To create the vertical scroll bars on the form and set their Min and Max properties:

1. Click the **VScrollBar** control on the toolbox.

2. Draw a scroll bar between the Burger check box and its quantity ordered label. Refer to Figure 3-7 for the placement of the scroll bars.

3. Activate the **Properties** window for the scroll bar and set its Name property to **vsbBurger.**

4. Set the value of the Max property to **0** and the Min property to **25.**

5. Create a second vertical scroll bar between the French Fries check box and its quantity ordered label. Set its Name property to **vsbFrenchFries,** its Max property to **0,** and its Min property to **25.** Remember if you copy and paste the scroll bar, the Max and Min properties are copied from the original scroll bar as well.

6. Create the third vertical scroll bar between the Soft Drink check box and its quantity ordered label. Set its Name property to **vsbSoftDrink,** its Max property to **0,** and its Min property to **25.** Your screen should look like Figure 3-7.

Figure 3-7 ◀
Completed
ScrollBar
objects

new scroll bars

You have completed setting the necessary properties for the scroll bars. Note that you did not need to change the SmallChange or LargeChange properties from their default values (1), because you want the quantity ordered to increase or decrease by 1 when any part of the scroll bar is clicked. You now are ready to create the next part of the user interface: the buttons to select the delivery zone.

Using Option Buttons

You now will learn how to use another control, the OptionButton control, to allow a clerk to select the correct delivery zone or to specify that the order would be eaten in the restaurant. For Master Burger the delivery cost is relative to the delivery address, so different rates are charged based on the delivery distance. Each store breaks the delivery area into three zones. While you could use a check box to select a delivery area, the CheckBox control would not ensure that the clerk marked only one delivery area in the group, so it would not be appropriate. Also, because the mouse must be the only means of input, a TextBox control is not a possibility either. The **OptionButton** control allows you to create a group of items from which a user can select only one item at a time. Option buttons often are called **radio buttons,** referring to buttons in car radios that allow you to press a button to select a station.

> *Tip:* Option buttons consume a large amount of space on the screen. Use option buttons only when the number of choices is fewer than 5; when the number of choices exceeds 5, consider using a list box or combo box, which will be discussed in Tutorial 6.

OptionButton objects usually are positioned and operate as a group inside another object known as a frame. When you draw a **Frame** object on a form and place option buttons inside the frame, the option buttons form an **option group.** Only one of the OptionButton objects in an option group can be selected at a time.

To implement Gill's design, you need to specify whether an order is delivered and if so, to which zone. To do so, you will add a frame and four option buttons to the form. When a clerk clicks one of the four option buttons, the other three option buttons in the group will be unselected automatically.

When you create a frame that will be used to group other controls like option buttons, you must draw the frame first, then draw the controls inside the frame. If you do not draw the controls inside the frame, the buttons will not belong to the same option group. Thus, it will be possible to click more than one button. If you draw an object outside a frame and then try to move the object inside the frame, it will appear on top of the frame but the buttons will not function as an option group. Finally, if you use the Clipboard to copy and paste buttons, you must make the frame the active object before pasting the button.

Creating a Frame

You create a Frame object in the same way that you created a Shape object in Tutorial 2. The size of the frame you draw must be large enough to hold the option buttons. Like other objects, a frame can be resized as needed. The standard prefix for a Frame object is "fra". If you do not write code to operate directly with the Frame object, you do not need to change the Name property. The Frame object also supports the Caption property; typically, the frame's caption provides the user with a descriptive message about the purpose of the option buttons it holds. To customize a frame's appearance you can set the BackColor, BorderStyle, and ForeColor properties. These properties have the same effect as the shape's properties.

REFERENCE window	ADDING A FRAME OBJECT TO A FORM
	▪ Click the Frame control on the toolbox.
	▪ Click and drag the mouse to draw the frame on the form.
	▪ Set the Caption property so it describes the purpose of the option buttons.
	▪ Set the Name property to the prefix "fra" followed by a meaningful description if you will write code to interact with the frame at run time.
	▪ Set the BackColor, BorderStyle, and ForeColor properties as needed.

You will create a Frame object, named fraDelivery that will contain four option buttons indicating the correct delivery zone.

To add the Frame object to the form:

1. Click the **Frame** control ⬜ on the toolbox, then draw a rectangular frame on the form below the CheckBox objects.

2. Set the Caption property of the frame to **Delivery**. Because you will not write any code for this object, there is no need to set the Name property. See Figure 3-8.

Figure 3-8 ◀
Creating a
Frame object

caption ⟶

new Frame object ⟶

Creating Option Buttons

When you create OptionButton objects, you are interested in finding out which single button is clicked from a group of buttons inside a frame. The OptionButton object supports the Caption property and has the standard naming prefix of "opt".

REFERENCE window

ADDING AN OPTIONBUTTON OBJECT TO A FRAME

- Click the frame that will contain the option button.
- Click the OptionButton control on the toolbox.
- Click and drag the mouse inside the frame to draw an option button in the frame.
- Set the Caption property to describe the object to the user.
- Set the Name property to a prefix of "opt" followed by a descriptive name.

You will create four option buttons (one for each delivery zone and one for an order eaten in the restaurant) inside the frame. These option buttons will make up an option group. Visual Basic will allow you to create multiple option groups by creating multiple frames and inserting option buttons in them. You will name the option button optDelivery, because it indicates the delivery location of the order; its caption, however, will be Zone 1.

To add the first option button to the Frame object:

1. Make sure the Frame object is active.

2. Click the **OptionButton** control on the toolbox.

3. Draw an option button inside the frame. Set the option button's Name property to **optDelivery** and its Caption property to **Zone 1**. Your form should look like Figure 3-9.

Figure 3-9 ◀
Creating an
OptionButton
object

new OptionButton object

You still need to create the remaining option buttons but before you do, you must learn about a way to create objects so that instead of each responding to a unique Click event procedure, they will all respond to a Click event by executing the same Click event procedure.

Creating Objects with the Same Name

The next step in developing the program is to create the other three option buttons. Until now, each object you have created on a form has had a unique name and unique event procedures. That is, two different command buttons will execute different Click event procedures. It is possible to group objects together, using a control array, so they all share the same name and event procedures. This process is particularly well-suited to working with the option buttons inside an option group, because you typically want to manipulate option buttons as a unit. A **control array** is a group of controls of the same type (like an option button) that share the same name and event procedures. Control arrays improve a program's efficiency. When you add an object, such as another option button, to a control array of option buttons, the new object shares the properties and event procedures with the other option buttons. Because the objects share event procedures, system memory is conserved. Control arrays also provide a way to overcome the programming limitations of Visual Basic controls. You can specify up to 256 different control names on a form. Even this small cash register program contains 33 instances of various controls. If you need more than 256 controls on a form, you can use control arrays. Each control array can contain a maximum of 32,767 objects.

Creating a Control Array

Depending on which option button is clicked, the program must apply the correct delivery charge or no charge if the order is eaten in the restaurant. You will use a control array for the option buttons so you only need to write one event procedure.

When you create objects in a control array, the objects share the same name; that is, they have the same value for the Name property. The **Index** property is an integer that Visual Basic uses in conjunction with the Name property to uniquely identify each object in a control array. The Index property starts at zero (0) for the first object and increments by one (1) for each subsequent object in the control array. Event procedures for control arrays receive an argument named Index, that contains the value of the Index property for the selected object. You can use the Index property to determine which option button is selected from an option group.

The easiest way to create a control array of option buttons is to copy and paste one object to create multiple instances of the object.

REFERENCE window	CREATING A CONTROL ARRAY OF OPTION BUTTONS
	▪ Create an instance of an option button on the form, then activate the option button.
	▪ Copy the option button to the Windows Clipboard by pressing Ctrl+C.
	▪ Click the Frame object to activate it.
	▪ Paste the copied option button into the frame by pressing Ctrl+V.
	▪ Be sure the option button appears at the top of the frame, not at the top of the form.
	▪ Click the Yes button in the message box that asks if you want to create a control array.
	▪ Move the new option button to the appropriate location.
	▪ Paste and move each option button you want to add to the control array.

You will copy the first option button and paste it into the Delivery frame three times to create the option buttons for delivery to Zone 2, Zone 3, and Eat In.

To create the remaining objects of the control array:

1. Click the **Zone 1** option button to select it.

2. Press **Ctrl+C** to copy the OptionButton object to the Windows Clipboard.

3. Click the **Delivery** frame to select it. The handles should appear around the frame.

4. Press **Ctrl+V** to paste the copied option button into the frame.

   A message box opens and asks if you want to create a control array.

5. Click the **Yes** button. The copy of the option button appears in the upper-left corner of the frame.

   TROUBLE? If the option button appears in the upper-left corner of the form rather than the frame, the option button is considered to be on the form rather than on the frame. For the buttons to work correctly, delete the option button, then repeat Steps 3 and 4.

6. Drag the new option button below the **Zone 1** option button, then set the Caption property of the new option button to **Zone 2**. Note that the value of the Index property is 1 and the name has not changed from optDelivery.

   Most controls have an Index property, which contains an integer number that you use with a control array to uniquely identify each member of the control array. You will use the Index property to identify which of the four option buttons on your form currently is selected.

7. Repeat Steps 3, 4, and 6 to create the third and fourth option buttons, and set the Caption properties to **Zone 3** and **Eat In**, respectively. Because the object you are pasting is now a member of a control array, you are not asked again if you want to create a control array.

Figure 3-10 ◄
Creating a
control array of
option buttons

option buttons
in control array

Gill suggests you run the program to verify that the option buttons are working correctly; that is, that only one button at a time can be selected.

To test the option buttons:

1. Save the project then start the program.

2. Click each of the option buttons. Only one button should be selected at a time.

TROUBLE? If you can click more than one option button at a time, the buttons are not all in the same option group. End the program. Click the frame and move it to another location on the form. The option button(s) that are not moved with the frame are in a different option group. Delete the button(s). Move the frame and buttons back into position. Activate a button that is inside the frame, then press Ctrl+C to copy it to the Clipboard. Click the frame to select it, then press Ctrl+V to paste the copied button into the frame. Repeat Steps 1 and 2.

3. End the program.

All the visible form objects are now in place. Next, you need to begin to write the Visual Basic code to compute and display the output in the different labels already drawn on the screen.

Using Boolean Values

To help a Master Burger clerk visually identify when an item has been ordered, Gill wants each scroll bar, its corresponding quantity ordered, and extended price labels to be visible only when the item's check box has been clicked. The scroll bar and labels should be invisible when an item's check box has not been clicked. You can accomplish this by setting the Visible property of the scroll bar and labels to True or False.

True and False are the valid Boolean values. A **Boolean variable** operates like an on/off switch; True signifies on and False signifies off. If you assign any value other than True or False to a Boolean variable, the value will be converted to True or False. If the value is 0, then it is converted to False. All other values are converted to True. Many properties accept Boolean values like True and False. Just as you can declare variables as Integer and Single, you can declare variables as the Boolean data type. The following list describes some of the more common properties that accept the Boolean values, True and False.

- The **Visible** property for an object determines whether or not the object appears on the screen when the program is running. As with other properties, you can set the Visible property for an object at design time using the Properties window, or by writing code in an event or general procedure that will be called at run time.

- The **Enabled** property for an object determines whether or not the object will respond to events. If you set the Enabled property of an object to False, clicking it will not generate a Click event.

- Option buttons support a **Value** property like a check box or scroll bar. But the value contains a Boolean value. If True, the option button in the option group is clicked and the others are not. When you explicitly set the Value of an option button to True with Visual Basic code, the button that was selected previously is no longer selected, and a Click event is generated. If you set the value of the selected option button to False, then none of the option buttons will be selected.

When the program first starts, Gill would like the most common option, an order being eaten in the restaurant, to be selected. To do this, you need to set the Eat In option button to True. This is the option button with the Index value of 3 named optDelivery.

To set the default option button to Eat In:

1. Open the Code window for the Form_Load event procedure and enter the following code shown in bold:

```
Private Sub Form_Load()
    optDelivery(3).Value = True
End Sub
```

This statement causes the Eat In option button to be selected when the form is first loaded. Notice the syntax of the statement. Like other controls you have used, you reference a specific property by typing the object's name, the object's Index value in parentheses, followed by a period (.), followed by the name of the property. The Index value specifies which specific option button in the array you want to set.

When the cash register program starts, no scroll bars or labels should appear on the form until a clerk clicks the corresponding check box. You could set the Visible property for each object individually, but this would be time consuming. Visual Basic allows you to select different types of objects and display only the properties common to all of the objects in the Properties window. You then can set any of the common properties all at once. In this case you need to change the Visible property for two different types of objects: scroll bars and labels. To select more than one object, you click the first object to display its handles; then you press and hold down the Shift key and click the additional objects. When you select and work with multiple objects, the Properties window does not display an object name.

To set the Visible property for the scroll bars and labels:

1. Make the Form window active. Press and hold down the **Shift** key as you click each scroll bar and each label for quantity ordered and extended price. As you activate an object, it is marked with blue handles and the other selected objects appear with dimmed handles. See Figure 3-11.

Figure 3-11
Selecting multiple objects

marked objects appear with handles

As shown in Figure 3-12, the Properties window displays only those properties that are common to both a label and a vertical scroll bar. Note that the object in the title bar may be different depending upon the last item selected.

Figure 3-12
Properties window for multiple selected objects

no object name displayed

only properties common to a label and vertical scroll bar are displayed

set this property to False

2. Set the Visible property for the selected objects to **False**.

The objects still are visible. The Visible property is applied at run time, so the objects will not disappear from the screen until the program is run.

3. Save the project and then start the program to test that the objects are not visible in run time. Your form should look like Figure 3-13.

Figure 3-13 ◄
Invisible
objects

scroll bars
are invisible

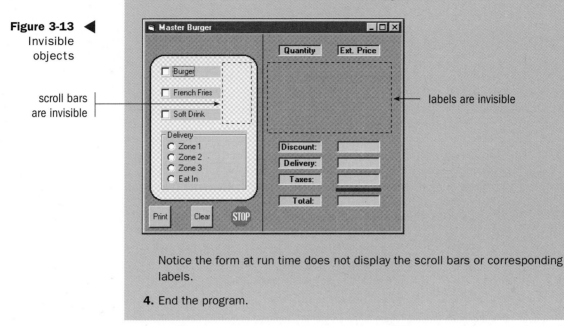

labels are invisible

Notice the form at run time does not display the scroll bars or corresponding labels.

4. End the program.

You now need to write the code to make the scroll bar, quantity ordered, and extended price labels visible when a clerk clicks the corresponding check box.

Writing Statements with Conditions

Now that your program starts running with the scroll bars and labels invisible, you need to write the code that will cause these objects to become visible if a corresponding check box is checked. You want the scroll bars and labels to remain invisible, or become invisible again, if the corresponding check box is not checked. Thus, you will set the Visible property of each object to a Boolean value of True or False. You also want the Initial value of the scroll bar to be set to 1.

The programs you have developed until now have all executed statements sequentially in the order they appear in the procedure, until the procedure reaches the End Sub statement. This is fine for simple tasks, but most programs need the capability to execute one set of statements in certain circumstances and another set of statements in different circumstances. Visual Basic allows you to write statements to address different conditions. For example, you can write a statement such as, "If a menu item check box is checked, then make its corresponding scroll bar and labels visible; otherwise, make these objects invisible." The following pseudocode shows the statement in generic form.

If some expression is True Then
    execute one group of statements.
Otherwise
    execute a different group of statements.
End of If statement

Using Comparison Operators

To determine which set of statements to execute, you use a conditional statement. A **conditional statement** allows you to execute one series of statements when a condition is True and another set of statements when a condition is False. When you write a conditional statement, you use comparison operators on two values or expressions. The values can be compared in many ways using **comparison operators**. The comparison operators used by Visual Basic are equal to (=), not equal to (<>), less than (<), greater than (>), less than or equal to (<=), greater than or equal to (>=), or contains the string (Like). The result of a conditional operation always must be either True or False and, therefore, produces a Boolean value. Comparison operators all have the same precedence. When used with arithmetic operators, however, the arithmetic operations are performed first then the comparison operations are performed.

To determine which statements to execute in your program, you will use the comparison operator equal to (=) with an If statement to determine if one value is the same as another. Comparison operators seldom are used by themselves. Rather, they are included as part of some statement. The simplest form of an If statement, which will execute a set of statements only if a specific condition is True, has the following syntax:

If *condition* **Then**

   statement(s)

End If

- The *condition* part of an If statement must evaluate to a Boolean value of True or False.

- The *statement(s)* part can be any valid Visual Basic statement(s), which is(are) executed when the condition is True.

- If the *condition* is False, the *statement(s)* before the **End If** is(are) not executed, and execution of the program continues at the statement following the End If.

The following pseudocode describes a simple If statement that will execute statements if the French Fries check box is checked.

```
If the French Fries check box is checked Then
  Make the corresponding scroll bar visible
  Make the corresponding label visible
  Set the value of the scroll bar to 1
End of If statement
```

This statement is useful, but it does not account for situations in which a different activity needs to be executed when a condition is False. The cash register program must make the scroll bar visible when a menu item is selected and invisible when the item is not selected. This type of If statement, often called an If...Then...Else statement, has the following syntax:

If *condition* **Then**

   statements executed when the condition is True

Else

   statements executed when the condition is False

End If

- If the *condition* is True, then the *statement(s)* before the **Else** statement is(are) executed, then execution continues at the *statement* following the End If statement.

- If the *condition* is False, the statements after the Else statement are executed.

This If…Then…Else statement is represented with the following pseudocode:

```
If the French Fries check box is checked Then
    Make the corresponding scroll bar visible
    Make the corresponding label invisible
    Set the value of the scroll bar to 1
Otherwise execute the following statements
    Make the corresponding scroll bar invisible
    Make the corresponding label invisible
    Set the value of the scroll bar to 0
End of If statement
```

You will write an If…Then…Else statement to make visible or invisible the scroll bars and the quantity ordered and extended price labels for each menu item when its corresponding check box is checked. For example, when the chkBurger object is checked, the Visible property for the vsbBurger, the lblQtyBurger and lblExtBurger output labels should be set to True; otherwise they should be set to False.

To make the user interface as intuitive and easy to use as possible, Gill wants the program to set the value of the corresponding scroll bar and quantity ordered label when the value of the check box changes. When the box first is checked, the quantity ordered scroll bar must be set to 1, the most likely quantity that will be ordered. You can do this by setting the Value property of the scroll bar to 1 when you set its Visible property to True. You will set the Caption of the label in a moment.

Occasionally, a customer will decide not to order a product that already has been checked. When a check box is unchecked, the scroll bar and the labels for quantity ordered and extended price need to be set to 0 and become invisible again.

Using Object Browser, you will see which intrinsic constants to use to express one of three valid check box values: 0 - Unchecked, 1 - Checked, or 2 - Grayed.

To use the Object Browser to examine the intrinsic constants applicable to a check box:

1. Open the **Object Browser**.

2. Click **CheckBoxConstants** in the Classes section of the Object Browser dialog box.

   The Members of 'CheckBoxConstants' section displays three constants—vbChecked, vbGrayed, and vbUnchecked, as shown in Figure 3-14.

Figure 3-14 ◀
Object Browser
dialog box

intrinsic constants
supported by
CheckBox object

3. Click **vbChecked**. Notice the value of the constant (1) is displayed at the bottom of the dialog box.

4. Click **vbGrayed** and notice the value of the constant is 2.

5. Click **vbUnchecked** and notice the value of the constant is 0.

6. Close the **Object Browser**.

When you use intrinsic constant names in a program, Visual Basic converts the names into their respective values when the program is run, which makes the program more readable and reliable. For example, if you needed to set the Value property to Unchecked, the following two statements would accomplish this; however, the statement containing the constant makes it clearer that you want the value to be Unchecked:

```
chkBurger.Value = 0
chkBurger.Value = vbUnchecked
```

You will use intrinsic constants to write the code to make the scroll bars and labels visible when a clerk checks a check box.

To set the Visible property for the scroll bars and labels based on the check box values:

1. Open the Code window for the chkBurger_Click event procedure and enter the following code (shown in bold):

```
Private Sub chkBurger_Click()
    If (chkBurger.Value = vbChecked) Then
        vsbBurger.Visible = True
        vsbBurger.Value = 1
        lblQtyBurger.Visible = True
        lblExtBurger.Visible = True
    Else
        vsbBurger.Visible = False
        vsbBurger.Value = 0
        lblQtyBurger.Visible = False
        lblExtBurger.Visible = False
    End If
End Sub
```

2. Repeat Step 1 for the chkFrenchFries_Click event procedure. Be sure you use the object names **vsbFrenchFries**, **lblQtyFrenchFries**, and **lblExtFrenchFries**. Remember, you can select the code you just wrote and use the copy and paste operations.

3. Repeat Step 1 for the chkSoftDrink_Click event procedure. Be sure you use the object names **vsbSoftDrink**, **lblQtySoftDrink**, and **lblExtSoftDrink**.

You now have written the code to make the scroll bars and labels visible when the value of a corresponding check box is 1 (vbChecked), and to set the Value property of the scroll bar to 1 when its box first is checked. This code also will reset the Visible and Value properties to False and 0, respectively, when the check box Value property is 0 (vbUnchecked).

Notice the parentheses in the If statement of the code you just wrote.

```
If (chkBurger.Value = vbChecked) Then
```

While not required to evaluate the statement correctly, parentheses can improve the readability of your program. They make it clear that chkBurger.Value is compared against the constant vbChecked first. If True, the statements before the Else are executed. If False, then the statements after the Else are executed.

Tip: Use parentheses liberally in your programs to improve readability and reduce logic errors caused by misunderstanding precedence. Note that adding parentheses will not slow down the execution of your program.

Now that the event code for each check box is complete, you have reached a milestone in your program. It is a good time to save your work, test your program, and correct any errors.

To test the check boxes:

1. Save the project and then start the program.

2. Click the **Burger** check box. The corresponding scroll bar, vsbBurger, and the labels, lblQtyBurger and lblExtBurger, become visible.

3. Click the **Burger** check box again. The objects are invisible again.

4. Repeat Steps 2 and 3 for the **French Fries** and **Soft Drink** check boxes.

TROUBLE? If the visibility of an object does not change in response to a click in the corresponding check box, end the program, then open the Code window for the CheckBox object's Click event procedure and verify that your code is identical to the code shown in the previous tutorial steps. Make any necessary corrections, then repeat Steps 1 through 4.

5. End the program.

The cash register screen now displays the corresponding scroll bars and quantity ordered fields when a check box is checked and makes those objects invisible when the corresponding check box is not checked. You are ready to begin programming the scroll bar objects so that when the user moves the scroll bars, the corresponding quantity ordered label is updated.

In this program, you need to know when the numeric value of a scroll bar changes, so the program can update the quantity ordered and extended price of an item and display the information in the corresponding Label objects. Whenever a clerk clicks part of a scroll bar and changes its value, a Change event is generated. You use a Change event with the Value property of the scroll bar in a computation to update the captions of the necessary labels. Figure 3-15 shows how each event causes the next event. Whenever the clerk clicks the check box representing a menu item, the scroll bar is set to 1; this also causes a Change event to be generated for the scroll bar.

Figure 3-15 ◀
Relationship between events (1)

Now you need to write the code to program the Change event that will update the caption in the quantity ordered label whenever the value of the scroll bar changes.

To write the code that will place the value of a scroll bar into its quantity ordered label:

1. Open the Code window for the vsbBurger_Change event and enter the following code (shown in bold):

```
Private Sub vsbBurger_Change()
        lblQtyBurger.Caption = vsbBurger.Value
End Sub
```

When one of the scroll arrows is clicked, the program generates a Change event for the vsbBurger object. The code in this Change event procedure copies the Value property of vsbBurger to the Caption property of lblQtyBurger.

You now need to create the same code for the scroll bars for the French Fries and Soft Drink items.

2. Repeat Step 1 for the vsbFrenchFries_Change event, using the names **lblQtyFrenchFries** and **vsbFrenchFries**.

3. Repeat Step 1 for the vsbSoftDrink_Change event, using the names **lblQtySoftDrink** and **vsbSoftDrink**.

Whenever a clerk clicks a scroll bar, the caption of the corresponding label will display the quantity ordered for the item, as indicated by the value of the scroll bar.

Gill suggests that you test the program to see whether or not the quantity ordered labels are updated correctly when a scroll bar is clicked. Testing the program also will give you an opportunity to see how the Change event works for a scroll bar. Because you have set the Max and Min properties, you cannot set the Value property outside the specified range.

To test the scroll bars and their corresponding quantity ordered labels:

1. Save the project and then start the program.

2. Click the **Burger** check box. The corresponding label displays the value 1.

3. Click the Burger scroll bar's **up arrow**. The corresponding label displays the value 2.

4. Click the Burger scroll bar's **down arrow**. The label displays the value 1. Because you did not change the SmallChange property from the default value of 1, the value of the scroll bar changes by 1 each time you click one of its arrows.

5. Repeat Steps 2 through 4 to test the French Fries and Soft Drink scroll bars and display labels.

   TROUBLE? If any quantity ordered label did not change, end the program, and open the Code window for the corresponding scroll bar. Check the code and make sure the Caption property is set for the correct Label object.

   If the value of an item incremented or decremented incorrectly, check the Min and Max properties of the corresponding scroll bar; Min should be 25 and Max should be 0. Make any necessary corrections, then repeat Steps 1 through 4.

6. End the program by clicking the **End** button ⬛ on the toolbar. You cannot use the stop sign icon because the code has not been written yet.

Note that when you click one of the scroll arrows for a menu item, the value of its scroll bar changes. This means that a Change event is generated for the scroll bar. This process is illustrated in Figure 3-16.

Figure 3-16 ◀
Relationship
between
events (2)

Creating User-Defined Constants

You still must create the code to compute and display the labels for the extended prices (unit price × quantity ordered), as described in the pseudocode Gill wrote for the program. Before you can compute the extended price, you need to include the price of each item in the program. You could declare variables for the prices and assign values to them as you did in Tutorial 2, or just use numbers in the computations. In this case, however, the price of an item will not change while the program is running, so a constant is more suitable for storing the prices. You used an intrinsic constant in the If statement you wrote to determine if a check box is checked. You also can create user-defined constants by using the **Const** (constant) statement. The syntax for a user-defined constant is:

[**Public** | **Private**] **Const** *constantname* [**As** *type*] = *expression*

- The **Public** keyword is used at the form level to declare constants that can be used by all procedures in all forms and other modules. You need this keyword only if you have more than one form in your project. The **Private** keyword is used at the form level to declare a constant that can be used only by procedures in the form where the constant is declared. Constants are Private if you omit the Public or Private keyword. You should use explicitly the Private keyword, however, to declare form-level constants and improve your program's clarity.

- You can declare constants in the general declarations section of a Form module or inside a procedure. Constants declared in the general declarations section are visible to the module in which they are declared when the Private keyword is used, and visible to the other modules in a project when the Public keyword is used. Constants declared inside a procedure are only visible to the procedure in which they are declared.

- The *constantname* assigned to a user-defined constant should follow the naming conventions for variables. That is, it begins with a three-letter prefix describing its data type, followed by a descriptive name. The entire constant name should be prefixed with the letter "c" indicating a constant.

- Constants can represent any of the Visual Basic data types by using the optional **As** *type* clause. If you don't explicitly declare the constant type using the **As** *type* clause, the constant has the data type that is most appropriate for the expression. Explicitly supplying the desired data type, however, will create more readable code and prevent possible type conversion errors.

- The *expression* represents a valid Visual Basic expression that becomes the value of the constant. The expression often is a simple value, such as a price, but it also can consist of other constants and operators. See the Visual Basic online Help for more information on the Const statement.

Because your program has only one form, the constants need to be visible only to the form in which they are declared, so you will declare them as Private. Each constant will be declared as a Single data type, because the prices contain a decimal point. The price constants will be used in various expressions throughout the program to compute the extended prices of products ordered.

Tip: Creating user-defined constants makes a program more readable and easier to maintain, because when the value of a constant changes, you only need to change the value once in the statement where the constant is created. For the cash register program, when the price of an item changes, you only need to change the constant once rather than searching for each occurrence of the price used in the program.

Next, you will declare the prices and the sales tax rate as constants in the general declarations section of the Form module so they will be available to all the procedures in the form.

To create the constants in the cash register program:

1. Open the Code window to the general declarations section of the Form module.

2. Type the following code shown in bold:

```
Option Explicit
Private Const csngPriceBurger As Single = 1.44
Private Const csngPriceFrenchFries As Single = 0.74
Private Const csngPriceSoftDrink As Single = 0.66
Private Const csngPercentTax As Single = 0.07
```

This code declares three constants for the item prices and another constant for the sales tax rate. The code also sets the data type and value for each constant.

Next, you must create the code to calculate the extended price and place it in the caption of the corresponding extended price label. The extended prices are computed and then stored as an intermediate result in a variable. Then, the intermediate result (the variable) is placed into the label. The variable is necessary so the program can use the value of the Label object to compute the order total. Because the contents of each label will be formatted with a leading dollar sign, if you had not used a variable, you would need to remove the dollar sign, and then call the Val function to convert the Label object's caption back to a number and calculate the order total. By creating the intermediate variable now, you will be able to use the variable to compute the order total. You also will need another variable to hold the delivery charges, if any.

To declare the variables for the extended prices:

1. In the general declarations section of the Form module, type the following four lines below the constants you just defined:

```
Private msngExtBurger As Single
Private msngExtFrenchFries As Single
Private msngExtSoftDrink As Single
Private msngDelivery as Single
```

The first three variables will store temporary information for the extended price of an item. Because these are form-level variables having a data type of Single, the prefix msng is used. The variable msngDelivery will be used to store the delivery charges, if any.

For each of the three different products, when either arrow of the scroll bar is clicked, the code you previously wrote executes in response to the VScrollBar_Change event and updates the caption of the corresponding quantity ordered label. When the label representing the quantity ordered of an item changes, the extended price also needs to change. Figure 3-17 shows how these events occur.

Figure 3-17 ◀
Relationship
between
events (3)

Now that you have declared the necessary variables, you can use them to write the code that will calculate the extended prices.

To write the code that will calculate and display the extended prices:

1. Activate the Code window for the lblQtyBurger_Change event. Make sure that you activate the Change event, not the Click event.

2. Enter the following code (shown in bold):

```
Private Sub lblQtyBurger_Change()
    msngExtBurger = lblQtyBurger.Caption * _
        csngPriceBurger
    lblExtBurger.Caption = Format(msngExtBurger, _
        "Currency")
End Sub
```

3. Repeat Steps 1 and 2 for the lblQtyFrenchFries_Change event procedure. Be sure to substitute **lblQtyFrenchFries** for lblQtyBurger, **msngExtFrenchFries** for msngExtBurger, **csngPriceFrenchFries** for csngPriceBurger, and **lblExtFrenchFries** for lblExtBurger.

4. Repeat Steps 1 and 2 for the lblQtySoftDrink_Change event procedure. Be sure to substitute **lblQtySoftDrink** for lblQtyBurger, **msngExtSoftDrink** for msngExtBurger, **csngPriceSoftDrink** for csngPriceBurger, and **lblExtSoftDrink** for lblExtBurger.

You now have written all the code to update the extended price of each item when the quantity ordered changes. The Format statement sets the output format as Currency, with a leading dollar sign and two decimal places. After being formatted with a leading dollar sign, this extended price label cannot be used by the Val function, as the Val function requires an argument to begin with a number (not a dollar sign). This is why you will use intermediate variables to calculate the order total. This is a good time to test your program, correct any errors, and save the form and project files.

To test the extended prices:

1. Save the project and then start the program.

2. Click each of the three check boxes. The extended prices are computed, placed in the labels, and formatted.

TROUBLE? If an extended price is not computed correctly, end the program, and activate the Code window for the Change event procedure of the corresponding quantity ordered Label object. Be sure that the code is the same as the code shown in the previous set of steps. Make any necessary corrections, then repeat Steps 1 and 2.

If an extended price is not formatted as currency, check that you wrote the correct Format statement for the correct corresponding extended price label. Repeat Steps 1 and 2.

3. End the program.

You have completed the cash register programming for this session. The user of the program can select items and specify the corresponding quantity ordered. Whenever the quantity ordered changes, the extended price of the item will be recomputed. Notice you took advantage of the Change event to determine when the extended price needs to be recomputed instead of forcing the user to explicitly click a command button to complete the extended price. In the next session you will learn how to compute the totals, the delivery charges, and the discount.

Quick Check

1 What is the function of a check box?

2 What values can a check box contain?

3 Define the following scroll bar properties: Min, Max, LargeChange, SmallChange, and Value.

4 What is a Boolean value?

5 Write the code for the following pseudocode statements:

If the Visible property of lblTaxes is equal to True, Then set the caption to 33.

If the Visible property of lblTaxes is not equal to False, Then set the value to 0.

If the January sales (lblJan) are greater than the February sales (lblFeb), Then add 1 to the value of the caption of January sales.

If yesterday is less than today, Then end the program.

6 Describe the difference between a Change event and a Click event.

7 Describe how one event can generate another event.

Now that you have completed Session 3.1, you can exit Visual Basic or you can continue to the next session.

In this session you will learn how to write more complex If statements and learn about a new statement called the Select Case statement. You also will create your own procedures, called general procedures, which are activated explicitly by your program rather than as a response to an event. You also will learn how to perform operations on String variables and display a message box to confirm an action.

Select Case Statements and Option Buttons

The option buttons on the cash register program should trigger a delivery charge only if the order will be delivered. For Zone 1 the delivery amount is $1.50, for Zone 2, $2.50, and for Zone 3, $3.50.

Earlier you used an If statement to test a condition and execute one set of the statements when the condition was True and another set when the condition was False. Sometimes the decision to be made has more than two possible outcomes. For example, the delivery decision has four outcomes—the order was eaten in the restaurant, or delivered to one of three different zones. The most efficient method in situations requiring three or more choices is to use one of two different statements: an If statement or a Select Case statement.

The If statement with more than two outcomes has the following syntax:

If *condition1* **Then**

    statement-block1

ElseIf *condition2* **Then**

    statement-block2

[ElseIf *condition-n* **Then**

    statement-block-n]

[Else

    [*statements*]]

End If

- If *condition1* is True, the statements contained in *statement-block1* up to the ElseIf clause are executed, then the entire If statement exits whether or not any of the other *conditions* are True and execution continues at the statement following the End If.

- If *condition1* is False and *condition2* is True, the statements contained in *statement-block2* up to the next ElseIf clause are executed. The entire If statement exits whether or not any of the remaining *conditions* are True and execution continues at the statement following the End If.

- The statement block following each successive ElseIf clause is executed if the previous conditions were False and it is True. The entire If statement exits whether or not any of the remaining *conditions* are True and execution continues at the statement following the End If.

- If none of the conditions is True, the statements inside the Else clause are executed if one exists, then the If statement exits. The Else clause is optional. If there is no Else clause, the If statement exits and execution continues at the statement following the End If.

Figure 3-18 illustrates how this type of If statement works by examining where an order will be eaten.

Figure 3-18 ◄
Analyzing the
If statement

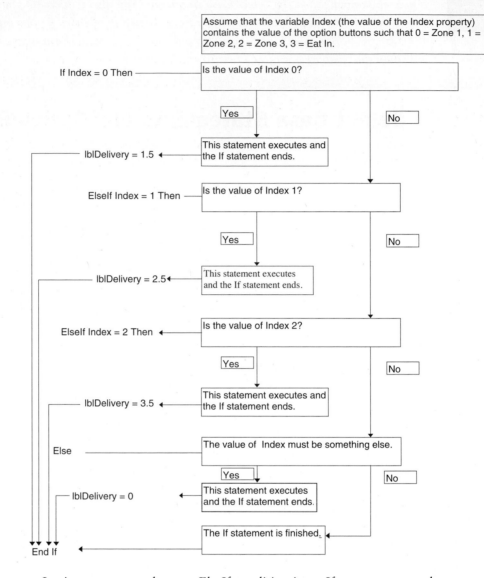

In circumstances where an ElseIf condition in an If statement uses the same expression and compares it to a different value, the Select Case decision structure can both simplify program logic and make a program more readable. **Select Case** statements are like If statements, but instead of testing multiple expressions, the Select Case statement tests only one expression and executes different statements based on the results of the expression. The following is the syntax of a Select Case statement:

Select Case *testexpression*

    Case *expressionlist1*

        statement-block1

    Case *expressionlist2*

        statement-block2

    Case *expressionlist-n*

        statement-block-n

  [Case Else

    [*statements*]]

End Select

- Visual Basic executes the Select Case statement by evaluating the *testexpression* once when the Select Case statement first starts. It then compares the *expressionlist1* with the *testexpression*. If they are the same, the statements in *statement-block1* are executed, then the entire Select Case statement exits. If they are not the same, the *expressionlist2* is compared with the *testexpression*. This process is repeated until there are no more expressions to be tested.

- If no expression matches the *testexpression*, the statements in the optional Case Else clause are executed. If no expression matched the *testexpression* and the Case Else statement is omitted, then no statement block will be executed.

- If more than one *expressionlist* is the same as the *testexpression*, only the statements in the first matching Case are executed.

- The *expressionlist* can be a list of values—such as 6,7,8—separated by commas. It also can be a range of values separated by the word To, as in 5 To 10. Refer to Visual Basic online Help for more information on the Select Case statement.

Figure 3-19 shows the If statement from Figure 3-18 written as a Select Case statement.

Figure 3-19 ◀
Analyzing the
Select Case
statement

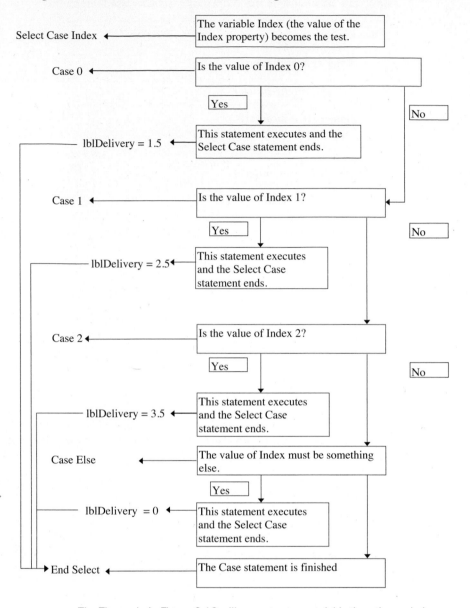

Tip: The code in Figure 3-19 will execute more quickly than the code in Figure 3-18 because Visual Basic only needs to check the Index once in the first line of the Select Case statement, rather than for each If and ElseIf. In addition, this Select Case statement will make your program easier to read than the longer If statement.

Using the Select Case Statement with a Control Array

You now need a way to check which Delivery option button is clicked and write a Select Case statement to update the delivery charges and order total accordingly. In the control array of option buttons, a specific option button is identified by its Index property. Visual Basic uses the Index property as an argument in the option buttons' Click event procedure to indicate which object in the control array caused the Click event to occur. When you call a procedure you send arguments to the procedure by enclosing the argument in parentheses, just like you did when you called functions like Val and FV. These procedures then receive the arguments and perform operations on them. Your Click event procedure will receive an argument, just as the Val procedure receives and processes arguments.

Like variables, an argument has a name and a data type, which are shown in the declaration for the argument. Figure 3-20 shows the argument for the optDelivery_Click event procedure.

Figure 3-20 ◀
Argument in
the event
procedure

Notice that the syntax of the argument looks like any other declaration statement except that the keyword, Dim or Private, is omitted. It contains a variable name, Index, and an As clause followed by the data type, Integer. Visual Basic stores the Index of the active option button as a local variable so you can use it in the event procedure. If you have more than one control array of option buttons on a form, each control array of option buttons uses a local variable of the name, Index. Like other local variables, this variable only exists while the procedure is running. This is the method of communicating information from one procedure to another or, in this situation, having the system communicate information to your event procedure. If the Zone 1 option button is clicked, Visual Basic will set the Index property to 0; if the Zone 2 option button is clicked, Visual Basic will set the Index property to 1; if the Zone 3 option button is clicked, Visual Basic will set the Index property to 2; and if the Eat In option button is clicked, Visual Basic will set the Index property to 3. This is how Visual Basic keeps track of, and shares code among, the control array's objects.

You will use this information to determine the delivery charge, if any, by writing the necessary Select Case statement in the Code window for the control array's Click event.

To write the Select Case statement to assign the necessary delivery charge:

1. Start Visual Basic, if necessary.

2. Open the project named **Master Cash Register.vbp** that you created in Session 3.1 and view the form, if necessary.

3. Activate the Code window for the **optDelivery_Click** event procedure and enter the following code (shown in bold):

```
Private Sub optDelivery_Click(Index As Integer)
    Select Case Index
        'Zone 1
        Case 0
            msngDelivery = 1.5
        'Zone 2
        Case 1
            msngDelivery = 2.5
        'Zone 3
        Case 2
            msngDelivery = 3.5
        'Eat In
        Case 3
            msngDelivery = 0
    End Select

    lblDelivery.Caption = Format(msngDelivery, "Currency")
End Sub
```

This sequence of statements is executed when any of the four option buttons is clicked. You determine which option button is clicked by looking at the value stored in the Index property. The Select Case statement works by first evaluating the value of Index, and then executing the statements for the respective case. The delivery charge then is formatted and displayed by setting the caption of lblDelivery. Because there is no other possibility, you did not need to include a Case Else statement.

The cash register program now computes a delivery charge if appropriate. You have reached another milestone in your program. You now should check that the Delivery option buttons and Delivery label work correctly.

To test the Delivery option buttons and Delivery label:

1. Save the project and then start the program.

2. Click each of the **option buttons** in the Delivery control array.

   The Delivery label changes with each option button clicked.

   TROUBLE? If the Delivery label does not reflect the changes when each option button is clicked, end the program. Check that the code in the option buttons' Click event matches the code in the previous set of steps, then repeat Steps 1 and 2.

3. End the program.

Creating a General Procedure

According to the program specifications written by Gill, the cash register program must compute the taxes and order total automatically whenever the extended price of a menu item changes. To accomplish this, you can use the same code for all three event procedures, lblExtBurger_Change, lblExtFrenchFries_Change, and lblExtSoftDrink_Change. Instead of writing the same lines of code in each of the three event procedures, you can create a procedure called a general procedure, and then call the general procedure with one line of code in the individual event procedures. A **general procedure** is like an event procedure, but you must explicitly call a general procedure because it does not respond to an event. One of the keys to writing successful programs is to divide tasks into logical components, such as general procedures, which then can be reused within the same program or in one or more different programs.

There are two types of general procedures: **Function procedures** (functions), and **Sub procedures** (subroutines). The difference between functions and subroutines is how they communicate their results to the procedure from which they were called. Functions return a result of a specific data type that you generally assign to a variable or appropriate property. Subroutines do not return a value.

When you create a general procedure like the one to compute the taxes and order total, you must specify the procedure name, type, and scope. Visual Basic will help you by creating a template for the procedure from information you supply in the Add Procedure dialog box.

To open the Add Procedure dialog box for the form:

1. Be sure the Code window is active then click the **Tools** menu, then click **Add Procedure**. The Add Procedure dialog box opens. See Figure 3-21.

Figure 3-21 ◄
Add Procedure
dialog box

Type section ──────►

Scope section ──────►

Name text box

TROUBLE? If the Add Procedure command is dimmed on the Tools menu, be sure the Visual Basic title bar displays [design], and that the Code window is the active window.

The Add Procedure dialog box consists of three sections—Name, Type, and Scope.

- In the **Name** text box you type a name for the general procedure. The requirements for procedure names are the same as for variables. You do not need to supply, however, the four-character prefix indicating the procedure's scope and type.

- The **Type** identifies whether the procedure is a Sub (subroutine) procedure, Function procedure, Property procedure, or Event procedure. **Sub** procedures communicate information to other parts of the program by setting form-level variables, but do not return values to the procedures from which they were called. **Function** procedures return values to the procedures from which they were called. **Property** procedures are used in a different type of module, called a class module, to create properties for the objects in a class module. **Event** procedures are used to create user-defined events.

- Public and Private are the keywords that describe the **Scope** of the procedure. If a procedure is **Private**, it can be called only from the form in which it is declared. If it is **Public**, the procedure can be called from anywhere in the project. Public procedures are useful only when a program contains more than one Form module or other modules.

You will use the Add Procedure dialog box to create the general procedure that will calculate the taxes and order total when any extended price changes. Because you do not need any value to be returned to the calling procedure, you will create a Sub procedure. Also, you will declare the general procedure as Private, because all the code for your program is contained in the same form.

To write the general procedure to compute the taxes and order total:

1. Type **ComputeTotals** in the Name text box.

2. In the Type section, click the **Sub** option button.

3. In the Scope section, click the **Private** option button.

4. Click the **OK** button.

   The Code window will become active; "(General)" will appear in the Object list box and "ComputeTotals" will appear in the Procedures list box. This indicates that the ComputeTotals procedure is not executed when an event occurs to a specific object, but is general to the Form module and can be called explicitly by any event or general procedure. Because the procedure is Private, it only can be called from event or general procedures in this form.

5. Enter the following code into the procedure:

```
Private Sub ComputeTotals()
    Dim psngSubtotal As Single
    Dim psngTaxes As Single

    psngSubtotal = msngExtBurger + msngExtFrenchFries + _
        msngExtSoftDrink

    psngTaxes = csngPercentTax * psngSubtotal
    lblTaxes.Caption = Format(psngTaxes, "Currency")
    lblTotal.Caption = Format(psngSubtotal + psngTaxes _
        + msngDelivery, "Currency")
End Sub
```

Now you can examine each line of the code in more detail.

```
Dim psngSubtotal As Single
Dim psngTaxes As Single
```

The variables psngSubtotal and psngTaxes are declared inside the ComputeTotals general procedure because you only need these variables when this procedure is running. These variables are considered local to the procedure, and other event or general procedures are not able to reference them. Furthermore, the memory for the variables exists only while the procedure is executing; it is allocated only when the procedure is called, and then it is released when the procedure terminates.

```
psngSubtotal = msngExtBurger + msngExtFrenchFries + _
    msngExtSoftDrink
```

This statement computes a subtotal by adding together the extended prices for each item. Remember that you declared the variables msngExtBurger, msngExtFrenchFries, and msngExtSoftDrink in the general declarations section of the Form module. These values were set by the Change event procedure of the corresponding quantity ordered label. Because the statements are too long to fit on a line, you needed to use the statement continuation character, as you did in Tutorial 2.

```
psngTaxes = csngPercentTax * psngSubtotal
```

Using the subtotal from the previous statement and the form-level constant representing the sales tax rate, this statement computes the sales tax.

```
lblTaxes.Caption = Format(psngTaxes, "Currency")
```

Because all the results representing a dollar amount need to be displayed with a leading dollar sign and two decimal places, this statement formats the sales tax and displays the formatted result in the label.

```
lblTotal.Caption = Format(psngSubtotal + psngTaxes _
    + msngDelivery, "Currency")
```

This statement computes the total using the local subtotal and sales tax variables, and the form-level delivery variable. Notice that rather than storing the order total in a separate variable, the computation was performed inside the first argument of the Format statement. This can be done because the value of lblTotal will never be used in another calculation, and because Visual Basic lets you embed expressions inside arguments. First psngSubtotal, psngTaxes, and msngDelivery are added together. Then the Format statement is called with the result and the second argument of Currency.

While the Add Procedure dialog box created a procedure template for you, it is not the only way to create a new Sub procedure in a module. You also can create a Sub procedure by typing the Private Sub and End Sub statements, if you desire.

Calling the General Procedure

Once you have created a general procedure, you need to call it from either a general or event procedure. Gill's design for the cash register program specifies that when the extended price of an item changes, the taxes and order total must recompute automatically. So, the ComputeTotals general procedure should be called in the Change event procedure for each extended price label. You need to call the ComputeTotals general procedure by typing its name in the appropriate event procedure. You also will format each extended price label as Currency.

To call the general procedure to compute the taxes and order total:

1. Activate the Code window for the **lblExtBurger_Change** event procedure. Be sure it is the Change event, not the Click event. Enter the following code:

```
Private Sub lblExtBurger_Change()
    ComputeTotals
End Sub
```

Calling the ComputeTotals general procedure in the Change event for this extended price label ensures that when the extended price changes, the taxes and order total will be updated.

2. Repeat Step 1 for the lblExtFrenchFries_Change event procedure. Be sure you select the object named **lblExtFrenchFries** instead of lblExtBurger.

3. Repeat Step 1 for the lblExtSoftDrink_Change event procedure. Be sure you select the object named **lblExtSoftDrink** instead of lblExtBurger.

Now that you have written all the code for the ComputeTotals general procedure and called the procedure whenever an extended price changes, you should examine the relationship between the events in the program. Figure 3-22 illustrates these relationships.

Figure 3-22
Event diagram for the cash register program

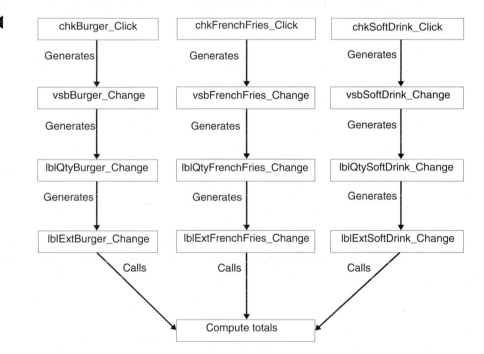

When a clerk clicks one of the check boxes, the value of the corresponding scroll bar is changed by the code in the Click event procedure causing a Change event to be generated for the scroll bar. The code for the scroll bar's Change event then updates the quantity ordered, generating another Change event. The Change event for the quantity ordered, in turn, updates the extended price. The Change event for each extended price label calls the ComputeTotals general procedure, which updates the taxes and order total labels. Understanding the relationship between multiple objects and the different events that occur is critical to writing Visual Basic programs. Now you will run the program and test it to verify that the order total is being computed correctly and being recomputed when necessary.

To test the general procedure to compute the taxes and order total:

1. Save the project and then start the program.

2. Enter an order and make sure the taxes and order total are computed correctly.

   TROUBLE? If the taxes and total do not change, be sure that each extended price object is calling the ComputeTotals general procedure.

3. Click the **Zone 1** option button.

   Notice that the order total does not change because you have not yet written the code to add the delivery charges to the order total.

4. End the program.

According to Gill's design specifications, the order total must be updated when the value of lblDelivery changes. Recall that the ComputeTotals general procedure adds together the subtotal, taxes, and delivery charges to get a total each time any extended price changes. To update the total when the delivery charge changes, the lblDelivery_Change event also must call the ComputeTotals general procedure.

To compute the total when the Delivery label changes:

1. Type the following code in the Code window for the **lblDelivery_Change** event procedure:

```
Private Sub lblDelivery_Change()
    ComputeTotals
End Sub
```

2. Save the project then start the program.

3. Enter an order, including a delivery zone. Make sure the total updates when you click the appropriate Delivery option button.

4. Test each of the option buttons.

   TROUBLE? If lblTotal does not update correctly when you click one of the option buttons, end the program. Make sure you have called the ComputeTotals general procedure from the lblDelivery_Change event procedure. Repeat Steps 2 through 4.

Now ComputeTotals updates the order total whenever the delivery charge changes.

As indicated in Gill's design specifications, Master Burger has been experimenting with keeping some stores open 24 hours a day. To increase sales volume between the hours of 1 A.M. and 8 A.M. Master Burger offers a 10% discount on the entire order. The discount, however, does not apply to the delivery charge. To accomplish this task you need to create another general procedure that will compute a discount. This time you will create a Function procedure, however, because the procedure will return a value—the amount of the discount. The Function procedure also will take an argument — the current subtotal of the order. The function will determine whether or not the order should be discounted, and apply the discount to the subtotal depending on the time of day. It then will return the amount of the discount. When a procedure returns a single value like this, writing a function reduces the number of variables you need to declare and improves the readability of the program.

To create a Function procedure to determine and compute the discount:

1. Open the **Add Procedure** dialog box. Remember the Code window must be active.

2. Set the Name to **ComputeDiscount**, the Type to **Function,** and the Scope to **Private**.

3. Click the **OK** button to close the Add Procedure dialog box.

Just as when you created a Sub procedure, Visual Basic creates a template for the procedure and activates the Code window. The procedure is declared as a Function, however. The Function statement, while similar to the Sub statement, has parts to define the data type of the value that will be returned to the calling procedure. The Function statement has the following syntax:

[**Public** I **Private**] **Function** *Name* [(*argumentlist*)] [**As** *type*]

    [*statementsName* = *expression*]

End Function

- The optional **Public** keyword indicates that the function can be used by the other forms in the program. The optional **Private** keyword indicates that the function is accessible only to the procedures in the form where it is declared.

- The required *Name* argument contains the name of the procedure and must be unique. The requirements for a Function procedure's name are the same as for a Sub procedure.

- The optional *argumentlist* describes the names and data types of the arguments passed to the function.

- The optional **As** *type* clause determines the data type of the value returned by the function.

- By assigning the *Name* of the function to an *expression*, the return value of the function is set.

- The **End Function** statement causes the function to terminate.

You now are ready to complete the code for the argument list, the return data type of the function, and the local variables. The ComputeDiscount function uses one argument —the order subtotal—to compute the discount. This is the value returned by the function. The argument is a Single data type and the function returns a Single data type because both numbers can contain a decimal point.

To declare the function's arguments:

1. Enter the code shown in Figure 3-23.

Figure 3-23 ◀
Creating
a function

argument name

The local variable psngDiscount is the function's argument name. The first "As Single" sets the data type of psngDiscount to Single; the second "As Single" sets the data type of ComputeDiscount to Single. In other words, the function ComputeDiscount will return a Single. Figure 3-23 shows the argument name, type, and return value.

To complete the procedure, you need to write the If statement that will determine whether or not the hour is between 1 A.M. and 8 A.M.

To accomplish this task you first must learn how to get the time of day from the computer's system. Visual Basic has several intrinsic functions that help you work with dates and times. When you work with dates, you generally use the Date data type. The information in a Date data type is stored as a number that can hold dates between January 1, 1000 and December 31, 9999. When you display a Date variable in a label, however, you see a string like:

```
12/12/99 3:33 PM
```

> *Tip:* For years between 1000 and 1999, Visual Basic only displays the last two digits of the year. For years 2000 or greater, Visual Basic displays all four digits of the year. Some older programs stored only the last two digits of the year. This problem, known as the millennium problem, will affect many programs when the year 2000 arrives.

There are three different functions that retrieve the date from the system. Each returns a Date and takes no arguments.

- The **Now** function returns the current date and time.

- The **Date** function returns the current date.

- The **Time** function returns the current time.

Figure 3-24 illustrates the functions that look at the different parts of a Date variable.

Figure 3-24 ◀
Date Functions

Function name	Description	Example
Day(*date*)	Return an integer between 1 and 31 representing the date of the month.	pintVar = Day(Now())
Month(*date*)	Returns an integer between 1 and 12 representing the month of the year.	pintVar = Month(Now())
Year(*date*)	Returns an integer representing the year; the full year is returned (that is, 1999, not 99).	pintVar = Year(Now())
Hour(*date*)	Returns an integer representing the hour of the day between 0 and 23.	pintVar = Hour(Now())
Minute(*date*)	Returns an integer between 0 and 59 representing the minute.	pintVar = Minute(Now())
Second(*date*)	Returns an integer between 0 and 59 representing the second.	pintVar = Second(Now())

For the cash register program, you are interested in the hour of the day so you need to use the Now function to first obtain the time of day. This can be accomplished by calling the Now function and using that result as the argument to the Hour function. Notice these functions are nested. That is, the Now function appears as an argument to the Hour function. When a function appears as an argument to another function, the function in the innermost parentheses is executed first.

To determine the hour of the day:

1. Enter the following code into the ComputeDiscount general procedure:

```
Dim pintHour As Integer
pintHour = Hour(Now())
```

This statement creates a local variable, pintHour. The current hour is computed by first calling the Now function, then calling the Hour function with one argument—the value returned by the Now function.

Creating an If Statement with Logical Operators

To create the If statement that will check the time of day you need to learn how to use a new kind of operator called a logical operator. **Logical operators** define the relationship between different expressions, much like conjunctions define the relationship between the parts of a sentence in English. The sentence, "If the hour of the day is earlier than 8 A.M. and equal to or later then 1 A.M., then compute a discount.", uses the conjunction and logical operator **And**. Thus, the statements on the leftmost and rightmost sides of the conjunction both must be True for the sentence to be True. If either or both of the statements are False, then the sentence is False. Figure 3-25 shows the more common logical operators.

Figure 3-25 ◀
Logical operators

Logical Operator	Definition	Example	Result

And	If both expressions evaluate to True, result is True. If either expression evaluates to False, result is False.	`If 2 > 1 And 3 > 1,Then`
		`    statements`
		`End If`
		`If 1 > 2 And 3 > 1,Then`
		`    statements`
		`End If`
			True
			
			False

Or	If either or both expressions evaluate to True, result is True.	`If 2 > 1 Or 3 > 1, Then`
		`    statements`
		`End If`
		`If 1 > 2 Or 3 > 1,Then`
		`    statements`
		`End If`
		`If 1 > 2 Or 1 > 3,Then`
		`    statements`
		`End If`
			True
			
			True
			
			False

Xor	If one, and only one, of the expressions evaluates to True, result is True. If either expression is Null, however, result also is Null.	`If 2 > 1 Xor 3 > 1,Then`
		`    statements`
		`End If`
		`If 1 > 2 Xor 3 > 1,Then`
		`    statements`
		`End If`
		`If 1 > 2 Xor 1 > 3,Then`
		`    statements`
		`End If`
			False
			
			True
			
			False

Not	If expression is True, then result is False. If expression is False, then result is True. If expression is Null, then result is Null.	`If Not 1 > 2,Then`
		`    statements`
		`End If`
		`If Not 2 > 1,Then`
		`    statements`
		`End If`
			True
			
			False

Like arithmetic operators, logical operators have an associated precedence. All operations involving arithmetic operators and comparison operators are performed first. Then the logical operations are performed in the following order: Not, And, Or, Xor.

You now can convert the sentence, "If the hour of the day is earlier than 8 A.M. and equal to or later then 1 A.M., then compute a discount.", and write the statement in the general procedure.

To compute the order discount:

1. Enter the following code into the ComputeDiscount general procedure after the declaration and assignment statements.

```
If (pintHour >= 1) And (pintHour < 8) Then
    ComputeDiscount = psngDiscount * 0.1
Else
    ComputeDiscount = 0
End If
```

The If statement you just wrote first determines if the variable pintHour is greater than or equal to 1. This result is either True or False. Then the variable pintHour is tested to see if it is less than 8. While not necessary, the parentheses help show that these operations are performed first. This result is either True or False. Finally, the two intermediate results are evaluated with the And. Thus, if both are True, then the If statement is True and the discount will be applied. Notice you set the amount of the discount to the name of the function. Thus, the discount amount will be returned to the calling procedure.

You have completed the code so the ComputeDiscount general procedure will determine whether the hour is between 1 A.M. and 8 A.M., and then calculate the discount accordingly. Now you need to call the function in the ComputeTotals general procedure so this discount will be subtracted from the total, if applicable.

To modify the ComputeTotals procedure to compute the discount and subtract it from the order total:

1. Open the Code window for the **ComputeTotals** general procedure and modify the following statements shown in bold.

```
Private Sub ComputeTotals ( )
    Dim psngSubtotal As Single
    Dim psngTaxes As Single
    Dim psngDiscount As Single

    psngSubtotal = msngExtBurger + msngExtFrenchFries + _
        msngExtSoftDrink
    psngDiscount = ComputeDiscount(psngSubtotal)

    psngTaxes = csngPercentTax * psngSubtotal
    lblTaxes.Caption = Format(psngTaxes, "Currency")
    lblDiscount.Caption = Format(psngDiscount * -1, _
        "Currency")
    lblTotal.Caption = Format(psngSubtotal + psngTaxes _
        + msngDelivery - psngDiscount, "Currency")
End Sub
```

The first new statement declares a local variable to hold the discount amount.

The second new statement calls the ComputeDiscount function and stores the result in the local variable psngDiscount. Remember that you declared the function to accept one argument, a Single, and returns a Single. Thus you used a variable containing the order subtotal as the function's argument and stored the result in the Single variable you just declared.

The next statement formats the variable and places it in the Label object's caption. The value is multiplied by -1 so it will be displayed as a negative number.

The addition to the final statement subtracts the discount amount from the order total.

You now should test the program to be sure the program is working correctly. Note that depending on the time of day, you may need to modify temporarily your If statement to a different time.

To test the discount:

1. Save the project.

2. Start the program and enter order values.

    TROUBLE? If the discount does not appear surrounded by brackets indicating a negative number, end the program and be sure that the code that places the discount in lblDiscount's caption multiplies the discount amount by –1, then repeat Step 2.

    TROUBLE? If the discount amount is not being subtracted from the order total, end the program and be sure that you added "- psngDiscount" to the statement that places the order total in lblTotal's caption.

TROUBLE? If the discount does not appear, the current time of day probably is not included within the hours 1 A.M. and 8 A.M.; temporarily modify your If statement so it includes the current time of day.

3. End the program.

Now that you have written the statements to compute the order discount, if applicable, you can proceed to program the Print and Clear command buttons.

Printing a Form Image

As part of the design specifications, the cash register program must be able to print each order to the default printer. To do this, you need to call a method of the Form object called **PrintForm**. The PrintForm method has the following syntax:

formname.**PrintForm**

- The **PrintForm** method prints an image of a form, as it appears on the screen.

- If *formname* is omitted, the current form is printed. If *formname* is specified, that form is printed.

Before calling this method, you must write the code for the Print command button that, when clicked, will print the form.

Creating a Command Button with Graphical Images

Gill would like to continue to use graphical pictures in all the buttons so the program has a consistent visual appearance. The CommandButton control will let you display a picture like the Image control. The command button, however, will let you display different pictures depending on the state of the control. To display pictures in a command button, you must learn about some new properties:

- The **DisabledPicture** property defines the picture displayed while the button is disabled and the Enabled property is False.

- The **DownPicture** property defines the picture displayed while the button is being clicked.

- The **Picture** property displays the bitmap or other picture when the button is enabled but not depressed.

- The **Style** property has two settings. When set to **0 - Standard**, the control displays the text stored in the Caption property as you have done before. When set to **1 - Graphical**, the control displays different graphical pictures depending on the state of the control. If a caption exists, it will be displayed in the command button along with the appropriate picture.

You now are ready to set the properties for the cmdPrint command button so it will display an image of a printer.

To display a picture in the cmdPrint command button:

1. Remove the text from the **Caption** property and set the Style property to **1 - Graphical**.

2. Set the Picture property to **A:\Tutorial.03\ImgPrint.bmp**; the name of the bitmap image on your Student Disk. Notice that the image will appear in the command button.

3. Open the Code window to the cmdPrint object's Click event then enter the following statement in the **Code** window:

```
frmMasterCashRegister.PrintForm
```

This statement prints the form named frmMasterCashRegister to the printer. Because this is the current form, the statement could have been written as:

```
PrintForm
```

In addition to the cmdPrint command button, Gill created a button to set up the cash register for a new order. This button, when clicked, must uncheck each check box, then set the quantity ordered (stored in the Value property of each scroll bar) to 0. Finally, you need to set the option button corresponding to the Eat In delivery status to True so that appears selected.

To program the cmdClearOrder command button:

1. Remove the text from the **Caption** property and set the Style property to **1 - Graphical.**

2. Set the Picture property to **A:\Tutorial.03\ImgClear.bmp**; the name of the bitmap image on your Student Disk. Notice that the image will appear in the command button.

3. Enter the following statements into the **Click** event procedure for the command button named cmdClearOrder:

```
chkBurger.Value = vbUnchecked
chkFrenchFries.Value = vbUnchecked
chkSoftDrink.Value = vbUnchecked
optDelivery(3).Value = True
```

The first three statements uncheck each of the check boxes. Remember the code you wrote for each check box's Click event to change the value of the scroll bars and make the scroll bars and corresponding labels invisible.

Because a Click event occurs whenever the value of a scroll bar changes, or the object is clicked explicitly, you do not have to clear explicitly the scroll bars to anything else. The code to respond to the different events already performs all the necessary tasks for you.

Because the option button corresponding to the Eat In delivery status has an Index value of 3, you set the Value property of this option button to True. This will cause this button to be selected. You have completed programming the Print and Clear command buttons. You now should test that these buttons are working properly.

To test the Print and Clear command buttons:

1. Save the project and then start the program.

2. Enter an order.

3. Click the **Print** button on the form. The form should be printed on the default printer.

4. Click the **Clear** button on the form. The order total, taxes, and discount should be set to 0 (zero), the labels and scroll bars should be invisible, and the Eat-In option button should be selected.

The final step in the cash register program is to program the stop program icon. When clicked, a message should be displayed asking the user if they actually want to exit the program or continue processing.

Creating a String Variable

In this session you need to display a message to verify that the clerk intended to exit the cash register program. Until now, you have not created a variable to contain text. The data type for a variable that contains text is String. You declare **String variables** using the Dim and Private statements just like Single and Integer numbers. There are two types of strings: fixed-length strings, which always store the same number of characters, and variable-length strings, which can store strings of different sizes. In this session you will store text strings of different lengths into String variables and the number of characters in the String variable will change at run time. Thus you will use variable-length strings.

When you assign text to the string, you surround the text in quotation marks. Just as you can perform operations on numbers, you also can perform operations on text strings. For example, you can append the contents of one string to another. This process is called **concatenation.** You concatenate strings together using the ampersand (&) operator. The following statement will concatenate two strings and store the result in the variable pstrPrompt2. Notice that a space character is stored between Gill and Clark.

```
pstrPrompt2 = "Gill" & " " & "Clark"
```

The variable pstrPrompt2 contains the string "Gill Clark". Every character in a string can be represented by a number between 0 and 255 or by a Visual Basic key code constant. The first 128 characters conform to a standard set of characters known as ASCII and represent all the standard characters on a keyboard. The other 128 characters are used for special characters and symbols. For example, a space is represented by the number 32 or by the constant, vbKeySpace. The KeyCodeConstants class in the Object Browser lists each of these constants. You also can refer to the Naming Appendix on your Student Disk for a chart of all ASCII characters and the corresponding KeyCodeConstants.

To use the numbers or constants as characters in a string, you must use the String function called Chr, which has the following syntax:

Chr(*charcode*)

- The function **Chr** converts a number or a key code constant into a character in a string.

- The charcode argument is a long integer between 0 and 255 or any valid Visual Basic constant defined by KeyCodeConstants.

Part of the ASCII character or key code constant set contains codes for characters that are not displayed on the screen. There are characters that perform special actions like starting a new line or inserting a tab. For example, a line feed character, represented by the number 13 causes the cursor to advance to the first column of the next line. You can use the return character to display a descriptive message on multiple lines. For example, the following statement will store the following sentences on two lines by embedding a return character between the two strings:

```
pstrPrompt = "You are about to exit the cash register." & _
    Chr(vbKeyReturn) & _
    "Are you sure you want to do this?"
```

The sentence enclosed in the first set of quotation marks will appear first in the variable, then the concatenation character, &, adds the return character, Chr(vbKeyReturn), to the string of text. The text within the second set of quotation marks will appear on a new line of text; this text also is joined by the concatenation operator. The following code would perform the same operation using the ASCII character code in place of the key code constants.

```
pstrPrompt = "You are about to exit the cash register." & _
    Chr(13) & _
    "Are you sure you want to do this?"
```

Displaying a Multiline Message in a Message Box

To prevent the program from exiting if a clerk accidentally clicks the stop sign image, Gill wants the program to display a message in a dialog box asking the clerk to confirm exiting the program. The dialog box will include a Yes button for exiting the program and a No button for not exiting it. Visual Basic supports a standard dialog box called a **message box** that will display a message, an icon to identify the importance of the message, and a standard set of buttons, like a Yes button and No Button or an OK button.

Based on the value returned, the program will use an If statement to determine whether or not the clerk wants to continue using the cash register program or exit it. The MsgBox function accepts arguments to control the message displayed in the box (prompt), any icons that can be displayed (buttons), and the caption for the message box (title). The MsgBox function has the following syntax:

    MsgBox(*prompt*[, *attributes*][, *title*])

- The **MsgBox** function displays a message box.

- The *prompt* is a string expression that controls the text displayed in the message box. This text is sent to the MsgBox function as an argument. The maximum number of characters allowed in a prompt is 1024. You can create the arguments for the text using String variables.

- The *attributes* argument is an expression containing intrinsic constants that define the behavior of the message box. The vbMsgBoxStyle class in the Object Browser lists each of these constants.

- You can include a *title* for the message box, which appears in the title bar of the message box in the same way as the form's Caption property.

Gill suggests that you use the online Help system to learn more about the MsgBox function.

To view information about the MsgBox function using Help:

  1. Start the online Help system and use the **Index** tab to search for **MsgBox function**.

  2. Print a copy of the Help page and close Help.

The first group of constants, those with the values 0 through 5, determines the buttons that appear in the message box. Notice that the constant to display a message box with Yes and No buttons can be represented either by the constant vbYesNo or the value 4. Inside the message box, you can include one of several different icons to help communicate the importance of the message. The second group of constants, those with the values 16 through 64, identifies the corresponding icons.

> *Tip:* You should carefully consider which icon to display in a message box. If you are asking a question, display a Warning Query icon using the vbQuestion constant. Use the Critical Message icon (vbCritical) to indicate only very serious problems or consequences. Use the Warning Message icon (vbExclamation) for less critical problems. Use the Information Message icon (vbInformation) when you are explaining something.

You can use one of three constants from the third group to define which button is the default. Pressing the Enter key as an alternative to clicking the button can activate the button assigned as the default. These constants are named vbDefaultButton1, vbDefaultButton2, vbDefaultButton3, and vbDefaultButton4. They correspond to the first, second, third, and fourth buttons in the message box. Assigning a default button is optional; if a default button does not make sense in your program, do not set a default value.

One constant from each group is added together to make up the attributes argument. If you do not want to select an item from a group, just omit the constant. Now you are ready to write the code for the message box that will appear when a clerk clicks the stop sign to exit the cash register program. The Warning Query message box will ask the clerk to confirm exiting the program. You will set No as the default button to minimize the possibility of accidentally exiting the cash register program.

To add a message box to the cash register program:

1. Open the Code window for the **imgStop_Click** event procedure and enter the following code:

```
Private Sub imgStop_Click()
    'Create arguments for MsgBox function.
    Dim pintAnswer As Integer
    Dim pstrPrompt As String
    Dim pintAttributes As Integer
    Dim pstrTitle As String

    'Set the values for the arguments.
    pstrPrompt = _
        "You are about to exit the cash register." & _
        Chr(vbKeyReturn) & _
        "Are you sure you want to do this?"
    pintAttributes = vbYesNo + vbQuestion + _
        vbDefaultButton2
    pstrTitle = "Cash Register"

    'Call the MsgBox function.
    pintAnswer = MsgBox(pstrPrompt, pintAttributes, _
        pstrTitle)

    'Test which button the user clicked.
    If pintAnswer = vbYes Then
        End
    End If
End Sub
```

The local variables will contain the returned value and arguments in preparation for calling the MsgBox function.

The attributes argument pintAttributes creates a message box with a Yes button and a No button and a Warning Query icon, and sets the No button as the default.

The Title statement sets the title of the message box to Cash Register. Finally, the MsgBox function is called and the returned value is tested to find out which button the clerk clicked.

Gill asks you to test the program again to make sure the message box works properly and the program is ending normally.

To test the message box function:

1. Save the project and then start the program.

2. End the program by clicking the **stop sign** image. The message box in Figure 3-26 opens.

Figure 3-26 ◀
Message box

3. Click the **No** button to continue running the cash register program.

4. Continue to test that the **Yes** button ends the program.

   TROUBLE? If the message box does not open, end the program, and compare the code for the imgStop object with the code in the previous steps. Make the necessary corrections, then repeat Steps 1 through 4.

5. Exit Visual Basic.

You now have completed the cash register program. It takes advantage of several different events to keep the extended price of items and the order totals up to date without making the user click a command button to recompute these values. Also, it satisfies the design requirements of using only controls that can operate without keyboard input. Gill is pleased with the prototype cash register and presents it to senior management.

Quick Check

1 What is a frame?

2 What is the relationship between a frame and a group of option buttons?

3 Write a statement to concatenate two strings "Do you want to" and "continue" displayed on separate lines. Store the result in a String variable named pstrPrompt.

4 Describe the difference between an If statement and a Select Case statement.

5 What is a control array?

6 What is the difference between a Function procedure and a Sub procedure?

7 Describe how message boxes are used in a program.

8 What is the purpose of logical operators?

Figure 3-27 lists and defines the new terms presented in this tutorial.

Figure 3-27 ◀
New terms

Term	Definition
Boolean variable	A Boolean variable is a variable that can have the value True or False. A Boolean variable operates like an on/off switch; True signifies on and False signifies off.
Comparison operators	Comparison operators are used to test whether or not a conditional statement is True or False. They are made up of equal to (=), not equal to (<>), less than (<), greater than (>), less than or equal to (<=), greater than or equal to (>=), or contains the string (Like).
Concatenation	Concatenation is the process of appending one string to another using the ampersand (&) operator.
Conditional statement	A conditional statement is a statement that is used to execute one series of statement when a condition is True and another statement when a condition is False. The If statement is an example of a conditional statement.
Control array	A control array is a term used to describe multiple objects that have the same name and event procedure. You reference the members of a control array using the object's name and its Index property.
Function procedure	A function procedure is a type of general procedure that performs a task using arguments supplied to the function, then processes those arguments. When complete, it returns a value to the calling procedure. The value returned by the function procedure is always of the same data type. Function procedures commonly are referred to as functions.
General procedure	A general procedure, like an event procedure, contains Visual Basic statements to perform some task. Unlike an event procedure, however, a general procedure is not called by the system in response to an event. Rather, you must explicitly call a general procedure.
Logical operators	Logical operators connect expressions together much like conjunctions connect sentences together in English. Logical operators consist of And, Or, Xor and Not.
Message box	A message box is used to open a pop-up message window. The user can click one of several buttons. A message box is displayed on the screen when the MsgBox function is called.
Option group	An option group is a way of creating option buttons so that only one button of the group may be selected at a time. This is accomplished by creating a frame, then creating each option button in the frame.
Radio button	A radio button is a common name for the option buttons contained in an option group. The name comes from the notion of the buttons on a car radio; only one button can be selected at a time.
String variable	A string variable is a data type that stores one or more characters.
Sub procedure	A Sub procedure is a type of general procedure that performs a task using arguments supplied to the function, then processes those arguments. It does not return a value when complete. Sub procedures commonly are referred to as subroutines.

Tutorial Assignments

Each Master Burger franchise has eight tables available for customers. In these Tutorial Assignments, you will create a program that clerks will use to determine if a table is occupied or needs cleaning, and what, if any, condiments are needed at the table. This information and the time of day needs to be recorded in the text boxes that represent each table.

When placing an eat-in order, the clerk assigns an available table to the customer and sets the table status to "Occupied". When the customer leaves, the table status is changed to "Needs cleaning". After it has been cleaned, the table status is "Clean". The clerk also can designate any condiments that are running low at a table. At Master Burger, table settings include the following condiments: catsup, mustard, salt, and pepper.

In the seating chart program, each table will have a table number from 1 to 8 and will be part of a TextBox control array that can display multiple scrollable lines. Table numbers will be selected with a vertical scroll bar. The status will be written to the current table's text box with the current date and time when a status change occurs. Because more than one condiment can be needed at the same time, the clerk will click one or more check boxes indicating the condiments needed, then click the Write table needs button to write a line containing the date and time. The program also will include a stop sign image that will exit the program. Figure 3-28 shows the completed user interface for the seating chart program.

Figure 3-28 ◀

1. Make sure your Student Disk is in the appropriate disk drive, then start Visual Basic.

2. Change the form's caption to **Master Burger - Seating Chart** and change its name to **frmMasterSeatingChart**.

3. Draw the first of eight text boxes for the Tables control array, then remove the initial text and set the name to **txtTable**. The text box should be able to display multiple lines of text and contain vertical scroll bars.

4. Copy and paste seven more text boxes for the control array on the form. Be sure that you answer **Yes** in the message box asking if you want to create a control array.

5. Draw two frames on the form to hold the option buttons and check boxes. Set the caption for each frame as shown in Figure 3-28. Because you will not write code to reference the Frame objects, you do not need to set the Name property.

6. Draw the first option button of the control array in the frame, then set its name to **optTableStatus** and its caption to **Occupied**. Copy and paste the option button to create the remaining two option buttons in the control array and set the captions as shown in Figure 3-28. Remember to select the frame before you paste, or the object will be contained by the form rather than the frame, and to answer **Yes** in the message box asking if you want to create a control array.

7. Create a control array of four check boxes named **chkTableNeeds** inside the second frame. Be sure to set the captions as shown in Figure 3-28.

EXPLORE

8. Draw a vertical scroll bar to the left of the frames and set the name to **vsbTableNumber**. The range of valid values should be between **1** and **8**. As the scroll bar is moved upward, the value should increase.

9. Draw a label to display the table number, then set its Name property to **lblTableNumber**. Change the background color to white. Clear the caption; the caption will be set at run time by the scroll bar.

10. Draw a label above lblTableNumber and set its Caption property to **Table Number**.

11. Draw two command buttons on the form as shown in Figure 3-28. Set the names to **cmdWriteTableNeeds** and **cmdClear**, respectively, and set the captions for each command button. Be sure also to create a ToolTip.

12. Draw an image on the form that holds the **stop.ico** file in the **TAssign** folder in the **Tutorial.03** folder on your Student Disk. Name the image **imgExit**, then write the code for a typical program exit. Set the Stretch property so the file will be sized to the image you drew on the form.

13. In the general declarations section in the Form Module, require that all variables be declared explicitly.

14. Create a Sub procedure named WriteTableNeeds that will accept two arguments named **pintTable** (the current table number displayed in the Table Number label) and **pstrTableNeeds** (the condiments checked in the Table needs frame). This Sub procedure will be used to display the message in a corresponding text box.

15. Enter code into the procedure that will:

   ■ Use pintTable as the Index argument for the txtTable control array. This will allow you to reference the current table.

   ■ Set the Text property of txtTable to a text string that includes: the current date and time with the Now function, then a space, then the pstrTableNeeds variable, then another space, then the current Text property of txtTable. This will cause the most current entry to appear at the beginning of the text box.

16. Open the Code window for the optTableStatus_Click event and declare a variable named **pstrTableStatus**. You will use this string to hold a text string identifying the current status of the table.

17. Write a Select Case statement that will set the variable **pstrTableStatus** to the text **Occupied, Clean**, or **Needs cleaning**, depending on which option button is checked.

18. Add the following statement to call the WriteTableNeeds function, with the current table number as the first argument and the message as the second argument, after computing pstrTableStatus. Note that you need to subtract one (1) from the value of the scroll bar because the scroll bar begins numbering at one (1) while the function you just wrote loads a control array of text boxes indexed from zero (0).

```
WriteTableStatus (vsbTableNumber.Value -1), _
    pstrTableStatus
```

19. Activate the cmdWriteTableNeeds_Click event procedure, then create the following If statement to call the WriteTableNeeds function using the current table number and the catsup condiment as arguments.

```
If chkTableNeeds(0) = vbChecked Then
    WriteTableNeeds (vsbTableNumber.Value - 1), _
    "Catsup"
End If
```

20. Write the necessary If statements to write a message for the other three check boxes. Be sure to change the check box's argument to the correct index and the text string to the correct condiment each time.

21. Write the necessary statements to clear the active option button and uncheck each of the check boxes. *Hint:* You need to set the Value property.

22. Set the caption of lblTableNumber so it holds the value of the scroll bar each time the scroll bar value changes.

23. Save the form as **frmSeatingChart.frm** in the **TAssign** folder in the **Tutorial.03** folder on your Student Disk. Save the project as **Master Seating Chart.vbp** in the same folder.

24. Test the program by selecting a table number, a table status, and table needs and clicking the Write table needs command button. Be sure to test different tables, different boxes, and different option buttons. Click the Clear command button to verify that the check boxes and option buttons are cleared. Exit the program using the stop sign.

25. The table number does not initially appear when you run the program. Why is this? Modify the program to display an initial value of 1 in the lblTableNumber object's caption. When you have corrected any errors and are satisfied that the program works correctly, click the stop sign to exit the program. *Hint:* When does the code move the table number to the Label object's caption?

26. Examine the code in WriteTableNeeds general procedure. On a piece of paper, write down the purpose of each block of code and describe how it performs its function.

27. Save the form and project again. Print the form and the code. Exit Visual Basic.

Case Problems

1. Easy Carpet Emporium Easy Carpet Emporium stores specialize in low-cost home carpeting. The company would like a carpet selecting program that its customers can use to select the color, fabric, and pile of carpeting after looking through the samples in the store. This system will allow Easy Carpet to have only one salesperson on the floor to process the order after it has been entered into the computer by the customer.

In response to the customer clicking the Select button, the carpet selector program will clear any existing text from the text box, examine the option buttons the customer has checked, and then build a text string describing the carpet in a text box.

The NEADT chart for the carpet selector program is stored on your Student Disk in the **Cases** folder in the **Tutorial.03** folder. First you will print the design specifications and then create a sample program for Easy Carpet to use as a prototype in one of their stores. When you are finished, the program's user interface should look like Figure 3-29.

Figure 3-29 ◀

Easy Carpet Emporium - Carpet Selector

Color
- ○ Brown
- ○ Tan
- ○ White
- ● Green

Fabric
- ○ Wool
- ● Nylon

Pile
- ● Short
- ○ Long

Select

Exit

You have selected Green carpet with Nylon fabric and Short pile.

1. Make sure your Student Disk is in the appropriate disk drive. Using Microsoft Word open and print the NEADT chart stored in the file **Easy.doc**, in the **Cases** folder in the **Tutorial.03** folder on your Student Disk. If you do not have Word, use WordPad to print the file **Easy.txt**. Close the word processing program.

2. Start Visual Basic and begin a new project, if necessary. Set the form's Name property to **frmEasyCarpetSelector** and its Caption property to **Easy Carpet Emporium - Carpet Selector**.

3. Create a frame for the Color options, then set the caption to **Color**, and the background color to **light blue**.

4. Create a control array of four option buttons in the Color frame. Name the option buttons **optColor**, change the background color to **light blue**, and set the Caption property of the option buttons to **Brown, Tan, White**, and **Green**, respectively. Make sure that you select the frame after you copy the first option button and before you paste each subsequent option button; otherwise the option group will not work correctly.

5. Create a frame for the Fabric options, then set the caption to **Fabric**, and the background color to **light yellow**.

6. Create a control array of two option buttons in the Fabric frame. Name the option buttons **optFabric**, change the background color to **light yellow**, and set the Caption property of the option buttons to **Wool** and **Nylon**, respectively.

7. Create a frame for the Pile options, then set the caption to **Pile**, and the background color to **orange**.

8. In the Pile frame, create a control array of two option buttons. Name the option buttons **optPile**, change the background color to **orange**, and set the Caption property to **Short** and **Long**, respectively.

9. Create a text box to display the customer's selection, then set the name to **txtCarpet**. The text box should display multiple lines of text. Clear the initial text.

10. Create a command button at the right of the form named **cmdSelect** and set the caption as shown in Figure 3-29. Use **S** as the hot key for the Select command button.

11. Draw an Exit command button below the Select command button, then write the code for a typical program exit. Use **X** as the hot key for the Exit command button.

12. In the general declarations section in the Form module, declare the variables **mintIndexColor**, **mintIndexFabric**, and **mintIndexPile** that will preserve the local variable Index that is passed to each of the option button's procedures for use in the text box. Require that all variables be declared before they can be used in code.

EXPLORE

13. Open the Code window for the optColor_Click event and type the statement that will assign the local optColor variable Index as a form-level variable mintIndexColor.

EXPLORE

14. Repeat Step 13 for the other two option buttons' Click events, using the variable names defined in the general declarations section.

15. Open the Code window for the cmdSelect_Click event and write the statement to remove the contents of the text box.

EXPLORE

16. Still in the cmdSelect_Click event, write the following If statement to verify that one button from each in the optColor option group is selected. Note that when the Exit Sub statement is reached, the procedure exits and no more statements in the procedure will executed.

```
If mintIndexColor = -1 Then
    MsgBox ("Select a color")
Exit Sub
End If
```

EXPLORE

17. Write If statements to check that selections were made for the other two option groups and display an applicable message.

EXPLORE

18. Create a string that will store the carpet selection information in a string like the following:

    You have selected *optColor(mintIndexColor).Caption*
        carpet with *optFabric(mintIndexFabric).Caption* fabric and
        optPile(mintIndexPile).Caption pile.

    Hint: Remember to use the concatenation character to combine text strings you enclose in quotation marks and the option button captions. Figure 3-29 shows a sample string.

EXPLORE

19. Store the contents of the variable pstrOutput into the text box.

20. Clear the Color option buttons by setting the Index variables back to -1 (no option button selected) using the following code:

```
optColor(mintIndexColor).Value = False
mintIndexColor = -1
```

21. Repeat the statements for the other two option groups.

22. Save the form as **frmCarpetSelector.frm** and save the project as **Easy Carpet Selector.vbp** in the **Cases** folder in the **Tutorial.03** folder on your Student Disk.

23. Test the program. When you have corrected any errors and are satisfied that the program works correctly, click the Exit button.

24. Print the Code and Form Image. Exit Visual Basic.

2. Nutrition Foods Nutrition Foods is a national chain of health food stores. They specialize in pesticide-free and artificial-fertilizer-free fruits and vegetables.

Nutrition Foods franchises allow one group manager to be in charge of up to four franchises. Each group manager receives a commission based on the overall sales of the franchises to which the manager is assigned. Nutrition Foods would like a calculator program to compute automatically the commission for each group manager.

The calculator program will include labels to identify and display the sales for each region, the commission, the total commission, and the total sales; scroll bars to enter the sales amounts in $100 increments; and a command button to exit the program.

The labels identifying and displaying the sales for each region will be a control array, as will the scroll bars for entering the sales amounts.

Each time a scroll bar's Change event occurs, the program will recalculate automatically the total commission and the total sales amounts in the appropriate labels. The manager's commission is paid at the following rates:

- For Sales < $5000, Commission = 0

- For Sales >= $5,000 and <= $50,000, Commission = 1% of Sales

- For Sales > $50,000 and < $250,000, Commission = 2% of Sales

- For Sales >= $250,000, Commission = 3% of Sales

Figure 3-30 shows the completed user interface.

Figure 3-30 ◀

1. Make sure your Student Disk is in the appropriate disk drive. Start Visual Basic and begin a new project, if necessary.

2. Set the form's name to **frmNutritionCommissionCalculator** and its caption to **Nutrition Foods - Commission Calculator.**

3. Create four labels across the top of the form and set their captions to **Store 1, Store 2, Store 3**, and **Store 4**, respectively. Align the text in the center of the labels.

4. Create a control array of four labels below the store number labels, and set the name to **lblRegionSales**, set the background color to **white**, and remove the text from the caption.

5. Create a control array of four horizontal scroll bars below the Label control array such that the smallest value, 0, is at the left of the scroll bar, and the largest value, 10000, is at the right. Name the object **hsbRegionSales**. Recall that you were asked that the sales be entered in $100 increments; later, you will multiply the scroll bar value by 100.

6. Create two identifying labels below the Store 3 column and set the captions to **Total Sales** and **Total Commission**, respectively.

7. Create two output labels below the Store 4 column, and set their properties to **lblTotalSales** and **lblTotalCommission**, respectively; set the background color to **white**; and remove the text from the caption.

8. Create an Exit command button with the appropriate code to end the program, in the lower-right corner of the form.

9. Open the Code window for the hsbRegionSales control array's Change event and declare the following variables: **plngSubtotal** will hold the subtotal of the sales for each region, and **psngCommissionPercent** will calculate and hold the percentage of sales the group manager has earned.

10. Open the Code window for the hsbRegionSales control array's Change event. Type the code that will set each lblRegionSales object's Caption property to the value of its corresponding scroll bar multiplied by 100 and format it as Currency. *Hint*: You need to use the Index argument to reference the correct label and scroll bar.

11. After you have set the caption of the lblRegionSales object, calculate plngSubtotal by adding together the value of each scroll bar and multiplying the sum by 100. *Hint*: You need to use the index of each scroll bar in the control array and the Value property.

12. Write an If statement to calculate the commission. Using the variable plngSubtotal, which you computed in Step 11, test the amount against the sales amount to determine the commission rate. Store the commission rate in the variable psngCommissionPercent.

13. Write the statement that will format plngSubtotal as currency and place it in the caption of lblTotalSales.

14. Write the statement that will calculate the commission and store the result in the Caption property of lblTotalCommission.

15. Save the form as **frmNutritionCommissionCalculator1.frm** and the project as **Nutrition Commission Calculator1.vbp** in the **Cases** folder in the **Tutorial.03** folder on your Student Disk.

16. Test the program by clicking each ScrollBar object and observing the results in the Total Commission and Total Sales labels. Verify with a calculator that the commission rules are being applied correctly. When you are satisfied that the program works correctly, click the Exit button.

17. Print the Form Image and the Code.

18. Change the If statement in the hsbRegionSales code to a Select Case statement and test the program.

19. Save the form as **frmCommissionCalculator2.frm** and the project as **Nutrition Commission Calculator 2.vbp** in the **Cases** folder in the **Tutorial.03** folder on your Student Disk. Print the Form Image and the Code. Exit Visual Basic.

3. Williams Lumber Company Williams Lumber Company sells a variety of lumber products to contractors in Dallas Texas. Most lumber, like 2 × 4's, 2 × 6's, and 2 × 8's are sold in fixed lengths, like 8', 10', 12', and 14', but are priced by the foot. The company would like you to create a program to determine the total feet and total cost for each type of lumber. Your form should be divided into an input and output section using two shapes. The input area needs a label for the customer name and a corresponding text box. You need to create three check boxes for the different types of lumber— 2 × 4, 2 × 6, and 2 × 8. Each product is sold in four lengths—8', 10', 12', and 14'. You need to create a check box for each length of each product. The programming process will be easier if you use a control array for each procedure length. Thus, you will have a control array of check boxes for the lengths of 2 × 4's, another for 2 × 6's, and another for 2 × 8's. Each check box needs to have a corresponding text box to specify quantity desired. These also should be created as control arrays. All the orders are delivered to one of four areas. The charge for delivery is based on the number of feet delivered and the delivery zone as follows:

- 1 to 499 feet = $10.00

- 500 to 999 feet = $20.00

- 1000 to 2000 feet = $30.00

- more than 2000 feet = $40.00

Add to these charges $10.00 for Delivery Area 1, $20.00 for Delivery Area 2, $30.00 for Delivery Area 3, and $40.00 for Delivery Area 4.

In the output section of the form, create labels to hold the number of feet of each product and the total cost. You will need another label to hold the delivery charge and the order total.

The charge for lumber is based on the number of feet ordered as follows:

- 2 × 4 = $0.16/foot

- 2 × 6 = $0.22/foot

- 2 × 8 = $0.31/foot

You should use constants for these values.

Your program needs three command buttons. One to compute the order total based on the input, another to clear each of the input and output fields in preparation for a new order, and an Exit button. Figure 3-31 shows the completed user interface for the program.

Figure 3-31 ◀

4. Ms. Phillips Grading Calculator This case problem is an extension of Case Problem 4 of Tutorial 2. One of your former teachers, Ms. Phillips, wants a program that will take in the name of a student and the student's three test scores from the term. The program then will calculate the average score and assign a letter grade based on the following ranges: A >= 90, B = 79 to 89, C = 69 to 78, D = 59 to 68, F < 59. Create the calculator program using the Select Case statement to assign a letter grade based on the average. Display the result in a label in response to the Click event for a Calculate command button. Also include a Clear button to clear the text and captions of all the necessary objects before the input of data for another student, set the focus back to the student's name, and code an Exit button. The code for the Exit button should display a message box asking Ms. Phillips if she wants to exit the program. Check to ensure that your input objects have the correct tab order. Print the Form Image and the Code. Save the form as **frmPhillipsGradingCalculator** and the project as **Phillips Grading Calculator.vbp** in the Cases folder in the **Tutorial.03** folder on your Student Disk.

Creating a Program to Manage Data

Developing a Contact Management System for Atlantic Marketing

OBJECTIVES

In this tutorial you will:

- Add a menu system to a program

- Connect to a database with a Data control

- Set properties of controls to interact with a database

- Write Visual Basic code to locate, add, change, and delete information in a database

- Locate records in a database using a search string

- Validate user input

- Write Visual Basic code to detect errors that occur while a program is running

CASE

Atlantic Marketing

Atlantic Marketing, headquartered in Egan, Minnesota, has been providing marketing services to companies in the greater Minneapolis/St. Paul area since 1978. The sales staff of Atlantic Marketing currently use a paper-based contact management system to keep track of a clients' name, telephone number, estimated sales, and notes describing the interaction between each client and the sales force. Each client also is assigned a unique client ID number. The current contact management system consists of a paper form for each client. Each salesperson keeps these forms in a binder, sorted by the client's last name; notes describing each interaction with the client are also written on the form. Because Atlantic Marketing now has more than 1,000 clients and approximately 2,500 prospective clients, the current paper-based system has become slow and burdensome.

Nina Valenza, a programmer for Atlantic Marketing, was asked to develop a program to automate the contact management system. Nina decided to use Visual Basic together with a Microsoft Access database to manage the information. A database makes any program that needs to manage large quantities of data much simpler to write. The contact management system must be able to store each client's name, ID number, telephone number, the date added, estimated sales, and client notes—all sorted by the client's last name. The system must operate with infinite clients and simplify client retrieval. A salesperson must be able to add, change, and remove clients from the database. Nina already has created the Access database, test data, and a form containing the necessary objects. You will help her complete the contact management system.

SESSION

4.1

In this session you will create a menu system containing items that will allow users to add, change, and delete records from a database file, locate different records in the database, and exit the program. You also will learn how to write code that will execute when a menu item is clicked.

Viewing the Program Documentation

Nina planned the contact management system based on the current paper form, which is shown in Figure 4-1.

Figure 4-1 ◀
Paper contact management form

Atlantic Marketing
Contact Management Form

Last Name: Allen   **Telephone Number:**   (208) 555-7986

First Name: Mary   **Date Added:**   3/22/99

Client ID   3   **Estimated Annual Sales:** $4200.00

Notes:

3/22/99 Referred by John Alexander. Client sells sporting equipment to the upscale
buyer.   Looking for a comprehensive marketing program to increase sales to the
midrange buyer.

4/7/99 First meeting with Mary. She wants a preliminary plan and proposal by 5/15.

5/13/99 Delivered and presented proposal. Will convene with senior management.

The paper form contains a client's name and ID number, telephone number, date added, and estimated annual sales revenue. There are several lines on the form to allow a salesperson to record notes. Nina has completed the NEADT charts for the contact management system. She suggests you review the design specifications so you can familiarize yourself with the project. The NEADT charts are stored in the file AM_CMS.doc on your Student Disk.

To view and print the NEADT charts for the contact management system:

1. Make sure your Student Disk is in the appropriate disk drive. Using Microsoft Word, open the file named **AM_CMS.doc** located in the Tutorial.04 folder on your Student Disk. Otherwise open the file **AM_CMS.txt** using WordPad.

2. Print the file then exit the word processing program.

Look at the NEADT charts for the program. Notice you will create a program to add, change, delete, and locate client information in an Access database using commands located on a menu bar. Keep the NEADT charts on hand for reference as you complete the program. You will begin by opening the project file named AM_CMS.vbp stored on your Student Disk.

To open the project file for the contact management system:

1. Start Visual Basic and open the project file named **AM_CMS.vbp** in the Tutorial.04 folder on your Student Disk. Activate the form named **frmAtlanticContact**.

2. Save the form as **frmAtlanticContact.frm**.

3. Save the project as **Atlantic Contact.vbp**.

As you look at the form, you can see that Nina created all the labels and text boxes needed to display the information contained in the database. The form is shown in Figure 4-2.

Figure 4-2 ◀
Initial contact
management
system form

Adding Menus to a Program

Although you could use command buttons to perform the tasks in this program—printing the form; exiting the program; adding, updating, deleting, and locating client information—you will find that as programs become larger, the number of command buttons can become excessive. In fact, a form with eight or ten command buttons would cause the form to appear cluttered and disorganized. Menus can be an integral part of the user interface of a Visual Basic program and provide users with another way to complete tasks. Menus also organize user tasks. For example, the File menu includes the Print and Exit commands. The Edit menu includes the commands to add, change, and delete data in the underlying database. The Find menu will be used to locate client information. If each of these menu items were command buttons, you would need to search through several buttons to locate the correct one. Menus you create in Visual Basic function in the same way as menus in any Windows 95 program. The menus you create will allow the user to: print a copy of the form; exit the program; add, update, and delete client information; and locate different clients.

The menus you create consist of several parts. Figure 4-3 shows the anatomy of a menu.

Figure 4-3 ◀
Anatomy
of a menu

menu title

menu item

separator bar

hot key

menu

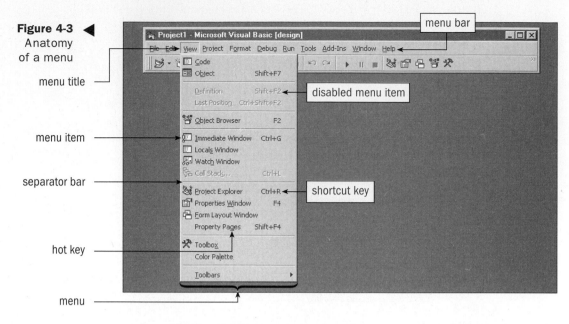

You will use the **Menu Editor** in Visual Basic to create the menu bar and menu items, as Nina requested. Each menu item has a name and caption, and can respond to a Click event procedure.

Windows 95 and Visual Basic menus support shortcut keys and hot keys (or access keys). A **shortcut key** is a function key (such as F5) or a key combination (such as Ctrl+A or Ctrl+X) that executes a command. Command buttons and menu items support shortcut keys; you cannot create a shortcut key for a menu title. A **hot key** is a key you press while holding down the Alt key to open a menu or carry out a command. For example, Alt+F opens the File menu in most Windows 95 applications.

Creating the Menu Titles for the Contact Management System

The first step in creating a menu is to create the menu titles that appear on the menu bar. Each menu title has a Caption property that contains the text the user sees on the screen. The first letter of a menu caption should be capitalized. You can create a hot key for a menu title by inserting the ampersand character (&) in the caption immediately to the left of the character you want to use as the hot key. Be careful not to specify the same hot key for two items on a menu. If you do, only the hot key for the first menu item will be recognized. Menu titles are objects and, as such, you should use the standard prefix "mnu" for the Name property followed by a descriptive name. The descriptive name should be the same as the menu's caption with any spaces removed. The program you are creating will have a single form. Because menus are bound to forms, each form in your program can have a unique menu associated with it.

REFERENCE
window

CREATING A MENU SYSTEM

- Click Tools on the menu bar, then click Menu Editor to activate the Menu Editor or click the Menu Editor button on the toolbar.
- In the Caption text box, type the title for the menu or the caption of the menu item. If you want to create a hot key for the menu or menu item, place the ampersand (&) character to the left of the character to be used as the hot key.
- In the Name text box, type the name for the menu title or menu item. Each menu name must be unique and should begin with the prefix "mnu".
- If you want to create a shortcut key for the menu item, select a shortcut key from the available keys displayed in the Shortcut list box.
- Indent the menu items below their appropriate menu titles by clicking the right arrow key.
- To enter another menu title or menu item, press the Enter key or click the Next button.
- To insert a new menu title or menu item between existing entries, click the appropriate existing entry, and then click the Insert button. The new menu item will be inserted before the active entry.
- To exit the Menu Editor, click the OK button.

Nina wants you to create the menu items necessary to add, update, delete, and select different clients. The menu titles for the contact management program are File, Edit, and Find. You will write the code for all of the menus in Sessions 4.2 and 4.3.

To create the menu titles for the program:

1. Make sure the form is displayed on your screen, and is active.

2. Click the **Menu Editor** button 🗐 on the toolbar to open the Menu Editor. See Figure 4-4.

Figure 4-4 ◀
Menu Editor
components

menu item properties ——▶

menu list box ——▶

TROUBLE? If the Menu Editor button is disabled, make sure the form is the active window and then repeat Step 2. Because menus are bound to a form, the form must be active before you can open the Menu Editor. Also, the Menu Editor is available only at design time; make sure the Visual Basic title bar says [design].

3. In the Caption text box, type **&File**. The & character to the left of the letter "F" identifies Alt+F as the hot key combination for the File menu.

4. In the Name text box, type **mnuFile**. Your screen should look like Figure 4-5.

Figure 4-5 ◀
Creating the
File menu title

menu title caption ⟶

menu title name ⟶

menu title appears
in menu list box ⟶

5. Click the **Next** button.

Notice that the File menu title has been added to the menu list box.

6. To create the second menu title, type **&Edit** in the Caption text box, type **mnuEdit** in the Name text box, then click the **Next** button.

7. To create the third menu title, type **F&ind** in the Caption text box, type **mnuFind** in the Name text box. (Notice that Alt+I is the hot key because Alt+F was used by the File menu.)

You have created the three menu titles for the contact management program. Your next task is to add the menu items to each menu.

Creating Menu Items

Now you must create the menus, and the items displayed on them when the user clicks on the menu title bar. When clicked, each menu item will generate a Click event and call the corresponding event procedure. This is just like clicking a command button to generate a Click event. Although the menu titles generate a Click event, you do not have to write any code to activate the menu when a menu title is clicked; Visual Basic does this for you.

> *Tip:* Several style guidelines will help you create menus that have a similar look and feel to menus in other Windows 95 programs. A menu item's caption should be short enough to appear on one line, but it can contain multiple words to convey its purpose. When menu items contain multiple words, the first letter of each word should be capitalized and each word should be separated by a space. The first letter of a menu item's caption always should be capitalized. If a menu item displays a dialog box or requires the user to complete other information, the item's name should be followed by an ellipsis (…).

You can create a hot key for a menu item with the & character, as you did for the menu titles. The name of a menu item also should begin with the prefix "mnu" and include the title of the menu on which it appears, for example, the Print menu item on the File menu will have the name "mnuFilePrint". Now you will create the Print and Exit menu items for the File menu and the menu items for the Edit menu.

To create the menu items for the File and Edit menu titles:

1. In the menu list box, click &Edit to select the Edit menu, then click the **Insert** button to insert a blank line before the Edit menu.

2. Type **&Print** in the Caption text box, then type **mnuFiiePrint** in the Name text box. This sets the hot key combination to Alt+P for the Print menu item.

3. Click the **right arrow** button [→] to change the indent level of the menu item. This causes the Print menu item to be an item on the File menu. Notice when a menu item is indented, it appears with four leading dots (....). See Figure 4-6.

Figure 4-6 ◀
Adding a
menu item

Print menu item on
File menu (indented)

4. Click the **Next** button then click the **Insert** button to insert a new menu item. Repeat Steps 2 and 3 using the caption **E&xit** and the name **mnuFileExit.** Note that Alt+X is the hot key for the Exit menu item rather then Alt+E. Windows 95 programs use this letter rather than the first character.

5. Click the **Next** button until the Find menu is highlighted, then click the **Insert** button to insert a new menu item before the Find menu.

6. Repeat Steps 2 and 3 using the following captions and names:

Caption	Name
&Add	**mnuEditAdd**
&Edit Record	**mnuEditRecord**
&Update	**mnuEditUpdate**
&Delete	**mnuEditDelete**
&Refresh	**mnuEditRefresh**

The Menu Editor looks like Figure 4-7.

Figure 4-7 ◀
File and Edit
menus
completed

File menu completed ⟶

Edit menu completed ⟶

Notice that the name mnuEditRecord violates the rule of using the Caption for the name. If you followed the rule, however, the name would be mnuEditEditRecord, which may seem confusing. In cases where the menu's caption may cause the name to be misleading or too long, change the name or abbreviate as necessary.

Menus have other characteristics to improve their appearance and make them more efficient for the user. For example, you can draw separator bars, and create shortcut keys.

Creating Submenus with Shortcut Keys and Separator Bars

Windows 95 programs also can separate menu items with a separator bar. A **separator bar** is a horizontal line that visually groups related menu items together to make the interface easier to use. Like all components of a menu, a separator bar must have a unique name or be a member of a control array. You create a separator bar by setting a menu item's Caption property to a hyphen (-).

Also, menu items can have submenus. A **submenu** is a menu item that displays another menu, rather than executing code in an event procedure. You can make a menu item display on a submenu by indenting it another level. Nina wants the Find menu to include the submenu Navigate, which will contain the items First, Last, Previous, and Next. The Find menu also needs to contain a menu item to search for last name. Nina would like the Navigate and Last Name items to be separated by a separator bar. The Last Name item should include a shortcut key definition so users can choose the item using both the keyboard and the mouse. A shortcut key is appropriate because the user then will enter the last name, which can eliminate the transition from the mouse to the keyboard. Also, searching for a last name is expected to be a commonly executed command. You specify the shortcut key for a menu item by selecting it from the Shortcut list box in the Menu Editor. You cannot create shortcut keys that are not listed in the Shortcut list box. For command buttons, you create shortcut keys by placing the ampersand character (&) in the button's caption immediately to the left of the character you want to designate as the shortcut; for example, the caption E&xit would set the shortcut key for the Exit button to Alt+X.

Tip: Create shortcut keys for the more frequently used menu items. This will minimize the number of keystrokes needed to activate a menu item. By allowing both mouse and keyboard input for the menus, the interface will appeal to the broadest number of users. When selecting characters for a shortcut key, use characters that are the same as those used in other common programs. For example, many programs use Ctrl+P as the shortcut key for printing. Using the first character of the menu caption also is common.

To create the menu items for the Find menu:

1. In the menu list box, click the blank line below the Find menu option.

2. Type **&Navigate** in the Caption text box, then type **mnuFindNavigate** in the Name text box.

3. Click the **right arrow** button [→] to indent the Navigate menu item.

4. Click the **Next** button. Notice that the next line in the menu list box automatically is indented and will place the next entry on the Find menu.

5. Create the separator by setting the caption to a hyphen (-) and the name to **mnuFindSep**.

6. Click the **Next** button.

7. Type **&Last Name...** in the Caption text box, then type **mnuFindLastName**.

8. Click the Shortcut list arrow, then select Ctrl+A. Notice that the menu list box for the Last Name item now contains the shortcut key for the last name.

The final step in creating the menus is to create the menu items that will be displayed when the Navigate submenu is selected. These items need to appear under the Navigate submenu item in the menu list box, so they will be indented with eight dots.

To create the items on the Navigate submenu:

1. Enter the following menu items such that they appear below the Navigate menu item and be sure you click the **right arrow** button [→] to indent each item.

Caption	Name	Shortcut
&First	mnuFindNavigateFirst	Ctrl+F
&Last	mnuFindNavigateLast	Ctrl+L
&Previous	mnuFindNavigatePrevious	Ctrl+P
&Next	mnuFindNavigateNext	Ctrl+N

Your screen should look like Figure 4-8.

Figure 4-8 ◀
Completed
menu

shortcut keys

The Find menu is complete. Later, you will write the code for these items in the appropriate event procedures. Nina asks you to check the accuracy of the menus. If you forgot to indent a menu item, it might appear on the menu bar rather than within the menu title. You also need to verify that the hot keys and shortcut keys appear. You can view all the menu items, hot keys, and shortcut keys at design time, so there is no need to run the program.

To view the menus:

1. Click the **OK** button to close the Menu Editor.

   TROUBLE? If you receive an error message indicating that a menu item must have a name, you may have neglected to assign a menu name. Click the OK button to close the message box. The menu item in question will be highlighted. Enter a valid name in the Name text box. If you receive the error message "Menu control array must have an index" you have assigned the same name to two menu items. Like other objects you have created, menu items can be created as a control array, each sharing the same event procedure. You need to assign an index to the menu using the Index text box or assign a unique name to each item. Visual Basic will not create a control array of menu items for you.

2. Save the project.

3. Click the **File** menu on your form. The menu items are displayed. See Figure 4-9.

Figure 4-9 ◀
File menu
displayed

File menu

4. Click the **Edit** menu on your form. The menu items are displayed. See Figure 4-10.

Figure 4-10 ◀
Edit menu
displayed

Edit menu

5. Click the **Find** menu on your form, then click the **Navigate** submenu to display its menu items. The menu items are displayed. See Figure 4-11.

Figure 4-11 ◀
Find menu
displayed

separator bar ——

Navigate submenu

shortcut key

> **TROUBLE?** If a menu title or menu item does not appear on the menu, open the
> Menu Editor and verify that the Visible check box for the item is checked.
>
> If a check mark appears to the left of a menu item, open the Menu Editor and, if
> the Checked check box is selected, click it to remove the check mark.
>
> If a menu title or item is dimmed, open the Menu Editor and verify that the
> Enabled check box for the item is checked.

Creating an Event Procedure for a Menu Item

The first menu item you need to program is the Exit menu item on the File menu. The
mnuFileExit object's Click event should end the program. You write the code for a menu's
Click event procedure in the same way as you would for a command button. That is, you
can locate the object and event procedure in the Code window.

> *Tip:* You can open quickly the Code window to a menu item's Click
> event procedure by clicking the menu title then clicking on the
> desired menu item rather than locating the event procedures in
> the Code window.

To write the code for the Exit menu item:

1. Click the **File** menu on your form. The menu items are displayed.

2. Click the **Exit** menu item. The Code window displays the mnuFileExit_Click event
   procedure.

3. Enter the **End** statement into the event procedure.

The Exit menu item is operational. Now you can proceed to write the code to print the
form. You need to use the PrintForm method, like you did in Tutorial 3, to print the form.

To write the code for the PrintForm method:

1. In the Code window, display the **mnuFilePrint_Click** event procedure.

   Enter the **PrintForm** statement into the event procedure.

2. Close the Code window.

3. Save the project.

You have completed the user interface for the contact management system. Nina suggests you run the program and test the Print and Exit menu items.

To test the PrintForm and Exit menu items:

1. Click **File** then **Print** to print an image of the form on the printer.

2. Click **File** then **Exit** to stop the program.

The menu system, and the code for each item on the File menu, are complete. The menu is a better interface than creating 12 command buttons, which would make the screen appear confusing and cluttered.

Quick Check

1. Describe the design criteria for menu item names.

2. What is the difference between a menu title and a menu item?

3. What are hot keys and shortcut keys?

4. What is a separator bar?

5. What is a submenu? How do you create a submenu?

The menu system is now complete. As you complete the different components of the program, you will add the necessary code to the proper event procedures. You have completed this session. You can now take a break or continue to Session 4.2.

SESSION
4.2

In this session you will create an instance of the Data control to communicate with an Access database. You will learn how to set additional properties of TextBox objects so they can display information contained in the database and store information in the database. You also will learn how to locate information in a database using the Data control, and how to add, update, and delete that information.

Understanding How Visual Basic Uses a Database

Before you can complete the program, you need to understand what a database is, and how Visual Basic objects interact with a database. A **database** is a set of information related to a particular topic or purpose. Information is stored in a database within a table. Most databases contain several tables. A **table** consists of rows and columns. The column defines a name for, and characteristics of, the stored information. The columns in a table are called **fields**. In the Atlantic Marketing database Nina created seven fields to hold the information. Client ID, Last Name, First Name, Telephone Number, Date Added, Estimated Sales, and Notes are the fields in the tblContact table. The actual information in the table is stored in the rows. The rows in a table are called **records**. Figure 4-12 shows the six rows (records) and column names (fields) in the table. As you can see, field names have the prefix "fld". So she could test the program, Nina entered six records as test data.

Figure 4-12 ◀
Database
table fields
and records

six records —

seven columns —

In a modern database, or database management system (DBMS), multiple users can access the information contained in the database at the same time. If two users add records at the same time, the DBMS keeps track of each request without causing an error or losing either user's information. When you are working in Visual Basic and Windows 95, the **Microsoft Jet database engine** is the DBMS that retrieves data from, and stores data in, an Access database. A database can organize and store information so it can be viewed and retrieved based on the needs of a particular user. For example, the contact management system represents only part of the data that Atlantic Marketing needs to manage. Another component of the company's data is its sales system. If information about sales accounts could be accessed by the contact management system, a salesperson could view sales history before talking with an existing client.

Most databases in use today are **relational**; that is, information is contained in several tables that can be related together in different ways. In other words, billing transactions could be stored in one table, and client information in another. A relational database management system (RDBMS) allows you to define the relationships between these different pieces of information. For example, in the Atlantic Marketing database, information in the tblContact table is related to the information in the tblSales table using a query. A **query** is an instruction to a database to return a set of records from one or more tables in a specific order. The use of an RDBMS to manage large volumes of data has become increasingly popular as the software technology has evolved and the computer hardware has become fast enough to run this complex software effectively. Refer to the Database Appendix for more information.

Using the Data Control to Open a Database

Before you can communicate with the database Nina created, you need to connect your program to the database. There are two ways to interact with a database from a program. One way is to write Visual Basic statements that will access a database; the other is to use the **Data control** in the toolbox. The Data control enables you to move from record to record and to display information inside other controls on the form. By setting the properties of the Data control you can use its buttons to locate different database records without writing any code at all. You cannot use the Data control to create new databases, only to connect to existing ones. You can create your own databases using Microsoft Access.

You need to create a Data control to establish communication with the database Nina created. The standard prefix for a Data control is "dat". Like a label, the Data control supports the Caption property. This controls the text displayed inside the Data control.

To create the Data control:

1. Start Visual Basic, if necessary, and open the project named **Atlantic Contact.vbp** from Session 4.1.

2. Click the **Data** control 🖳 on the toolbox and draw an instance of the Data control across the bottom of the form. See Figure 4-13.

Figure 4-13 ◄
Creating the
Data control

caption

Previous
Record button

First Record button

draw Data
control here

Next Record button

Last Record button

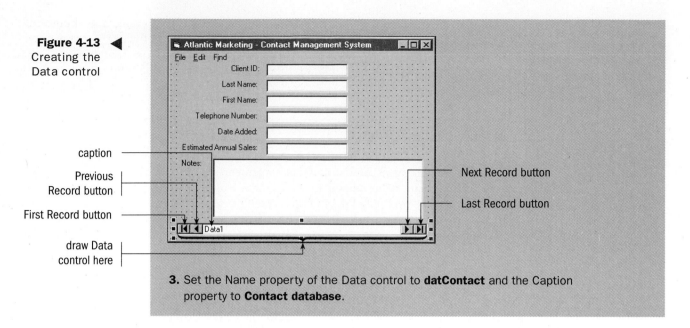

3. Set the Name property of the Data control to **datContact** and the Caption
property to **Contact database**.

The database Nina created contains the tables and other information you need to complete your program. Although the form now contains an instance of the Data control, it cannot store or display the information in the existing database until you set the necessary properties to connect the Data control to the database.

The properties of the Data control that allow you to communicate with the database are the Connect, DatabaseName, RecordSource, and RecordsetType properties.

- The **Connect** property provides the information about the kind of database. The Data control can operate with Access, dBASE, FoxPro, and Paradox databases using the Connect property. The Connect property is set to Access by default.

- The **DatabaseName** property identifies the name and location (folder) of the database file. Note that Microsoft Access database files have the extension ".mdb".

- The **RecordSource** property identifies the table or query in the database that you want to use.

- The **RecordsetType** property determines what operations can be performed on the table or query you identified when you set the RecordSource property. By default, the RecordsetType property is set to 1 - Dynaset.

When you set these properties, the Data control creates the necessary objects to access a table in the database at run time.

REFERENCE window

USING A DATA CONTROL TO CONNECT TO AN EXISTING DATABASE

- Draw an instance of a Data control on the form containing the objects that will display data from the database.
- In the Properties window, be sure the Connect property is set to Access.
- Set the DatabaseName property to the name and folder of the database.
- Set the Name property with a prefix of "dat" followed by a descriptive name.
- Set the RecordSource property to the name of the table.
- For a browser, the Data control should be visible and enabled. To edit records in a database, the Data control either should be invisible or disabled so the user will not save changes unintentionally.

The order in which you set the Data control properties is important. You should select the database (DatabaseName property) before you select the table (RecordSource property). Then, when you set the RecordSource property, Visual Basic connects to the database and shows you a list of its available tables. The file that contains the contact management test database is named AM_CMS.mdb and is stored in the Tutorial.04 folder on your Student Disk.

To connect the Data control to the contact management database:

1. In the Properties window for the Data control you just created, make sure the value of the Connect property is **Access**.

2. Click the value column of the **DatabaseName** property.

3. Click the **Properties** button [...] and choose the file **AM_CMS.mdb** in the Tutorial.04 folder on your Student Disk.

4. The Properties window should look like Figure 4-14.

Figure 4-14 ◀
Setting the
DatabaseName
property

You have identified the database you want to use so the Data control can establish a connection with the database for the contact management system. Now you need to identify the database table or query you want. To do so, you set the RecordSource property to a table or query that exists in the database. The Properties window will display a list of available tables or queries in the database from which you can select. The standard prefix for a table object is "tbl". The query for the contact management system is named qryContact. The standard prefix for a query is "qry".

To view the tables in the AM_CMS database and set the RecordSource property:

1. Click the value column of the **RecordSource** property, then click the **Properties** button [▼] to display the list of tables. Your Properties window should look like Figure 4-15.

Figure 4-15 ◀
Setting the
RecordSource
property

set the Record
Source property
to qryContact

TROUBLE? If no information appears when you click the Properties button ▼ for the RecordSource property, then the database is not selected properly. Verify that the DatabaseName property is set to the correct path and filename, A:\Tutorial.04\AM_CMS.mdb, and that the file exists on your Student Disk. Then repeat Step 1.

2. Click **qryContact** to select the table. Check that the RecordsetType property is set to **1 - Dynaset**, the default setting.

3. Click the **Properties** button ▼ for the RecordsetType property to see the other options for this property.

Note the default setting of 1 - Dynaset for the RecordsetType property. A **dynaset** is a dynamic view of the information contained in a database table or query. You can create dynasets to view and change the contents of rows from one or more tables, depending on the needs of the program.

The Recordset Object

When you set the properties of the Data control, it uses that information to create an object called a recordset. A reference to this object is stored in the Recordset property of the Data control when the program is run. The Data control is set indirectly at run time, thus does not appear in the Properties window. You use the Recordset object at run time to locate different records and to add, change, and delete records.

A **Recordset object** is a view of the data stored in the database. When you look at records stored in the Recordset object, only one record can be active at a time. The **current record pointer** indicates the active record in a Recordset object. You do not access the current record pointer explicitly. Rather, you move the current record pointer indirectly using the Recordset object's methods.

You can find out if the current record pointer is at the beginning or end of the recordset using the BOF and EOF properties of the Recordset object.

- When the current record pointer is positioned just before the first record, **BOF** is True, and the recordset is at the beginning of file. Otherwise, BOF is False.

- When the pointer is positioned just after the last record, **EOF** is True, and the recordset is at the end of file. Otherwise, EOF is False.

The buttons on the Data control call different procedures that act on the Recordset object. A procedure that acts on an object is called a **method**. Figure 4-16 illustrates how a Recordset object is created by the Data control and shows some of its properties and methods.

Figure 4-16 ◀
The Recordset
object

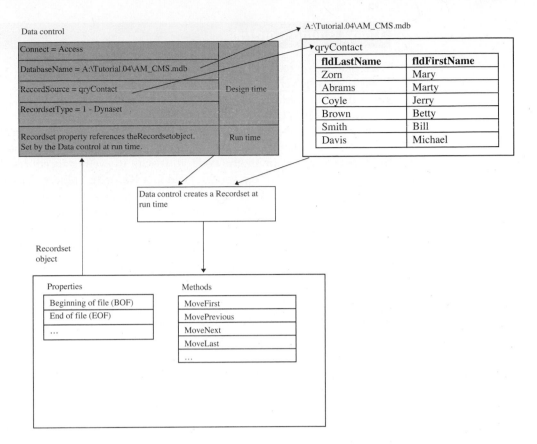

By setting the Connect, DatabaseName, RecordSource, and RecordsetType properties at design time, the Data control will be able to retrieve information from the query named qryContact at run time. It does this by creating a Recordset object and storing the object in the Recordset property of the Data control. Once the Recordset object is created by the Data control you can locate records and perform other operations.

Objects and Their Methods

An object is made up of properties, events, and methods. The methods of an object contain code that is built inside the object to accomplish a task. Consider a television's remote control as an object. The remote control is capable of a specific number of methods, or actions, such as changing a channel or adjusting the volume. You could use the ChannelUp and ChannelDown methods to set the CurrentChannel property. Likewise there are methods that apply to the Recordset object. Methods supply functionality to an object.

The Data control simplifies the process of working with a Recordset object by providing buttons that navigate through the records in the Recordset object without explicitly calling methods. There are limitations to the Data control, however. For example, it does not support a method to remove a record from a Recordset object. To do this you need to call the methods of the underlying Recordset object (stored in the Recordset property of the Data control).

So you can learn more about the methods applicable to the Recordset object, Nina suggests you look at the Help system. Using the Index tab, find information on recordsets, then Recordset Object, Recordsets Collection Summary (DAO). Print the information for future reference.

A Recordset object is considered a **Data Access Object**. Data Access Objects (DAO) enable you to use a programming language to access and manipulate data in databases, and to manage databases, their objects, and their structure.

The Data control allows you to click buttons located on the control to navigate through records without writing any code. In essence, it calls methods for you. Nina wants the user to be able to use the menu items you created in the first session to move forward and backward through the client list. This requires the fields to be connected to the text boxes.

Using Bound Controls

Each field in the recordset needs to be displayed in the corresponding TextBox object that Nina already has created on the form. No code needs to be written to accomplish the task. All you need to do is set some new properties for each TextBox object and it will display information from the database table.

The TextBox objects on your form are the same as those you created in previous tutorials. The Text property of these TextBox objects, however, will not be explicitly set in the Properties window or by the code you write in event procedures. Rather, each TextBox control will be bound to a specific field in a Recordset object. A **bound control** displays the changes in the current record of the Recordset object on the form. When a text box is bound to a Recordset object, changes in the current record of the Recordset object are reflected in the TextBox object. Each bound TextBox object corresponds to a field in the Recordset object. Bound controls often are referred to as **data aware** controls. Many different controls that can hold text (such as the Label or ListBox control) and graphics (such as the ImageBox or PictureBox control) can be bound to a field in a Recordset object.

The process of binding an object to a Recordset object requires setting properties you have not used yet. These properties are common to all bound controls. When you create a bound control such as a text box, these properties initially are blank; you must set them explicitly.

- The **DataField** property is set to a field inside the table or query. When you select a field with the Properties button, Visual Basic looks in the database table or query, which you specified with the DataSource property to see the list of available fields. By using the standard prefix "fld", you can immediately determine the type of object you are working with.

- The **DataSource** property of a bound control is set to an instance of a Data control drawn on the same form. To see the list of available choices for this property, you click its Properties button. In the contact management program, this property will be set to datContact (the name you assigned to the Data control). If a form will interact with multiple tables or queries, you can create multiple Data controls, then select the desired Data control.

> *Tip:* When you create instances of bound controls and set their properties at design time, it is important that you set the properties of the Data control first. If the Data control does not reference an existing table or query in a database, the bound TextBox objects will not display the table names and field names. Set the DataSource property before setting the DataField property when creating a bound text box. If you try to set the DataField first, Visual Basic cannot look into a table and show the list of available fields.

REFERENCE
window

BINDING A CONTROL TO A DATABASE FIELD

- Create an instance of a valid control (text box, label, etc.) on the form.
- In the Properties window for that object, set the DataSource property to the name of the Data control.
- Set the DataField property to the corresponding field in the database table.
- For a browser, the bound control either should be invisible or disabled so the user will not unintentionally make changes. To edit records in a database, the bound control should be both visible and enabled.

Figure 4-17 shows the properties used to bind controls to interact with fields in a Recordset object.

Figure 4-17 ◀
Bound controls

You will set the DataSource property for all the TextBox objects on your form as a group, because they all must be set to datContact, the only Data control on the form. Then you will set the DataField property for each TextBox object to its corresponding field in the database table. At run time, each object will interact with a field in the Recordset object created by the Data control.

To set the properties for the TextBox objects:

1. Press and hold down the **Shift** key and click all seven **TextBox** objects to select them. Your form should look like Figure 4-18.

Figure 4-18 ◀
Selecting
multiple
text boxes

2. In the Properties window, set the DataSource property to **datContact**, the name of the Data control. This is the only available option because there is only one Data control on the form. The Properties window should look like Figure 4-19.

Figure 4-19 ◀
Setting the
DataSource
property

no object displays
in Object list
box

when multiple
objects are selected

3. Click any blank area of the form to deactivate the selected objects.

4. Click the text box for **Client ID**.

5. Click the Properties button ▼ for the DataField property. Your Properties window should look like Figure 4-20.

Figure 4-20 ◄
Setting the
DataField
property

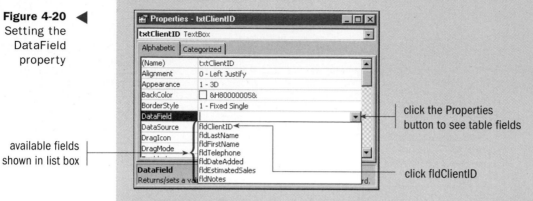

click the Properties
button to see table fields

available fields
shown in list box

click fldClientID

TROUBLE? If clicking the Properties button does not display the fields in the database or you get an error message, the DataSource property is not set correctly. Be sure the DataSource property is set to datContact. Also, check that the DatabaseName property of the Data control is set to the file AM_CMS.mdb in the Tutorial.04 folder on your Student Disk, and that the database exists there.

6. In the displayed list of fields, click **fldClientID**.

The text box txtClientID now is bound to the field fldClientID in the table tblContact. When you run your program, the information contained in this record will be displayed in the text box.

7. Repeat Steps 4 through 6, setting the DataField property as follows:

Object	Property
txtLastName	**fldLastName**
txtFirstName	**fldFirstName**
txtTelephoneNumber	**fldTelephoneNumber**
txtDateAdded	**fldDateAdded**
txtEstimatedSales	**fldEstimatedSales**

Nina also created a text box for notes. The table includes a Notes field, which contains notes the salesperson writes about interactions with the client. You need to modify the properties for the txtNotes object so that it will display several lines of text from the Notes field of the database.

8. For the **txtNotes** object, set the MultiLine property to **True**, the ScrollBars property to **2 - Vertical**, and the DataField property to **fldNotes**.

The program now will display the appropriate information from a database record in the text boxes when you run the program, and you can move from record to record using the buttons on the Data control. This is a good time to save the project, check that the program works, then correct any errors. When Nina created the database and the table containing the clients, she designed it so the table records would appear sorted by last name. When you run the program, the records then will be displayed alphabetically by last name.

To run and test the program:

1. Save the form and project files.

2. Start the program. The first record in the Recordset object is displayed. See Figure 4-21.

Figure 4-21 ◀
Form with
multiline
text box

information from
Notes field displayed
in text box

scroll bar displayed

The record for Marty Abrams is displayed because Abrams is the first last name alphabetically in the database.

3. Drag the scroll box in the Notes text box to the bottom of the scroll bar. The rest of the information from the Notes field is displayed.

   TROUBLE? If you cannot scroll through the Notes field information, you probably neglected to set the MultiLine property to True. Stop the program, set the MultiLine property for the Notes text box to True, and then repeat Steps 1 and 2.

4. Click the **Next Record** button ▶ in the Data control. The form now displays the information for Betty Brown.

5. Click the **Previous Record** button ◀ in the Data control. The form displays the information for Marty Abrams again.

6. Click the **Last Record** button ▶| in the Data control. The form displays the information for Mary Zorn.

7. Click the **First Record** button |◀ in the Data control. The form displays the information for Marty Abrams again.

8. End the program.

The text boxes now connect to the database table using the Data control and display the client ID, name, telephone number, date added, estimated annual sales information, and notes from the Recordset object in the text boxes.

In addition to using the buttons on the Data control, you can call the methods of the Recordset object explicitly. The methods of the Recordset object operate on data in the database table or query. For example, you can locate records in the table using the following four methods:

- The **MoveFirst** method locates the first record in the Recordset object.

- The **MoveLast** method locates the last record in the Recordset object.

- The **MoveNext** method locates the next record in the Recordset object.

- The **MovePrevious** method locates the previous record in the Recordset object.

These four methods are not supported explicitly by the Data control. Rather, they are supported by the Recordset object, which is stored in the Recordset property of the Data control at run time. Thus, you could use the following statement to find the next client stored in the Recordset object created by the Data control named datContact. When you call an object's methods, you include a period (.) between the object and method names.

```
datContact.Recordset.MoveNext
```

This statement calls the MoveNext method on the Data control's (datContact's) Recordset property, which is the Recordset object. While this statement is valid, you can save a considerable amount of typing by creating an object variable to store a Recordset object. The three-character prefix for a Recordset object is "rst". To create an object variable you use the following syntax:

Private *varname* **As [New]** *Object*

- The name of the object variable is specified with *varname* and must follow the standard naming conventions for variables.

- The **New** keyword is used to create new objects. In this session you will use the object variable to reference an existing object, the Recordset object, so you will not use the New keyword.

- *Object* is a placeholder for the kind of object you want to reference.

After you create an object variable, the variable must be set to point to an existing object or to create a new instance of an object. You accomplish this using the Set statement, which has the following syntax:

Set *varname* = [[**New**] *objectexpression* | **Nothing**]

- The *varname* can be any valid object variable name.

- The **New** keyword creates a new instance of the object.

- The *objectexpression* can be any existing instance of an object, such as a recordset, a form, or an instance of a control, when the New keyword is not used.

- The **Nothing** keyword is used to disassociate an object variable from an actual object. When you assign Nothing to an object variable, the variable will no longer refer to an actual object. If there are multiple object variables that reference the same object, setting all of them to Nothing will free the memory and system resources used by the object.

Thus, you could use the following statements to declare an object variable, then set that variable to a valid instance of a recordset:

```
Private mrstContact as Recordset
Set mrstContact = datContact.Recordset
```

The first statement creates a Recordset object variable named mrstContact. Like other variables you have created, it contains nothing until you store information in it.

The second statement stores information in the object variable using the Set statement. Then you could call the MoveNext method on the mrstContact recordset.

You now can create an object variable and assign it to the existing Recordset object. Because you will use this variable in many different event procedures, it should be declared in the general declarations section of the Form module.

To create an object variable:

1. Enter the following statement in the general declarations section of the Form module after the Option Explicit statement.

   Private mrstContact As Recordset

Now that you have created a variable to hold the Recordset object, you must assign it to a valid recordset instance before it can be used. Normally you would assign a value like this once, when the form was loaded. There is an event, however, called the Reposition event that occurs each time you locate a different record in a recordset and occurs before the Load event for the form. You will need to write code for this event that will reference the recordset before the form is loaded, so you must assign the variable in this event procedure.

While you could set the value of the object each time the recordset is repositioned, it only needs to be done once. Thus you need to create a variable and an If statement to test the variable to determine whether or not it is the first time the event has occurred. You cannot use a local variable because its value is lost each time the procedure exits. A form-level variable would work but there is another way of creating the variable that is better suited to this purpose. The **Static** statement works much like the Private and Dim statements. It creates variables that, like form-level variables, retain their value whenever the form is running. Like variables declared inside a procedure using the Dim statement, however, the variable only can be referenced by that procedure. The **Static** keyword has the following syntax:

Static *varname* [**As** *type*]

- *Varname* can be any valid variable name.
- *Type* can be any valid data type or object type.

> *Tip:* When the value of a variable must be retained whenever a module is running, declare it as a Static variable inside the appropriate event or general procedure. As programs get larger, form-level variables may be used by several procedures. It becomes difficult to keep track of each procedure that is manipulating the variable, and logic errors easily can happen. Using a Static variable, no other procedure can reference it and any possible side effects are eliminated.

Nina suggests that you write the If statement that will determine if the Reposition event is occurring for the first time.

To set the object variable to a recordset instance:

1. Enter the following statements in the Reposition event for datContact:

```
Static pblnFirst As Boolean
    If pblnFirst = False Then
        Set mrstContact = datContact.Recordset
        pblnFirst = True
    End If
```

The Static statement declares the variable pblnFirst as a Boolean variable. While only visible from this general procedure, the value of the variable remains while the program is running. The first time the procedure is executed, the value of the variable is False, so the statements inside the If block are executed. The next time the procedure is executed, the value of the variable is True so the statements in the If block are not executed.

Now that the object variable is assigned to the active recordset, you can proceed to call the methods to locate different records from the menu item's event procedures.

To write the code for the items on the Find menu:

1. Open the Code window for the menu named **mnuFindNavigateFirst** and select the **Click** event procedure. Remember you can click **Find, Navigate, First** to select the Click event procedure for this menu item.

2. Enter the following code in the window:

```
Private Sub mnuFindNavigateFirst_Click()
    mrstContact.MoveFirst
End Sub
```

3. Enter the following statements into the respective event procedures:

for the mnuFindNavigateLast object's Click event,

```
mrstContact.MoveLast
```

for the mnuFindNavigatePrevious object's Click event,

```
mrstContact.MovePrevious
```

for the mnuFindNavigateNext object's Click event,

```
mrstContact.MoveNext
```

4. Save the project then run the program.

5. Test the items on the Navigate submenu to be sure they are locating different records in the database.

6. End the program.

While the buttons on the Data control allow the user to browse through the data in the database, there is a side effect. If a user makes changes to a record and then locates a different record using the Data control's buttons, those changes will be saved to the database table or query. If you want to let the user abandon changes to a record, you can use properties supported by the recordset. Therefore, Nina would like the commands on the menu bar to be used for all database navigation and updating. There are two ways to prevent the user from interacting with the Data control. You could disable the Data control, to prevent it from responding to user activity, or you can make it invisible. Nina suggests that you make the Data control invisible. Although the user cannot see the Data control, your program can continue to set properties and call methods at run time.

To make the Data control invisible at run time:

1. Set the Visible property of the Data control to **False**.

Sometimes the decision to make an object invisible, or to disable it, is subjective. As a general rule, if the visible object provides no information to the user, make it invisible; otherwise, disable it.

Understanding the Beginning and End of File

Nina would like to disable the Previous Record menu item when the recordset is at the beginning of the file and the Next Record menu item when the recordset is at the end of the file. That is, the menu items should appear gray and not respond to the Click event. This will give the user a visual clue that these operations cannot be performed.

Nina also would like the Next and Previous items on the Navigate submenu to be disabled when the BOF or EOF properties are True, respectively. Any visible object, like a command button, text box, or menu item can be disabled at run time by setting its Enabled property to False. The objects you have used always have been enabled (the Enabled property is set to True). When disabled, a control cannot receive focus although it does remain visible. That is, a command button or menu item will do nothing (not cause an event to occur) when clicked. The object also will appear with a gray foreground. Nina would like you to write the necessary statements to enable and disable the menu items.

CREATING A PROGRAM TO MANAGE DATA   TUTORIAL 4   VB   4.25

To accomplish this task, you need to know when the position of the current record pointer changes. The Reposition event for the Data control occurs whenever the current record pointer is moved. Thus, you can write the statements in this event procedure to determine if the BOF or EOF properties of the recordset are True, and disable the corresponding menu items.

To disable and enable a visible object:

1. Open the Code window for the **datContact** object's **Reposition** event procedure and enter the following code into the window after the existing code:

```
If mrstContact.BOF = True Then
     mnuFindNavigatePrevious.Enabled = False
Else
     mnuFindNavigatePrevious.Enabled = True
End If

If mrstContact.EOF = True Then
     mnuFindNavigateNext.Enabled = False
Else
     mnuFindNavigateNext.Enabled = True
End If
```

The first If statement determines if the current record pointer is at the beginning of file and enables or disables the Previous menu item accordingly. The second If statement determines if end of file has been reached and enables or disables the Next menu item accordingly. Nina would like you to test this code you have just written.

To test the menu items:

1. Save the project and run the program.

2. Click the **Find** menu then click **Navigate** then **Last**.

3. Click the **Find** menu then click **Navigate** then **Next**. The current record pointer is now at the end of file.

4. Click **Find**, then **Navigate** again to verify the Next menu item is disabled.

5. End the program.

If you disable the Data control rather than making it invisible, you can enable and disable its buttons. This depends on the value of two properties that determine what happens when you try to locate the previous record when the first record is current, or try to locate the next record when the last record is current. The **BOFAction** property defines the behavior of the Data control when the user tries to locate the beginning of file (BOF) and can have one of two values:

■ When set to **0 - Move First**, clicking the Previous Record button when the first record is the current record, will cause the first record to remain the current record.

■ When set to **1 - BOF**, the current record will be set to the beginning of file (there is no current record) and the Data control's Previous Record button will be disabled. The BOF property of the recordset also will become True.

The **EOFAction** property works similarly and controls the action taken when the Next Record button on the Data control is clicked when the current record is the last record in the recordset.

■ When set to **0 - MoveLast**, clicking the Next Record button when the last record is current will cause the last record to remain the current record.

- When set to **1 - EOF** the current record will be set to the end of file (there is no current record) and the Data control's Next Record button will be disabled. The EOF property of the recordset will become True.

- When set to **2 - Add New**, a new record will be added. (This is just like calling the recordset's AddNew method.)

Now that you have programmed the menu items to navigate through the database records, Nina suggests you proceed to write the code to modify the contents of the database.

Adding, Updating, and Deleting Database Records

By creating objects on a form and setting the necessary properties, you have created a Visual Basic program that will operate with a database. So far you only can navigate through the records in a Recordset object. Now that your program and its objects are communicating with the database, you can proceed to the next phase of the program's development: providing add, update, and delete capabilities to the user. You need to write the necessary Visual Basic statements for each menu item's Click event procedure to add, update, and delete records in the Recordset object.

Adding New Database Records

The Recordset object has a method that allows you to add records to a database. When the AddNew method is called, a new blank record is created, which you then can edit. After entering the information for the new record, you need to call the Update method to store the new record in the database. The syntax for the Recordset object's AddNew method is:

*Object.***AddNew**

- *Object* must be a valid instance of a recordset.

- The **AddNew** method acts on a Recordset object and will create an empty database record to be edited.

The RecordsetType property of your Data control is set to 1 - Dynaset; therefore, all new records will be inserted at the end of the Recordset object, even if it was sorted. You need to write the code to add a new blank record to your database when the Add menu item is clicked.

To write the code to add new database records:

1. Open the Code window for the object named **mnuEditAdd** and select the **Click** event procedure.

2. Enter the following code in the window:

```
Private Sub mnuEditAdd_Click()
    mrstContact.AddNew
End Sub
```

The AddNew method operates on a Recordset object. When the program calls the AddNew method, a new blank record is created. A user then can enter data into each of the bound text boxes to identify the new client for Atlantic Marketing.

Updating Existing Database Records

When you want to change information in an existing record, you first must make the current record editable using the Edit method of the Recordset object. This places the information in the current record into a temporary storage area in the computer's memory called the copy buffer. The **copy buffer** stores the current record and any changes made to it before those changes actually are written to the underlying database table or query. By storing the changes in the copy buffer, you can choose not to update the database if you made an error. After making changes, you can save them explicitly, using the Update method of the Recordset object. When you move from one record to another by explicitly calling the methods of the Recordset object, such as MovePrevious or MoveNext, or if you close the Recordset object without calling the Update method, your changes will be lost. Sometimes this is what you want to do. For example, if you make changes to the data and notice a mistake, you can leave the record without saving the changes. The syntax for the Edit and Update methods are:

Object.**Edit**

Object.**Update**

- *Object* must be a valid instance of a recordset.

- The **Edit** method must be called to edit an existing record before the Update method, to allow editing on the record.

- The **Update** method acts on the recordset and writes the changes of a record created by the AddNew method or an edited record to the database.

To put a new record in sorted order, you also need to use the Requery method of the Recordset object. If you do not call the Requery method, newly added records always will appear at the end of the Recordset object until the program is run again, causing the Recordset object to be refreshed. The syntax of the Requery method is:

Object.**Requery**

- *Object* must be a valid instance of a recordset.

- The **Requery** method reloads the contents of the underlying table or query into the recordset. When the Requery method is called, the query is run again and any changes made by you, or another user, will be reflected in the recordset. So that any bound text boxes will display information from the new recordset, you should call a method like MoveFirst after calling the Requery method.

You now can proceed to write code for the Edit Record, Update, and Refresh menu items.

To write the code to edit, update, and sort the database records:

1. Activate the Code window for the **mnuEditRecord_Click** event procedure and enter the following code:

```
Private Sub mnuEditRecord_Click()
    mrstContact.Edit
End Sub
```

2. Activate the Code window for the **mnuEditUpdate_Click** event procedure and enter the following code:

```
Private Sub mnuEditUpdate_Click()
    mrstContact.Update
End Sub
```

3. Activate the Code window for the **mnuEditRefresh_Click** event procedure and enter the following code in the window:

```
Private Sub mnuEditRefresh_Click()
    mrstContact.Requery
    mrstContact.MoveFirst
End Sub
```

Examine the code you wrote to update the database any time a user adds or changes a record.

```
mrstContact.Edit
```

The Edit method operates on a Recordset object. When the program calls the Edit method, the current contents of the record are stored in the copy buffer. Any changes made by the user will be reflected in the contents of the copy buffer but not in the table saved on the disk until the Update method is called.

```
mrstContact.Update
```

When the Update menu item is clicked, the contents of the copy buffer are written to the Recordset object and therefore saved to the underlying table in the database. In other words, they become permanent. This menu item needs to be called after adding a new record or editing an existing record.

```
mrstContact.Requery
mrstContact.MoveFirst
```

The Requery method causes the Recordset object to be reinitialized so it will continue to be in sorted order. The MoveFirst method repositions the current record to the first record in the database, giving the user a visual clue that the recordset has been resorted. If you wanted to resort the recordset if a name was changed, or a new contact was added, you could have called the Requery and MoveFirst methods in the Add and Update menu item event procedures.

As you add and edit records, a property is set that contains the status of the current record. The **EditMode** property is supported by the Recordset object and can assume one of three values.

- The constant **dbEditNone** indicates that no editing operation is in progress.

- The constant **dbEditInProgress** indicates that the Edit method has been called and the current record is in the copy buffer.

- The constant **dbEditAdd** indicates the AddNew method has been called, and the current record in the copy buffer is a new record that has not been saved to the database table or query.

Nina wants you to use the Add, Edit Record, and Update menus to add a new record to the test database to make sure the program is working correctly.

To use the Add and Update menu items on your form to add a record to the database:

1. Save the project then start the program.

2. Click the **Edit** menu on your form, then click **Add** to create a new blank record.

3. Enter the information shown in Figure 4-22.

Figure 4-22 ◀
Adding
a record to
Contact table

Data control
is invisible

4. Click **Update** on the Edit menu on your form to save the new record to the database. The form displays the information for Marty Abrams again and the record you just added is stored at the end of the recordset.

> **TROUBLE?** If you receive a run-time error, you probably tried to update the database without completing all the fields. End the program and then repeat Steps 1 through 4.

5. Type **Ctrl+L** to locate the last record. Because you have not run the Requery method, Clark Biddleford appears at the end of the recordset.

6. Click the **Edit** menu then **Refresh** to reload the recordset in sorted order.

7. Locate the record for Clark Biddleford.

The new record was added between the records for Marty Abrams and Betty Brown.

8. End the program.

When the program calls the Update method, the changes are stored immediately in the underlying table in the database. If the power goes out or the computer crashes, none of the changes made will be lost. When you start the program again, Clark Biddleford's record will remain.

You now are ready to program the Delete menu item that will allow salespeople to remove obsolete records from the database.

Deleting Database Records

You need to write the necessary statement for the Click event procedure to delete an existing record from the database. To do this, you will use the Delete method of the Recordset object. The syntax for the Delete method is:

Object.**Delete**

- *Object* must be a valid instance of a recordset.

- The **Delete** method is used to delete the current record from a Recordset object, which removes the corresponding row from the underlying database table. When the program calls the Delete method on a Recordset object, the information from the deleted record still appears in the text boxes on the form.

After the Delete method removes the current record, you explicitly should move the current record pointer to another record with the MoveNext or MoveFirst methods of the Recordset object. Now you will write the code for the Delete menu item's Click event procedure.

To write the code to delete database records:

1. Open the Code window for the **mnuEditDelete** menu's Click event procedure.

2. Enter the following code in the window:

```
Private Sub mnuEditDelete_Click()
    mrstContact.Delete
    mrstContact.MoveNext
End Sub
```

The first statement calls the Delete method to delete the current record of the Recordset object. The second statement positions the current record pointer on the next record of the Recordset object and clears the deleted record from the screen.

You now can manipulate information in the database with Visual Basic in addition to navigating through the existing information. A user can add, update, and delete information with a simple click of a menu. You have reached another milestone in the development of your program, so this is a good time to save your completed work, and test the code you have written for the Delete menu item.

To test the code for the Delete menu item:

1. Save the project then start the program.

2. Click **Find** then **Navigate** then **Next** to locate the record for Clark Biddleford.

3. Click **Edit** then **Delete** to delete the record. After deleting the record, notice the form displays the record for Betty Brown, the next record in the Recordset object.

   TROUBLE? If you receive a run-time error, you might have tried to delete a record when no record was displayed in the form. End the program and then repeat Steps 1 through 3.

4. End the program.

Your program now can locate, add, change, and delete records. These functions are common to nearly every program you will ever create to manage data in a database.

Quick Check

1. What properties does the Data control use to communicate with an existing Access database?

2. What is a bound control and what are the properties used to bind a control to data? What is a Recordset object?

3. What are the properties and the settings for those property values needed to create a text box in which you can display and navigate through multiple lines of text?

4. List and describe the methods to add, update, and delete information in a database.

5. What is the difference between the Enabled and Visible properties?

Now that you have completed Session 4.2, you can exit Visual Basic or you can continue to the next session.

SESSION

4.3

In this session you will learn how to locate records using a search string, how to validate user input, and how to prevent user errors from crashing a program when a run-time error occurs.

Searching for Records

Nina knows that moving from record to record using the Navigate submenu is sufficient only when working with a small number of records. But the contact management system will ultimately contain about 3,500 client records. The salespeople need to locate a specific record quickly, without scrolling through 3,500 records.

You can use the FindFirst method, which acts on a Recordset object, to locate a specific record easily. The method will be familiar because the current paper-based system is organized by last name. The syntax for the FindFirst method is:

*Object.***FindFirst** *criteria*

- The *Object* can be any valid Recordset object.

- The **FindFirst** method locates the first record in a recordset that satisfies the criteria. The current record pointer is moved to that record.

- The *criteria* defines which records in the database will be located. If several records match the criteria, the first record found will become the active record.

- You can use the **FindNext** method after the FindFirst method to locate subsequent occurrences of records matching the criteria. The FindNext method has the same syntax as the FindFirst method. See the Help system for more information on the FindFirst and FindNext methods.

Locating a Record Using an Input Box

Nina wants the form to include a dialog box in which the user can enter a last name, and a corresponding command button that, when clicked, will locate and display the record with the specified last name. You can do this without placing any other objects on the form by using a window that will appear only when called. This approach is consistent with the Windows 95 user interface. When a user wants to locate a specific record, the user will click the Find menu item and a temporary window, called an input box, will appear. An **input box** is similar to a message box; however, an input box sends a text string back to your program. Thus, the user can enter the last name of the client to search for and click a button in the input box. The input box will close and then, using the string returned by the input box function, the FindFirst method is called and the client's record will be displayed on the screen, if it exists.

To display an input box, you call the InputBox function, which has the following syntax:

string = **InputBox**(*prompt*[,*title*][,*default*])

- When the **InputBox** function is called it displays a prompt, a text box to enter input, and two command buttons—OK and Cancel. The InputBox function always returns a value. If the user clicks the OK button, the contents of the input box are returned to the program and stored in a variable. If the user clicks the Cancel button, the InputBox function returns a *string* with no characters in it. This is known as a zero-length string. You can use an input box for any task that must prompt the user to enter a text string.

- The *prompt* argument contains descriptive text that will appear inside the input box.

■ The optional *title* argument will appear in the title bar of the input box.

■ If the optional *default* argument contains a value, that is displayed in the input box's text box when it appears. This value then is returned to the program when the user clicks the OK button unless changed by the user. When there is a common response to the prompt, a *default* can save users time.

Figure 4-23 shows the parts of an input box.

Figure 4-23 ◀
Parts of an
input box

input box title ─
descriptive text ─

user types text here

The InputBox function will return a string, containing a last name, which you will store into a String variable. The string containing the last name is only part of the criteria, however. You also must define the name of the field you want to use. The criteria is made up of a string that contains the field name you want to search, followed by an operator like (=), followed by the search text (in this case a client's last name) enclosed in single quotation marks. It also is possible to create much more complex criteria. To look for the name "Smith", the format of the string containing the criteria needs to be:

```
fldLastName = 'Smith'
```

Notice that the word *Smith* is enclosed in single quotation marks. This tells the Microsoft Jet database engine that the contents are a string. If you were searching for a number, you would not use any quotation marks. To create this criteria string, you need to use the string concatenation operator.

To improve the user interface further, you should write an If statement to determine whether or not the program actually should try to find a record in the database depending on whether the user clicked the Cancel or OK button in the input box. Remember, if the Cancel button was clicked, a zero-length string will be returned.

It also is possible that the user entered a name that is not in the database. In that case, Nina would like the program to display a message box to the user. Whenever the FindFirst method is called, it sets the **NoMatch** property of the Recordset object.

■ If one or more records were found, the NoMatch property is set to False.

■ If no record is found, then the NoMatch property is set to True.

After calling the FindFirst method, you should check the value of the NoMatch property and, if it is True, display a message box to the user.

> *Tip:* A message box provides a visual clue to the user about the results of a request, such as the database engine is not able to locate a specific record in the database. If the code does not check that a record was found, it would appear to the user that the program did not look for a record. Whenever the program cannot perform a task as requested, it should advise the user what happened and why. Also, if possible, you should suggest to the user how to achieve the desired results.

Now you will use the FindFirst method of the Recordset object and the InputBox function together to display the information for a specific record in the TextBox objects. Your input box should have the title "Find" and the prompt "Enter the last name." If the database engine does not find a match for the last name, the user should see a message box that says "Cannot find (last name)." You need to declare a variable to determine whether the user clicked the OK or

Cancel button and to hold the value returned by the InputBox function (the last name the user types). This variable only will be used by this procedure; it will be named pstrLastName.

To write the code to display an input box and locate a specific record:

1. Open the Code window for the **mnuFindLastName** object's **Click** event procedure.

2. Enter the following code in the window:

```
Private Sub mnuFindLastName_Click()
    Dim pstrLastName As String
    pstrLastName = InputBox("Enter the Last Name", "Find")
    If pstrLastName <> "" Then
        mrstContact.FindFirst "fldLastName = " & "'" & _
            pstrLastName & "'"
        If mrstContact.NoMatch = True Then
            MsgBox "Cannot find " & pstrLastName, _
                vbInformation, "Atlantic Marketing"
        End If
    End If
End Sub
```

Examine the statements you just wrote. The code will execute in response to a Click event for the Find menu's Last Name item.

```
Dim pstrLastName As String
pstrLastName = InputBox("Enter the Last Name", "Find")
```

First, you declared a local variable named pstrLastName to hold the value returned by the InputBox function. Then you called the InputBox function using the prompt "Enter the Last Name" and the title "Find". A default value would not be appropriate in this case, because each user will most likely search for a different record each time.

```
If pstrLastName <> "" Then
```

This statement provides the error checking for the procedure. In this case, you want the program to try to locate the record only if the user supplied a last name, so the program must test to make sure pstrLastName is not blank. Remember that <> means "not equal to."

```
mrstContact.FindFirst "fldLastName = " & "'" & _
    pstrLastName & "'"
```

This statement provides the functionality for the FindFirst method. You need to tell the FindFirst method what to find by building a text string that will be processed by the FindFirst method. Remember the & character concatenates strings.

```
FindFirst fldLastName = 'Smith'
```

If the variable pstrLastName contained the text "Smith", the string evaluates the above statement.

```
If mrstContact.NoMatch = True Then
    MsgBox "Cannot find " & pstrLastName, _
        vbInformation, "Atlantic Marketing"
End If
```

After the FindFirst method was called, you checked to see that a client was found in the database. If no client exists with the specified name, the FindFirst method sets the recordset's NoMatch property to True. The If statement tests to see if this happened and displays a message box if no record was found.

This is a good time to test the Last Name menu item to see if it calls the InputBox function and FindFirst method correctly.

To test the code for the Last Name menu item:

1. Save the project then start the program.

2. Click the **Find** menu on your form then click **Last Name**. The Find input box appears.

3. Enter the last name **Zorn** in the Find input box as shown in Figure 4-24.

Figure 4-24 ◄
Find input box

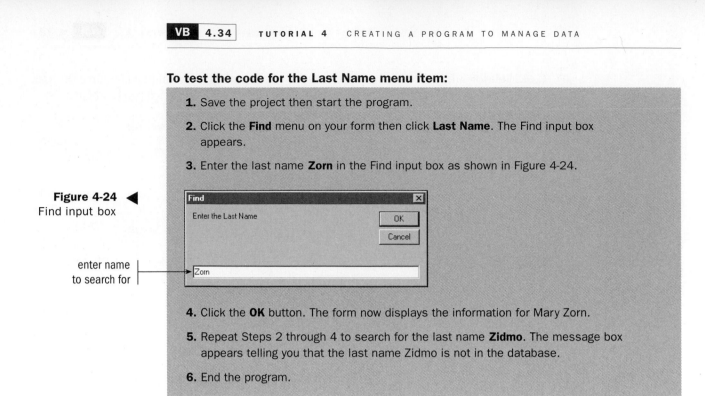

enter name
to search for

4. Click the **OK** button. The form now displays the information for Mary Zorn.

5. Repeat Steps 2 through 4 to search for the last name **Zidmo**. The message box appears telling you that the last name Zidmo is not in the database.

6. End the program.

Verifying the Correctness of Data with the Validate Event

In addition to notifying the user when the beginning and end of file have been reached, Nina would like to make sure the user enters valid data. For example, before a record is changed in the database, she wants to make sure that both a first and last name were entered, that the value entered for the date is in the correct format, and that a valid number was entered for the estimated annual sales. Visual Basic supports several classification functions that determine the characteristics of a variable or object property like the Text property of a text box. A **classification function** is a function that determines the data type of a variable.

You can use the IsDate function to determine if a date value is a date or can be converted to a valid date, and the IsNumeric function to determine if a number value is valid (that is, it contains only numbers and an optional decimal point). The IsDate and IsNumeric functions use the following syntax:

IsDate(*string*)

IsNumeric(*string*)

- Each of these functions takes one argument, *string*.

- Each of these functions returns a Boolean value. If *string* is a valid date or number, **IsDate** and **IsNumeric** return True, respectively. If *string* is not a valid date or number the respective function returns False.

You can use the IsDate and IsNumeric functions in an If statement in the contact management system to determine if input is valid. While you could place these If statements in the LostFocus events for each text box, the Data control supports an event called the Validate event that is well-suited for this purpose. The Validate event uses the following syntax:

Private Sub *Object*_**Validate** ([*index* **As Integer**,] *action* **As Integer**, *save* **As Integer**)

statements

End Sub

- *Object* is any instance of a Data control.

- Several different actions cause a **Validate** event to occur. Whenever the current record is repositioned, a record is updated, or a record is deleted, the argument is passed to the Validate event using an argument named *action*.

- The optional *index* argument identifies the Data control, if it is a member of a control array.

- The *action* argument is an integer that indicates the operation causing this event to occur. Each of these actions can be expressed as a constant. The *statements* in the Validate event procedure determine to which constant the *action* argument should be set. Valid constants for the *action* argument are: vbDataActionCancel, vbDataActionMoveFirst, vbDataActionMovePrevious, vbDataActionMoveNext, vbDataActionMoveLast, vbDataActionAddNew, vbDataActionUpdate, vbDataActionDelete, vbDataActionFind, vbDataActionBookmark, vbDataActionClose, and vbDataActionUnload. Refer to the Help system for more information about these constants.

- The *save* argument is a Boolean expression specifying whether bound data has changed.

In this session, you will need to cancel the current action, like updating a record, whenever invalid data is detected. If the input is valid, then the update will proceed. If not, you can display a message box to the user describing the nature of the problem and then cancel the update. To do this you set the action argument to the constant vbDataActionCancel when invalid data is detected. When the end of the event procedure is reached, the Update method that caused the Validate event will be canceled.

Nina would like you to program the Validate event for the Data control to make sure that both the First Name and Last Name text boxes contain text, that the Date Added text box contains a valid date, and that the Estimated Annual Sales text box contains a valid number. You first will declare variables that only will be used within the Validate procedure: pstrMessage will hold the message the user sees if there is invalid data and pintReturn will hold the return value of the MsgBox function. Because these variables only are used by this procedure, they are declared as local variables.

To validate the user input and display a message if necessary:

1. Open the Code window for the **datContact** object's **Validate** event procedure.

2. Enter the following code in the window:

```
Dim pstrMessage As String
Dim pintReturn As Integer
If Action = vbDataActionUpdate Then
    If txtLastName.Text = "" Or txtFirstName.Text = _
        "" Then
        pstrMessage = _
            "You must enter both a first and last name"
        Action = vbDataActionCancel
    End If
    If IsDate(txtDateAdded.Text) = False Then
        pstrMessage = pstrMessage & Chr(vbKeyReturn) & _
            "The date " & txtDateAdded.Text & _
            " is not a date"
        Action = vbDataActionCancel
    End If
```

```
        If IsNumeric(txtEstimatedSales.Text) = False Then
            pstrMessage = pstrMessage & Chr(vbKeyReturn) & _
                "The estimated sales " & _
                txtEstimatedSales.Text & " is not a number"
            Action = vbDataActionCancel
        End If
        If Action = vbDataActionCancel Then
            pintReturn = _
                MsgBox(pstrMessage, vbOKOnly, "Input error")
        End If
    End If
```

These statements test the value of each user input field. Notice the MsgBox function is called only once. You could have called it each time you detected invalid input, but that could confuse the user with several message boxes appearing one after another.

```
    If Action = vbDataActionUpdate Then
```

The statement to test for valid input only needs to be executed when the user is trying to update a record. If a record is repositioned, or is being deleted, there is no need to verify these changes. In other words, when the Update method is called, the Action argument is set to vbDataActionUpdate and the Validate event occurs. Thus, you checked this argument to determine whether or not to validate the input.

```
    If txtLastName.Text = "" Or txtFirstName.Text = _
        "" Then
        pstrMessage = _
            "You must enter both a first and last name"
        Action = vbDataActionCancel
    End If
```

The If statement determines if either txtLastName or txtFirstName contains no text. If either of these conditions is True, then the string pstrMessage changes accordingly. By setting the variable Action to the constant vbDataActionCancel, the Update method that causes this event will be canceled when the event procedure ends.

```
    If IsDate(txtDateAdded.Text) = False Then
        pstrMessage = pstrMessage & Chr(vbKeyReturn) & _
            "The date " & txtDateAdded.Text & _
            " is not a date"
        Action = vbDataActionCancel
    End If
```

This If statement calls the IsDate function to determine whether or not the date added contains a valid date value. If it does not (that is, IsDate is False), then additional information is appended to the existing contents of the message, and the Update action will be canceled. The next If statement behaves identically but uses the IsNumeric function to check that the Estimated Annual Sales text box contains a valid number.

```
    If Action = vbDataActionCancel Then
        pintReturn = _
            MsgBox(pstrMessage, vbOKOnly, "Input error")
    End If
```

Finally, the contents of the argument Action are checked to see if the pending method that caused this Validate event needs to be canceled. If so, the message box is displayed.

Nina suggests you test the code for the Validate event.

To test the code for the Validate event:

1. Save the project then start the program.

2. Click **Edit** then **Add.**

3. Enter **10** as the client ID. Leave the first and last names blank. Enter **1/1/1/3** as the date. Enter **22.3.3** as the estimated annual sales amount.

4. Click **Edit** then **Update** to attempt to save your changes.

5. A message box should appear describing the input errors, as shown in Figure 4-25.

Figure 4-25 ◀
Input error
message box

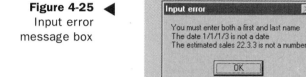

Developing an Error Handler

Because this program will be used by the entire sales force of Atlantic Marketing, Nina does not want the program to generate a run-time error if a user tries to perform an impossible action. The three most likely offenses a user will commit in the contact management system are trying to update a record that has not been edited, trying to delete a nonexistent record, and entering incorrect data in the name fields. Nina created the database such that each record must have a first name and a last name. Nina has asked you to find a way to avert these problems.

These problems can be solved by writing a set of Visual Basic statements that will execute when a run-time error occurs. This set of statements is referred collectively to as an error handler. An **error handler** is made up of a set of statements inside a procedure that executes when a run-time error occurs. An error handler in a procedure is said to be enabled when an error handler is included in that procedure. When a run-time error occurs, the error handler becomes active; that is, it begins to execute the statements that make up the error handler. Figure 4-26 illustrates the processing that takes place by a procedure's error handler.

Figure 4-26 ◀
Control flow of
an error handler

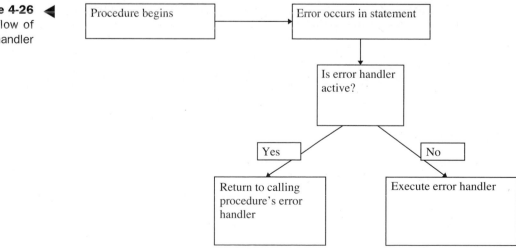

If the error handler is enabled but not active, then the statements in the calling procedure's error handler are executed. If another run-time error occurs while the error handler is executing, control returns to the calling procedure. This process continues until an enabled but inactive error handler is found.

The code in an error handler is not a separate Function or Sub procedure but rather a set of statements inside a procedure. Depending on the cause and severity of the error, your error handler may display a message box describing the cause of the error to the user or it may reset the variables. The error handler then can continue execution of the program.

Trapping Errors Resulting from an Update Statement

One of the problems that can occur when working with a database is when a user tries to update a record when no current record exists or when duplicate records would violate rules contained in the database. Trying to update a record before making it available for editing also will cause an error. Entering invalid data for a field also will cause a run-time error but you already have solved that problem by checking the input in the Data control's Validate event. You need to create a means by which errors will not stop the program from running. Nina wants the program to tell the user what is wrong and allow the user to continue.

You can use the On Error statement to identify errors and optionally a Resume Next statement to tell the program where to continue processing. The On Error statement creates an enabled error handler for the procedure. The Resume Next statement, when executed, will cause execution to continue at the statement following the statement that caused the error. If the Resume Next statement is omitted, then statements will continue to be executed until an End Sub or Exit Sub is reached. The On Error statement has the following syntax:

On Error GoTo *ErrorHandler*

   statements

Exit Sub

ErrorHandler:

   statements

[Resume Next]

- The **On Error** statement tells Visual Basic that when a run-time error occurs in this procedure, the *ErrorHandler* will be called. You do not explicitly call the error handler. Rather, Visual Basic calls it when an error occurs. If an error occurs, Visual Basic uses the **GoTo** statement to determine the code that will be executed in response to the error.

- The name *ErrorHandler* is called a line label. The line label is used to define a location in your program. It identifies a single line of code. Line labels must begin in the first column, must start with a letter, and end with a colon (:). In this case, when the error handler is called, the next statement that will be executed is the statement following the line:

   `ErrorHandler:`

- After the statements in the error handler have executed, the optional **Resume Next** statement tells Visual Basic to continue execution at the statement immediately following the statement that caused the error. Otherwise, execution continues in the error handler until an End Sub or Exit Sub statement is reached.

- Usually, a procedure exits when the last line of the procedure (End Sub) is reached, which means Visual Basic would continue execution of the procedure, causing the statements in the error handler to be executed even if there was no error. The **Exit Sub** statement can occur anywhere in a procedure and does not have to be part of an error handler. When the Exit Sub statement is reached, the procedure will exit. Because the error handler usually appears at the end of a procedure, the Exit Sub statement is necessary to exit a procedure when no error occurs. Otherwise, the error handler would execute every time the procedure was called.

When an error occurs in the contact management system, Nina wants the program to execute code in response to the error and display a message in a message box that explains the cause of the error to the user.

When an error occurs, a numeric code and description of the error is stored in a predefined object called the **Err object**. A predefined object works just like other objects you have used. You do not create an instance of the Err object, however. It is created by Visual Basic for you. This information is stored in the Err object's properties as follows:

- The **Description** property contains a short description of the error.

- The **Number** property contains a numeric value representing the error.

- The **Source** property contains the name of the object or program that originally generated the error.

The error handler you create will display a general message for run-time errors that occur in the mnuEditUpdate object's Click event procedure. The message will tell the user the number and the description of the error encountered.

To display a message when a run-time error occurs and continue program execution:

1. Open the Code window for the **mnuEditUpdate** object's **Click** event procedure.

2. Enter the following code in the window (shown in bold):

```
Private Sub mnuEditUpdate_Click()
    Dim pstrMessage As String
    On Error GoTo mnuEditUpdate_Error
    mrstContact.Update
    Exit Sub

mnuEditUpdate_Error:
    pstrMessage = "Cannot perform operation" & _
        Chr(vbKeyReturn) & "Error #" & _
        Err.Number & ":" & Err.Description
    MsgBox pstrMessage, vbExclamation, _
        "Atlantic Contact - Database Error"
End Sub
```

Examine the code you just wrote. The code will be executed whenever clicking the Update menu item causes a run-time error. This will happen if a user tries to update a record when no current record exists, a duplicate client ID is found, or the record has not been made available for editing.

```
On Error GoTo mnuEditUpdate_Error
```

The first line of code identifies the line label for the error handler (mnuEditUpdate_Error) in the procedure. When an error occurs, the statement following the line label named mnuEditUpdate_Error: will be executed. Remember that run-time errors still occur, but the program is dealing with the errors. This also is known as error trapping. **Error trapping** is a programming concept that you use to prevent run-time errors from ending a program.

```
Exit Sub
```

Notice the location of the Exit Sub statement. This causes the procedure to exit and return to the calling procedure or, in this case, wait for more events. Without this statement, Visual Basic would continue execution of the procedure. This would cause the statements in the error handler to be executed, even if there was no error.

```
mnuEditUpdate_Error:
```

This statement is the line label for the error handler. A line label is used to provide a reference for the GoTo statement. In this example, when an error occurs, Visual Basic will go to the line label causing execution to continue at the statement following the line label. Notice that the line label appears in the first column and ends with a colon.

```
pstrMessage = "Cannot perform operation" & _
    Chr(vbKeyReturn) & "Error #" & _
    Err.Number & ":" & Err.Description
MsgBox pstrMessage, vbExclamation, _
    "Atlantic Contact - Database Error"
```

These statements are the essence of the error handler. You used another object provided by Visual Basic, the Err object, to describe the nature of the error to the user. In your program, the message box will display the Number property of the error and its corresponding Description property.

This is a good time to see how the error handler works when the program is running. To test the error handler, make an intentional error. Because you cannot update before clicking the Edit Record menu item, the Update menu item will generate a run-time error.

To test the error handler:

1. Save the project then start the program.

2. Click the **Edit** menu then **Update** to attempt to update the record. The error handler displays a message box describing the error. See Figure 4-27.

Figure 4-27 ◄
Message box displayed by Update error handler

> **Atlantic Contact - Database Error**
>
> ⚠ Cannot perform operation
> Error #3020:Update or CancelUpdate without AddNew or Edit.
>
> [OK]

As you can see from Figure 4-27, you cannot perform an update without having first called the Edit or AddNew method.

3. Click the **OK** button to close the message box.

4. End the program.

Trapping Deletion Errors

When a user tries to delete a record, but no record is current, an error also will occur. Nina wants the program to display an error message while continuing to run the program. To accomplish this you can use the On Error statement just like you did for errors caused by the Update method.

To display a message when a user tries to delete a record with no record current:

1. Open the Code window for the **mnuEditDelete** object's **Click** event procedure.

2. Enter the following code in the window:

```
Private Sub mnuEditDelete_Click()
    Dim pstrMessage As String
    On Error GoTo mnuEditDelete_Error
    mrstContact.Delete
    mrstContact.MoveNext
    Exit Sub
```

```
mnuEditDelete_Error:
    pstrMessage = "Cannot perform operation #" _
        & Err.Number & ":" & Err.Description
    MsgBox pstrMessage, vbExclamation, _
        "Atlantic Contact - Database Error"
    mrstContact.MoveFirst
End Sub
```

This error handler is nearly identical to the one you wrote for the mnuEditUpdate event procedure. This error handler will be called, however, when an error occurs in the mnuEditDelete_Click event procedure (called by the Delete menu item).

Now you need to test the error handler for mnuEditDelete_Click. This error handler will be activated when a user tries to delete a record when there is no current record. This would happen if the user deleted the record at the end of the Recordset object and then clicked the Delete menu item again.

To test the error handler:

1. Save the project then start the program.

2. Click **Edit** then **Add**.

3. Enter **14** as the client ID.

4. Enter **Zyl** as the last name, **Bill** as the first name, today's date for the date added, and **1000.00** for the estimated annual sales, then click **Edit** then **Update**.

5. Click **Find** then **Navigate** then **Last** to display the record for Zyl.

6. Click **Edit** then **Delete** to delete the record from the database. All the text boxes on the form now are empty.

7. Click **Edit** then **Delete** again to cause the error. The error handler displays the message box shown in Figure 4-28.

Figure 4-28 ◄
Message box
displayed
by Delete
error handler

As you can see from Figure 4-28, there is no current record.

8. Click the **OK** button. You return to the blank form.

9. End the program.

Another error will occur if you call the Edit method when there is no current record to edit. The error handler for this event procedure looks like the other two you already have written. Nina suggests you complete this error handler and test it.

To display a message when a user tries to edit a record with no record current:

1. Open the Code window for the **mnuEditRecord** object's **Click** event procedure.

2. Enter the following code in the window:

```
Private Sub mnuEditRecord_Click()
    Dim pstrMessage As String
    On Error GoTo mnuEditRecord_Error
    mrstContact.Edit
    Exit Sub

mnuEditRecord_Error:
    pstrMessage = "Cannot perform operation #" _
        & Err.Number & ":" & Err.Description
    MsgBox pstrMessage, vbExclamation, _
        "Atlantic Contact - Database Error"
End Sub
```

3. Save the project.

4. Run the program.

5. Test the handler by typing **Ctrl+L** to locate the last record. Type **Ctrl+N** to locate the end of file.

6. Click **Edit** then **Edit Record** to try to edit the nonexistent record. The message box should appear.

7. End the program.

The contact management system now is complete. Nina is certain various objects on the form—Data control, text boxes, menu—will make it easy for the Atlantic Marketing salespeople to enter, locate, and maintain information about clients. The error handlers will help users correct errors while running the program. Nina knows the contact management system is a great improvement over the paper-based system, and is confident it will be well received by the salespeople.

Quick Check

1 What is the purpose of the FindFirst method of the Recordset object, and how would you use it in a Visual Basic statement?

2 What is the purpose of an input box?

3 What is the purpose of an error handler and what Visual Basic statements are used to create an error handler?

4 What is the purpose of data validation?

5 What is the Resume Next statement used for?

6 What is the difference between the End Sub and Exit Sub statements?

Figure 4-29 lists and defines the new terms presented in this tutorial.

Figure 4-29 ◀
New terms

Term	Definition
Bound control	A bound control displays the changes in the current record of the Recordset object on the form. A bound control can provide access to a specific field in a database through a Data control by setting the DataSource and DataField properties. Also called data aware controls.
Classification functions	Classification functions determine the characteristics of a variable or object property, such as the IsDate and IsNumeric functions.
Copy buffer	The copy buffer stores the current record and any changes made to it before those changes actually are written to the underlying database table or query.
Current record pointer	The current record pointer indicates the active record in a Recordset object. You do not access the current record pointer explicitly. Rather, you move the current record pointer indirectly using the Recordset object's methods.
Data Access Objects	Data Access Objects (DAO) enable you to use a programming language to access and manipulate data in a database, and to manage tables, their objects, and their structure.
Data aware controls	Also called bound controls. A data aware control displays the changes in the current record of the Recordset object on the form. A data aware control can provide access to a specific field in a database through a Data control by setting the DataSource and DataField properties.
Data control	The Data control is a control that is used to bind the data in a Microsoft Access database to other controls in your Visual Basic program.
Database	A database is a collection of related information organized in tables.
Dynaset	A dynaset is a dynamic view of the information contained in a database table or query.
Error handler	An error handler is made up of a set of statements inside a procedure that executes when a run-time error occurs.
Error trapping	Error trapping is a programming concept that you use to prevent run-time errors from ending a program.
Field	A field is a column of data stored in a table.
Hot key	Also called access key. The underlined character of a menu title or menu item that allows the title or item to be activated by pressing the Alt key and the hot key at the same time.
Input box	An input box is like a message box. An input box returns a string that can be used by your program.
Menu Editor	The Menu Editor is a dialog box that allows you to create a menu system for your program.
Method	A method is a procedure that acts on an object. It contains code that is built inside the object to accomplish a task.
Microsoft Jet database engine	The Microsoft Jet database engine is the DBMS that retrieves data from, and stores data in, an Access database.
Query	A query is an instruction to a database to return a set of records from one or more tables in a specific order.
Record	A record is a row of data stored in a table.
Recordset object	Recordset objects are created at run time by the Recordset property of the Data control. They are a view of the data stored in the database.
Relational database	A relational database stores information in several tables that can be related together in different ways.
Separator bar	A separator bar is a horizontal line that visually groups related menu items together to make the interface easier to use.

Figure 4-29 ◄
New terms
(continued)

Term	Definition
Shortcut key	A shortcut key, is a function key (such as F5) or a key combination (such as Ctrl+A or Ctrl+X) that executes a command.
Submenu	A submenu is a menu item that displays another menu, rather than executing code in an event procedure.
Table	A table consists of rows and columns. The column defines a name for, and characteristics of, the stored information.

Tutorial Assignments

Nina has asked you to design a program for Atlantic Marketing that can be used by each salesperson and the sales manager to look at the sales records of each client. Each client may have one or more sales records. The program needs to be able to locate a specific client using an input box. After a client is located, the user needs to be able to continue to look at the sales records for the selected client. You will need to create command buttons to accomplish this. The first will display the input box and locate the first record if it is found. The second should locate the next record given the selected criteria. The information is stored in a query based on the contact table and the sales table. The query is named qryContactSales. Users will locate records in the query using the command buttons, so the Data control should be invisible. Figure 4-30 shows the completed form for the program.

Figure 4-30 ◄

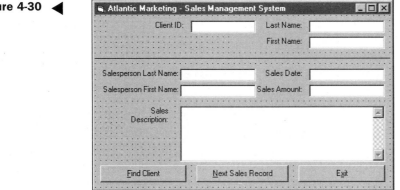

1. Make sure your Student Disk is in the appropriate disk drive, then start Visual Basic.

2. Create a new project and save the form with the name **frmAtlanticSales.frm** and the project with the name **Atlantic Sales.vbp** in the **TAssign** folder in the **Tutorial.04** folder on your Student Disk.

3. Change the form name to **frmAtlanticSales**, and its caption to **Atlantic Marketing - Sales Management System**.

4. Draw a Data control on the form. Set the Visible property so that the Data control will not be visible when the program is run. Set the properties of the Data control so it will connect to the table named **qryContactSales** in the Access database named **AM_CMS.mdb** in the **TAssign** folder in the **Tutorial.04** folder on your Student Disk. The Recordset object created should be a **Dynaset** type recordset. Name the Data control **datContactSales**. *Note:* Because it will be invisible when the program runs, it does not matter where you draw the Data control; you will just use its functionality to connect to the database.

5. Draw eight text boxes and their corresponding labels so your form looks like Figure 4-30. The Sales Description text box must be able to display multiple lines and should contain vertical scroll bars. Set the name for each text box as follows:
   txtClientID
   txtLastName
   txtFirstName
   txtSalesLastName
   txtSalesFirstName
   txtSalesDate
   txtSalesAmount
   txtSalesDescription

6. Set the necessary properties for each text box so it can communicate with the Data control you created in Step 5. The corresponding field names in the table are as follows:
   fldClientID
   fldLastName
   fldFirstName
   fldSalesLastName
   fldSalesFirstName
   fldSalesDate
   fldSalesAmount
   fldSalesDescription

7. Create three command buttons on the form to find a client, find the next sales record, and exit the program as shown in Figure 4-30. Be sure each command button has a hot key as shown in Figure 4-30. The command buttons should be named, **cmdFindClient**, **cmdNextSalesRecord**, and **cmdExit**.

8. Declare a String variable named **mstrLastName** such that it can be used by all the event procedures in the program. This variable will be used to build a search string for record retrieval from the database. Require that all variables be declared explicitly.

9. Activate the Code window for the cmdExit object's Click event procedure. Write the code to end the program.

10. Activate the Code window for the cmdFindClient object's Click event procedure. Write the statement to display an input box that will ask the user what last name to find. The return value of the input box should be the last name the user is searching for, stored in the string named mstrLastName. Include a descriptive prompt and title for the input box.

11. In the same event procedure in the Code window write the statement that will create the search string. You will use this string when you call the FindFirst method in the next step.

12. Write the statement to locate the first record in the recordset having the specified criteria. To do this you will need to call the FindFirst method of the recordset.

13. Activate the Code window for the cmdNextSalesRecord object's Click event and write the statement to locate the next record in the recordset having the specified criteria. To do this you will need to call the FindNext method of the recordset.

14. Save the project.

15. Test the program by clicking the **Find Client** button and entering the name **Zorn**. Click the **Find Next Sales Record** button to locate the other records for the client Zorn.

16. Repeat Step 15 for the client named **Cantor**.

17. Exit the program by using the **Exit** command button.

18. Print the Form Image and Code.

19. Exit Visual Basic.

Case Problems

1. Neptune Warehouse Neptune Warehouse stores a variety of goods for the auto parts industry. Lou Ortiz is in charge of creating a simple system that will allow the company to manage its inventory. She has asked you to create the menu system for the program. Later, the code will be written for each of the menu items you create. She has designed the appearance of the menus on paper as shown in Figure 4-31, and wants you to use the Menu Editor to create the actual menu items.

Figure 4-31 ◀

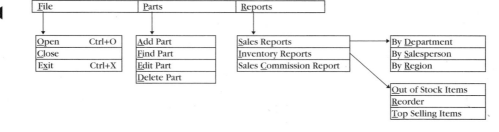

1. Make sure your Student Disk is in the appropriate disk drive, then start Visual Basic.

2. Create a new project and change the form name to **frmNeptuneInventory**, and its caption to **Neptune Warehouse - Inventory**.

3. Save the form with the name **frmNeptuneInventory.frm** and the project with the name **Neptune Inventory.vbp** in the **Cases** folder in the **Tutorial.04** folder on your Student Disk.

4. Create the menus according to the specifications in Figure 4-31. Be sure to choose appropriate names for each menu item and set the shortcut and hot keys as described.

5. After you have created the menus, be sure to check that each menu item is in the correct place.

6. Save the form and project.

7. Exit Visual Basic.

2. Henderson Music Henderson Music is a small music store in a college town. Valerie Henderson, the store's owner, wants a program to display items from its music collection database. The music collection database was created using Microsoft Access. The three items to be displayed are **Music Category**, **Recording Artist Name**, and **Recording Title**. Valerie has asked you to create a test program with the title, **Henderson Music**. She wants the program to contain three text boxes and three Data controls. Each text box will be bound to one of the three Data controls so when a user clicks a Data control, one of the categories will be displayed in the matching bound text box. You do not have to write any code for the Data controls to access the database in this program, but you should provide descriptive labels for the objects. Each data control also should contain a caption that describes the table in the database. You will write only one line of code for the working **Exit** button. Make sure you use valid names for the objects on the form. Each of the three Data objects will connect to **Music.mdb**, which is located in the **Cases** folder in the **Tutorial.04** folder on your Student Disk. The RecordSource for each Data control should be set to **tblMusicCategory**, **tblRecordingArtistName**, and **tblRecordingTitle**, respectively. The DataSource and DataField properties for the bound text boxes should be set to the name of the appropriate Data control, as follows:

tblMusicCategory	**tblRecordingArtist**	**tblRecordingTitle**
fldMusicCategory	**fldRecordingArtistName**	**fldRecordingTitle**
	fldRecordingLabel	
	fldFormat	
	fldNumberofTracks	

When your form and code are complete, test the program, and save the form as frmHendersonMusic and the project as Henderson Music in the Cases folder in the Tutorial.04 folder on your Student Disk. Print the Form Image and the Form as text.

3. Galaxy Personnel Galaxy Personnel is a payroll and personnel services company in Denver, Colorado. Each day hundreds of weekly time sheets need to be entered into a database. Because the volume of data entry in payroll is so large, and accuracy is so important, they need a form that will validate all user input before adding records. Also, to minimize the number of keystrokes, or mouse buttons, the user needs to type to add a time sheet, the program needs to validate automatically when the last data entry field loses focus. If correct, the program should add the record to the database, then clear the text boxes of their contents in preparation for the next record, and set the focus to the first data entry field. If there are any errors in the input, then the program should display a message box, cancel the update, and set the focus back to the first input field. The program will operate in two modes. While in Browse mode, the user should be able to click the buttons on the data control to locate different records but not change the contents of the text boxes. When in Add mode, the data control should be invisible, and the text boxes enabled so the user can add records. When the program is first started, the form should be in Browse mode. The following table shows the names of the fields, their valid values, and a brief description of the field.

Figure 4-32 ◀
Field names and valid values

Field name	Description	Valid values
fldEmployeeID	Employee identification number	Between 100 and 1000
fldHoursWorked	Number of hours worked	Must be greater than 0 and less than 60
fldPayRate	Rate of employee pay	Between 4.25 and 32.5
fldPayDate	Date paid	Must be a valid date value

When complete your form should look like Figure 4-33.

Figure 4-33 ◀

1. Make sure your Student Disk is in the appropriate disk drive and start Visual Basic.

2. Create a new project and save the form with the name **frmGalaxyPayroll.frm** and the project with the name **Galaxy Payroll.vbp** in the **Cases** folder on your Student Disk.

3. Create a Data control, four labels, and corresponding text boxes as shown in Figure 4-33. Set the Name property of the text boxes to **txtEmployeeID**, **txtHoursWorked**, **txtPayRate**, **txtPayDate**, and the name of the Data control to **datPayroll**.

4. Connect the Data control to **tblPayroll** in the **Payroll.mdb** database in the **Cases** folder in the **Tutorial.04** folder on your Student Disk. Bind the text boxes to the corresponding fields.

5. Create two command buttons named **cmdStartAdding** and **cmdBrowse**, and set their captions.

6. Write the statements for the datPayroll_Validate event to validate the data in each of the input fields according to the requirements in Figure 4-32. Remember, the Validate Event occurs before a new record becomes the current record, and when the Update method is called on a recordset. You will need to execute the validation statements when the Validate event is triggered by the Update method. This information is stored in the Action argument. When the event is triggered by the Update method, the Action argument is set to the constant vbDataActionUpdate.

7. The first field to validate is txtEmployeeID. Write an If statement to verify that the employee ID number is between 100 and 1000. If it is not, write the statement to cancel the action, and append a message to the string describing the problem to the user.

8. Next write the If statement to validate the hours worked. If the hours worked are not between 0 and 60, then the action should be canceled. Append a message to the String variable describing the problem to the user.

9. Create another If statement to validate that the pay rate is between $4.25 and $32.50.

10. Create another If statement to validate the pay date using the IsDate classification function.

11. Finally write an If statement that tests whether or not the action was canceled. If it was, then display a message box to the user.

12. Write the statements for the cmdStartAdding_Click event to add a new record to the database. Because the first three fields will hold numbers, VB automatically inserts a 0 in the text boxes. Write the statements to remove the text from the text boxes. Also, when adding records, the Data control needs to be invisible, because the program is in Add mode rather than Browse mode.

13. To make the user interface as fast as possible for the user, set the initial focus to the text box containing the Employee ID.

14. Now the Browse command button must be programmed. When Browse mode is selected, you first need to test that the user is not editing a record. If he or she is, then the update should be canceled. Write an If statement to determine if the EditMode property of the recordset is equal to the constant dbEditAdd. If it is, cancel the update by calling the CancelUpdate method. Finally, write the statement to locate the first record in the recordset and make the Data control visible.

15. You need to save the new record that was added each time the txtPayDate text box loses focus (when the user presses the Tab key in this text box). Enter the statement to update the current recordset record into the LostFocus event procedure for the txtPayDate text box.

EXPLORE

16. If the update action was not canceled by the Validate event, then the EditMode property of the recordset still will be dbEditAdd and the contents of the text boxes should be cleared. Immediately following the update statement, enter a statement that will determine whether or not the update succeeded; that is, whether the EditMode property still is dbEditAdd, and clears the contents of the text boxes.

17. The final statement in the txtPayDate_LostFocus event should reset the focus to the Employee ID text box. Write the statement to accomplish this.

18. Save the form and project.

19. Test the program by clicking the **Start Adding** button. Enter several records to test that each text box is being validated correctly; that is, you should enter numbers that are both valid and invalid for each field.

20. Click the **Browse** command button. Be sure the Data control becomes visible and use its navigation buttons to test that the valid records you entered actually were added and that invalid records were ignored.

21. Correct any errors and repeat Steps 14 through 16.

22. Print the Code.

23. Exit Visual Basic.

4. Perfect Printing Perfect Printing makes photocopies and provides other printing services. The price of a copy depends on the size, color, weight, and quality of the paper. The price per copy also depends on the number of copies made. The price break table is as follows:

1 – 100 copies

101 – 500 copies

more than 500 copies

The complete price break table is stored in a database named **Perfect.mdb** in the **Cases** folder in the **Tutorial.04** folder on your Student Disk. The database has the following table and fields:

tblPrice
fldPaperSize
fldPaperColor
fldPaperWeight
fldPaperQuality
fldPrice1
fldPrice100
fldPrice500

Raj Venkat would like you to create a program that will allow the user to select a type of paper, the number of copies, and whether the copies are single-sided or double-sided. When double-sided copies are made, instead of charging for two copies, Raj charges for 1.9 copies, because only 1 piece of paper is used. Figure 4-34 shows the completed user interface.

Figure 4-34 ◀

1. Start Visual Basic and create a new project.

2. Name the form **frmPerfectPrinting**, and give it an appropriate caption.

3. Save the form as **frmPerfectPrinting.frm** and the project as **Perfect Printing.vbp** in the **Cases** folder in the **Tutorial.04** folder on your Student Disk.

4. Draw an instance of the Data control and set its properties to connect to the table named **tblPrice** in the database named **Perfect.mdb** stored in the **Cases** folder in the **Tutorial.04** folder on your Student Disk.

5. Create the necessary text boxes, labels, and command buttons as shown in Figure 4-34. Set the Caption and Name properties as necessary. Remember to use meaningful names for all objects.

6. Set the necessary properties of the text boxes so they are bound to the fields in tblPrice.

7. Create a frame with two option buttons. The option buttons should be members of a control array named **optSides**. Set the captions to **Single-sided** and **Double-sided**.

8. In the **Form_Load** event procedure set the value of the Single-sided option button to True so it will be checked when the program is started.

9. The remainder of the processing takes place in the Click event procedure for the command button named **cmdComputePrice**.

10. Write the necessary If statement to determine the appropriate price based on the quantity ordered and store the extended price in a local variable.

11. Next write an If statement to determine which option button is selected. If the Double-sided button is selected, multiply the extended price by 1.9.

12. Store the final result in the Quantity text box.

13. Write the statement in the Click event procedure for the Exit command button to end the program.

14. Create a command button to add new records to the database. Set the Caption and Name properties as appropriate.

15. Create a command button to update existing records and write the necessary error handler.

16. Create a command button to refresh the recordset.

17. Create a command button to delete records from the database. Set the Caption and Name properties as appropriate. Be sure to write an error handler that will trap errors if the user tries to delete a record when there is no current record.

18. Save and run the program.

19. Using the navigation buttons on the Data control select different records and specify quantities that will test the three different possible prices. Be sure to test both option buttons. Correct any errors and save your work again.

20. Print the Form Image and Code and exit Visual Basic.

Working with Multiple Forms and Printing Reports

Creating an Inventory and Sales Reporting Program for Pacific Electronics

OBJECTIVES

In this tutorial you will:

■ Add existing forms to a program

■ Create a general procedure that will execute when your program first is started

■ Understand the different events that are applicable to forms

■ Add forms to a program using templates

■ Add a form to a program that operates with database data using a wizard

■ Print reports to a printer

■ Move sequentially through each record in a recordset using a Do loop

■ Write code to reference individual fields in a recordset

CASE

Pacific Electronics

Pacific Electronics is an electronic parts distributor that has been doing business in Seattle, Washington, since 1991. In addition to selling transistors, wiring, and other parts used by the electronics industry in the area, the company recently has increased its inventory to include selected computer chips and expanded its territory to serve all of Washington and Oregon. As part of this expansion, the management wants to develop an inventory and sales reporting system. Mary Deems, an analyst for the company for many years, already has created a Microsoft Access database of parts inventory and sales records. Now she wants a Visual Basic program that, together with the database, will allow the salespeople to view inventory and sales information and to print reports of their sales. This information will be used by the salespeople to identify which items are selling well and which items are not. Also, the sales manager will use the sales reports to determine the commission for each salesperson.

To accomplish this task, you will need to add several forms to the program. Mary would like a splash screen that will appear whenever the program is started. After the splash screen appears, she wants the user to enter his and her name and employee ID into another form. If correct, the Main form should be displayed. Additionally, she would like another form to display parts data.

For every product, the salespeople need to be able to print a sales report containing the product ID, a description of the product, the quantity of the product sold so far this year, the sales price of the product, and the extended price. Also, the salespeople need to know the total number of orders, the total items sold, and the total annual sales in dollars.

The program also must have a menu system like other Windows 95 programs. The menu system needs to have commands to display the different forms, and print the sales and inventory reports. Mary already has created the Main form and the menu system.

SESSION

5.1

In this session you will add a splash screen to the project Mary already has created. You will also add a form to your project then modify it to fit a particular purpose. You will use the Data Form Wizard to create a login form and forms that will interact with a database. You also will write the necessary code to display these different forms.

Reviewing the Program Design

Mary already has completed the NEADT charts for the program that describe both the processing performed by the different forms and that processing required to print the sales report. She suggests you now review this documentation to become more familiar with the project.

To view and print the NEADT charts for the inventory and sales program:

1. Make sure your Student Disk is in the appropriate disk drive. Using Microsoft Word open the file **Pacific.doc** in the **Tutorial.05** folder on your Student Disk. Otherwise, open the file **Pacific.txt** using WordPad.

2. Print the NEADT charts and close the word processing program.

As you can see from the NEADT charts, the program consists of four separate forms. The first form, called a splash screen, will appear while the rest of the program is being loaded. A **splash screen** is used to provide the user a brief description of the program and its purpose. After the splash screen is displayed, a second form that works much like an input box, will be used to get the name and employee ID of the user. Once the user has specified this information and clicked the OK button, the Main form will be displayed. The Main form will have a menu to exit the program, another to print the sales report, and another to display the form to interact with a database.

Instead of creating the forms and each of their objects from scratch, you will learn how to add a form using templates and wizards provided by Visual Basic. Visual Basic supplies you with several forms that perform common tasks. You can add these forms to your program, and modify them rather than creating new forms and objects from scratch.

Adding an Existing Form to the Program

Mary already has created the Main form for the program. You now need to begin by adding the splash screen to your project file. Remember the project file contains a list of all the different forms in your program. With the exception of the demonstration project in Session 1.1, the programs you have created so far have contained a single form. This program will contain the four forms mentioned above when you are finished.

You often can simplify the programming process by adding an existing form to a project and modifying it slightly, if necessary, to fit a particular purpose. In this case Mary has created the splash screen, but you must add it to the project before it can be used by your program. The splash screen is the initial screen that appears on your computer when a program first is started. It often displays the company name, logo, and program name, each time the program starts. Displaying a splash screen while the rest of the program is loading can reassure the user that the computer has not frozen. You see the Visual Basic splash screen each time you start Visual Basic.

The splash screen Mary created contains the Pacific Electronics name and logo and the name of the program, Inventory and Sales Program.

> *Tip:* Most programs begin by displaying a splash screen that identifies the program name, program purpose, and copyright information. To adhere to Windows 95 standards, you should display a splash screen for each program you write.

When Visual Basic runs a program, it either loads a form and displays it on the screen or executes a general procedure. This is called the startup object. The **startup object** can be a single form or general procedure that is executed when the program is run. In the programs you have created so far, you have used only a single form, which, by default, has been the startup object. The splash screen you now add must be displayed before the Main form, however, so you will need to change the startup object.

To add a second form to a project:

1. Start Visual Basic and open the project named **Pacific.vbp** in the **Tutorial.05** folder on your Student Disk.

2. Click the **Project Explorer** button 📇 on the toolbar to open the Project Explorer, if necessary. Click the **plus sign** ⊞ to the left of the Forms folder to open it, if necessary. Note there is only one form in the project named frmMain. This form will be used to open the parts form that will interact with the database, print a sales report, and exit the program. Because it is the Main form in the program, Mary used the name frmMain. Do not open frmMain at this time.

3. Click **Project** then **Add Form** on the menu bar to add a new form to the project. The Add Form dialog box will appear as shown in Figure 5-1.

Figure 5-1 ◀
Add Form
dialog box

click the Existing
tab to locate
an existing form

4. Click the **Existing** tab to locate the splash screen Mary already has created.

5. Click the file named **frmSplash.frm** in the **Tutorial.05** folder on your Student Disk then click **Open** to add the form to your project.

   Notice the form will be added to the Project Explorer as shown in Figure 5-2.

Figure 5-2 ◀
Adding
the splash
screen form

frmSplash added
to project

6. View **frmSplash**.

7. Save the project as **Pacific Sales Report.vbp** in the **Tutorial.05** folder on your Student Disk. Accept the default names, **frmMain.frm** and **frmSplash.frm** if prompted.

The purpose of the splash screen is different from the other forms you have created. The splash screen only provides a visual message to the user while the rest of the program loads and then it disappears without any input from the user. There is no need for many of the form elements you have created in the past—a title bar, a border, or any input objects—because the user will not need to do anything to the form.

A Form object has properties that allow you to control the appearance of a form. The **BorderStyle** property of the Form object works differently from the BorderStyle property of the Shape object in that it is read-only at run time. You can change the settings of the BorderStyle property to modify the behavior of forms.

- When set to **0 - None**, the form will not display a border or title bar at run time.

- When set to **1 - Fixed Single**, the form only can be resized using the Maximize or Minimize buttons on the form's title bar.

- When set to **2 - Sizable** (the default setting) the form displays a border and a title bar, allowing the user to resize the form while the program is running.

- When set to **3 - Fixed Dialog**, the form cannot be resized and no Maximize and Minimize buttons are displayed on the form's title bar.

In addition to changing the form's border, you can set the form's position on the screen. While you could set the Left and Top properties of the form, the Form object supports another property called the **StartUpPosition** property.

- When set to **0 - Manual**, the form appears as defined by the Left and Top properties.

- When set to **2 - CenterScreen**, the form is centered on the whole screen.

- When set to **3 - WindowsDefault**, the window appears on the upper-left corner of the screen.

There are other BorderStyle and StartUpPosition property settings you can use in your program. Look at the Help screens for the BorderStyle property and the StartUpPosition property of the Form object for further information.

Mary suggests you now set the splash screen properties so it appears in the center of the screen with no border at run time. Because you now have two forms in your program, you must be careful to set the properties for the correct form and object. Only one Properties window can be active at a time. The Properties window sets the property values for an active form. Thus, you can click on a form to activate it, then change the properties as necessary.

To remove the form's borders and set the startup position:

1. Activate the Properties window for the object named **frmSplash**. Be sure the title bar of the Properties window says "frmSplash" or you will set the properties for the wrong object.

2. Set the BorderStyle property to **0 - None**. Note that the form has no caption. Because the title bar will not appear at run time, the caption is not relevant.

3. Set the StartUpPosition property to **2 - CenterScreen**.

Although the splash screen has been added to your program, it will not appear on the screen when the program first is started, because the project still will load its default startup form, frmMain. You now need to learn how to control the startup object that is displayed when a program is started. When a program is started, Visual Basic can display any form in the project or call a Sub procedure with the name Main.

The procedure Sub Main is not contained inside a Form module like the other procedures you have seen. Rather it is contained in a different kind of module called a standard module. A **standard module** is like a Form module but contains only general procedures and variable declarations commonly accessed by other modules within a program. Standard modules also are called bas modules. You can write general procedures in standard modules that are used by different forms in your program. It also is in a standard module that you write the procedure Sub Main. Before you can write the Sub Main procedure, you must create the new standard module.

To add a standard module to your program:

1. Click **Project** then **Add Module** on the menu bar. The Add Module dialog box will appear as shown in Figure 5-3.

Figure 5-3 ◀
Adding a standard module to the project

New tab is active ——

click Module to add a bas module ——

click Open to add the module to the project

2. Be sure the **New** tab is active, click the **Module** icon then click the **Open** button. Notice that the general declarations section of the Code window is activated and a new module will be inserted into the Project Explorer as shown in Figure 5-4. Note that the shape and relative position of your windows may vary.

Figure 5-4 ◀
Project Explorer with standard module added

new standard module ——

module name shown in title bar of Code window ——

The module you created by default has the name Module1. It has not been saved on the disk, however. Before proceeding, you should save both the module and the project files.

3. Save the project. Accept the default module name, **Module1.bas**, when prompted.

Now that the new standard module and project have been saved, Mary would like you to insert the procedure to display the splash screen when the program is started.

The programs you have created so far have had a single form and a single form module, so the startup module was set to the single Form object by default. This program now has three modules, however. There is a Form module for the splash screen, another for the Main form, and another for the standard module you just created. Visual Basic will allow you to open one Code window for each module in your program. For example, you could open three different Code windows—one for each of the two Form modules, and one for the standard module. Thus, it is important you write code to show the form in the correct module.

Like the Properties window, the Code window displays the Form or standard module name in the title bar to help you verify that you are interacting with the correct module.

To create a startup procedure you will need to insert a new Sub procedure like you have done before, and write the necessary statements to display the splash screen. This Sub procedure must be named Main to operate as a startup procedure.

Because Sub Main will be the startup procedure, no form will be displayed on the screen until you explicitly write a statement to display the form. The Form object supports a method called Show that will display the form. When the Show method is called, form events like Form_Load occur and any code in those event procedures are executed. The Show method has the following syntax:

object.**Show** [*style*]

- The *object* can be any Form object.

- When the **Show** method is called, the specified form is displayed on the screen and becomes the active form (has focus).

- The optional *style* argument is an intrinsic constant that determines if the form is modal or modeless. A **modal form** must be closed before focus can switch to another form in the program. Modal forms, however, do not prevent the user from interacting with other applications, like Microsoft Word or Excel. Forms that allow a user to change focus from one to another are called **modeless forms**. If you call the Show method with no style argument, then the form is modeless. If you call the Show method with the intrinsic constant vbModal as the style argument, then the form is considered modal and must be unloaded or hidden before another form in the program can receive focus. A message box is an example of a modal form.

When the Show method is called, several different events occur, depending on the existing state of the form. The following steps describe what happens when a form first is loaded and becomes the active object:

1. When Visual Basic creates the instance of the Form object at run time, the Initialize event occurs first. This event only occurs the first time a form is loaded.

2. The Load event occurs next as Visual Basic begins to make the form the active object. When the form is a startup form, this event occurs only when a program starts and the form is loaded. Loading the form merely places the form and its objects into the computer's memory; it does not display the form on the screen. Once a form is loaded, you can write Visual Basic statements to interact with the form's objects like setting run-time properties even though the form may not be visible. This is useful if you want to set properties before the form first is displayed on the screen.

3. The Activate event occurs for the form after the form is loaded. A startup form is activated automatically after it is loaded. Each time the Show method is called or the form gets focus, the Activate event occurs.

4. After the form is activated, it becomes the active object and the GotFocus event occurs for the object with the TabIndex property of zero (0). A form can become active by user action, such as clicking the form, or by using the Show or SetFocus methods in code.

To display the startup form, you will call the Show method for the splash screen named frmSplash in the Sub Main procedure. This will cause the form to be initialized, loaded, and then activated.

To create the Sub Main procedure and write the statement to display the splash screen:

1. Be sure the Code window for the module named **Module1.bas** is active.

2. Click **Tools** then **Add Procedure** to open the Add Procedure dialog box.

3. Enter the name **Main**.

4. Click the **Sub** and **Public** option buttons, then click the **OK** button. The new procedure is activated in the Code window.

5. Enter the following statement, shown in bold, into the Code window to display the form named frmSplash:

```
Public Sub Main( )
    frmSplash.Show
End Sub
```

6. Save your changes to the module and project.

The final step to display the splash screen is to tell Visual Basic to start executing the procedure Sub Main when the program first is run rather than displaying the Main form that Mary already created. What happens first when a program is started is controlled by the startup object. When a project first is created with a single form, the startup object is set to the name of the form by default. You can change the startup object to any form in the program or the procedure Sub Main by modifying the project's properties.

REFERENCE window

SETTING THE STARTUP OBJECT

- Click **Project** then **Project1 Properties** on the menu bar to open the Project Properties dialog box.
- Be sure the **General** tab is active.
- Use the **Startup Object** list arrow to select the correct startup form or the Sub Main procedure.
- Click the **OK** button.

While you could make the splash screen the startup object, then have the splash screen load and display the next form, putting all the necessary statements to manipulate the forms in one procedure (Sub Main) will help improve the modularity of the program. Mary suggests you now change this project's properties so the Sub Main procedure you just wrote will be called when the program is run.

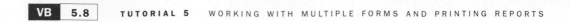

To change the startup object:

1. Click **Project** then **Project1 Properties** on the menu bar to open the Project Properties dialog box as shown in Figure 5-5.

Figure 5-5 ◀
Setting the
startup object

General tab is active ──

```
Project1 - Project Properties                              [x]

 General │ Make │ Compile │ Component │

  Project Type:                      Startup Object:
 [Standard EXE            ▼]        [frmMain              ▼]  ──→ Startup
  Project Name:                                                  Object list box
 [Project1                        ]
  Help File Name:                    Project Help
                                     Context ID:
 [                          ] [...]  [0        ]
  Project Description:
 [                                          ]

                         ┌─ Unattended Execution ──────────┐
                         │  ○ Thread per Object             │
 ☑ Upgrade ActiveX Controls │ ⊙ Thread Pool [1  ⬍] threads │
 ☐ Require License Key    └──────────────────────────────────┘

                    [   OK   ] [ Cancel ] [  Help  ]
```

2. Be sure the **General** tab is active, then click the **Startup Object** list arrow.

   Notice there are three objects listed in the Startup Object list box corresponding to each module in the project.

3. Select **Sub Main** then click the **OK** button.

4. Save the project.

You now have completed the necessary steps to display the splash screen when the program is started rather than displaying the Main form. Mary suggests you test your work to be sure the splash screen is being displayed.

To test that the splash screen is being displayed:

1. Start the program. The splash screen shown in Figure 5-6 should be displayed in the center of the screen.

Figure 5-6 ◀
Splash screen
at run time

TROUBLE? If the splash screen does not appear, you may have set the wrong project properties or written the statements in the wrong module. End the program and be sure you have set the startup object to Sub Main and the statement to call the Show method for the object named frmSplash in the Sub Main procedure. Repeat Step 1.

TROUBLE? If the form did not appear in the center of the screen, you did not set the form's properties correctly. End the program and set the frmSplash object's StartUpPosition property to 2 - CenterScreen. Repeat Step 1.

Notice the splash screen has no title bar or border because you set the BorderStyle property to 0 - None.

2. End the program.

Your program now uses the Sub Main general procedure to display the splash screen and then the Main form. You now are ready to insert and display the other forms needed by the program.

Inserting a Form from a Template

When the program starts, after the splash screen is displayed, Mary would like another form to be displayed. This second form, called a login form, will ask the user to enter a name and employee ID. This user information will be displayed on the printed reports, and ultimately will be recorded to database tables when changes are made.

While you could create the login form by adding a blank form to the project and creating the necessary labels, text boxes, and command buttons, Visual Basic supplies several templates of common forms that you can add to your project and modify slightly to perform a specific task. This makes the program development process much easier. A **template** is an existing form that provides a way for you to reuse components, like forms, and add them to projects. One template that Visual Basic provides is a login form template. This form is used to obtain a user name and password from the user before continuing to execute the program.

REFERENCE window	ADDING A TEMPLATE FORM TO YOUR PROJECT
	■ Click Project then Add Form on the menu bar to display the Add Form dialog box. ■ Click the New tab, if necessary. ■ Click the desired form template to add an About Dialog, Log In Dialog, Options Dialog, or Splash Screen. ■ Click Open to add the template to your project.

You now need to add the login template form to your program, and modify it to get the employee ID and employee name.

To add a login template to your project:

1. Click **Project** then **Add Form** on the menu bar to open the Add Form dialog box.

2. Click the **New** tab, if necessary.

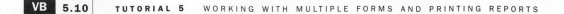

3. Click the **Log In Dialog** icon to add a login form to your program as shown in Figure 5-7.

Figure 5-7 ◄
Adding a
login form

New tab is active

select Log In
Dialog icon

TROUBLE? If the Log In Dialog icon does not appear, the template forms are not installed on the computer. Contact the administrator of your computer system.

4. Click the **Open** button.

The login form will appear as shown in Figure 5-8.

Figure 5-8 ◄
Login form

5. Save the project. Accept the default form name, **frmLogin**, when prompted.

If you show the splash screen then immediately show the login form, the login form may be displayed before the splash screen is painted completely because of the way Windows 95 processes events. To solve this problem, you can repaint completely the form using a method called Refresh supported by the Form object. The Refresh method has the following syntax:

Object.**Refresh**

■ *Object* is any valid form or control name.

■ The **Refresh** method will repaint completely the object on the screen.

After the splash screen is loaded and repainted on the screen, you need to load the login form. To load a form into the computer's memory without activating or displaying it on the screen, you use the Load statement. The Load statement has the following syntax:

Load *formname*

■ The *formname* can be any form in the project.

■ The **Load** method will place the form in the computer's memory, but not display it on the screen. You must call the Show or the SetFocus methods after the Load statement to display the form.

One technique used to speed up the process of displaying different project forms while the program is running is to load all the forms while the splash screen is displayed. Then you would call the Show method on a form to make it visible. It takes significantly less time to show a loaded form than to load it for the first time.

Before the login form is displayed on the screen, the splash screen needs to be hidden. There are two ways to make a form invisible.

- The first is to call the **Hide** method on a Form object. When the Hide method is called, the Visible property of the form is set to False, and the form no longer is visible on the screen. Thus, the user cannot interact with the form or any objects drawn on it. When a form is hidden, its objects still exist and can be referenced with Visual Basic code. If the Show method is called on a hidden form that has been loaded, then the Activate and GotFocus events will occur. Because the form already has been loaded, the Initialize and Load events will not occur again. The Hide method has the same syntax as the Show method.

- Another way of removing a form is to use the Unload statement. The **Unload** statement has the effect of removing the form and its associated objects from memory. When a form is unloaded, its objects no longer exist and cannot be referenced using Visual Basic code. If the Show method is called on a form that has been unloaded, then the Initialize, Load, Activate, and GotFocus events will occur again. The Unload statement has the same syntax as the Load statement.

> *Tip:* When a form will no longer by used by a program, call the Unload statement to free up the memory allocated to the form and its objects. This will help improve the performance of the program and other programs running on the computer.
>
> When a form may be used repeatedly in a program, but does not need to remain visible all the time, use the Hide and Show methods to make the form invisible and visible. It takes less time to show a form that is hidden than to load a form that has been unloaded.

Once the splash screen is removed from the screen, the login form can be displayed. When the login form is displayed, the user must be required to enter both their employee ID and name before continuing. Therefore, the login form needs to function like an input box. That is, the user must click a button on the login form and the form closed before the user can interact with another form in the program. To make the login form a modal form, you will call the Show method with the intrinsic constant vbModal as an argument.

Mary suggests you load all the forms in the project immediately after displaying the splash screen. Then, once the forms have been loaded, you can continue to unload the splash screen and then display the login form.

To load the project's forms and display the login form:

1. Add the following code to the Sub Main procedure in Module1 after the statement that displays the splash screen:

```
frmSplash.Refresh
Load frmLogin
Load frmMain
Unload frmSplash
frmLogin.Show vbModal
```

2. Save the project.

The first statement calls the Refresh method to force the splash screen to be repainted before continuing. After the splash screen has been painted, the login form and Main form are loaded into memory. After the login and Main forms are loaded, the splash screen is

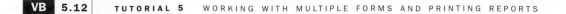

removed from the screen and the computer's memory with the Unload statement. If you had used the Hide method, the splash screen would continue to take up memory. Because the splash screen will not be used again, there is no need for it to remain in memory. Finally, the login form is displayed as a modal form using the Show method with the vbModal argument.

You now have completed the statements to display the splash screen, load the forms into memory, then display the login form. Mary suggests you now run the program to see that the login form is being displayed after the splash screen and that the splash screen is being removed from the screen.

To test that the login form is being displayed:

1. Start the program. The splash screen appears for a moment then disappears. After the splash screen is unloaded, the login form appears.

   TROUBLE? If the login form does not appear, make sure you called the Show method on the frmLogin object in the Sub Main procedure.

   TROUBLE? If the splash screen still is visible, be sure you called the Unload statement on the frmSplash object in the Sub Main procedure.

2. End the program.

Now that the login form appears in your program, you must modify the labels and statements to make sure the user enters the correct information. First, you need to change the contents of the labels and the names of the text boxes.

To modify the properties of the login form's objects:

1. Be sure the **login form** is the active window.

2. Change the Caption property of the first label from User Name: to **Employee ID**.

3. Change the Caption property of the second label from Password: to **Employee Name**.

   TROUBLE? If your new captions do not fit, you may need to resize the form, labels, and/or text boxes. Use the sizing handles to size the objects so the new captions will fit.

4. Change the Name property of the first text box from txtUserName to **txtEmployeeID.**

5. Change the Name property of the second text box from txtPassword to **txtEmployeeName**.

   The PasswordChar property is used to prevent the characters typed by the user from being displayed on the screen. If a character is placed in this property, that character will be displayed in the text box for each character typed by the user.

6. Delete the **asterisk** (*) from the PasswordChar property of the txtEmployeeName text box.

7. Save the project.

Next you need to write the code to hide the login form. Before you can write this code you need to learn to reference the current form. The **Me** keyword allows you to reference the current form without retyping the form name over and over. Thus, if you wanted to call the Hide method on the current form, you could write the following statement:

```
Me.Hide
```

This statement gives you a way to hide the current form after the information is entered. Remember the login form either must be hidden or unloaded before the user can interact with the rest of the program because it was displayed as a modal form. You need a way to check whether the user clicked the OK button or the Cancel button on the form. You can accomplish this by storing the value True or False in a Boolean variable declared in the login form, and then checking the value of that variable in the Sub Main procedure.

In the past, your programs have had only one form. When a variable needed to be used by more than one event or general procedure on a form, you have declared the variable in the general declarations section of the Form module using the Private keyword. Variables declared with the Private keyword, however, cannot be used by other forms or standard modules. To accomplish this, you must use the **Public** keyword. To declare a Public variable, you use the same syntax as you have used to declare Private variables. Thus, to declare a Public variable named LoginSucceeded that has a data type of Boolean you would use the following statement:

```
Public LoginSucceeded As Boolean
```

Public variables behave differently depending on whether they are declared in a Form module or a standard module. If they are declared in a Form module, they are referenced just like the properties of an object. Thus, when you want to reference the Public variable named LoginSucceeded in the Form module named frmLogin you will use the following statement:

```
frmLogin.LoginSucceeded
```

If a Public variable is declared inside a standard module, it can be referenced by any module in your program and is not considered a property. Rather it is called a global variable. A **global variable** is a variable that can be referenced by any module in a program and whose value exists while the program is running. It is referenced like the Private variable you already have used.

Because the Public variable is declared in a Form module and is treated as a property, you did not use the standard prefix for the variable. Rather, you used a name that looks like a property. Property names generally use complete words with the first letter of each word capitalized.

The Public variable was declared in the login form by the template, so you now are ready to write the statements to check that the user entered both an employee ID and a name when the OK button is clicked. If the information was entered, you need to set the variable LoginSucceeded to True. If not, you need to display a message box asking the user to enter the information. If the Cancel button is clicked, you need to set the variable LoginSucceeded to False. The login form template has code in it to validate the user name and password. This code needs to be modified to verify that the user entered a value in both of the text boxes when the OK button is clicked.

To modify the statements to validate the user input:

1. Activate the Code window for the **cmdOK_Click** event procedure in the login form. Remember your program has multiple forms, so be sure you are entering the code into the correct form.

2. Remove the existing code and replace it with the following statements:

```
Private Sub cmdOK_Click( )
    If txtEmployeeID.Text <> "" _
        And txtEmployeeName.Text <> "" Then
        LoginSucceeded = True
        Me.Hide
    Else
        MsgBox ("Enter your employee ID and name")
    End If
End Sub
```

The code for the cmdCancel button's Click event already has been written.

3. Activate the **cmdCancel_Click** event procedure and note that the statements set the variable LoginSucceeded to False and then call the Hide method.

4. Save the project.

This If statement tests that both of the text boxes contain data. If they do, then the variable LoginSucceeded is set to True. Otherwise a message box is displayed telling the user to enter his or her employee ID and name.

Now that you have programmed the OK button on the login form, you must write the necessary statements to determine whether the OK or Cancel button was clicked. This code needs to be written in the Sub Main procedure. After the user has filled in the information in the login form, the code will test the value of the variable LoginSucceeded and display the Main form in the program if it is True and end the program if it is False.

You now are ready to write the statements to determine whether or not the login was successful. Otherwise the program should exit. Remember, because this is a Public variable in a Form module it is treated just like any other form property. You will hide the form rather than unloading it because you will need to reference the LoginSucceeded property in the Sub Main procedure to determine if the login was successful and later when the report is printed. Remember, when a form is unloaded, its objects and variables are removed from the computer's memory and can no longer be used.

To add the statements to test that the login was successful:

1. Append the following statements to the end of the Sub Main procedure just before the End Sub statement:

```
If frmLogin.LoginSucceeded = False Then
    End
Else
    frmMain.Show
    frmLogin.Hide
End If
```

2. Save the project.

The If statement tests to determine the value of the Public variable named LoginSucceeded in the frmLogin form. Because this variable is considered a property of the form, you specify the object name (frmLogin) followed by a period (.), followed by the property name (LoginSucceeded). If the value of this variable is False, then the program will end. If it is True, then the Main form (frmMain) will be displayed. Even though the frmLogin form no longer appears on the screen, the form and its objects still exist. Because the information in the text boxes in frmLogin will be used when you print the reports in the next session, you hide the form rather then unloading it so the objects still exist.

You now have completed all the code to display the splash screen, the login form, and then the Main form. Mary suggests you run the program to test that each form is being displayed.

To test the program:

1. Start the program. The splash screen is displayed briefly while the other forms are loaded, then disappears and the login form is displayed. The login form appears as shown in Figure 5-9.

Figure 5-9 ◀
Login form
at run time

Employee ID ⟵ enter 100 here

Employee Name ⟵ enter your name

OK   Cancel

2. Enter **100** as the employee ID, then your name, then click the OK button to continue to display the Main form.

3. End the program.

Mary would like you to create two additional forms—one will display inventory data, and the other sales data. These forms each will use a Data control to establish a connection with a database table and bound text boxes to display that data just like the form you created in Tutorial 4. Instead of creating a new form, however, and then all the necessary objects, you can use a wizard. A **wizard** is a tool that leads a user step-by-step through an unusually long, difficult, or complex programming task. The wizard you will use to create the form for you is called the Data Form Wizard. The Data Form Wizard works by asking you to complete a series of questions in several dialog boxes that tell the wizard the database, table, and fields you want to use. After you have answered the questions, the wizard will create the form for you. It will not only create the Data control and bound text boxes, but also can create and write code for command buttons to insert, update, and delete records.

Mary suggests you now use the Data Form Wizard to create a form that will display data from the inventory table.

To use the Data Form Wizard to create a form:

1. Click **Project** then **Add Form** to display the Add Form dialog box.

TROUBLE? If you get an introductory Add Form dialog box, click the Don't show this dialog in the future check box and click OK.

TROUBLE? If you are using Visual Basic 5.0 Learning Edition, there are no Wizards. You will have to create a form that resembles Figure 5-16 on your own and connect it to the appropriate fields in the database Pacific.mdb in the Tutorial.05 folder on your Student Disk.

2. Click the **New** tab, if necessary, then double-click **VB Data Form Wizard**. When the Data Form Wizard – Introduction dialog box displays, click the Next button. The Database Type dialog box will appear as shown in Figure 5-10.

Figure 5-10 ◀
Database Type
dialog box

select Access to set
the Data control's
Connect property

click Next to proceed

3. Select **Access**. This sets the Connect property for your Data control. Click the **Next** button. The Database dialog box shown in Figure 5-11 appears on your screen.

Figure 5-11 ◀
Database
dialog box

enter Database Name here
to set the Data control's
DatabaseName property

click Next to proceed

4. Set the Database Name to **Pacific.mdb** in the **Tutorial.05** folder on your Student Disk. This sets the DatabaseName property for your Data control. Click the **Next** button to display the Form dialog box shown in Figure 5-12.

Figure 5-12 ◀
Form
dialog box

preview of form

Single record option
button selected

click Next to proceed

The Form dialog box is used to tell the Data Form Wizard how the data should appear on the form. You can select from three different option buttons:

- If the Single record option button is selected, the form will be created so only one record will be displayed at a time. This is like the form you created in Tutorial 4.

- If the Grid (Datasheet) option button is selected, the form will display several records at a time in a grid. Each record will appear on a single line and each field will appear in a column.

- If the Master/Detail option button is selected, the form will operate with two tables.

Mary would like a single record to appear on the form at a time so you will select the Single record option button.

To create a form that will display a single record:

1. Click each of the option buttons and observe the display preview.

2. Click the **Single record** option button, then click the **Next** button to display the Record Source dialog box shown in Figure 5-13.

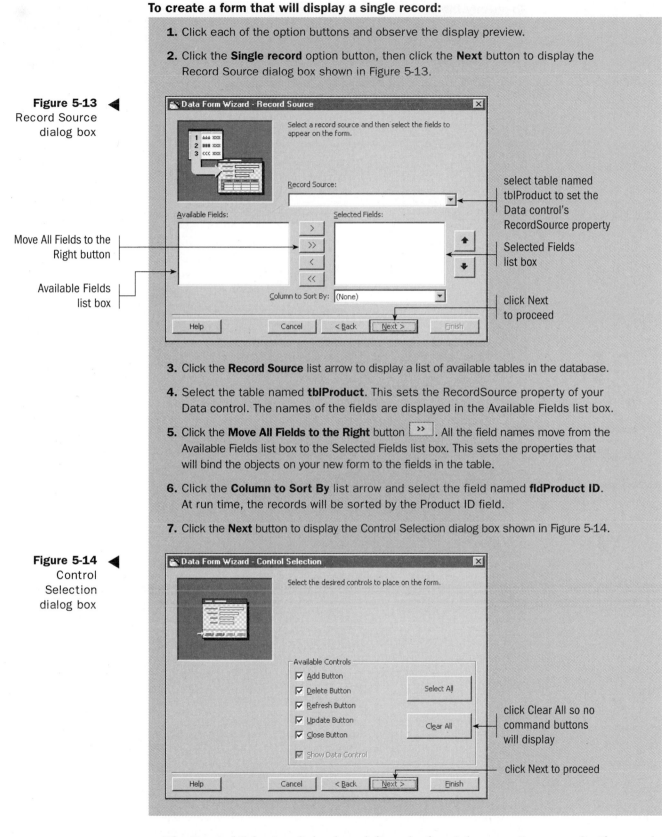

Figure 5-13 ◄
Record Source
dialog box

Move All Fields to the
Right button

Available Fields
list box

select table named
tblProduct to set the
Data control's
RecordSource property

Selected Fields
list box

click Next
to proceed

Figure 5-14 ◄
Control
Selection
dialog box

click Clear All so no
command buttons
will display

click Next to proceed

3. Click the **Record Source** list arrow to display a list of available tables in the database.

4. Select the table named **tblProduct**. This sets the RecordSource property of your Data control. The names of the fields are displayed in the Available Fields list box.

5. Click the **Move All Fields to the Right** button. All the field names move from the Available Fields list box to the Selected Fields list box. This sets the properties that will bind the objects on your new form to the fields in the table.

6. Click the **Column to Sort By** list arrow and select the field named **fldProduct ID**. At run time, the records will be sorted by the Product ID field.

7. Click the **Next** button to display the Control Selection dialog box shown in Figure 5-14.

The Control Selection dialog box defines the form's buttons. For example, if you only wanted the user to see the navigation buttons on the Data control, you would not check any of the boxes. Mary wants the salespeople only to look at product information, so you will not add any command buttons to the form.

To specify the buttons that will be created on the form:

1. Click the **Clear All** button so all the Available Controls check boxes are not checked, then click the **Next** button to display the Finished! dialog box shown in Figure 5-15.

Figure 5-15 ◀
Finished
dialog box

use form's
default name

click the Finish button
to create the form

2. The Data Form Wizard has provided a default name for the form. Click the **Finish** button to accept the default name and create the form. The Data Form Wizard creates the form and adds it to your project.

TROUBLE? If you see a dialog box telling you that the form has been created, the Visual Basic setup on your computer is slightly different. Click the OK button.

The new form is shown in Figure 5-16.

Figure 5-16 ◀
Completed
form

bound text boxes

Data control

3. Save the form and the project. Accept the default form name when prompted.

The Data Form Wizard has created the Data control to communicate with a table in the database. Also, four bound text boxes have been created, corresponding to each of the fields in the table, and labels were created based on the field names. You now should change the title of the form and the caption of each label to improve the appearance of the form.

To change the form's title and the captions of each label:

1. Change the form's caption from tblProduct to **Pacific Electronics - Product Table**.

2. Remove the 'fld' prefix from each label's caption.

Although the form has been created, the Data Form Wizard has not written the code to display the form on the screen. Mary would like the form to be loaded with the other forms when the program is started and displayed when the user clicks the product item on the Main form's View menu. Therefore you need to call the Show method in the mnuViewProduct object's Click event procedure. The form should be loaded in the Sub Main procedure. While this form could be displayed as a modal form, Mary would like the user to be able to interact with the Main form and this form at the same time, so you will not display it as a modal form.

To write the code to load and display the Product form:

1. Activate the Code window for the **mnuViewProduct_Click** event procedure on the form named frmMain.

2. Enter the following statement, shown in bold, into the event procedure:

```
Private Sub mnuViewProduct_Click( )
    frmtblProduct.Show
End Sub
```

3. Activate the Code window for the **Sub Main** procedure in Module1.

4. Add the following statement to the Sub Main procedure immediately after the statement to load the Main form.

```
Load frmtblProduct
```

5. Save the project.

Now that you have created the form to display the list of products and wrote the code to open the form, Mary suggests you test the program to be sure it is working properly.

To test the View Product menu item and the Product form:

1. Start the project.

2. Enter **100** as the employee ID, then your name into the login form, then click the **OK** button. The Main form appears.

3. Click **View** then **Product** on the Main form's menu bar. The Product Table form appears as shown in Figure 5-17.

Figure 5-17 ◀
Completed
form at
run time

4. End the program.

The program for Pacific Electronics now displays the splash screen and login form. After the login form is displayed, and the user enters an employee ID and name, the Main form is displayed. The user can click the menu items to display the other forms as necessary.

Quick Check

1 What is the purpose of the startup object?

2 What is the purpose of a splash screen?

3 Describe the events that occur when the Show method is called?

4 What is the difference between the Hide method and the Unload statement?

5 What is a modal form?

6 What is the Data Form Wizard used for?

You have completed this session; you can take a break or continue on to Session 5.2.

SESSION 5.2

In this session you will design a sales report of sales records contained in a database. You will connect to the database using a Data control on the Main form, write code to print each record by enclosing the statements in a loop, write code to interact directly with the fields in the Recordset object, and use a counter and an accumulator to compute total orders and sales totals.

Specifying the Information for the Sales Report

In Session 4.2 you used the Data control to create a Recordset object based on the information you specified for the DatabaseName and RecordSource properties. In Session 5.1 you also used the Data control but it was created for you by the Data Form Wizard. In this session you again will use the Data control to create a Recordset object at run time. This Recordset object, however, will be based on information from two tables instead of one.

You can combine information from two or more tables by creating a query. Mary already has created the query using Access. Refer to the Database Appendix for more information on creating a query. Figure 5-18 shows the records and fields in the query.

Figure 5-18 ◀
Pacific
Electronics
sales query

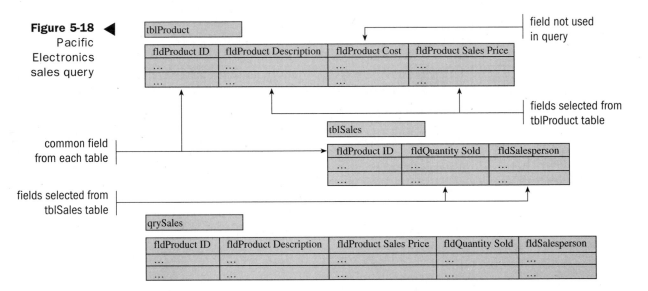

The query contains information from the tables named tblProduct and tblSales. The tblProduct table contains the Product Description, Product Cost, and Product Sales Price fields. The tblSales table contains the Quantity Sold and Salesperson fields. The Product ID is contained in both tables and is used to join them together in the query.

Before you can print any sales reports, you must connect the Main form to the database, Pacific.mdb, in the Tutorial.05 folder on your Student Disk. The user will not use this form to view the records in the database, only to print a report.

To connect the Main form to the sales query:

1. Start Visual Basic and open the project file named **Pacific Sales Report.vbp** in the Tutorial.05 folder on your Student Disk. If necessary, display the Main form.

2. Click the **Data** control ▦ on the toolbox and draw an instance of the Data control across the bottom of the form. See Figure 5-19.

3. Set the DatabaseName property of the Data control to **Pacific.mdb** in the **Tutorial.05** folder on your Student Disk, and set the RecordSource property to **qrySales**.

4. Set the Caption property to **datSales** and the Name property of the Data control to **datSales**.

5. Set the Visible property to **False**. Because Mary does not want the user to use the buttons on the Data control, it should not be visible at run time. Your form looks like Figure 5-19.

Figure 5-19 ◀
Creating the
Data control on
the Main form

Data control ────────

You can use the Recordset object created with the Data control to access the information in the sales database. In the form you opened, Mary already has created menu items to print the sales report. Now you can begin to design and create the sales report based on the information in the sales database.

Designing a Report

Just as a well-designed form makes the user interface of a program easy to use, a well-designed report makes the report easy to read and understand. In general, a report should have a page title that describes the report. Reports often are organized into columns. Each column should have a title that describes the information contained in the column, and the columns should be spaced evenly on the page. That is, the left and right margins should be the same, the spacing between the columns should be uniform, and numeric data should be aligned such that the decimal points are aligned under each other. Figure 5-20 illustrates the sales report you will create in this session.

Figure 5-20 ◀
Sales Report
layout

page title ───

column titles ───

report totals ───

detail lines ───

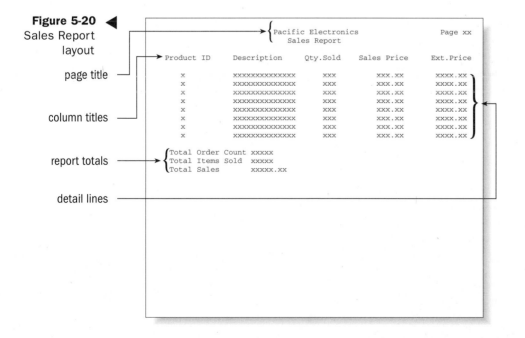

In addition to the page title and column titles, the report includes detail lines. When you print the detail lines of your report, you print a line for each record in the recordset. To do this, you execute the same statements repeatedly for each record printed in the report. When you print the detail records, you use variables to count the number of orders and accumulate the number of items ordered and total sales. After all the records have been processed, the report prints the totals below the detail lines.

Refer to your NEADT charts. The page and column titles need to print first. Then each detail line needs to print. After each record has been processed, the report totals print. All these activities will occur when the user clicks the Sales Report item on the Reports menu.

Some reports are more complicated than the one you will create, but the basic logic of printing a report is useful for beginning nearly every report you print. Although you could write all the code to print the report in a single event procedure, you instead will divide the code into different general procedures, as you did in Tutorial 3 when you computed the order totals in the cash register program. This process of dividing a task into multiple subtasks is called **modularization**. Dividing your programs into multiple procedures, also called **component modules**, simplifies the debugging process, because you can identify the procedure containing an error and focus on only those few lines of code. As your program grows, you can use component modules in other sections of the program or in other programs. This will save time in the development process. The program you will complete for Mary will include one general procedure to print the titles, one to print the detail lines, and one to print the report totals.

Printing a Report with the Printer Object

There are several ways of printing text and graphics in Visual Basic. In this session you will learn how to print using the **Printer** object, which initially is set to the default system printer from the Printers collection. A **collection** is an object that contains similar objects. It is simply a way of grouping like objects together. Although you have not worked with them explicitly, the Controls collection lists all the controls on a form and the Recordsets collection identifies the open Recordset objects in a database. The Printers collection contains each of the printers defined on your system. Visual Basic sets the Printer object to the default printer on your system. Just as the Recordset object supports several methods to manipulate data in a database table or query, the Printer object supports different methods to control how your output will be printed on the page. In this tutorial you will use the Font property, and EndDoc, NewPage, and Print methods of the Printer object.

The Font property sets the font for the printer. Depending on the type of printer attached to your computer, different fonts may be available. You can use the Windows 95 Control Panel to view the different fonts on your printer. The Font property has the following syntax:

object.**Font** = "*font name*"

- The *object* can be a Form, Printer, or any other object that supports the **Font** property.

- The *font name*, enclosed in quotation marks, can be any valid font installed on your computer. Note that the screen fonts that apply to a Form object and the printer fonts that apply to the Printer object may differ.

Many fonts are proportional. That is, the space used by a character depends on the size of the character. Thus, the letter "I" will take up less space than the letter "W". When printing reports, this is not always desirable because it is difficult to align a decimal point exactly when printing columns of numbers. Monospace fonts can be used in this situation. A monospace font uses the same amount of space for each character. One of the most common monospace fonts is named Courier New, and is available on nearly every computer and printer. Mary suggests you set the font in the Form_Load event procedure so all printing in this program will use this font.

To set the printer font:

1. Activate the Code window for the form named **frmMain**.

2. Enter the following statement, shown in bold, into the Form_Load event procedure:

```
Private Sub Form_Load( )
    Printer.Font = "Courier New"
End Sub
```

One method supported by the Printer object is the Print method. You will use the Print method of the Printer object more than any other method. The Print method has the following syntax:

[*object.*]**Print** *outputlist*

- The **Print** method prints text to the *object*—a form, printer, or the Immediate window. If you call the Print method without an object, the text will be printed to the form from which it is called. The Print method accepts optional arguments that define the text to be printed and the format of the text. If an object is specified, the object and Print method are separated by a period.

- The *outputlist* describes the text to be printed, and how that text is formatted. It has the following syntax:

[**Spc**(*number*) | **Tab**(*number*)] *expression* [*character-position*]

  - The *expression* represents the data to print. It can be a text string enclosed in quotation marks, a variable, or a reference to a property of an object.

  - If the optional **Spc** argument is included, space characters will be inserted in the output before the *expression* is printed. The space characters are inserted after the previously printed characters. The number of space characters inserted is specified by the *number* argument. The **Spc** argument is useful for inserting a fixed number of spaces between the column titles in a report.

  - If the optional **Tab** argument is included, the *expression* will be inserted at the absolute column number specified by the *number* argument. The **Tab** argument is useful for aligning all the detail lines to the correct column. Using **Spc** or **Tab** is often a matter of personal preference.

  - The optional *character-position* argument specifies the insertion point for the next *expression*. If you place a semicolon here, the insertion point of the next *expression* immediately follows the last character displayed. The default *character-position* is the first absolute column on a new line.

The NewPage method ends the current page and advances to the next page on the printer. The NewPage method has the following syntax:

Printer.NewPage

- The **NewPage** method advances to the next printer page and resets the print position to the upper-left corner of the new page. If you have printed only a partial page when the NewPage method is called, the partial page is printed and any other text you send with the Print method appears on the next page.

- The **Printer** object also supports a **Page** property that keeps track of the current page number. The Page property initially is set to one (1). Each time the **NewPage** method is called, it increases the Printer object's Page property by one (1). Also, if a page becomes full, and a new page is started, the Page property will be incremented by one (1).

The EndDoc method ends a print operation sent to the Printer object. The EndDoc method has the following syntax:

Printer.EndDoc

- When the **EndDoc** method is called, any unprinted text sent to the **Printer** object with the Print method is printed. If you have printed only a partial page when the EndDoc method is called, the partial page is printed.

- After the **EndDoc** method is called, the Page property of the **Printer** object is set to one (1) again.

Each time you call the Print method, the information is not immediately sent to the printer. Rather the information is stored in the printer buffer. The **printer buffer** is an area of the computer's memory that holds printed output before it is sent to the printer. When this buffer is full, or the EndDoc method is called, the information is sent to the printer. You will use the EndDoc method to send any information remaining in the printer buffer to the printer after the titles, detail lines, and report totals have been printed.

Printing a Page Title on a Report

The first step in printing the report is to print the page title across the top of the page and then the column titles spaced evenly across the page. You will create a general procedure to do this. Remember, you should name a general procedure so you can recognize easily what it does. In this case, Mary suggests you name this general procedure PrintTitles. As with any general procedure, it must be called explicitly from a general or event procedure. Mary suggests you place these procedures in the Main form containing the Sales Report menu item because they only will be used by this form. You could create a standard module for the general procedures, and then the module could be used by more than one program easily.

You need to print the report titles in the PrintTitles general procedure, as shown in Figure 5-21. Notice the page titles are positioned using the Tab( ) argument and the column titles are positioned relative to each other using the Spc( ) argument.

Figure 5-21 ◄
Sales report
headings

15 spaces; Spc(15)

column 31; Tab(31)

column 34; Tab(34)

5 spaces; Spc(5)

To print the page and column titles on the Sales Report:

1. Activate the Code window for the form named **frmMain**.

2. Click **Tools** on the menu bar, then click **Add Procedure**. The Add Procedure dialog box opens.

3. In the Name text box, type **PrintTitles**. Click the **Sub** and **Public** option buttons, then click the **OK** button. The new procedure is activated in the Code window.

WORKING WITH MULTIPLE FORMS AND PRINTING REPORTS   **TUTORIAL 5**   **VB** **5.25**

4. Enter the following code into the procedure (shown in bold):

```
Private Sub PrintTitles( )
    Printer.Print Tab(31); "Pacific Electronics";
    Printer.Print Spc(15); "Page ", Printer.Page
    Printer.Print Tab(34); "Sales Report"
    Printer.Print ""
    Printer.Print Tab(6); "Product ID";
    Printer.Print Spc(5); "Description";
    Printer.Print Spc(5); "Qty. Sold";
    Printer.Print Spc(5); "Sales Price";
    Printer.Print Spc(5); "Ext. Price"
    Printer.Print ""
End Sub
```

When the statements in the PrintTitles general procedure are executed, they will print the page and column titles shown in Figure 5-21 to the printer. Remember, nothing actually may be sent to the printer until the Printer.EndDoc method is called. Information only is sent to the printer when the printer buffer becomes full or the EndDoc method is called.

The first three statements use the Print method of the Printer object to print a title on the report containing the company name (Pacific Electronics), page number, and report name (Sales Report), respectively. The Tab argument is used to position the text on the lines; the first line is indented 31 characters and the second line is indented 34 characters so the page title will be centered on the lines. Notice that each Tab argument is followed by a semicolon so the next argument (the company name or report name) will print on the same line, immediately following this argument. If a semicolon (;) does not appear, the Printer object moves to the leftmost column of the next line. The page number is printed at the right margin. The fourth statement uses the Print method of the Printer object with a null string so the page title will be separated visually from the column titles by a blank line.

The next five statements print the column titles. You could have called the Print method once to print the line of column titles; however, if you placed all these titles on the same line of code, it would not fit in one screen and would be difficult to read. Breaking the task down into several statements that call the Print method improves the readability of your program. In these statements, the Spc argument prints five spaces between each of the columns. The first four lines end with semicolons because you want to print each of the five column titles on the same line. After printing the last column title (Ext. Price), the Printer object moves to the next line. The final statement prints a blank line to separate the column titles from the detail records that will be printed.

Printing the Detail Lines on a Report

Now that you have written the code to print the page and column titles in the sales report, you must write the code to print each of the sales records. You will use an object variable to set the Recordset object to access the sales data contained in the database Mary created.

Creating an Object Variable

As in Tutorial 4, you will create an object variable to reference the Recordset object. You will declare a Private object variable in the general declarations section of the Form module for the form named frmMain, because the variable will be used by several procedures in this form but will not be used by any other forms. Using this variable will save typing, because you will be able to use a short variable name in place of datSales.Recordset each time you reference the recordset. The mnuReportsSalesReport_Click event procedure needs to perform all the tasks to print the sales report. One of these tasks is initializing the object variable. Therefore, you will set the value of the object variable to the current recordset in this event procedure.

The first step is to declare the object variable that will reference the Recordset object created by the Data control at run time.

To create an object variable that points to the datSales.Recordset object:

1. Activate the general declarations section of the Form module for the form named **frmMain**.

2. Append the following statement to the general declarations after the Option Explicit statement:

```
Private mrstSales as Recordset
```

3. Activate the Code window for the **mnuReportsSalesReport** object's **Click** event procedure.

4. Enter the following code in the window:

```
Set mrstSales = datSales.Recordset
```

The statement in the general declarations section creates a new Recordset object variable named mrstSales, which can be used wherever you would use datSales.Recordset. The prefix "m" indicates that this is a module-level variable, and "rst" indicates that the variable references a Recordset object. This will help reduce typing and make your program easier to read. The Private statement you wrote only creates an object variable.

The Set statement you wrote in the mnuReportsSalesReport_Click event points the variable mrstSales to an existing Recordset object, which is created for you by the Data control at run time. This Recordset object variable can be used by all the procedures in this form because you declared it as a Private variable in the general declarations section of the Form module.

Now that you have created the mrstSales object variable and set it to the Recordset property of the Data control, mrstSales references a valid instance of a Recordset object at run time. You can use this variable to reference the contents of the current record and send the different fields of the record to the printer buffer. To do this, you need to use this object variable in a set of statements that will print each record of the database in turn.

Creating a Do Loop

Because the program must examine, compute totals for, and print each record from the sales query, you need a way to execute the same statements repeatedly. A **Do loop** repeats a block of statements while a condition is True or until a condition becomes True. The Do loop has the following syntax:

Do [While|Until] *condition*

   statements

Loop

- The **Do** statement evaluates the *condition* before any of the statements are executed.

- If you use the **While** keyword, the *statements* are executed while the *condition* is True, the *condition* is tested again and, if it still is True, the *statements* are executed again. Whenever the *condition* becomes False, the loop exits, and the statement after the **Loop** statement is executed.

- If you use the **Until** keyword, the *statements* are executed until the *condition* is True. Then the loop exits and the statement after the **Loop** statement is executed.

You will use a Do loop to move one by one through each sales record in the new Recordset object you created, until there are no more records in the recordset. When there are no more records in the Recordset object, the end of the recordset has been reached. Every Recordset object has an **EOF** (End Of File) property that is False whenever there are more records in the Recordset object and True when the end of the file has been reached. You will use the EOF property of the mrstSales object variable to determine when there are no more sales records to process. You also will use the MoveNext method of the Recordset object like you did in Tutorial 4 to move one by one through each sales record in a Do Until loop. The Do loop you will use has the following format:

```
Do Until mrstSales.EOF = True
    statements
    mrstSales.MoveNext
Loop
```

This syntax shows only a prototype for moving through the Recordset object. You will insert statements to print each of the sales records contained in the current Recordset object.

You will test the Do loop and Print method statements for the detail lines of your report as you develop them. This way, you can locate and correct errors by looking at small pieces of code rather than having to debug a large procedure. First, you will test the loop structure by printing a test string to the Immediate window. (For more information on the Immediate window and the Debug.Print method refer to Appendix A.) The menu item must initialize the object variable before it does anything else, so you will add the Do loop after the Set statement in the Sales Report menu item's Click event procedure.

To create the Do loop structure for the sales report:

1. Activate the Code window for the **mnuReportsSalesReport** object's **Click** event procedure in the form named frmMain.

2. Append the following statements to the end of the procedure, just before the End Sub line:

```
Do Until mrstSales.EOF = True
    Debug.Print "RecordFound"
    mrstSales.MoveNext
Loop
```

3. Save the project.

This loop first checks the EOF property of the Recordset object. If the EOF property is not True, it executes the statements and tests the condition again.

```
Do Until mrstSales.EOF = True
```

The Do Until statement looks at the EOF property of the Recordset object. If the end of file has not been reached (EOF = False), the statements inside the loop are executed. If the end of file has been reached (EOF = True), there are no more records in the Recordset object and the loop exits.

```
Debug.Print "RecordFound"
```

The Debug.Print statement uses the Print method of the Debug object. You can print information in the Immediate window by using the Print method of the Debug object. The Print method of the Debug object works just like the Print method of the Printer object, except that you do not need to call the EndDoc method to send the text to the Immediate window. The Print method of the Debug object can be called only at run time. Refer to the Debugging Appendix for more information about the Debug.Print statement.

The text string RecordFound is the argument to the Debug.Print statement. It will be printed in the Immediate window every time the loop executes. In addition to text strings, you can print variables and object properties to the Immediate window at run time. If your program is not working properly, you can include Debug.Print statements inside any general or event procedure to trace the execution of the program and look at the values of variables and objects.

```
        mrstSales.MoveNext
Loop
```

After the text string is printed to the Immediate window, the MoveNext method positions the current record pointer at the next sales record in the Recordset object. When the Loop keyword is reached, the Do Until statement is executed again and the EOF property of the Recordset object variable is tested to determine if there are more records to process.

You have written enough code at this point to test the program and determine if the loop is accessing each of the records in the Recordset object and terminating correctly.

To test that the Do Until loop is working properly:

1. Click **View** then **Immediate window** on the menu bar to open the Immediate window.

2. Start the program, then run it.

3. Position and size the Immediate window so you can see it and the form named frmMain at the same time.

4. Enter **100** as the employee ID entry, then your name into the login form. Click the **OK** button.

5. Click **Reports** then **Sales Report** on the Main form's menu bar.

   The text "RecordFound" prints in the Immediate window seven times, once for each sales record.

   TROUBLE? If your program displays the line of text without stopping after the seventh time, you have created an error called an infinite loop. This is a common problem with Do loops. In this case, it would happen if the Recordset object never reached the end of file. End the program by pressing Ctrl+Break and make sure that the Do loop matches the code in the previous steps and that the MoveNext method is being called inside the Do loop. Save the project and repeat Steps 2 through 5.

6. End the program.

Mary is satisfied that the Do loop works correctly and finds each record. Because the Do loop and the Debug.Print statement work, you can continue to develop the program. You will replace the Debug.Print statement with the statements that will print the detail lines for the report. The statements to print each record in the Recordset object will be enclosed in a general procedure, just as the titles were. The Click event procedure for the Sales Report command button will call this general procedure once for each record to print the report. Therefore, the code in the Click event procedure will be much shorter and simpler to comprehend.

Printing the Detail Lines

The general procedure you will create will print each record in the Sales Report each time the loop is executed. For each record, you need to print the Product ID, Product Description, and other fields in columns so each field appears under its corresponding column title. To align each field to the exact position of its column title, you will use the Tab( ) argument of the Print method. The information you need to print will come from the fields of the Recordset object.

Before you can print a field inside a Recordset object, you need to learn how to write the syntax to reference the field in Visual Basic. The fields that make up the Recordset object are considered members of the Fields collection of the Recordset object. Referencing a collection member is similar to referencing the different properties of an object. When you refer to an object's properties, you use the following syntax:

ObjectName.PropertyName

When you reference a particular object in a collection, you use an exclamation point (!) instead of a period (.). So, to reference a specific member (field) in a Recordset object, you use the following syntax:

RecordsetName!FieldName

Unlike Visual Basic variable and object names, field names in Access databases can contain spaces. So that the Microsoft Jet database engine knows you are using a field with an embedded space, you must put the field name in brackets. When field names do not contain spaces, the brackets are optional.

> *Tip:* Using brackets will help the reader of your program know that you are referring to a field name.

To reference the Product ID field in the Recordset object mrstSales, you would use the following statement:

```
mrstSales![Product ID]
```

Before you can write the procedure, you need to know the different fields in the Recordset object. Figure 5-22 shows the fields you need to print in the Sales Report.

Figure 5-22 ◄
Fields in the
Recordset
object

Field name	Description
fldProduct ID	Product identification number
fldProduct Description	Description of product
fldQuantity Sold	Quantity sold of product
fldProduct Sales Price	Sales price of product

The extended price is not a field stored in the database. Rather, you will compute this value by multiplying the quantity sold by the product sales price.

You will create a general procedure to print the current record's fields. In this general procedure you will use a variable to calculate and hold the temporary value of the extended price. Again, this general procedure should be Private because it only will be used by this module. It also should be declared as a Sub procedure because it does not return any information to the calling procedure.

Because the product sales price and extended price fields contain currency information, each column should be formatted such that the decimal points are aligned. This will give the report a professional appearance. To do this you need to learn about a new statement and how to use a fixed-length string. Until now each string you have created has been a variable-length string; that is, the size of the string depended on the number of characters stored in the string. You now need a way, however, to allocate a fixed number of characters to hold the product sales price and extended price and align the information into the rightmost characters of the string.

To declare a fixed-length string, you use the following syntax.

Dim *varname* **As String** * *size*

- The *varname* can be any valid variable name.
- The *size* argument represents the exact size of the string. For example, to declare a string that will store three characters you would set *size* to 3.

For example, the statement:

```
Dim pstrQuantitySold As String * 3
```

always will store three characters in the pstrQuantitySold variable. If the quantity sold is 4, pstrQuantitySold will store two placeholder characters in addition to the "4". You also need a way to store characters in the string so they are stored in the rightmost characters. By default, when you store characters in a fixed-length string, they are stored in the string from left to right. If there are not enough characters to fill the string, spaces are stored in the remaining characters. This can be accomplished using the RSet statement. The **RSet** statement has the following syntax:

RSet *stringvar* = *string*

- The **RSet** statement takes two arguments.
- The *string* argument contains the source string or input string.
- The *string* then is stored in *stringvar* such that the rightmost characters are filled first. Spaces are stored in any remaining characters in a fixed-length string.

For example, the statement:

```
RSet pstrQuantitySold = Str(mrstSales![fldQuantitySold])
```

will send to the printer the quantity sold fixed string such that the rightmost characters are filled first, that is, "4" on the far right, then the two spaces to the left.

You now will add the statements that will print and format the detail lines for your report.

To write the statements to print the current record's fields:

1. Activate the Code window for **frmMain**.

2. Click **Tools** on the menu bar, then click **Add Procedure** to open the Add Procedure dialog box.

3. In the Add Procedure dialog box, create a form-level Sub procedure named **PrintDetail**.

   The Code window activates the procedure you just created.

4. Enter the following code into the procedure (shown in bold):

```
Private Sub PrintDetail( )
    Dim pcurExtPrice As Currency
    Dim pstrQuantitySold As String * 3
    Dim pstrSalesPrice As String * 6
    Dim pstrExtPrice As String * 7

    pcurExtPrice = mrstSales![fldQuantity Sold] * _
        mrstSales![fldProduct Sales Price]

    Printer.Print Tab(5); mrstSales![fldProduct ID];
    Printer.Print Tab(21); _
        mrstSales![fldProduct Description];
    RSet pstrQuantitySold =
        Str(mrstSales![fldQuantity Sold])
```

```
    Printer.Print Tab(39); pstrQuantitySold;
    RSet pstrSalesPrice = _
        Format(mrstSales![fldProduct Sales Price], "Fixed")

    Printer.Print Tab(53);
    Printer.Print pstrSalesPrice;
    RSet pstrExtPrice = Format(pcurExtPrice, "Fixed")
    Printer.Print Tab(68); pstrExtPrice
End Sub
```

5. Save the project.

When the statements in the PrintDetail general procedure are executed, they will print the contents of each field in the current record to the printer buffer. Remember, nothing actually may be sent to the printer until the Printer.EndDoc method is called. You want the page and column titles, the detail lines, and the totals to be printed together, so you will not call the EndDoc method until you have printed all the information by calling the general procedures.

```
Dim pcurExtPrice As Currency
Dim pstrQuantitySold As String * 3
Dim pstrSalesPrice As String * 6
Dim pstrExtPrice As String * 7
```

These statements declare the variables. The variable pcurExtPrice will hold the value of the extended price for the current record. The Currency data type is used to store variables representing dollars and cents. The variables pstrQuantitySold, pstrSalesPrice, and pstrExtPrice are the fixed-length strings that will be used to display the output.

```
pcurExtPrice = mrstSales![fldQuantity Sold] * _
    mrstSales![fldProduct Sales Price]
```

This statement computes the total sales amount for an item (the extended price) by multiplying the quantity sold by the product sales price and storing the result in the local variable pcurExtPrice.

```
Printer.Print Tab(5); mrstSales![fldProduct ID];
Printer.Print Tab(21); _
    mrstSales![fldProduct Description];
RSet pstrQuantitySold = Str(mrstSales![fldQuantity Sold])

Printer.Print Tab(39); pstrQuantitySold;
RSet pstrSalesPrice = _
    Format(mrstSales![fldProduct Sales Price], "Fixed")

Printer.Print Tab(53);
Printer.Print pstrSalesPrice;
RSet pstrExtPrice = Format(pcurExtPrice, "Fixed")
Printer.Print Tab(68); pstrExtPrice
```

These Printer.Print statements look similar to the statements you wrote to create the page title. Instead of simply printing text strings enclosed in quotation marks, however, these statements print information from the mrstSales object. Each Printer.Print statement moves to the appropriate column, as specified by the Tab function, and prints the contents of the fixed-length string the current record. The Product Sales Price value will be formatted with two decimal places using the Fixed argument and then stored in the fixed-length string right-justified. Because the Tab and field name arguments end with a semicolon, each argument is printed on the same line. The final Printer.Print statement moves to the final column, prints the value of the temporary variable, formatted with two decimal places, and moves to the first column of the next line.

Now you can modify the Sales Report menu item's Click event procedure to print the report. All you need to do is call the general procedure PrintTitles to print the report titles and the general procedure PrintDetail, where the Debug.Print statement currently is called to print the detail lines when the menu item is clicked.

To modify the Click event procedure to call the print procedures:

1. Activate the Code window for the **mnuReportsSalesReport** object's **Click** event procedure.

2. Change the contents of the event procedure as shown in bold:

```
Private Sub mnuReportsSalesReport_Click( )
    Set mrstSales = datSales.Recordset
    'Print the report title and column titles
    PrintTitles
    Do Until mrstSales.EOF = True
        'Print a detail line on the report
        PrintDetail
        mrstSales.MoveNext
    Loop
    'Send the contents of the printer buffer to the
    'printer
    Printer.EndDoc
End Sub
```

3. Save the project.

The first statement you added calls the PrintTitles general procedure. It is called only once, because the titles should appear only once on the report. Therefore, this statement is outside the Do loop.

Next, the Do loop prints the contents of each record by calling the PrintDetail general procedure, and steps through each record in the Recordset object by calling the MoveNext method. The MoveNext method must be called after the PrintDetail general procedure is called. If the program called the MoveNext method first, it would skip over the first record in the Recordset object before printing, and the first record would never be printed.

```
Printer.EndDoc
```

This statement calls the EndDoc method. All the information stored in the printer buffer is sent to the Printer object—your default printer.

Mary suggests you test the program at this point to verify that the Sales Report is working properly.

To test the Sales Report:

1. Start the program, then complete the information in the login form.

2. Click **Reports** then **Sales Report** on the Main form's menu bar. Your Sales Report looks like Figure 5-23.

Figure 5-23 ◀
Sales Report
with detail lines

```
                     Pacific Electronics            Page    1
                       Sales Report

  Product ID      Description      Qty. Sold   Sales Price    Ext. Price

  1               Fuse .05 Amp         1          1.33          1.33
  1               Fuse .05 Amp         3          1.33          3.99
  2               Fuse .10 Amp         1          1.45          1.45
  3               Power Supply 150w   10         64.51        645.10
  4               Power Supply 200w    4         83.27        333.08
  5               Chip UART           13         30.00        390.00
  6               Resistor 3332        9         13.34        120.06
```

Notice that the Product ID number 1 is printed twice. This is because there were two sales records for the item.

TROUBLE? If the detail lines on the report are not formatted correctly, check the PrintDetail general procedure.

TROUBLE? If the alignment is not correct, verify that the tab positions are correct.

TROUBLE? If you receive a run-time error telling you that an item is not found in the collection, make sure the field names are spelled correctly.

3. End the program.

Mary viewed the report and is satisfied it will print the page title, the column titles, and the detail lines for each record in the Recordset object. Now she would like you to print the order count, number of items sold, and total sales below the detail lines. Just below these lines, she would like the employee name and employee ID printed.

Computing Totals with Counters and Accumulators

To compute the order count, number of items sold, and total sales, you will create variables to hold these three values. Each time a record is printed, the program must add one (1) to the order count and then update the items sold and total sales by the value of the respective field in the current record. You can do this using variables that work as counters and accumulators.

A **counter** is a variable that increases by one (1) each time some activity occurs, such as a record being printed. You first initialize the value of the counter to zero (0). Then the counter describing the number of records is increased, or incremented, by one (1). Incrementing a program counter has the following syntax:

MyCounter = MyCounter + 1

- Each time the program executes this statement, the existing value of *MyCounter* is replaced by its previous value plus one (1).

An **accumulator** is like a counter but instead of increasing the variable by one (1), accumulators are used to tally values. Updating an accumulator has the following syntax:

MyAccumulator = MyAccumulator + value

- Each time the program executes this statement, the existing value of *MyAccumulator* is replaced by its previous value plus *value*.

- In your program, each time a sales record is printed the following should occur:

  - The counter representing the total orders should increase by one (1).

  - The accumulator representing the total items sold will increase by the quantity of items in the current record.

  - The accumulator representing the total sales will increase by the dollar value of the current record.

Figure 5-24 shows how the counter and accumulators will work in your program.

Figure 5-24 ◀
Counters and
accumulators

You need to create the counter, mintTotalOrderCount, and the first accumulator, mintTotalQuantitySold, as Integer data types. The second accumulator, mcurTotalSales, will be a Currency variable to hold the two decimal places needed for dollar amounts. Because the counter and accumulators will be used by multiple procedures in your program, you need to declare them as form-level variables. Counters and accumulators often are initialized when the form loads. If you initialized these values in the Form_Load event procedure, however, the report would be correct the first time it was printed. But, if you printed the report again without reloading the form, the values would not reset, and the report totals would be incorrect.

To declare and initialize the counters and accumulators:

1. Activate the general declarations section of the Form module for the form named **frmMain** and append the following declarations to the end of the existing declarations:

```
Private mintTotalOrderCount As Integer
Private mintTotalQuantitySold As Integer
Private mcurTotalSales As Currency
```

2. Activate the Code window for the **mnuReportsSalesReport** object's **Click** event procedure.

3. Enter the following code immediately below the Set statement:

```
mintTotalOrderCount = 0
mintTotalQuantitySold = 0
mcurTotalSales = 0
```

The first three statements create the form-level variables. After processing each of the sales records and updating the counter and accumulators, the program needs to print the contents of these variables.

Whenever a user clicks the Sales Report menu item at run time, the second three statements will set the value of the counter and accumulators to zero (0). You initialize these values in the menu item's Click event procedure so they will be reset and the report will produce the correct values every time it is printed.

Now you can write the statements to update the counter and accumulators each time a detail line is printed. Because the incrementing must take place each time a record is printed, it makes sense to place this code inside the PrintDetail procedure you already wrote.

To update the PrintDetail procedure to increment the values of the counter and accumulators:

1. Activate the Code window for the **PrintDetail** general procedure in frmMain.

2. Insert the following lines to update the counter and accumulators to the PrintDetail general procedure just before the End Sub statement:

```
mintTotalOrderCount = mintTotalOrderCount + 1
mintTotalQuantitySold = mintTotalQuantitySold + _
    mrstSales![fldQuantity Sold]
mcurTotalSales = mcurTotalSales + pcurExtPrice
```

3. Save the project.

Each time a detail record is printed, the total order count is incremented by one (1). The value of the total items sold accumulator increases by the contents of the Quantity Sold field of the current record, and the value of the total sales accumulator increases by the contents of the pcurExtPrice variable for the current record.

You now need to print the totals after all the sales records have been processed. You can place the statements for printing the counter and accumulators in a general procedure and then call them with one simple statement in the command button's Click event procedure. This will keep the Click event procedure small and easy to read.

To create the procedure to print the counter and accumulators:

1. Be sure the Code window for the form named frmMain is active.

2. Click **Tools** on the menu bar, then click **Add Procedure** to open the Add Procedure dialog box.

3. In the Add Procedure dialog box, create a form-level Sub procedure named **PrintTotals**.

   The Code window activates the procedure you just created.

4. Enter the following code into the procedure (shown in bold):

```
Private Sub PrintTotals( )
    Printer.Print ""
    Printer.Print " Total Order Count "; Tab(20); _
        mintTotalOrderCount
    Printer.Print " Total Items Sold "; Tab(20); _
        mintTotalQuantitySold
    Printer.Print " Total Sales "; Tab(20); mcurTotalSales
End Sub
```

5. Save the project.

As with any other general procedures, you need to call explicitly the PrintTotals procedure. When called, it first will print a blank line as specified by the double quotation marks, to visually separate the totals from the detail lines. Then the procedure will print the total order count prompt and value. The Printer object then will move to a new line, print the total items sold prompt and value, move to a new line, and print the Total Sales prompt and value.

In addition to printing the totals, you also need to print the employee name and ID of the person printing the report. Remember, this information is stored in the text boxes of the login form that is loaded but not visible. Whenever you reference an object in a different form, you must precede the object name with the form name separated by a period. This is the same as referencing a Public variable in a different form. Thus, to reference the Text property of the object name txtEmployeeName in the form named frmLogin you use the following syntax:

```
frmLogin.txtEmployeeName.Text
```

You now can write the statements to print the totals, employee name, and employee ID to the sales report. Because these lines should appear once on the report after the totals are printed, the code should appear after the PrintTotals procedure is called. If you placed these statements in the PrintTotals procedure the program would have produced the same results. Because the procedure, name PrintTotals implies that totals are being printed on a report, however, the statements were placed here. Deciding how to organize the procedures in your program and what each of them does can be subjective at times.

To call the PrintTotals general procedure and print the employee name and ID on the Sales Report:

1. Activate the Code window for the **mnuReportsSalesReport** object's **Click** event procedure.

2. Append the following statements to the event procedure, just before the Printer.EndDoc statement:

```
PrintTotals
Printer.Print ""
Printer.Print " Employee name: "; _
    frmLogin.txtEmployeeName.Text
Printer.Print " Employee ID: "; _
    Tab(17); frmLogin.txtEmployeeID.Text
```

3. Save the project.

The first statement you added calls the PrintTotals procedure and sends the totals to the printer after all the records have been read. The next three statements print a blank line then a line containing the employee name then a line containing the employee ID, each aligned and preceded by a descriptive message.

You now have completed all the components of the Sales Report for Pacific Electronics. Because you divided the tasks of printing the report into several different general procedures, Mary can make changes to the report titles, the formatting of the detail lines, or the report totals without having to look at unrelated code. Now Mary asks you to test the completed program to see if the report prints correctly. You already have tested the code to print the report titles and detail lines, so any problems that might exist would be due to errors in the code for the counter and accumulators.

To test the completed Sales Report:

1. Start the program then complete the login form.

2. Click the **Reports** menu on the Main form then click **Sales Report** to print the Sales Report. Your report should look like Figure 5-25.

Figure 5-25 ◀
Completed
Sales Report

```
                          Pacific Electronics                Page    1
                             Sales Report

      Product ID        Description      Qty. Sold     Sales Price    Ext. Price

      1                 Fuse .05 Amp          1           1.33           1.33
      1                 Fuse .05 Amp          3           1.33           3.99
      2                 Fuse .10 Amp          1           1.45           1.45
      3                 Power Supply 150w    10          64.51         645.10
      4                 Power Supply 200w     4          83.27         333.08
      5                 Chip UART            13          30.00         390.00
      6                 Resistor 3332         9          13.34         120.06

      Total Order Count  7
      Total Items Sold   41
      Total Sales        1495.01

      Employee Name: Mary Deems
      Employee ID:   100
```

TROUBLE? If the counter and accumulators do not appear on the report, be sure the program calls the PrintTotals procedure in the mnuSalesReport_Click event procedure before the EndDoc method is called.

TROUBLE? If the values of the counter or accumulators are not correct, be sure they are being updated correctly in the PrintDetail general procedure.

TROUBLE? If the output is not formatted correctly, verify that the PrintTotals general procedure is correct.

3. Then save any changes and repeat Steps 1 and 2.

4. End the program.

The Pacific Electronics Sales Report now is complete. Salespeople can click the Sales Report command button to print a report based on the underlying database. The report contains the page title required by Pacific Electronics, which includes the company name and the report title. It also includes the Product ID, Description, Quantity Sold, Sales Price, and Extended Price value for each record in the Recordset object. Finally, the report counts the number of orders and accumulates the total items sold and the total sales.

Mary will distribute the sales reporting program to the sales managers for testing so they can verify that the information in the Sales Report is correct and is organized and formatted in a way that is most useful to them.

Quick Check

1. Describe the purpose of the NewPage and EndDoc methods of the Printer object.

2. What is the difference between the Tab and Spc arguments of the Print method?

3. What is the difference between a Do Until and a Do While loop?

4. Write the Visual Basic statements for the following pseudocode:

   Execute the following two statements while there are more records in the Recordset object named rstPacific:

   Print the field named fldProductID to the Immediate window

   Move to the next record

5. What are the purposes of a counter and an accumulator?

Now that you have completed Session 5.2, you can exit Visual Basic. Figure 5-26 lists and defines the new terms presented in this tutorial.

Figure 5-26 ◄
New terms

Term	Definition
Accumulator	An accumulator is like a counter but instead of increasing *the variable* by *one (1)*, accumulators are used to tally values.
Collection	A collection is an object that contains similar objects. It is simply a way of grouping like objects together.
Component modules	Component modules are the multiple general procedures used to accomplish a specific task.
Counter	A counter is a variable that increases by one (1) each time some activity occurs, such as a record being printed. You first initialize the value of the counter to zero (0). Then the counter describing the number of records is increased, or incremented, by one (1).
Do loop	A set of statements including a Do While and Do Until statement that will be executed until or while a condition is True.
Global variable	A global variable is a variable that can be referenced by any module in a program and whose value exists while the program is running.
Modal form	A modal form is a form that must be closed (hidden or unloaded) before another form in the program can receive focus.
Modeless form	A modeless form is a form that can lose focus without being closed.
Modularization	Modularization is the process of dividing a large task into multiple subtasks.
Printer buffer	The printer buffer is an area of the computer's memory that holds printed output before it is sent to the printer. When this buffer is full, or the EndDoc method is called, the information is sent to the printer.
Splash screen	The splash screen is the initial screen that appears on your computer when a program first is started. It provides the user with a brief description of the program and its purpose.
Standard module	A standard module is like a Form module but contains only general procedures and variable declarations commonly accessed by other modules within a program. Standard modules commonly are called bas modules.
Startup object	The startup object can be a single form or general procedure that is executed when the program is run.
Template	A template is an existing form that provides a way for you to reuse components, like forms, and add them to projects.
Wizard	A wizard is a tool that leads a user step-by-step through an unusually long, difficult, or complex programming task.

Tutorial Assignments

Pacific Electronics requires a product report describing the items it sells, the cost to Pacific, and what Pacific charges for it. The report must contain the Product ID, the Product Description, the Product Cost, and the Product Price for each item. The report also must total the number of items sold and allow the user to specify whether the report will be printed to the screen or printed on the printer. The report will contain a final line stating that you tested the program.

This report is a prototype for a more complex report, so the underlying database does not have a large number of items. Therefore, you do not have to consider page or screen breaks.

You need to create a menu item to generate the report. You will enter your name into the program using a login form. The finished Main form will look like Figure 5-27 while the report is printed on the screen, and the login form like Figure 5-28.

Figure 5-27 ◀

```
Pacific Electronics - Product Report                    _ □ ✕
File  Print

                    Pacific Electronics
                      Product Report

Product ID        Product Description     Product Cost      Product Price

   1               Fuse .05 Amp               0.88              1.33
   2               Fuse .10 Amp               0.92              1.45
   3               Power Supply 150w         44.22             64.51
   4               Power Supply 200w         66.83             83.27
   5               Chip UART                 21.34             30.00
   6               Resistor 3332              8.43             13.34


Tested by: Mary Deems

Number of items sold:  6
```

Figure 5-28 ◀

```
Login                                    ✕
Tester Name:   Mary Deems

        OK              Cancel
```

1. Make sure your Student Disk is in the appropriate disk drive, then start Visual Basic.

2. Create a new project named **Pacific Product Report.vbp** in the **TAssign** folder in the **Tutorial.05** folder on your Student Disk.

3. Write the statements in the Form_Load event procedure for the Main form that will set the Font property for both the Printer object and the Main form to a proportional spaced font.

4. Change the form's caption to **Pacific Electronics - Product Report** and its name to **frmMain,** then save the form. Accept the default name.

5. Draw a Data control named datProduct on the form and set the necessary properties to connect to the database named **Pacific.mdb** in the **TAssign** folder in the **Tutorial.05** folder on your Student Disk. Connect to the table named **tblProduct.** Because the user only will be using the Data control to print the product report, it should be invisible at run time.

6. Create a Recordset object variable named **mrstProduct** that will be used by all the procedures in the form. Create a form-level Integer variable named **mintItemCount** that will be used to tally the number of items sold. Require that all variables be declared explicitly.

7. Add a login form to the project. Modify the login form and its boilerplate code so that it requires the tester to type in his or her name. If the user clicks the OK button on the form, set a Public variable LoginSucceeded to True if a name was entered and display a message box asking for the tester name if none was entered. If the user clicked the Cancel button, set the value of LoginSucceeded to False. You will use another procedure to test the value of LoginSucceeded. Save the form. Accept the default name.

8. Add a standard module to the project. Save the standard module as **Module1.bas** in the **TAssign** folder in the **Tutorial.05** folder on your Student Disk.

9. In the standard module, create a general Sub procedure named **Main**. Add the statements to display and repaint the login form, then test the LoginSucceeded variable and either go on to the Main form or end the program. Set the startup object to the Sub Main procedure. *Hint:* You will need to access the tester name that is typed into the login form's text box when you print the report, so do not unload the login form entirely.

10. Create a form-level general Sub procedure named **PrintTitles** on the Main form. This procedure will print the page title. The first line of the page title should be blank. The second line of the page title should contain the text **Pacific Electronics** centered on the page. The third line should contain the text **Product Report** centered on the page. The fourth line should be blank. The fifth line should contain four column heads: **Product ID, Product Description, Product Cost,** and **Product Price**. Format the columns so that the space between the columns is the same, and the left and right margins are equal. Refer to Visual Basic Help for the Print method, if necessary.

11. Create another general Sub procedure named **PrintDetail** to print the detail lines for the report. The information for each line is stored in a field in the Recordset object named **mrstProduct**. The names of the fields are **fldProduct ID, fldProduct Description, fldProduct Cost,** and **fldProduct Sales Price**, respectively. The detail lines should appear under the corresponding column titles. Write the statement to increment the counter variable, **mintItemCount**, containing the number of different items on the report. Be sure to align output for the fields **fldProduct Cost** and **fldProduct Sales Price** so each is formatted with two decimal places and the decimal point is aligned.

12. Create another general procedure named **PrintFooter**. Write the necessary statements to print two blank lines, then the text **Tested by:** followed by the name of the program tester from the login form. The PrintFooter procedure then should print the text **Total items sold:** followed by the value of the variable **mintItemCount**.

13. Using the Menu Editor, create a menu with two titles, **File** and **Print**. Create an **Exit** menu item under the File menu title that will end the program. The Print menu title should have two menu items, **Print to Printer** and **Print to Screen**. Be sure to use appropriate names, captions, shortcuts, and access keys for each menu.

14. In the Click event procedure for the Print to Printer menu item, write the statement that will assign the Recordset object variable **mrstProduct** to the existing Recordset object, stored in the current Data control named datProduct.

15. In the same event procedure, call the general procedures to print the headings.

16. In the same event procedure, create a Do loop in which you call the general procedure to print the detail lines and increment the counter, then write the statement to move to the next record, until the end of file is reached.

17. In the same event procedure, call the general procedure to print the report footer so that appears one time, after all the detail lines have been printed.

18. Call the EndDoc method to empty the contents of the printer buffer.

19. Write the code for the Print to Screen menu item to print the same report you just created to the form instead of the printer. *Hint:* If you call the Print method without an object, the arguments of the Print method will print to the form.

20. In the Code window for the mnuExitItem_Click event, add the code that will end the program.

21. Save the form and the project.

22. Run the program. Execute the **Print to Screen** menu item and verify that the report is correct. If the report contains any errors, correct them. If necessary, change the width and position of the form on the screen. Repeat Steps 17 and 18.

23. When the report prints correctly to the screen, execute the **Print to Printer** menu item and verify that the report is correct. If the report contains any errors, correct them, and repeat Steps 17 and 19.

24. Click the **Exit** menu item to end the program.

25. Exit Visual Basic.

Case Problems

1. Helping Hand Incorporated Helping Hand Incorporated organizes and solicits contributions for various charities in the northern United States and Canada. As part of their business activities, Helping Hand staff members often write letters to possible donors. The same letter is written and then sent to a large number of donors, and Helping Hand would like to have a program to speed up this process. The program will allow staff members to compose a letter and add a closing on one form, and use another form to capture the donor name and address information. You can print the letter or exit the program from either form. Because many people receive the same letter, the program should clear the address fields after the letter is printed, but contents of the letter should remain the same in preparation for the next letter. The volunteer's name will be added to the letter from the information gathered on the login form. You will create the program for Helping Hand.

Figure 5-29 shows the completed form for composing the letter and Figure 5-30 shows the form for entering the address.

Figure 5-29 ◀

Figure 5-30 ◀

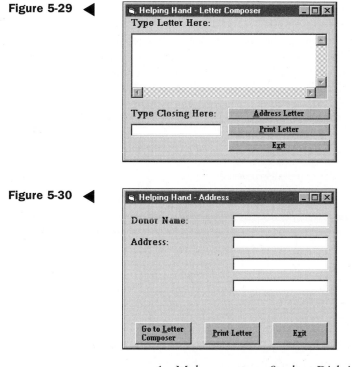

1. Make sure your Student Disk is in the appropriate disk drive, then start Visual Basic and create a new project.
2. Change the form name to **frmHelpingLetter** and change its caption to **Helping Hand - Letter Composer**.
3. Save the form using the default name in the **Cases** folder in the **Tutorial.05** folder on your Student Disk. Save the project using the name **Helping Hand Letter Generator.vbp**.
4. Draw a large multiline text box with both vertical and horizontal scroll bars in the middle of the form to hold the text of the letter. Name the text box **txtLetter**. Remove the initial text from the object. Draw an identifying label with the caption **Type Letter Here:**.

5. Draw a text box in the lower-left corner of the form; the text box will be used to add a standard closing to a letter. Remove the initial text from the text box and change the name to **txtClosing**. Draw an identifying label with the caption **Type Closing Here:**.

6. Draw three command buttons in the lower-right corner of the form as shown in Figure 5-29 with the captions **Address Letter**, **Print Letter**, and **Exit**, respectively. Give the buttons appropriate names and hot keys. Add the appropriate code for the Exit button.

7. Open the Code window for the Address Letter button's Click event and add code to hide the frmHelpingLetter object and show the frmHelpingAddress object.

8. Create a second form with the name **frmHelpingAddress** and the caption **Helping Hand - Address**. Save the form using the default name in the **Cases** folder in the **Tutorial.05** folder on the Student Disk.

9. Draw two identifying labels on the leftmost side of the form with the captions **Donor Name:** and **Address:**, respectively.

10. Draw four blank text boxes down the rightmost side of the form. Change the Name property to **txtDonor**, **txtAddress1**, **txtAddress2**, and **txtAddress3**, respectively.

11. Draw three command buttons along the bottom of the form (refer to Figure 5-30). Change their captions to **Go to Letter Composer**, **Print Letter**, and **Exit**, respectively. Give the buttons appropriate names and hot keys. Add the appropriate code for the Exit button.

12. Open the Code window for the Go to Letter Composer button's Click event and type the code that will show the frmHelpingLetter object and hide the frmHelpingAddress.

13. Use the Add Module dialog box to add a standard module to the project. Save the module as **Helping.bas** in the **Cases** folder in the **Tutorial.05** folder on the Student Disk. Save the project.

14. Create a general procedure named **PrintLetter**. Type the code that will print a letter to the printer with the layout show in Figure 5-31. *Hint:* Remember to reference the form name for the text boxes when you call the Print method. Remember, you can use the Date function to print the current date on the letter.

Figure 5-31 ◀

```
                              Helping Hand Incorporated

        Blank line

                                                          Today's date


        Blank line

        Donor's Name

        Address

        Blank line

        Dear Donor's Name:

        Blank line

        Text of letter

        Blank line

        Closing

        4 blank lines

        Volunteer's Name
```

15. Open the Code window for the Click event procedure for the Print Letter command button. Write the code to call the PrintLetter general procedure.

16. Add the necessary statements to clear the contents of the input text boxes on the frmHelpingAddress form just after the letter is printed.

17. Write the statements to print the letter from the Print Letter command button on the form named frmHelpingLetter.

18. Use the Add Form dialog box to add a splash screen to the project. In a label that fills the form, type the title **Helping Hand Incorporated**. Change the font and colors to a style you like. Save the form as **frmHelpingSplash.frm** in the **Cases** folder in the **Tutorial.05** folder on the Student Disk.

19. Use the Add Form dialog box to add a login form. Change the form and its boiler-plate code to require the user to type a volunteer name in the txtVolunteerName text box. The identifying label for the text box should have the caption **Volunteer Name:**. Write the code that will display the frmHelpingLetter object after the volunteer types a name in the text box and clicks the OK button, and that will end the program if the volunteer clicks the Cancel button. Save the form as **frmHelpingLogin.frm** in the **Cases** folder in the **Tutorial.05** folder on the Student Disk.

20. Use the Add Procedure dialog box to add a project-level Sub procedure named **Main**. Add code to the Sub Main procedure to display and repaint the splash screen, load all the forms in the program, then display the login form and hide the splash screen.

21. Set the project properties so Sub Main is the startup object.

22. Save the project.

23. Run the program. The first form displayed is the splash screen, then the login form. Type your name in the Volunteer Name: text box and click the OK button.

24. The Letter Composer form appears. Type a thank you letter in the letter text box, then add a closing. Click the Address Letter command button.

25. Type information of your choice in the Donor Name and Address text boxes. Click the Print Letter button. Check that all the fields correctly print what you entered in each form.

26. Enter another address and generate another letter, then go back to the first form and change the letter you already wrote. Test the Print Letter button on the Letter Composer form.

27. When you have finished testing the program, exit it by clicking the Exit button.

28. Print the Form Image and Code for all the forms. Save any changes to the project.

29. Exit Visual Basic.

2. Toys, Toys, Toys, and More Toys Toys, Toys, Toys, and More Toys is a toy manufacturer operating in western Europe. The company has decided to begin work on a comprehensive stock control application. The anticipated system will use an Access database to store information about the toys currently being manufactured, how many toys of each type are in stock, and delivery estimates for toy orders currently in production. Because this is a new application, you will design the startup screen, create a second screen, and then test the links between the two screens. You will use a Data control to retrieve the toy names from a test database.

Figure 5-32 shows the completed startup splash screen for the program.

Figure 5-32 ◄

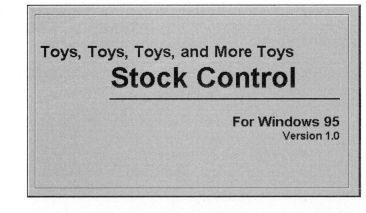

1. Make sure your Student Disk is in the appropriate disk drive, then start Visual Basic. Create a new project.

2. Use the Add Form dialog box to add a splash screen to the project file. (Use the splash screen template.) Change the properties of the labels and remove the extra labels so the splash screen looks like Figure 5-32. Add a Line object to the splash screen. Set the Name property to **frmToysSplash** and save the form with the default name in the **Cases** folder in the **Tutorial.05** folder on your Student Disk.

3. Save the project using the name **Toys Stock Control.vbp**.

4. Remove the code from the Form_Load event procedure on the splash screen.

5. Using the Data Form Wizard, create a form based on the table **tblToyProducts** in the database named **Toys.mdb** in the **Cases** folder in the **Tutorial.05** folder on your Student Disk. Use all the fields in the table and sort the information using the field **fldProductName**. The form should have Add, Delete, Refresh, and Update buttons. Change the caption of this form to **Toys, Toys, Toys, and More Toys - Stock Control**. Change the caption of the labels so they are more meaningful to the user.

6. Create a command button on the form named **cmdExit** and write the code to end the program. If necessary, move the existing command buttons so they all appear on the same line.

7. Save the form using the default name in the **Cases** folder in the **Tutorial.05** folder on your Student Disk.

8. Use the Add Module dialog box to add a new standard module to the project.

9. Save the standard module using the name **Toys.bas** in the **Cases** folder in the **Tutorial.05** folder on your Student Disk.

10. Use the Add Procedure dialog box to insert a project-level Sub procedure named **Main** to the module.

11. In the Code window for the **Sub Main** procedure, write the necessary statements to display and repaint the splash screen, then display the frmtblToyProducts object and unload the splash screen.

12. Change the startup object to Sub Main.

13. Save the project.

14. Run the program. The splash screen appears, then the Stock Control form appears. Click the Data control arrows to view the stock information.

15. Click the Exit button to end the program.

16. Print the Form Image and Code for both forms. Exit Visual Basic.

3. Jill Jones Distribution Jill Jones is a marketing representative for a distributor of kitchen supplies. Her sales territory consists of the southwestern United States although she sometimes services clients outside that region. She presently has a database listing customer names, telephone numbers, and information. She spends much of her time traveling to customer's sites to sell products. Just before she leaves on a trip, she looks at a list of the clients in a particular city, and makes notes about the client to optimize her itinerary and make sure she does not forget to contact a client. She would like a program that would facilitate this review for her by allowing her to select a city, then display all the clients in that city. She needs to be able to edit the information and then print the report. To do this, you will need to connect a form to her database using the Data control. Then locate all the records in a particular city. If a customer record is in that city, then you will need to add a line containing the customer's name and telephone number to a multiline text box. Otherwise, you should ignore the record. She also would like the option of displaying all the customer records, regardless of city. When complete, the form for this program should look like Figure 5-33.

Figure 5-33 ◄

1. Start Visual Basic and create a new project.
2. Set the form name to **frmJillJones** and the caption to **Jill Jones Distribution - Itinerary Planner**. Save the form file using the default name to the **Cases** folder in the **Tutorial.05** folder on your Student Disk.
3. Save the project using the name **Jill Jones Itinerary.vbp** in the **Cases** folder in the **Tutorial.05** folder on your Student Disk. Remember to save your work frequently in case you make a mistake.
4. Create a multiline text box with a vertical scroll bar. Name the text box **txtNames**.
5. Create three command buttons at the bottom of the form. Be sure to assign meaningful names and hot keys to each of the buttons as illustrated in Figure 5-33.
6. Create a Data control that will access the table named **tblCustomers** in the database named **dbJill.mdb** in the **Cases** folder in the **Tutorial.05** folder on your Student Disk. Because Jill will not interact with the Data control at run time, make it invisible. Name the Data control **datCustomers**.

7. Use the Add Form dialog box to add a login form to the project.
8. Change the object on the form so there is one label and a text box for Jill to enter the desired city. The text box should be named **txtCity**. Remove the Cancel button. Create a frame with two option buttons in a control array named **optSelect**. The captions for the option buttons should be **One City** and **All Cities**, respectively.
9. Change the caption of the OK button to **Lookup Names**.

10. Change the code for the Lookup Names command button form so it requires Jill either to click the One City option button and enter the city's name in the text box or click the All Cities button to continue. If the correct information is entered, hide the form and set the value of the global variable LoginSucceeded to True.

11. Create a standard module named **JillJones.bas**. Create a general Sub procedure named Main and change the project properties so this is the startup object. The procedure should display the login form as a modal form. Then write another statement in this procedure to display the other form. Because the login form must be hidden before control can revert to another form and the form will not be hidden until correct information is entered into the login form, there is no need to check in the Main procedure that the correct information was entered.

EXPLORE

12. You need to write an If statement to determine which option button is selected, locate the customers from one city or all cities, then display the selected records in the text box you created each time the Main form is activated. Display the fields named **fldFirstName, fldLastName,** and **fldTelephone** for the matching items in the Main form's text boxes. *Hint:* If Jill selected a single city you will need to use the FindFirst method to locate the first record matching the selected city. Then, in a loop, use the FindNext method to locate additional matching records. Remember, the NoMatch property is set to True when the FindNext method cannot locate another record. If Jill is selecting all of the customers, then you need to set the current record pointer to the first record in the recordset, then write a loop to locate each record in the table. Remember to use the concatenation characters, space constant characters, and carriage return line feed constant characters to format the output and move to a new line every time you add a name.

13. Write the code for the Click event for the Reset button on the Main form to clear the contents of both forms, reposition the recordset to the first record, hide the Main form and show the login form.

14. Write the statements for the Print button on the Main form to use the Print method of the Printer object to print the contents of the txtNames object. Be sure to call the EndDoc method to flush the printer buffer.

15. Write the statements so the Exit button will unload the form and exit the program when it is clicked.

16. Save the project before testing.

17. Test the program by selecting all cities, then click the Reset button to clear the information. Select the city **Las Vegas** and click the Lookup Names button again. You see a list of six names and telephone numbers.

18. Correct any errors, save the project, and print both forms as text and code. Exit Visual Basic.

4. Mort Enterprises   Mort Enterprises is a small auto loan company in Central California. Their customers frequently request loan amortization schedules. A loan amortization schedule displays the payment amount of a loan. Then for each payment made, a line is printed on a report that displays the beginning balance of the loan, the interest charged for the period, the amount of the payment applied to the principal of the loan, and the new balance. Thus, a line needs to be printed for each payment to be made. After the last payment is made, the balance on the loan is zero. Thus, for each payment, you need to compute the amount of interest. This can be computed by multiplying the beginning balance of the loan by the interest rate. Then you can compute the principal by subtracting the interest amount from the payment. The new balance is computed by subtracting the amount of the payment applied to the principal from the beginning balance. You need to perform these computations for each payment using the new beginning balance. You can perform these computations inside a loop that will execute once for each payment.

You need to create a program with two forms. The startup form is shown in Figure 5-34. It contains three labels and corresponding text boxes. There is an Exit command button and a button to compute the amortization schedule. When this button is clicked, the current form should be hidden and the output form displayed. Using the information from the text boxes on the other form, you need to display the output. This output should include the payment amount, and column titles for the month, beginning balance, interest, principal, and ending balance.

Figure 5-34 ◀

Reading and Writing Text Files into List Boxes and Arrays

Creating a Quotation System for Star Plant Supply

OBJECTIVES

In this tutorial you will:

■ Create instances of controls that work with lists

■ Read information from a text file and load it into a combo box at run time

■ Create arrays to store a series of variables

■ Add and remove items in a list box

■ Create a For loop that will execute statements a fixed number of times

■ Write information to a text file

CASE

Star Plant Supply

Rose Blain is the owner of Star Plant Supply, a company that has been supplying plants to landscaping firms in Naples, Florida, since 1986. Currently Rose employs nine people. Eight of the staff members perform deliveries, unload shipments, and track inventory. Rose also has an assistant to help her manage the business.

Before Rose's customers place an order, they require a verbal or written price estimate, or quotation. Her customers want to make sure they are getting the best price for each item they buy, so they shop around. They also need to meet deadlines for their landscaping projects, so they must obtain quotations quickly. Rose currently maintains a price list and uses a quotation form and calculator to write customer quotations. Her business is growing so rapidly that she often cannot write all the requested quotations. This means she loses the sale. Also, because Rose needs to look up the price of each item by hand when she writes quotations, the current system is prone to errors. Furthermore, she has noticed she makes occasional errors when computing and adding extended prices. Rose wants a computerized system that will 1) help her keep up with the volume of quotations she has to write and, 2) compute the pricing information for her automatically.

Rose's friend, Mack Woolard, has been helping her to develop the quotation system in Visual Basic. Mack has been creating a program for her, but he does not have time to complete it, so they have asked you to finish it. Rose is not very familiar with computers and she is a poor typist, so she wants to be able to select an item from a list of the products she carries, enter the quantity requested, then have the program compute the extended price of the item. Most customers want a running total of the items they have requested, so she also wants the program to add together the extended prices of all the items and compute a quotation total each time an item is added to the quotation.

Rose's assistant, Joan Grayson, used WordPad to create a price list of all Star Plant Supply's products. Each product is listed on a separate line followed by the corresponding price for the item. Joan updates this file when the prices change or new items are added. Mack explains that the quotation program can read this text file and use the information to produce the quotations for the customers after some modifications have been made to the text file.

SESSION

6.1

In this session you will read information from a text file into a series of variables stored as one unit called an array. You also will insert items into a list box and combo box using code, and access the items of a list box using the List and ListIndex properties. Also, you will write a For loop to step through the items in a list box.

Analyzing the Program

Mack already has written the NEADT charts, and designed the screen for the quotation program. Also, he has created a form with most of the objects he plans to use. He has not written any code yet or set many of the properties for the objects he created. Before you begin working on the program, you should review the design specifications.

To view and print the NEADT charts for the quotation program:

1. Make sure your Student Disk is in the appropriate disk drive. Using Microsoft Word, open the **Star.doc** file in the **Tutorial.06** folder on your Student Disk. If you do not have Word, open the **Star.txt** file using WordPad.

2. Print the file then exit the word processing program.

Examine the NEADT charts. All the product descriptions will be stored in a list that Rose can use to choose products. Rose will be able to add a product to the quotation by clicking the product in the list, typing the quantity requested, and then clicking a button to add the item to the output section of the price quotation. The program also includes a Remove Item command button, which will delete a product from the output lists and recompute the quotation total whenever an item is deleted. The Write Quotation command button will allow Rose to print the quotation to a text file. Then Rose can use the text file in her word processing program to format and print quotations for customers. The New Quotation command button will clear the contents of all the output list boxes and quotation total so Rose can enter a new quotation. The program will include four list boxes for output: Product Description, Quantity, Price Each, and Extended Price. Keep the printed NEADT charts next to you while you complete the program. So that Rose can give customers immediate feedback about the quotation total, the extended price of an item and the quotation total will be computed each time an item is added to the quotation. Mack has completed the screen design for the program, as shown in Figure 6-1.

Figure 6-1 ◀

Screen design
of the quotation
form

Product prompt		Add Item command button	
Product combo box		Remove Item command button	
Quantity prompt		Write Quotation command button	
Quantity text box		New Quotation command button	
Discount check box		Quit Program command button	

Product Description prompt	Quantity prompt	Price Each prompt	Extended Price prompt	Picture prompt
Product Description list box	Quantity list box	Price Each list box	Extended Price list box	Picture

Quotation Total prompt	Quotation Total text box

Following good user-interface design principles, Mack divided the screen into two sections—the upper section for input and the lower section for output. Each section is bordered by a frame for visual identification. In this case, the frames are not being used to group together option buttons. Rather, they are used only to visually separate the input and output sections of the program.

When Rose clicks the Add Item command button, the program will look up the price of the selected item, and then multiply it by the quantity requested in order to compute the extended price. Then, the item, quantity ordered, price, and extended price will be displayed in the output section of the form. Finally, the quotation total will be computed and displayed in the output section of the form.

You will begin by opening the project file that Mack already created.

To open the partially completed quotation program:

1. Start Visual Basic and open the project file named **Star.vbp** in the **Tutorial.06** folder on your Student Disk. Activate the form named **frmStar.frm**. Your form should look like Figure 6-2.

Figure 6-2 ◀
Initial quotation
screen

input section ──▶

output section ──▶

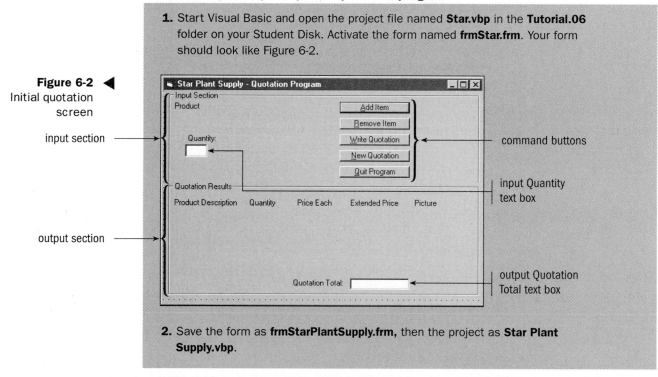

command buttons

input Quantity
text box

output Quotation
Total text box

2. Save the form as **frmStarPlantSupply.frm,** then the project as **Star Plant Supply.vbp**.

Mack suggests you begin by creating the remaining controls on the form.

Displaying a List of Items in a Combo Box

Remember, Rose wants to select a product from a list of items she has in inventory. She does not want to have to type the name of each item every time she prepares a bid. The solution to this problem is to use a combo box. A **ComboBox** control can display a list of items from which the user can select one item. There are three styles of combo boxes you can use by setting the object's **Style** property:

- Setting the Style property to **0 - Dropdown Combo** allows a user either to select an item from a dropdown list of suggested choices or type in a new item. No options appear until the user clicks the list arrow at the right of the combo box.

- Setting the Style property to **1 - Simple Combo** displays a text box and a list, which does not drop down. All the choices appear in the list at all times. Whenever the list will not fit inside the region of the object, a scroll bar is displayed. The user can specify a value for the combo box that is not in the list of suggested choices.

■ Setting the Style property to **2 - Dropdown List** only allows a user to select an item from a preset dropdown list of choices. As in a dropdown combo box, no options appear until the user clicks the list arrow at the right of the combo box.

Figure 6-3 shows how the different combo boxes will appear on a form.

Figure 6-3 ◀
Types of
ComboBox
objects

Dropdown and
Dropdown List
ComboBox objects

Simple ComboBox
object

In addition to the Style property, there are other properties that determine contents of the combo box and how those contents appear to the user.

■ The **List** property specifies the items stored in the combo box. It is used to add items to the combo box at design time. If you want to add items at run time, you do not need to use the Properties window to set the List property.

■ The **Sorted** property, when set to True, causes the items to be displayed in alphabetical order even if the items were not added in alphabetical order.

■ The combo box can be used as a bound control; that is, it can reference a record in a Recordset object by setting its **DataSource** and **DataField** properties. This is identical to the process you used to bind the TextBox object to a database.

■ The **ItemData** property is a list of long integer values with the same number of items as the control's List property. You can use the numbers associated with each item to identify the list items. The most common use of the ItemData property is as an index into another array. When you insert an item with the AddItem method, an item also is inserted into the ItemData array.

■ The **NewIndex** property works with the ItemData property. If you are adding items to a list that is sorted, each new item is added to the list in alphabetical order. To determine where an item was inserted, you use the NewIndex property. The NewIndex property returns the item most recently added to a combo box or list box.

■ The **ListIndex** property is an integer value that identifies the currently selected item in a list box. The first item in the list has a ListIndex property value of zero (0), the second item has a value of one (1), and so on. If no item has been selected, the ListIndex property has a value of minus one (-1).

■ The **ListCount** property is an integer value that returns the number of items in a list. If the list is empty, the ListCount is zero (0); otherwise, the value of ListCount is the number of items in the list.

In your program you will add the items to the combo box when the program is run so you do not need to set the List property in the Properties window at design time. Also, because the quotation program will not interact with a database, there is no need to set the DataSource and DataField properties. Because the items will appear in the list in the same order as they appear in the input file, you will not set the Sorted property or use the ItemData property. Because Rose only will select items from the list rather than adding new items, and because there is not room on the form to display each item in the list, you will use a dropdown combo box. The standard prefix for a combo box is "cbo".

To create the ComboBox object for your program:

1. Click the **ComboBox** control on the toolbox and draw an instance of a combo box as shown in Figure 6-4.

Figure 6-4 ◄
Creating the
ComboBox
object

new ComboBox
object

list arrow

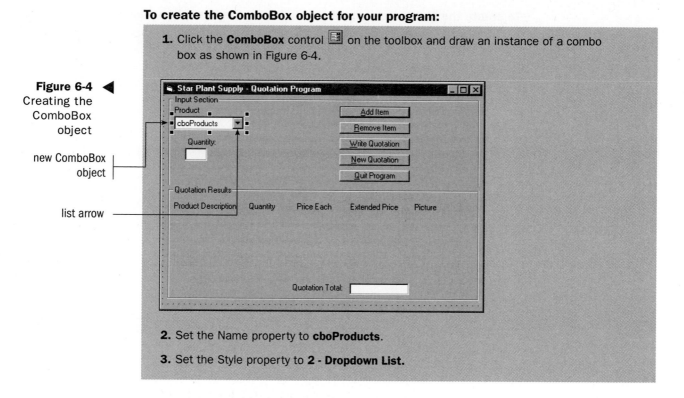

2. Set the Name property to **cboProducts**.

3. Set the Style property to **2 - Dropdown List**.

You will add the items to the combo box when the program is run from information contained in the price list Joan created.

The ListBox Control

After Rose selects a product from the combo box, she wants the item, quantity ordered, price, and extended prices to be displayed in the output section of the program. Because there will be several items in any given quotation, the control must be able to display several items. There is another control that is similar to a combo box called the **ListBox** control. They share almost the same properties. The user cannot enter new items into a list box by typing in information, however. Rather items must be added either at design time by setting the List property or at run time by calling a method of the list box. You now will create the list boxes that will be used to display the quotation information. The standard prefix for a list box is "lst". Because you are creating list boxes to store the products that are quoted, quantity selected, price, and extended price, you will name the objects lstQuotedProduct, lstQuotedQty, lstQuotedPrice, and lstQuotedExtPrice.

To create the ListBox objects that will display the items in a quotation:

1. Click the **ListBox** control on the toolbox and draw an instance of a list box as shown in Figure 6-5. Set the Name property to **lstQuotedProduct**.

Figure 6-5 ◀
Creating the
ListBox objects

<table>
<tr><td colspan="2">🔲 Star Plant Supply - Quotation Program   _ □ ✕</td></tr>
</table>

Input Section
Product
[cboProducts ▼]

Quantity:
[   ]

Add Item
Remove Item
Write Quotation
New Quotation
Quit Program

Quotation Results

Product Description ↓   Quantity ↓   Price Each ↓   Extended Price ↓   Picture

lstQuotedProduct   lstQuotedQty   lstQuotedPrice   lstQuotedExtPrice

→ ListBox objects

Quotation Total: [   ]

2. Create three more list boxes as shown in Figure 6-5 and set the Name property to **lstQuotedQty**, **lstQuotedPrice**, and **lstQuotedExtPrice**, respectively.

The price list, which Joan created in WordPad, lists each of Star Plant Supply's products on a separate line followed by the corresponding price for each product. Joan updates this list when the prices change or new items are added to the inventory. Figure 6-6 shows the first nine items of the text file.

Figure 6-6 ◀
Price list for
Star Plant
Supply

Flower - Iris	4.37
Flower - Lilac	5.22
Herb - Mint	1.88
Shrub - Juniper	4.18
Shrub - Boxwood	9.22
Tree - Ash	43.80
Tree - Pine	28.60
Tree - Oak	33.84
Tree - Olive	19.20

The quotation program you are creating can read and use this text file. Joan needs to make some changes to the formatting, however, so Visual Basic can read the file. To use the text file with Visual Basic, Joan must remove the tabs and enter commas with no spaces, to separate the products from the prices. Also, the product names must be enclosed in quotation marks because they contain text rather than numbers.

Loading a Text File into a Program

When the quotation program starts, the first thing it must do is load all the products into the Product combo box. There are three options available for loading the product and price list. First, you could store the product information in a database and use a Data control and its Recordset property with a Do loop to add each item. Second, you could load the product and pricing information into the computer's memory from a text file when the program first starts. Third, you could set the List property at design time to load the items.

The decision to use a text file or a database to store the data is based on several factors. When the number of items to be used is relatively small, they can be read effectively from a text file and stored in the computer's memory using list boxes and combo boxes without slowing down your system. Reading the information from a database each time a product is accessed would take longer than finding the information in a list or a variable. The information in your input list is read-only; that is, once the information is loaded into the program, it will not be changed. So, there is no need to write individual records back to a database. Also, Rose wants to continue using the text file containing the price list. In this way if the computer is not available because of a disk failure, or if she is preparing a quotation outside the office, she can refer to a printout of the price list to prepare quotations manually. Your program will read the product information from the text file that Joan created.

In Tutorials 4 and 5 you accessed a table in a database by creating an instance of a Data control and using the methods of the Data control and the Recordset object to navigate through the records. Unlike a database, a text file is not an object. Instead of calling the methods of an object like a recordset, you use a Visual Basic statement to open a text file. Once a text file is open, you can read the file from beginning to end. This way of accessing a text file is called **sequential access**. A program cannot explicitly locate a specific line in a text file without reading all the lines preceding it. Also, it is not possible to move backward through a file when reading it sequentially.

Opening a Text File

When you open a text file, you must open explicitly the file and tell Visual Basic what operations you want to perform on it. You open a text file with the **Open** statement, which has the following syntax:

Open "*pathname***" For [Input | Output | Append] As #***filenumber*

- The *pathname* contains a string describing the name and location of the file you want to open. It must be enclosed in quotation marks if you enter text, but the quotation marks should be omitted if you use a variable.

- One of three options—Input, Output, or Append—must be included in the Open statement or Visual Basic will generate a syntax error.

- If the file is opened **For Input**, it already must exist. You can read information contained in the file but you cannot write to the file when it is opened For Input. This is the method you will use to read the file for the Star Plant Supply quotation program.

- If the file is opened **For Output**, you can write to the file but you cannot read it. If the file does not exist, Visual Basic will create it for you. If the file does exist, the existing contents will be deleted. The user will not be asked to confirm the deletion. You can create a message box to ask for confirmation from the user with the MsgBox function. The **For Output** option is useful if you want to rewrite an existing file entirely.

- If the file is opened **For Append**, information you write to the file will be appended to the end of the file, but you cannot read from it. If the file does not exist, Visual Basic will create it for you. Unlike opening a file For Output, the existing contents of a file opened **For Append** will not be deleted.

- The *filenumber* is an arbitrary integer number you assign as a reference to the file while it is open. The *filenumber* must be preceded by the **#** character. If you do not specify a *filenumber*, Visual Basic will generate a syntax error.

- If you want to read a file opened For Output or For Append, or write a file opened For Input, you must close the file and open it again using the desired option.

> *Tip:* Although you can use any integer number, starting the filenumber at #1 for the first open file and #2 for the second open file will make your program more understandable. Although you can have several files open at once, you cannot open an infinite number of files. Windows 95 determines how many total files you can have open at once, which varies from system to system. It is a good practice to close a file once you are done reading it or writing to it.

| REFERENCE window | **OPENING A TEXT FILE** |

> - To open a file for reading, type the Open statement followed by the filename and the For Input clause after the filename in quotation marks.
> - To assign a filenumber to the file, type As #*n* at the end of the Open statement, where *n* is an integer number not already assigned to an open file. To make your programs more readable, the first file you open should have a filenumber of 1.

Because the information contained in the text file must be loaded before Rose can begin preparing any quotations, the program should read the text file and place the information into the combo box in the form input section in the Form_Load event procedure.

To write the code to open the text file:

1. Open the Code window for the **Form_Load** event procedure.

2. Enter the following code in the window (shown in bold):

```
Private Sub Form_Load( )
    Open "A:\Tutorial.06\Product.txt" For Input As #1
End Sub
```

This statement opens the price list file, Product.txt, in the Tutorial.06 folder on your Student Disk. Because you will be reading information into the program, you opened the file For Input. It is the first open file, so its filenumber is #1.

Reading a Text File

After opening the file For Input, the program can read each of the products from the file into the Product combo box. You could enter all the items at design time by setting the combo box's List property, but if you did so, any changes to the list of products would have to be made by changing the properties using the Properties window. Because Rose and Joan are not very familiar with computers, they do not want to have to modify the program. Reading the products from a file is the best solution, because Joan can update the text file in WordPad when products are added and removed or the prices change. As long as Joan keeps the price list current, every time Rose runs the program it will read the current information from the text file.

> *Tip:* If the contents of a combo or list box are likely to change, you should read the items at run time from a text file or database table. If the contents will not change, set the List property at design time.

The **Input #** statement is used when each line of the file contains information separated by commas, and any text strings in the file are enclosed in quotation marks. The Input # statement has the following syntax:

Input #filenumber, varlist

- The **Input #** statement reads a line of text from an open file. When an input file has information separated by commas, each item of information can be thought of as a field, like in a database. Each field of information in the text file must be separated by a comma and any text strings in the file must be enclosed in quotation marks.

- The *filenumber* can be any valid filenumber assigned by the Open statement, preceded by the **#** character.

- The *varlist* is a list of variables, separated by commas, which are assigned values read from the file. The data type of each variable should correspond to the data type in the respective field.

REFERENCE window	**READING A TEXT FILE**
	■ Make sure the file is open for input.
	■ To read information from a file into different variables, use the Input # statement followed by the filenumber describing the open file.
	■ Append a variable name for each field in the record.

Visual Basic can read text files using an Input # statement when each field in a line is separated, or delimited, by a comma, and string information is enclosed in quotation marks. This type of file is called an **ASCII-delimited file** and is supported by most word processing, spreadsheet, and database programs. Joan has converted the WordPad text file into a form suitable for reading by your Visual Basic program. Figure 6-7 shows part of the ASCII-delimited file for the quotation program.

Figure 6-7 ◄
ASCII-delimited file with two fields

"Flower - Iris",4.37
"Flower - Lilac",5.22
"Herb - Mint",1.88

Numeric field
comma separator

Text field enclosed in quotation marks

As shown in Figure 6-7, the input file contains two items of information separated by a comma. Each of these items can be thought of as a field. The first field contains text enclosed in quotation marks. The second field is numeric; it is not enclosed in quotations. Each line in the file can be thought of as a record. In Figure 6-7 there are three records.

When you create an ASCII-delimited file, you need to be sure that each record contains the correct number of fields. If there is no information for the field, a blank entry should be created with two commas next to each other. Each line must end with a carriage return, including the last line. Typically, if the input file is not correct, your program will generate a run-time error indicating that you tried to read past the end of file.

REFERENCE window	**CREATING A TEXT FILE**
	■ Using WordPad or NotePad, create a new file.
	■ Enter each line (record) such that Text fields are surrounded by quotation marks and numbers are not.
	■ Make sure each field is separated by a comma and that you have accounted for each field.
	■ After the last line press the Enter key to insert a final carriage return.
	■ Verify that there are no blank lines at the end of the file.

Generally you want the text to be read just after the file is opened, so the program should read the file immediately after opening it in the Form_Load event procedure. To do this, you will create a variable that will store temporarily the information before adding it to the Product combo box.

To read the text file, you will create a Do loop that calls the Input# statement repeatedly until the end of file has been reached. To determine when the end of file has been reached, you will use the EOF function. The EOF function takes one argument—the filenumber assigned to the file. The function returns the value True when the end of the input file has been reached; otherwise, it returns the value False.

To read the text file into the variables:

1. Make sure the Code window for the **Form_Load** event procedure still is active.

2. Enter the following code in the window (shown in bold):

```
Dim pstrProduct As String
Dim psngPrice As Single
Open "A:\Tutorial.06\Product.txt" For Input As #1
Do Until EOF(1) = True
    Input #1, pstrProduct, psngPrice
Loop
```

These statements read the input from the text file and load the items into the variables named pstrProduct and psngPrice.

```
Dim pstrProduct As String
Dim psngPrice As Single
```

The Dim statements declare two variables. The variable pstrProduct will store the name of each product. The variable psngPrice will store the price of each product, which you will be using later in the session. You must include the Dim statements before the Open statement because all variables must be declared before they are used.

```
Do Until EOF(1) = True
    Input #1, pstrProduct, psngPrice
Loop
```

The EOF function works with a text file in the same way that the EOF property works with a Recordset object. The EOF function determines when the end of file is reached. This is used to exit the Do loop. The EOF function returns the value False unless the end of file has been reached; then it returns the value True. The argument 1 is the filenumber corresponding to the open file.

In the Input statement, the filenumber #1 is associated with the file you opened when you executed the Open statement. Each time the program reads a line from the file, the values read are stored in the variables pstrProduct and psngPrice. If the input file included more than two fields on a line, you would have stored the fields in additional variables separated by commas. Because the number of variables in the Input statement must correspond to the number of fields in the file, the variable psngPrice must be included here, even though the program is not using this variable at this point.

The Loop statement sends the program back to the Do statement to determine if the end of file has been reached.

The AddItem Method

The text file has been read into the computer's memory, but the items need to appear in the combo box. The AddItem method acts on both ComboBox and ListBox objects and is used to add an item to the list of choices for each at run time. The AddItem method has the following syntax:

object.**AddItem** *text*

- *object* represents any valid combo box or list box.

- The **AddItem** method adds an item to the list of choices at run time.

- The *text* represents the item to be added to the list, which will appear in the combo box or list box when the program is running. So, if you wanted to add five different items to a list you would call the AddItem method five times with different text strings.

You now can write the statement to call the AddItem method that will store the contents of the variable pstrProduct into the combo box. This statement needs to be executed each time a record is read from the input file, so it should be inside the Do loop.

To add each product to the combo box:

1. Make sure the Code window for the **Form_Load** event procedure still is active.

2. Enter the following code into the event procedure just after the Input # statement and before the Loop statement:

```
cboProducts.AddItem pstrProduct
```

Whenever a program finishes using a file, the program should close the file. Because Windows 95 limits the number of files you can have open at one time, closing files that are not being used will ensure there are adequate filenumbers remaining. Also, each open file consumes some memory. So, too many open files can slow down your computer, depending on the amount of memory it has.

Closing the File

When the program finishes reading a file, the program should close the file explicitly using the Close statement. The **Close** statement has the following syntax:

Close [[#]1][,[#]2]...

- The **Close** statement is used to close explicitly one or more files.

- The arguments can be one or more filenumbers separated by commas. So, to close file #1 and #2 you would write the following statement:

```
Close #1, #2
```

- If you do not specify a *filenumberlist*, any files opened with the Open statement are closed. If you are working with several files, including such a Close statement just before the program exits will guarantee that all files have been closed.

> *Tip:* Whenever you are finished processing a file, use the Close statement to close explicitly the file. This will prevent corruption of a file in the event of a power failure or a program being terminated improperly.

You currently have one file open, Product.txt, which is associated with the filenumber #1. You now need to write the code to close this file.

To close the open text file:

1. Open the Code window for the **Form_Load** event procedure.

2. Enter the following line of code, just before the End Sub statement:

```
Close #1
```

When the running program reaches this statement, the program will close the Product.txt file. The filenumber #1 will no longer be associated with the file. If a program needs to read the file again, the program must open the file again with the Open statement.

You now should test the Do loop to see if the products in the text file are being read into the Product combo box.

To test the Do loop:

1. Save the project then start the program.

2. Click the list arrow on the rightmost side of the combo box. Your screen should look like Figure 6-8.

Figure 6-8 ◀
Combo box
with products

products from text file
stored in combo box

Notice the Product combo box now contains the products that Rose sells. Because all the products will not fit into the combo box, scroll bars appear so she can scroll through the list.

TROUBLE? If the products are not being loaded in the combo box, make sure the code you wrote matches the code in the previous steps. If incorrect information is being loaded, make sure both variables are listed in the Input # statement. Make any necessary corrections, then repeat Steps 1 and 2.

3. Test the **Quit Program** button to end the program.

Now, every time you run the program, the information in the first field of the Product.txt file will be stored in the Product combo box.

Creating an Array to Store Information

In each program you have written until this point, you have declared variables that can store only a single item of information, such as a price. In the quotation program, you need to store the prices for each product sold by Star Plant Supply. When Rose selects an item from the combo box containing the products, the program needs to look up the corresponding price. The company sells many different products, so you would need many different variables to store the information. Although creating different variables does not present a problem in this case, consider a company that sells 500 or 5,000 products. The problem becomes more complicated when you need to add new products, because you would need to create new variables.

You have seen how several objects of the same type can be grouped together in a control array. Each object in a control array has the same name and is referenced with its Index property value, which is unique. You can group variables together in the same way using an array. An **array** is a variable that contains a list of several items of the same data type. Each item in an array is called an **element**. Each individual element is referenced by a unique index number, called a **subscript**. When you want to access an individual element in an array, you use the array name and the subscript to reference the element.

You can create an array to store the prices of each item in one variable, just as you can store many items in one combo or list box. Figure 6-9 shows the relationship between the information stored in the array and the combo box.

Figure 6-9 ◀
Relationship
between an
array and a
combo box

first array item

third array item

array containing
prices

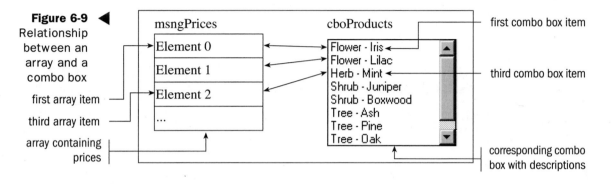

In Figure 6-9 the array msngPrices contains three elements, numbered 0 through 2, that correspond to the product descriptions stored in the cboProducts combo box. Thus, the price for the first product, Flower - Iris, is stored in the first element of msngPrices, which is element 0.

When you create an array, you use the Dim, Private, and Public statements, just as you do when you declare any variable. An array is simply a variable that contains many elements of the same data type.

To declare an array that can be used in a single module, you use a Private statement in the general declarations section of the Form module with the following syntax:

Private *array-name*([*lower-bound* **To**]*upper-bound*) **As** *datatype*

- The *array-name* can be any valid variable name.

- The *lower-bound* defines the first element of the array. If you do not specify a lower-bound, it will be set to 0 by default. The keyword **To** specifies the range of the array.

- The *upper-bound* defines the last element of the array.

- The array can be declared as any valid *datatype* using the keyword **As**.

You need to create an array to store the price for each of the products loaded into the Product combo box. Like any variable, an array declared in the general declarations section of the Form module is available to all procedures in the module if the Private keyword is used, and all procedures in all modules if the Public keyword is used. If you declare an array inside a procedure using the Dim statement, the array is considered local to the procedure and can be referenced inside that procedure only. Because the array you create will be used by many procedures on the form, you must declare the array in the general declarations section. Because there is only one form, the array should be Private.

Like variables, arrays consume memory. If you make an array too large, memory will be wasted because Visual Basic allocates memory for each element in the array whether or not the program stores values in each element. So, you should try to estimate accurately the number of elements in the array. Rose estimates she will sell at most 100 different products, so the array should be declared to hold 100 items. You do not need to store a value in each element of an array right away. You can add values later. Running the program with some empty array elements will not cause an error. Because the array is a form-level array that will hold prices, you will use the Single data type and the name msngPrices.

To declare an array to contain the prices of the products:

1. Activate the general declarations section of the Code window for the Form module.

2. Enter the following statement in the Code window after the Option Explicit statement:

```
Private msngPrices(0 To 99) As Single
```

The array msngPrices contains 100 elements. The first element is 0 and the last element is 99. Each element in the array is defined as a Single data type, which is the appropriate data type because the prices will contain a decimal point.

Storing Information in an Array

Once the array has been declared, you need to store information in it. This information will consist of the price for each item. Each price will correspond to an item in the Product combo box, as shown in Figure 6-9, but the array will include 100 elements instead of three.

When you store information in an array and retrieve information from an array, you are interested in a specific element rather than the contents of the entire array. In this case, the array stores the price for each product in the inventory. When you need to look up a price in the array, you are looking for the price of a particular item, rather than all the prices.

Next, you need to load the prices into the array. The price of each product must be stored in the array such that the first item in the Product combo box will correspond to the price contained in the first element of the array.

The procedure for loading the prices into the array is similar to the procedure you used to load the products into the combo box. Because all the products and corresponding prices must be loaded into the computer's memory before Rose can begin writing a quotation, the array should be loaded at the same time that the products are loaded into the combo box. So, you can modify the existing Form_Load event procedure to add the necessary statements for loading prices into the array. In fact, you can expand the Do loop that reads the products into the Product combo box so it also loads the prices into the array. So you can keep track of the current array element, you need to create a variable to be used as a subscript. Because a subscript always contains a whole number, you will declare it as an integer. Each time through the Do loop, the subscript must be incremented by one (1) much like a counter.

To write the code for loading the prices into the array:

1. Activate the Code window for the **Form_Load** event procedure.

2. Add the following statements to the event procedure (shown in bold):

```
Dim pintCurrentItem As Integer
pintCurrentItem = 0
Open "A:\Tutorial.06\Product.txt" For Input As #1
Do Until EOF(1)
    Input #1, pstrProduct, psngPrice
    cboProducts.AddItem pstrProduct
    msngPrices(pintCurrentItem) = psngPrice
    pintCurrentItem = pintCurrentItem + 1
Loop
```

The code you just entered will load the prices from the text file into the array.

```
Dim pintCurrentItem As Integer
pintCurrentItem = 0
```

The variable pintCurrentItem is used as an array subscript, which is always a whole number. Because you want the program to load the first line of the text file into the first element of the array, you initialized the pintCurrentItem variable to one (0).

```
msngPrices(pintCurrentItem) = psngPrice
pintCurrentItem = pintCurrentItem + 1
```

Each time a line is read from the file, the variable used in the Input # statement, psngPrice, is assigned to the element in msngPrices corresponding to the product contained in the Product combo box. Whenever you reference an array, you use the subscript to identify the element of the array you are referring to. Because the variable pintCurrentItem was initialized to zero (0), the first value of psngPrice will be stored at element position 0. This is the lower bound, or first element, of the array. Next, pintCurrentItem is incremented explicitly by one (1) so the next time through the loop, the value of psngPrice will be stored in the next element.

All the products and prices will be loaded into the program when it starts. When Rose clicks a product in the combo box, the program must determine which item she selected so it can find the corresponding price from msngPrices. The program also needs to copy this information into the ListBox objects used for output when the Add Item command button is clicked. The ListIndex property of the ComboBox object solves this problem.

The **ListIndex** property is an integer value that identifies the currently selected item in a list or combo box. The expression List1.ListIndex returns the integer index for the currently selected item in the ListBox object named List1. This is similar to the way you reference an element in an array with a subscript, but with an array you are not using a property. You can assign a value to the ListIndex property for a list or combo box. When you do, you set the active item for the list. For example, if you wanted to make the currently selected item the first item of a list box, you would set its ListIndex property to zero (0). If you wanted to deselect all items in the list, you would set the ListIndex property to minus one (-1).

Adding an item to the quotation is the most common event that Rose will trigger in this program. To allow Rose to press the Enter key to add an item to the quotation, Mack set the Default property of the Add Item command button to True in the Properties window. You now need to program the Add Item command button to look up the price for the selected product and store the product and price information in the output list boxes. The selected product is stored in the Text property of the cboProducts combo box. This must be added to the Product Description output list box. You also need to add the item's price to the Price Each output list box. This information should be formatted with two decimal places so you will use the Format statement with the Fixed argument.

To program the Add Item command button to look up prices and add both product and price information to the output ListBox objects:

1. Activate the Code window for the **cmdAdd_Click** event procedure.

2. Enter the following code in the window (shown in bold):

```
Private Sub cmdAdd_Click( )
    lstQuotedProduct.AddItem cboProducts.Text
    lstQuotedPrice.AddItem _
        Format(msngPrices(cboProducts.ListIndex), "Fixed")
    cboProducts.ListIndex = -1
End Sub
```

Each time Rose clicks a product in the Product combo box and then clicks the Add Item command button, the code you just wrote will add the information into the Product Description and Price Each output list boxes.

```
lstQuotedProduct.AddItem cboProducts.Text
```

This statement adds the text of the currently selected item in the Products combo box to the output list box lstQuotedProduct.

```
lstQuotedPrice.AddItem _
    Format(msngPrices(cboProducts.ListIndex), "Fixed")
```

This statement uses the array you created to locate the price for the selected product. To do this, the value of the ListIndex property of the currently selected product in the Products combo box is referenced, and that value becomes the subscript referenced in the msngPrices. Figure 6-10 shows how this process works. To display the prices with two decimal places, you used the Format function with the Fixed argument.

Figure 6-10 ◀
Adding the product and price to the output lists

third item (Herb - Mint) is selected; this is cboProducts.text

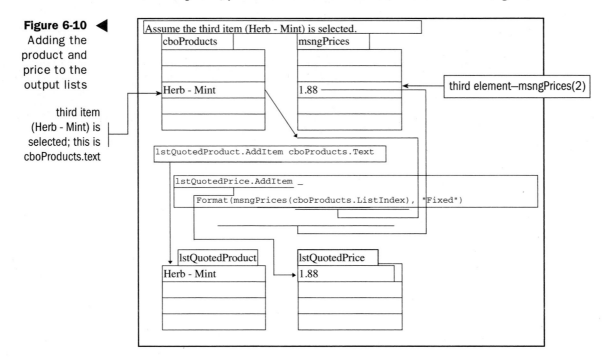

```
cboProducts.ListIndex = -1
```

This statement sets the ListIndex property of the combo box to -1, which deselects the item in the Product combo box so it is clear for the next product selection.

You now should test the program to determine if the Add Item command button is working properly. When clicked, this button should add the selected product and its corresponding price to the quotation, and then deselect the active item in the Product combo box.

To test the Add Item command button:

1. Save the project then start the program.

2. Click the list arrow in the Product combo box, then click the product **Herb - Mint**.

3. Click the **Add Item** command button. Your screen should look like Figure 6-11.

Figure 6-11 ◀
Testing the Add
Item command
button

no active item after
clicking Add Item
command button

output product
description

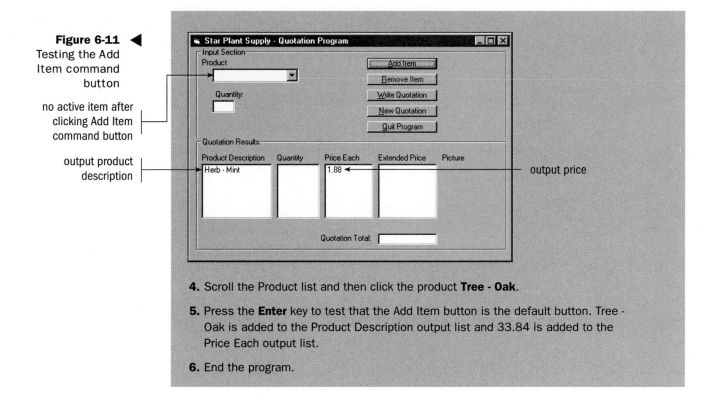

output price

4. Scroll the Product list and then click the product **Tree - Oak**.

5. Press the **Enter** key to test that the Add Item button is the default button. Tree -
Oak is added to the Product Description output list and 33.84 is added to the
Price Each output list.

6. End the program.

Now you are ready to add the quantity ordered and the extended prices to the corresponding output list boxes. This also needs to occur when the Add Item command button
is clicked. The quantity ordered will be typed in the text box and must be added to the
Quantity output list box. The extended price needs to be stored in a local variable. Because
the variable only is used by this procedure, it is declared as a local variable. Because the
variable will store prices, it must be declared as a Single data type. The variable will be
named psngExtPrice. The extended price is computed by looking up the correct price in the
msngPrices array, and multiplying that value by the quantity ordered. The output should
be displayed with two decimal places, so you will use the Format statement with the Fixed
argument. The result then is displayed in the Extended Price output list box.

To write the code for the Quantity Ordered and Extended Price output list boxes:

1. Activate the Code window for the **cmdAdd** object's **Click** event procedure.

2. Add the following statements to the event procedure (shown in bold):

```
Dim psngExtPrice As Single
lstQuotedProduct.AddItem cboProducts.Text
psngExtPrice = (txtQty.Text * _
    msngPrices(cboProducts.ListIndex))
lstQuotedPrice.AddItem _
    Format(msngPrices(cboProducts.ListIndex), "Fixed")
lstQuotedQty.AddItem txtQty.Text
lstQuotedExtPrice.AddItem Format(psngExtPrice, "Fixed")
cboProducts.ListIndex = -1
txtQty.Text = ""
```

The code you added will copy the quantity from the Quantity text box in the input section to the Quantity list box in the output section. It also will compute the extended price
and place it in the Extended Price list box in the output section.

```
Dim psngExtPrice As Single
psngExtPrice = (txtQty.Text * _
    msngPrices(cboProducts.ListIndex))
```

The first statement creates a local variable, psngExtPrice, to store the temporary extended price used in this procedure. The local variable you declared then is used to store the extended price of the product. To produce the extended price, you use the ListIndex property of the Product combo box as the subscript of the array, and multiply the value stored in each element of the array by the quantity ordered value stored in the Text property of the txtQty object. After computing the extended price, the program can add the items to the output list boxes.

```
lstQuotedQty.AddItem txtQty.Text
lstQuotedExtPrice.AddItem Format(psngExtPrice, "Fixed")
```

The first statement adds the quantity of the specific item (stored in the Text property of the Quantity text box) to the lstQuotedQty list box. The second statement adds the computed extended price to the lstQuotedExtPrice list box by calling the AddItem method. To display the extended price with two decimal places, you called the Format function with the Fixed argument.

```
txtQty.Text = ""
```

This statement sets the Text property of the txtQty text box to a blank value, which clears the Quantity text box and makes the form ready for the next product and quantity to be added.

Now you should test the program to verify that the output is being added to the correct ListBox objects, that the extended prices are being computed properly, and that the input combo and text boxes are being reset.

To test the extended price and quantity output:

1. Save the project and start the program.

2. Enter the products and quantities shown in Figure 6-12.

Figure 6-12 ◀
Completed output list boxes

input section cleared for next selection

output list boxes completed

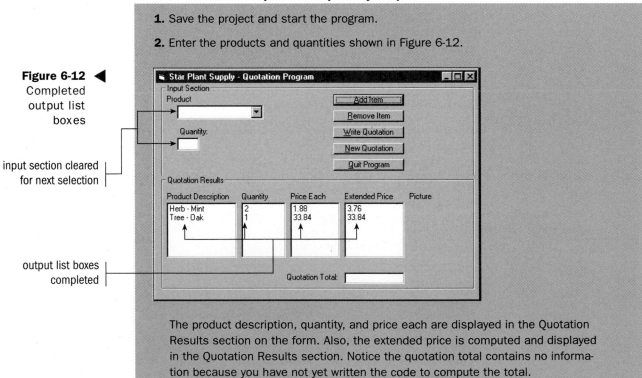

The product description, quantity, and price each are displayed in the Quotation Results section on the form. Also, the extended price is computed and displayed in the Quotation Results section. Notice the quotation total contains no information because you have not yet written the code to compute the total.

> **TROUBLE?** If you do not enter a valid number in the Quantity text box, the program will generate a run-time error when it tries to multiply the quantity requested by the price. End the program and then repeat Steps 1 and 2, making sure you enter the number "2" in the Quantity text box.
>
> **3.** End the program.

You have completed the statements to store the product description, quantity, price each, and extended price in the output list boxes. Your next task is to update the quotation total each time an item is added.

Looping Through the Items in a List Box

In previous tutorials you used the Change or LostFocus event of an object to call a general procedure that calculates totals each time the value of the object changed or the focus moved to a different object. In this case, unlike a TextBox object, the ListBox object does not support the Change event. So, the program must update the total when the Add Item command button is clicked.

You have seen how to use a Do loop with the EOF function to examine each line of a text file repetitively until the end-of-file condition is reached. In that situation the program does not know how many lines are in the text file. Rather, the loop terminates when the end-of-file condition is true.

You still could use a Do loop to step through each item in the Extended Price list box as well, by creating a variable used as an index. Another ListBox property, the ListCount property, is an integer that contains the number of items in a list. If the list or combo box is empty, the ListCount is zero (0); otherwise, the value of ListCount is the number of items in the list.

Your Do loop would use a variable to represent the ListIndex property. It would contain a statement to increment the variable each time through the loop. Before executing the loop again, the condition in the Do loop would test that the variable representing the current ListIndex property is less than the number of items in the list box (represented by the ListCount property), and exit the loop when it has examined all of the items.

Visual Basic provides another kind of looping structure that works like a counter. Each time the statements in the loop are executed, a counter is incremented until the counter is the same as some value you assign. This type of looping structure is called a **For loop** and it uses the For statement.

You can use a For statement when you know in advance how many times the statements in the loop need to be executed. Because your program includes items in a list box, the number of items (represented by the ListCount property) are known at any given time. So, a For loop is appropriate for stepping through each item in the list box. When you use a For loop, you do not have to write any statements to increment the variable you are using as a counter. Instead, the For statement does this for you. The For loop has the following syntax:

For *counter* = *start* **To** *end* [**Step** *increment*]

    [*statement-block*]

    [**Exit For**]

    [*statement-block*]

Next [*counter*]

Consider the For loop as a structure that works with counters, as illustrated in Figure 6-13.

Figure 6-13 ◀
The For loop

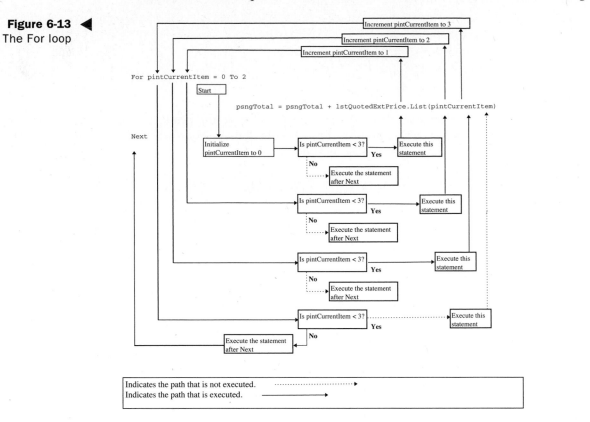

When you execute a For loop, the following happens:

1. The *counter* is initialized to the value of *start* the first time the For loop is executed. The counter is a variable of the Integer data type that you already declared using a Dim, Private, or Public statement. To look at the first item in a list box, *start* should have a value of zero (0), the lower bound of the list box.

2. Every time through the loop, the value of the counter is increased by the *increment*. If the increment is not specified, the default value is one (1). So, after the statements in the loop are executed, the counter must be incremented by one (1) to look at every item in the list box.

3. When the value of the counter is greater than *end*, the For loop exits and the *statement-block* in the loop is not executed again. This will happen after all the items in the list box have been examined.

4. If the counter is less than *end*, the first *statement-block* is executed; *end* would be the number of items in the list box.

5. If an Exit For statement is reached, usually enclosed in an If statement as the result of an abnormal condition, the For loop will exit. Otherwise the next *statement-block* is executed. A For loop does not require an Exit For statement. For example, if you are adding to the contents of the list boxes and wanted to make sure each list box contained a number, you could use an Exit For statement to stop the loop if one of the list boxes contained invalid data. Because the prices are taken from a text file and the extended prices are computed by the program, rather than entered by the user, you do not need to check for valid data. So, an Exit For statement is not necessary.

6. When the Next statement is reached, the *counter* is incremented and the For loop is tested again.

The List property of the ListBox and ComboBox objects, used with an index, acts like an array. The List property has the following syntax:

object.**List**(*index*)

- The **List** property references the text in each item of the list or combo box.

- You use the List property with an *index* of the item just as you use the subscript for an array. The first list item has an index of zero (0). If you wanted to reference the text of the second item (remember, its ListIndex property is one (1)) to the list box named lstMyList, you would use the following statement:

```
lstMyList.List(1)
```

For the quotation program, you want to create a loop that will step through all the items in the Extended Price list box so the program can compute the quotation total. The first item in the list box has an index of zero (0). The ListCount property tells you how many items are in the list. You can compute the index value of the last item in the list by subtracting one (1) from the ListCount property. You now have the information for the start and end conditions of the For loop. You can use the List property with the index to reference the item you want the program to look at. This index should be the *counter* from the For loop. The index of the first item in a list box is always zero (0), so the For loop should start at zero (0) and end when all the items have been examined (ListCount - 1).

Using a For loop and the properties of the list box, you can compute the quotation total by adding together each extended price in the Extended Price list box. You need to declare a variable to be used as an accumulator that will store the quotation total. This variable will be named psngTotal. Because the variable only will be used by the procedure, it will be declared as a local variable. Each time through the loop, the program must add the extended price to the accumulator. When the loop is complete (each item has been examined), the result should be formatted with two decimal places and a leading dollar sign and displayed in the lblTotal label. Thus, you will use the Format statement and store the result in the Caption property of lblTotal.

Because the program also must compute the quotation total when products are removed, you can write the necessary code once in a general procedure and call the general procedure whenever the total needs to be recomputed. You will name the procedure ComputeTotal to communicate its purpose. Because the program consists of a single form and the general procedure will be used by multiple procedures, you will declare the procedure as Private. You need to use the Insert Procedure dialog box to create this procedure before writing the code.

To compute the quotation total using a For loop:

1. Make sure the Code window is active. Because you are going to create a new general procedure, it does not matter which object and event procedure currently are active in the Code window.

2. Click **Tools** on the menu bar, then click **Add Procedure** to open the Add Procedure dialog box.

3. In the Name text box, type **ComputeTotal**.

   You will create a Sub procedure because it will not return a value.

4. In the Type section, click the **Sub** option button.

   You will declare the procedure as Private because it only will be used by this form.

5. In the Scope section, click the **Private** option button.

6. Click the **OK** button.

7. Enter the following statements in the Code window (shown in bold):

```
Private Sub ComputeTotal( )
    Dim psngTotal As Single
    Dim pintCurrentItem As Integer
    psngTotal = 0
    For pintCurrentItem = 0 To _
        lstQuotedExtPrice.ListCount - 1
        psngTotal = psngTotal + _
            lstQuotedExtPrice.List(pintCurrentItem)
    Next
    lblTotal.Caption = Format(psngTotal, "Currency")
End Sub
```

With the For loop, these statements use a counter (pintCurrentItem) to look at each value in the Extended Price list box and add the value to an accumulator (psngTotal).

```
Dim psngTotal As Single
Dim pintCurrentItem As Integer
psngTotal = 0
```

These statements declare two local variables, which exist only while the procedure is running. The variable psngTotal is used as an accumulator. Each time the program steps through an item in the Extended Price list box, it adds the extended price to psngTotal. The variable pintCurrentItem is used as the counter in the For loop. You initialize the variable by setting the value of psngTotal to zero (0). The For loop initializes the value of the counter pintCurrentItem.

```
For pintCurrentItem = 0 To _
    lstQuotedExtPrice.ListCount - 1
    psngTotal = psngTotal + _
        lstQuotedExtPrice.List(pintCurrentItem)
Next
```

> *Tip:* It is a good practice to initialize variables explicitly before the program begins processing. This gives the reader of your program a clear indication of what the value of the variable should be when the procedure starts.

The For loop steps through each item in the lstQuotedExtPrice list box by starting at item zero (0). This is the start value of the For loop. You could use a similar For loop to go through all of the elements in an array, because you know the number of elements (represented by the array subscript).

The List property of the list box retrieves the contents of the list box, in this case the extended prices, and adds them to the variable for the total. Remember, the List property is like an array; it requires an index of the element. In this case, the index is the loop's counter, pintCurrentItem.

When the Next statement is reached, the value of the counter pintCurrentItem is incremented by one (1). If the new value of the counter is less than or equal to ListCount - 1, then the statements in the loop are executed again. This process continues until there are no more items in the list box, which means that the counter has reached the end value, ListCount, and the For loop will exit. Recall that no Exit statements are needed to exit a For loop—it exits automatically when the end value of the counter is reached.

```
lblTotal.Caption = Format(psngTotal, "Currency")
```

This statement formats the quotation total with two decimal places and a leading dollar sign.

Now that you have written the ComputeTotal general procedure, you need to call it explicitly. The cmdAdd_Click procedure controls what occurs when a product is added to the quotation. If you want the quotation total to be updated whenever a product is added to the quotation, you need to call the general procedure from the cmdAdd_Click event procedure.

To call the ComputeTotal general procedure:

1. Activate the Code window for the **cmdAdd_Click** event procedure.

2. Add the following statement to the procedure, just before the End Sub statement:

```
ComputeTotal
```

You should run the program to verify that the quotation total is being computed correctly.

To test the quotation total:

1. Save the project then start the program.

2. Enter the products and quantities shown in Figure 6-14.

Figure 6-14 ◀
Testing the
quotation total

enter these quantities ——

select these products ——

displays total of
extended prices

3. Make sure your extended prices and quotation total match those shown in Figure 6-14.

TROUBLE? If the quotation total is not being computed, make sure you called the ComputeTotal procedure in the cmdAdd_Click event procedure.

TROUBLE? If the quotation total is not correct, check the code for the For loop in the ComputeTotal procedure. Make any necessary corrections, then repeat Steps 1 through 3.

4. End the program.

You have completed the first phase of the quotation program. Rose now can add products, quantities, and prices to a quotation and see the new total of the quotation each time she adds a product. Rose also can create her quotations electronically, with a minimal amount of typing. By preserving the contents of the text file containing the product and price information, she still can print a copy of the file when she needs to use a hard copy.

1. Describe the difference between using a database and sequential access for processing. Describe the advantages and disadvantages of each method.

2. What is the purpose of the Open statement, the Input # statement, and the Close statement?

3. What is the EOF function used for?

4. Declare an array named Prices with 20 elements and a lower bound of 1.

5. Describe the purpose of the List, ListCount, and ListIndex properties of a list box.

6. Write a For loop that will count from 20 to 100 and print the value of the counter.

7. What is the purpose of the Exit For statement?

SESSION

6.2

In this session you will learn how to remove one specific item from a list box and how to remove all the items in a list box at once. You also will create a two-dimensional array, use the Variant data type for storing multiple kinds of data, display pictures at run time in a PictureBox control, and write program results to a text file.

Modifying the Program

Rose spent some time reviewing and testing your program with Mack. Rose still needs to be able to clear all the output list boxes so she can prepare a new quotation. Also, when she is preparing a quotation, she needs the capability to delete specific products from the quotation if the customer decides to omit items to maintain the budget for a project. For this, Mack included a Remove Item button that needs the code to delete a quoted product from the output and recompute the total whenever an item is removed. Finally, Rose wants a way to write the quotation results to a file she can format and then print the quotation using her word processing program.

Rose and Mack also have some suggestions to improve the program so it more closely models Rose's business activities. Rose often gives customers a discount depending on their annual purchasing volume, so she wants the program to be able to apply the discount. You will add a new Apply Discount check box that will enable Rose to apply a discount to the prices she charges, when appropriate. She also would like to display pictures of the different products on the form for those times when the customer is in the office. In this way customers can see the products they are ordering. Mack suggests you complete the development of the program. Next to the output list boxes, you will need to include a picture box, which will display pictures of the different products. You need to complete the programming for the Remove Item, Write Quotation, and New Quotation buttons, and the new check box and picture box.

Clearing the Contents of a List Box

After Rose completes a quotation, she needs to reset all the output list boxes and the quotation total to begin a new quotation for another customer. The New Quotation command button Mack created will be used to reset the list boxes used for output in preparation for another quotation. You needed to delete all the items from the ListBox objects and set the quotation total to zero (0) again. You can delete all the items from the list boxes using the Clear method for each of the four ListBox objects. The Clear method has the following syntax:

object.**Clear**

- The *object* can be any valid ListBox or ComboBox object.

- The **Clear** method removes all items from the object.

You now can write the code for the New Quotation command button. You will call the Clear method for each of the list boxes and reset the total to zero (0).

To program the New Quotation command button:

1. Open the project file named **Star Plant Supply.vbp** in the **Tutorial.06** folder on your Student Disk, if necessary.

2. Open the Code window for the **cmdNewQuotation_ Click** event procedure.

3. Enter the following code in the window (shown in bold):

```
Private Sub cmdNewQuotation_Click( )
    lstQuotedProduct.Clear
    lstQuotedQty.Clear
    lstQuotedPrice.Clear
    lstQuotedExtPrice.Clear
    lblTotal.Caption = ""
    txtQty.Text = ""
    cboProducts.ListIndex = -1
End Sub
```

These statements clear the input and output objects in preparation for another quotation.

```
lstQuotedProduct.Clear
lstQuotedQty.Clear
lstQuotedPrice.Clear
lstQuotedExtPrice.Clear
```

The Clear method deletes all the items in a list box, and is called in these four statements for each of the four output list boxes.

```
lblTotal.Caption = ""
txtQty.Text = ""
cboProducts.ListIndex = -1
```

These statements erase the value of the Caption property of the Label object used for the quotation total, clear the contents of the Quantity text box, and deselect the active item in the Product combo box. You need to clear the Quantity text box and the Product combo box because if Rose selects a new product or enters a new quantity, but does not click the Add Item button to add those selections to the output and clear these objects, they still would be selected.

Now you should run and test the program to be sure the code for the New Quotation command button is working properly.

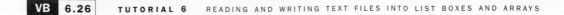

To test the New Quotation command button:

1. Save the project then start the program.

2. Enter the products and quantities shown in Figure 6-15.

Figure 6-15 ◀
Testing the
New Quotation
command
button

objects will be blank
after clicking New
Quotation button

3. Click the **New Quotation** command button. Each line in the output list boxes is erased. The Quotation Total label is blank and no product is selected in the Product combo box.

   TROUBLE? If the output lists and quotation total did not clear, check the code for the New Quotation command button and make sure you called the Clear method for each of the output ListBox objects and set the text box's Text property to an empty string. Make any necessary corrections, then repeat Steps 1 through 3.

4. End the program.

Now that you have used the Clear method to remove all the items from a list box, you can proceed to write the statements that will allow Rose to remove an individual item from one of the output list boxes.

Removing a Specific Item from a List Box

Just as you used the AddItem method to add an item to a list box, you can use the **RemoveItem** method to delete an item from a list box. The RemoveItem method has the following syntax:

object.**RemoveItem** *index*

- The *object* is any valid list or combo box.

- The **RemoveItem** method takes one argument—the *index* of the item you want to delete. If you want to remove the first item, the index is zero (0); if you want to remove the second item, the index is one (1), and so on.

The program needs to call the RemoveItem method for each output list box when the Remove Item command button is clicked. You will use a temporary procedure-level Integer variable representing the ListIndex property as the index argument for each call to the RemoveItem method. Whenever an item is removed from the quotation, you need to recompute the total, so you will call the ComputeTotal general procedure you wrote earlier.

To write the code to delete an item from the output list boxes:

1. Activate the Code window for the **cmdRemove_Click** event procedure.

2. Enter the following code in the window (shown in bold):

```
Private Sub cmdRemove_Click( )
    Dim pintIndex As Integer
    pintIndex = lstQuotedProduct.ListIndex
    If pintIndex > -1 Then
        lstQuotedProduct.RemoveItem pintIndex
        lstQuotedQty.RemoveItem pintIndex
        lstQuotedPrice.RemoveItem pintIndex
        lstQuotedExtPrice.RemoveItem pintIndex
        ComputeTotal
    End If
End Sub
```

These statements remove a selected item from the output ListBox objects and recompute the quotation total.

```
Dim pintIndex As Integer
pintIndex = lstQuotedProduct.ListIndex
```

These two statements declare the variable pintIndex and store the index of the currently selected item into that variable. When the program calls the RemoveItem method on the active item in the list, the ListIndex property is set to minus one (-1) because the active item no longer exists. If you try to use the ListIndex property, rather than the temporary variable, as the argument to the RemoveItem method when its value is -1, the program would generate a run-time error because you would be attempting to remove a nonexistent item.

```
If pintIndex > -1 Then
    lstQuotedProduct.RemoveItem pintIndex
    lstQuotedQty.RemoveItem pintIndex
    lstQuotedPrice.RemoveItem pintIndex
    lstQuotedExtPrice.RemoveItem pintIndex
    ComputeTotal
End If
```

This code uses an If statement to determine if an item is selected in the lstQuotedProduct list box. If no item is selected, the value of the ListIndex property and of pintIndex is minus one (-1), so no attempt will be made to remove an item when none has been selected. Next, the RemoveItem method is called for each of the four output list boxes. Then, because the program removed an item, it computes the quotation total again by calling the ComputeTotal general procedure.

You now should test your program to determine if the cmdRemove_Click event works properly.

To test the Remove Item command button:

1. Save the project then start the program.

2. Enter the products and corresponding quantities into the quotation, as shown in Figure 6-16.

Figure 6-16 ◀
Testing the
Remove Item
command
button

enter these two
products and
quantities

select this item
to be removed

total will update
after clicking Remove
Item button

3. Click the product **Tree - Oak** in the output list box, as shown in Figure 6-16.

4. Click the **Remove Item** command button. The program removes the item Tree - Oak from the output lists and recomputes the quotation total.

   TROUBLE? If you receive a run-time error or if the item Tree - Oak was not deleted from the list and the quotation total was not recalculated, make sure your code for the cmdRemove_Click event procedure is the same as the code in the previous steps. Make any necessary corrections, then repeat Steps 1 through 4.

5. Make sure no product is selected in the Product Description list box.

6. Click the **Remove Item** command button. No item is removed from the lists and no error is generated because the If statement tested that nothing was selected.

7. End the program.

Rose has looked at the program and thinks it is very easy to use. She quickly can look up each product she sells and see a quotation without worrying about looking up the wrong price or making a computational error. And, with the Remove Item command button, she can delete items from the quotation without starting over. She also would like the program to compute a discount for customers with a large annual sales volume. To do this, you need to create a check box to indicate whether or not a discount needs to be applied and an array that can hold both the regular and discounted prices.

Creating a Two-dimensional Array

One way to tell the program when to use the regular price and when to use the discounted price is to include a second price list array that contains the discounted prices. But you also can create an array with two columns for each product. One column will contain the regular price and the other column will contain the discounted price.

The array you need to create, with one column for the regular prices and another for the discounted prices, is called a **two-dimensional array**. Two-dimensional refers to rows and columns. The one-column array you created in the previous session to contain the prices for the products is a one-dimensional array because it contains only rows. In the two-dimensional array for regular and discounted prices, one dimension, the rows, will hold the information for each element in the array, and the other dimension, the columns, will hold the regular prices in one column and the discounted prices in the second column. Figure 6-17 shows part of the two-dimensional array for the regular and discounted prices.

Figure 6-17 ◄
Two-
dimensional
array

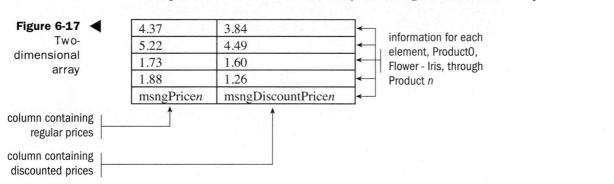

4.37	3.84
5.22	4.49
1.73	1.60
1.88	1.26
msngPrice$n$	msngDiscountPrice$n$

information for each
element, Product0,
Flower - Iris, through
Product n

column containing
regular prices

column containing
discounted prices

Like the one-dimensional array you created in the first session, a two-dimensional array is not an object. Rather it is a variable that contains elements. In a two-dimensional array, you make a reference to an individual element using a subscript, just as you do with a one-dimensional array. You must supply, however, a subscript for each dimension of the array. So, a two-dimensional array has two subscripts. One subscript identifies the row number and the other identifies the column number. The syntax to create a two-dimensional array is similar to the syntax to create a one-dimensional array:

Private *array-name*([*lower-bound* **To**] *upper-bound*, [*lower-bound* **To**] _
    upper-bound) **As** *datatype*

- This statement declares a form-level array with the name *array-name*, which can be any valid variable name.

- The first subscript is the range of rows and the second is the range of columns. The first *lower-bound* defines the element in the first row of the array. The second *lower-bound* defines the element in the first column of the array. If you do not specify a lower-bound, it will be set to zero (0) by default.

- The first *upper-bound* defines the element in the last row of the array. The second *upper-bound* defines the element in the last column of the array.

- The *datatype* can be any valid Visual Basic data type.

You need to change the price array msngPrices so it has two columns. The first column will store the regular prices and the second column will store the discounted prices.

To declare the two-dimensional array:

1. Activate the general declarations section of the Code window for the Form module.

2. Change the declaration of the msngPrices in the window (shown in bold):

```
Dim msngPrices(0 To 99,0 To 1) As Single
```

This statement declares a two-dimensional array made up of 100 rows and two columns. There are 100 products that can be stored in the rows for each of the two different prices.

Now you need to write the statements to load the array. Joan already has changed the contents of the text file to contain the discounted prices separated by commas. You need to create a variable named psngDiscountPrice, which is needed to store the discounted prices, and modify the Input # statement in the Form_Load event procedure so it reads all the contents of the new file. The first subscript refers to the rows, as in the original array. The second subscript refers to the columns. The first column can be referenced using a subscript of zero (0). The second column has a subscript of one (1).

To declare the discounted price variable, modify the Input # statement, and load the discounted prices into the array:

1. Activate the Code window for the **Form_Load** event procedure.

2. Change the Open statement so it reads the file named **Product2.txt** rather than Product.txt.

3. Enter the following variable declarations into the **Form_Load** event procedure just after the other variable declarations:

```
Dim psngDiscountPrice As Single
Dim pstrPicture As String
```

Note that you will use the variable pstrPicture later in the session to store the file-names containing pictures of the products Rose sells. Because it is in the text file, you have to read it now.

4. Modify the Input # statement as follows (shown in bold):

```
Input #1, pstrProduct, psngPrice, _
    psngDiscountPrice, pstrPicture
```

5. Change the existing msngPrices statement in the event procedure, and add the new msngPrices statement to match the following code (shown in bold):

```
msngPrices(pintCurrentItem, 0) = psngPrice
msngPrices(pintCurrentItem, 1) = psngDiscountPrice
```

The changes you just made to the Form_Load event procedure will load the price information into a two-dimensional array.

```
msngPrices(pintCurrentItem, 0) = psngPrice
msngPrices(pintCurrentItem, 1) = psngDiscountPrice
```

These statements store the values of the variables into each column of the msngPrices. The first statement stores the regular prices into the first column (column 0), and the second statement stores the discounted prices into the second column (column 1). The row is defined by the variable pintCurrentItem and is set by the For loop.

Now you can create the Apply Discount check box and make the necessary modifications to the Add Item command button so the correct price will be used depending on whether or not the Apply Discount check box is checked. To do so, you need to write an If statement to determine the value of the check box. You will use this information to determine whether to use the regular or discounted price.

To add the discount check box and code the Add Item command button to assign the appropriate price:

1. Create a check box as shown in Figure 6-18.

2. Set the Caption property to **Apply Discount** and the Name property to **chkDiscount**.

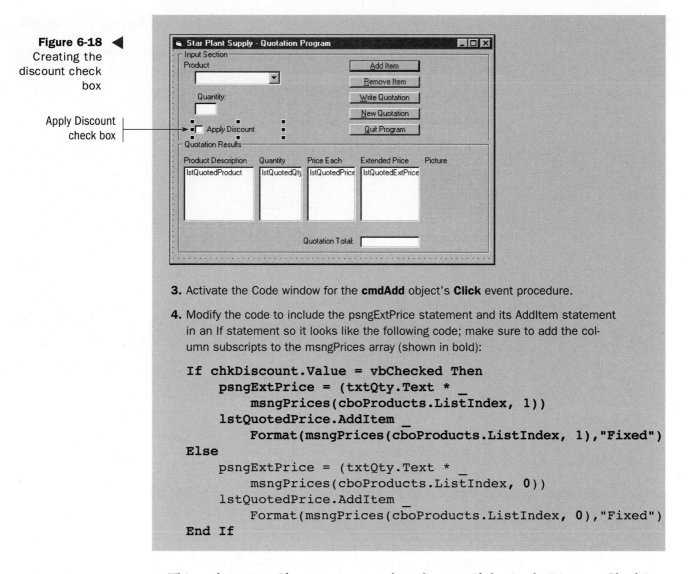

Figure 6-18 ◀
Creating the
discount check
box

Apply Discount
check box

3. Activate the Code window for the **cmdAdd** object's **Click** event procedure.

4. Modify the code to include the psngExtPrice statement and its AddItem statement
   in an If statement so it looks like the following code; make sure to add the column subscripts to the msngPrices array (shown in bold):

```
If chkDiscount.Value = vbChecked Then
    psngExtPrice = (txtQty.Text * _
        msngPrices(cboProducts.ListIndex, 1))
    lstQuotedPrice.AddItem _
        Format(msngPrices(cboProducts.ListIndex, 1),"Fixed")
Else
    psngExtPrice = (txtQty.Text * _
        msngPrices(cboProducts.ListIndex, 0))
    lstQuotedPrice.AddItem _
        Format(msngPrices(cboProducts.ListIndex, 0),"Fixed")
End If
```

This code uses an If statement to apply a discount if the Apply Discount CheckBox
object is checked. If the object is not checked, the regular prices are used. You now can
test the program to determine if the regular and discounted prices are being computed
correctly.

To test the discounted prices:

1. Save the project then start the program.

2. Click the **Apply Discount** check box to select it.

3. Enter the products and corresponding quantities into the quotation, as shown in Figure 6-19.

Figure 6-19 ◀
Testing the
discount prices

enter these products ⟶

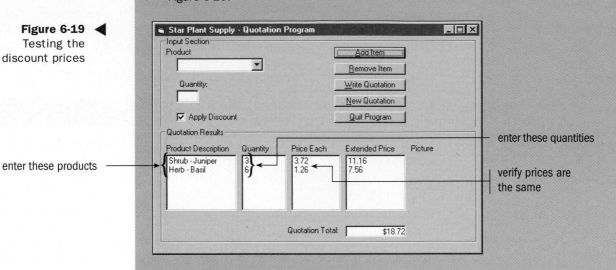

enter these quantities

verify prices are
the same

The program applies the discount and displays the discounted price for each selected product.

4. Be sure the discounted prices are the same as those in Figure 6-19.

TROUBLE? If you receive a run-time error, make sure you changed the number of dimensions of the array in the general declarations section of the Form module. Also make sure you changed the dimensions of the array in the Form_Load event procedure and added the statement to load the discounted price. Finally, be sure you changed the open statement to read Product2.txt. Check to make sure the If statement in the cmdAdd_Click procedure is correct. Make any necessary corrections, then repeat Steps 1 through 4.

5. End the program.

Now the program can calculate the quotations at the regular price or at the discounted price. Rose also would like to display pictures of the products to her customers when they are in the office as she prepares their quotations. At some point, she will have pictures of all the products, but currently she has only a few images that were supplied as samples by different vendors.

Adding Pictures to a Form

You can use either a PictureBox object or an Image object to display pictures on a form. The **PictureBox** object supports more events and properties than the Image object. For example, a picture box can respond to a Change event in addition to a Click event.

Unlike the Image control, the PictureBox control cannot resize pictures with the Stretch property. The pictures Rose intends to use will all be the same size, so you can create a PictureBox control that is the same size as the pictures.

As with the Image control, you could assign the pictures to the picture box by setting the Picture property in the Properties window at design time. But then your program would contain only one picture. You want the picture displayed to depend on the active product; therefore, you should set the Picture property with code, rather than in the Properties window.

Joan has changed the price list file, Product2.txt, so it includes a field containing the filename of the picture. The program must be able to load the file containing the picture when an item in the Product combo box is selected. You could create another array of the String data type. When you load the price, you could write another statement to load the file-name of the picture using the filename contained in the other array. In this case the other array would be a one-dimensional array.

You have learned that all the elements in an array must be of the same data type. You want to store numbers with a decimal point—regular prices in one column and discounted prices in another—and strings (picture filenames), in the third column. On the surface, this seems to break the Visual Basic "rule" of using variables of the same data type. Another option, however, will allow you to include prices and filenames in the same array.

Arrays of Variant Data Type

Visual Basic supports a data type called **Variant**, which can store all the different data types such as Integer, Single, and String. However, the Variant data type cannot store Fixed length strings or user-defined types. For example, Var1 declared as a Variant data type could contain the values 1, 1.05, TRUE, "Hello", or "c:\windows\waves.bmp". Visual Basic accomplishes this by storing the data type of the variable in the variable itself. If you store an integer into a variant array or variable, the variable is an Integer Variant data type. If you later store a string in the variant, the variable becomes a String Variant data type. Variant variables, and members of variant arrays, can change their data type while a program is running.

So, to hold both the prices and the picture filenames, you can create a two-dimensional variant array and use the first and second columns as Single Variant data types for the regular prices and discounted prices, and the third column as a String Variant data type for the picture filenames.

To declare an array of the Variant data type you use the Private, Public, or Dim statements, as you have done before.

> *Tip:*   Because Visual Basic stores the data type of a variable inside
> the variable, and must determine the type of data stored in a
> Variant variable whenever it is referenced, operations on Variant
> variables are much slower than operations on Integer or Single
> variables. Thus, you should use Variant variables only when
> necessary.

To develop the code to work with the pictures as well as the prices, you need to change the two-dimensional array msngPrices, which contains prices (Single data type), to a two-dimensional array of variants (Single and String data types). You also need to specify a third column to hold the picture filenames from the text file.

To change the msngPrices to a Variant array:

1. Open the general declarations section of the Code window for the Form module.

2. Change the declaration for msngPrices in the window (shown in bold):

```
Dim msngPrices(0 To 99,0 To 2) As Variant
```

Now that you have declared the three-column array of a Variant data type, you can write the code to load the picture filenames into the third column of the array. The specific picture should be loaded when Rose clicks a product so a customer in the office can see the product being quoted. To do this, you need to modify the Form_Load event procedure. In your array the first subscript still represents the rows, and the second subscript represents the columns. The regular prices are represented by the column subscript zero (0); the discounted prices are represented by the column subscript one (1); and the picture filenames are represented by the column subscript two (2).

To load the filenames into the Variant array:

1. Create a PictureBox object as shown in Figure 6-20.

Figure 6-20 ◀
Creating the
PictureBox
object

2. Set the Name property to **picFlower**.

3. Activate the Code window for the **Form_Load** event procedure.

4. Add the following line of code to the Do loop immediately after the Input # statement and the first two msngPrices statements to store the filename of the picture into msngPrices:

```
msngPrices(pintCurrentItem, 2) = pstrPicture
```

This statement stores the picture filenames into the third column of the array. Now you can write the code for displaying a picture in the picture box when an item in the Product combo box is clicked. When Rose clicks a product in the Product combo box, the program must load the corresponding picture using its filename. You can do this by calling the **LoadPicture** function at run time. The LoadPicture function supports one argument, the filename of a picture, and has the following syntax:

object.**Picture** = **LoadPicture**(*filename*)

- The **Picture** property of any valid *object* can be set using the **LoadPicture** function.

- The *filename* can be any filename containing a picture.

The third column of the array contains the filenames of the pictures you want to show in the quotation program. You will use the ListIndex property of the cboProducts ComboBox object as a subscript of the array to look up the correct filename.

To load the pictures into the picture box:

1. Activate the Code window for the **cboProducts_Click** event procedure.

2. Enter the following code in the window:

```
Private Sub cboProducts_Click( )
    If cboProducts.ListIndex > -1 Then
        picFlower.Picture = _
            LoadPicture(msngPrices _
            (cboProducts.ListIndex, 2))
    End If
End Sub
```

When an item in the Product combo box is clicked, the code you just wrote will display the corresponding picture in the picture box. The first statement determines if an item is selected in the Product combo box. The subsequent statements are called only if an item is selected (ListIndex > -1). The second statement calls the LoadPicture function with one argument—the filename of the picture to load. The filenames are stored in the third column of the msngPrices. The current row is determined by using the current index (ListIndex property) of cboProducts.

Now you should test the new picture box and the code you added to the cboProducts_Click event procedure.

To test the picture box:

1. Save the project then start the program.

2. Click **Flower - Iris** in the Product combo box. The picture of the selected product appears in the PictureBox object, as shown in Figure 6-21.

Figure 6-21 ◀
Testing the picture box

selected product

picture appears in PictureBox object

TROUBLE? If you receive a run-time error, you probably did not change the dimensions of the array or you might have forgotten to change the data type from Single to Variant. Check your code, make sure you added the LoadPicture function to the Click event, make any necessary corrections, and then repeat Steps 1 and 2.

3. End the program.

Your program now will display pictures for those items that have pictures available by setting the Picture property of the PictureBox object at run time.

Writing a Text File

Some of Rose's customers want a printed copy of a quotation. Rose currently uses a word processing application to format the information. She likes the layout she has created and sometimes customizes the printout for an individual customer's needs. She wants to use the information produced by this quotation program in her word processing documents.

Visual Basic supports a **Write #** statement that will write text to ASCII-delimited files, which then can be read by most word processing, spreadsheet, and database programs. This is the same type of file you used to read text into the quotation program when you called the Input # statement.

When you write a text file, just as when you read one, you first must open the file using the Open statement. You used the Open statement For Input in the previous session to read the text file containing the product and price information. This time you need to use the Open statement with the For Output argument so you can write a file. Then, you can use the Write # statement to write information from the program to the text file. Remember, if the file already exists when you open it For Output, it will be overwritten.

As with other files you open, you must close a text file when you are finished writing to it. The syntax of the Write # statement is:

Write #*filenumber*, [*outputlist*]

- The **Write #** statement writes to a file that already has been opened For Output or For Append. It also inserts commas between each item in the *outputlist* and places quotation marks around strings as they are written to the file. Numeric data always is written using the period (.) as the decimal separator. Files written with the Write # statement can be read easily with the Input # statement.

- The *filenumber* is a valid filenumber created by an Open statement.

- Each item in the *outputlist* is usually a variable or object property in your program separated by a comma. The *outputlist* is similar to the *inputlist* of the Input # statement.

- In the file, Visual Basic will insert commas between the fields and surround String variables with quotation marks.

REFERENCE window	**WRITING A TEXT FILE**
	■ Make sure the file is open for output or append.
	■ Create a Write # statement with the filenumber you specified in the Open statement and multiple variables or expressions separated by commas.
	■ To finish writing a file, use the Close statement with the filenumber you need to close.

You need to add the statements to the Write Quotation command button so clicking this button will create a text file of the quotation output. Rose then will be able to read the file into her word processing program so she can format it. To do this you need to open the file For Output and create a For loop to examine every item in the output list boxes, just as you did to include every item in the ComputeTotal general procedure. Inside the For loop, you need to use the Write # statement to write the contents of each output list box—Product Description, Quantity, Price Each, and Extended Price—to the text file. Because you have no open files, you can reuse filenumber 1.

To write the code to create a text file of the current quotation output:

1. Open the Code window for the **cmdWriteQuotation_Click** event procedure.

2. Enter the following code in the window:

```
Private Sub cmdWriteQuotation_Click( )
    Dim pintCurrentItem As Integer
    Dim pstrFileName As String
    pstrFileName = _
        InputBox("Enter the filename", "Write File")
    If pstrFileName <> "" Then
        Open pstrFileName For Output As #1
        For pintCurrentItem = 0 To _
            lstQuotedExtPrice.ListCount - 1
            Write #1, _
                lstQuotedProduct.List(pintCurrentItem), _
                Val(lstQuotedQty.List(pintCurrentItem)), _
                Val(lstQuotedPrice.List(pintCurrentItem)), _
                Val(lstQuotedExtPrice.List(pintCurrentItem))
        Next
```

```
        Close #1
        End If
End Sub
```

The code to write an ASCII-delimited file is similar to the code to read one. You open the file, using a loop to write each line in the file, and close the file once all the lines have been written. So Rose can specify the folder and filename she wants to use, you call the InputBox function to get a string that will be used as a filename.

```
pstrFileName = _
    InputBox("Enter the filename", "Write File")
If pstrFileName <> "" Then
    Open pstrFileName For Output As #1
```

This statement opens the file using the Open statement if a filename was specified and assigns the active filenumber. Instead of opening the file For Input (reading the file) you need to open the file For Output (writing the file). When opened For Output, the contents of the file are overwritten if the file already exists. If you want to append information to a file, you use the For Append option.

```
For pintCurrentItem = 0 To _
    lstQuotedExtPrice.ListCount - 1
    Write #1, _
        lstQuotedProduct.List(pintCurrentItem), _
        Val(lstQuotedQty.List(pintCurrentItem)), _
        Val(lstQuotedPrice.List(pintCurrentItem)), _
        Val(lstQuotedExtPrice.List(pintCurrentItem))
Next
```

The For loop steps through each item in the output list box lstQuotedExtPrice, starting at zero (0) and ending at the end of the list (ListCount -1). A line is written for each of the items quoted. Each line written contains the four items from the output list boxes. Visual Basic will insert a comma between each item. Because the items in a list box are treated as strings, these statements call the Val function on the quantity, price, and extended price fields so they are converted to numbers and written without quotation marks.

Now you need to test the program one more time to make sure the Write Quotation command button works correctly.

To test the Write Quotation command button:

1. Save the project then start the program.

2. Enter the products and corresponding quantities, as shown in Figure 6-22.

Figure 6-22 ◀
Testing the
Write Quotation
command
button

enter these products
and quantities

3. Click the **Write Quotation** command button.

4. Enter the filename **A:\Tutorial.06\Quote.txt,** then click the OK button.

The program output is written to the file Quote.txt in the Tutorial.06 folder on your Student Disk.

The file Quote.txt contains the information shown in Figure 6-23. You can open it in WordPad or any word processing program.

Figure 6-23 ◀
Contents of
text file

```
"Herb - Basil",3,1.88,5.64
"Flower - Iris",2,4.37,8.74
"Flower - Lilac",3,5.22,15.66
```

5. End the program then exit Visual Basic.

6. Open Quote.txt in your word processing program and compare it to Figure 6-23. Exit your word processing program.

The quotation program now is complete. When Rose starts the program, the text file containing the price list will be loaded into the computer's memory. When she selects a product in the Product combo box, a picture of the product (if one exists) will be displayed in the picture box. Rose can enter a quantity and click the Add Item command button to display the product description, the quantity, the price per product, and the extended price in the output section of the form. The price per product either can be the regular or the discounted price, based on the customer's volume of sales. All Rose needs to do to determine which price to use is click the Apply Discount check box. Rose can clear one or all products from the output section of the quotation program. The quotation total will be updated with every change to the output section of the form. Finally, Rose can write the quotation to a text file, which she can use to format the quotation in her word processing program and print a copy for the customer.

Quick Check

1 What is the purpose of the RemoveItem method and the Clear method of the ListBox and ComboBox objects?

2 What is the difference between a one-dimensional and a two-dimensional array?

3 How does the procedure to open a file for writing differ from the procedure to open a file for reading?

4 What is the Variant data type?

5 What is the purpose of the Write # statement?

Figure 6-24 lists and defines the new terms presented in this tutorial.

Figure 6-24 ◀
New terms

Term	Definition
Array	An array is a variable that contains a list of several items having the same data type. You create an array using the Dim, Public, or Private statements. The number of items in an array is defined by the array's lower and upper bounds.
ASCII-delimited file	An ASCII-delimited file is a text file that contains one or more fields separated by commas. Text fields are enclosed in double quotation marks. The period (.) is used as the decimal point in numbers containing a fractional part.
Element	An element is a specific item in an array.
For loop	A For loop is a statement that works with a counter variable that increments each time the loop is executed. When the counter does not meet some condition, the For loop exits. The loop will increment the counter for you.
Sequential access	Sequential access is the process of reading a text file from beginning to end using the Open, Input #, and Close statements.
Subscript	A subscript is an integer value that is used to reference a specific element in an array.
Two-dimensional array	A two-dimensional array is an array made up of rows and columns. Two-dimensional arrays use two subscripts to reference an element. One subscript defines the row; the other defines the column.
Variant	The Variant data type is a data type that can contain any of the other Visual Basic data types. The type of data contained in a Variant variable can be changed at run time.

Tutorial Assignments

One of Star Plant Supply's customers, Maria Cepada, works for a large software company. She suggested that Rose provide an information display computer in her store so customers could use it to find out about the many varieties of flowers and plants that Star Plant Supply carries. Rose is somewhat hesitant to purchase such a computer, and she asks you to create a sample program that initially will show pictures of three types of roses and supply both background and planting information to the customer. Rose will evaluate the sample program to determine if she wants to provide an information display computer.

Figure 6-25 shows the completed form design for the program. Eventually, this program could be expanded to include hundreds of graphic and text files for Star Plant Supply, which Rose hopes will attract a large number of new customers. The program will use a PictureBox object to display the pictures of the roses, a frame containing option buttons to select the flower types, and a multiline text box to display a description of the flowers.

Figure 6-25 ◀

1. Make sure your Student Disk is in the appropriate disk drive, and then start Visual Basic.
2. Change the Caption property to **Star Plant Supply - Flower Display** and the Name property to **frmStarFlowerDisplay.**
3. Create a frame on the form with the caption Flower Types. See Figure 6-25 for object positions and sizes.

4. Create a control array of three OptionButton objects named **optFlowers** in the frame. Set the caption of the three option buttons to **Red Rose**, **Yellow Rose**, and **White Rose**, respectively.

5. Create a working Exit command button with Alt+X as the hot key.

6. Draw a PictureBox object on the form and set its name to **picFlowers**. Adjust the size of the form as needed to add the objects.

7. Draw a multiline text box with vertical scroll bars to hold the flower information on the form. Set the Name property to **txtInfo**, then clear the Text property.

8. Draw three identifying labels above the three objects you just created, and set the Alignment property of the labels to **2 - Center**. From left to right, set the captions of the labels to **Select a Flower**, **Picture**, and **Flower Information**.

9. Open the general declarations section of the Code window for the form module and create a one-dimensional array of the String data type with three elements named **mstrFlowerInfo**. Create two other String variables named **mstrRoseInfo** and **mstrOutInfo**; these will be used to load the values into the array. Require that all variables be declared explicitly.

10. To load the names of the three different roses into the mstrFlowerInfo array when the form is loaded, write the necessary code in the Form_Load event procedure. Store the filename **A:\Tutorial.06\TAssign\RedR.bmp** into the first element of the array, **A:\Tutorial.06\TAssign\YellowR.bmp** into the second element, and **A:\Tutorial.06\TAssign\WhiteR.bmp** into the third element. The file path names must be in quotation marks.

11. When the form is loaded, the program must load the description of the flowers into the Flower Information text box. This information is stored in the file **Rose.txt** in the **TAssign** folder in the **Tutorial.06** folder on your Student Disk. Add to the end of the Form_Load procedure the statement to open the file for input. Because this is the only file open, use filenumber 1.

12. Now you can read the records into the string mstrOutInfo. You need to append a carriage return character and a new line character to the end of each line so the message box will display the text correctly. Remember you can use the constant **vbCrLf** to accomplish this. Write a Do loop to input filenumber 1 into the variable named mstrRoseInfo. Write another statement to concatenate to the existing contents of the variable mstrOutInfo, a carriage return and line feed and the contents of mstrRoseInfo.

13. The String variable mstrOutInfo now contains the text describing the flowers and planting instructions. You now need to store this text in the Text property of the txtInfo text box. Write this statement after the loop you just created.

14. Write the statement to close filenumber 1.

15. Now you can write the code to load the pictures of the different roses. A picture will be loaded into the picture box when a user clicks one of the option buttons. So, the code should be executed when an option button is clicked. Because the option buttons belong to a control array, the same code will execute when any one of the option buttons is clicked. You need to call the LoadPicture function. The argument should be stored in the array mstrFlowerInfo(*subscript*) where *subscript* is 0, 1, or 2—the same as the index of the control array. You should store the result in picFlowers.Picture.

16. Write the statements to clear the value of the option button when the program starts. This will cause no picture to be loaded until an option button is selected.

17. Save the project as **Star Flower Display** in the **TAssign** folder in the **Tutorial.06** folder on your Student Disk.

18. Run your program. Click any option button to see the corresponding picture of the rose that was copied using the Copy function of the Microsoft Encarta software package and the Paste and Cut functions of Paint. Note that the picture display would be much faster if the .bmp files were stored on the hard disk. Scroll through the Flower Information text box to read the roses text that was loaded from Microsoft Encarta as a text file. Click the Exit command button to exit the program.

19. Print the Form Image and Code, then exit Visual Basic.

Case Problems

1. Valley Computer Supply Valley Computer Supply carries a wide variety of computers and computer accessories. Joe Kent, the business manager, keeps a list of all the different computers and accessories in a sequential file, with each computer listed on a separate line. This file is used for a variety of reports and to answer customer questions about what vendors Valley Computer Supply does business with. Joe would like to use this file for a report, but the list is not sorted alphabetically by product name, as the report requires. You will write a program to sort the list using the Sort property of an invisible list box. Figure 6-26 shows the completed form.

Figure 6-26 ◀

```
Valley Computer Supply - Sort          _ □ ×

lstSort                           ┌──────────┐
                                  │ Start Sort │
                                  └──────────┘

                                  ┌──────────┐
                                  │   Exit    │
                                  └──────────┘
```

1. Start WordPad or any word processing program and examine the file **Computer.txt** in the **Cases** folder in the **Tutorial.06** folder on your Student Disk. This file contains the unsorted list of computer names. Exit WordPad or the word processing program without saving the file.
2. Start Visual Basic.
3. Change the form's caption to **Valley Computer Supply - Sort** and change its name to **frmValleySort.**
4. Draw a command button, with the caption **Start Sort** and the name **cmdStartSort**. Make this the default button for the form. Position and size all objects as shown in Figure 6-26.
5. Create a working Exit command button with Alt+X as the hot key.

6. Draw a list box on the form. Set its name to **lstSort**. Set its properties so the list box will be sorted and invisible at run time.
7. All the processing will occur when the cmdStartSort button is clicked, so you need to write all your code and declare all your variables in its Click event procedure. Open the Code window for the cmdStartSort_Click event and declare three local String variables: **pstrComputerName** will hold the computer name as it is placed into the list box, **pstrInputFileName** will hold the name of the input file, **pstrOutputFileName** will hold the name of the output file. Declare a local Integer variable named **pintCount** that will be used within a For loop that writes to the output file.
8. Using the InputBox function with the prompt: **"Enter Input Filename"**, store the user's response in the variable called **pstrInputFileName**.
9. Using the InputBox function with the prompt: **"Enter Output Filename"**, store the user's response in the variable called **pstrOutputFileName**.
10. Open **pstrInputFileName** for input using the results of the InputBox function. Remember to assign the file a valid filenumber.

11. Create a Do loop to read each computer name and add it to the list box you already created. Because there is one computer name on a line, the Input # statement should store the field in the variable **pstrComputerName**. To store the computer names in the list box, you need another statement that will add an item to the lstSort list box. The text of the item you want to add is in the variable **pstrComputerName**.
12. Open **pstrOutputFileName** for output using the results of the InputBox function.
13. Write a For loop that will loop through all the items in the list box and write the items to the output file. Remember, the first item in a list box is 0. You can use the ListCount property to find out how many items are in the list box. Inside the For loop, create a Write # statement that will write the correct item to the output file. Remember, you can use the List property with the pintCount variable as its argument, which is set by the For loop to indicate the correct item.

14. Close all the files.

15. Change the caption of the Start Sort command button to contain the number of records sorted followed by a space and the string **Records Sorted**. You will need to concatenate the two strings to do this. Remember, the ListCount property of the lstSort object contains the number of items in the list box. This is the number of items sorted.

16. Save the project as **Valley Computer Sort** in the Cases folder in the Tutorial.06 folder on your Student Disk.

17. Run the program. Click the **Start Sort** command button. The program will request an input filename. Type **A:\Tutorial.06\Cases\Computer.txt** in the input box.

18. The program will request an output filename. Type **A:\Tutorial.06\Cases\Sorted Computer.txt** in the second input box. The program will sort the Computer text file and create the Sorted Computer file on your Student Disk. The Start Sort button now should say 11 Records Sorted.

19. Open WordPad or any word processing program and look at the **Sorted Computer.txt** file in the Cases folder in the Tutorial.06 folder on your Student Disk. Note that the names of the computers have been sorted by the invisible list box's Sort property.

20. Print the list, then close the word processing program and return to Visual Basic. Print the Code and Form Image, then exit Visual Basic.

2. Sundown Hospital Sundown Hospital is a small regional hospital that serves as a primary care center. Sundown Hospital admits approximately 20 individuals per day and would like a method of storing and recalling admitted patient information. The program will display previous patient information and accept new patient information. The program also will store the information in a sequential file for later use and be able to call up the information quickly for an admitted patient at any time by storing the sequential file as a two-dimensional array. Occasionally the hospital loses power to the admitting station. The staff would like to be able to start the program and recover all the admitted patient data. Therefore, after each new patient is added, the program will append that information to the sequential file and close the file so it cannot be corrupted. The admitting interface form already has been completed. You now have to add the code that will perform the tasks. Figure 6-27 shows the completed form.

Figure 6-27 ◀

Sundown Hospital - Patient Admitting
Patient Number:
Patient Name:
Date of Birth:
Doctor Name:
Diagnosis:
Date Admitted:

Click to See Patient Data

Print Data

Write Data to File

Exit

1. Make sure your Student Disk is in the appropriate disk drive, then start Visual Basic.

2. Click **Project** then click **Remove Form1** to clear the default Form1. Click **Project** then **Add File**. Load the form **frmSunDN.frm** in the **Cases** folder in the **Tutorial.06** folder on your Student Disk, then change the startup form to this new form.

3. Save the form as **frmSundownHospital** and the project as **Sundown Hospital – Patient Admitting** in the **Cases** folder in the **Tutorial.06** folder on your Student Disk.

4. Open the general declarations section of the Code window for the Form module. Declare a two-dimensional string array of 50 rows and 6 columns named **mstrPatients**. The first element of the array should be (1,1), not (0,0).

5. Open the Code window for the Form_Load event procedure and open the **A:\Tutorial.06\Cases\Patient.txt** file for input using filenumber 1. Write a Do loop to load the information in the file into the two-dimensional array mstrPatients you just created. Use the variable **pintRow** as a counter that will be incremented by one (1) each time through the loop. The Do loop should end when the end of file is reached.

6. Inside the Do loop, write an Input # statement to read the file into the different rows and columns of the array mstrPatients. The file **Patient.txt** has six fields, so there will be six arguments to the Input # statement. The first argument will be **mstrPatients(mpintRow,1)**. Remember, the lower bound of the array is 1,1, not 0,0. Increment the counter before the Loop statement.

7. Write the code to close the text file.

8. Create a general procedure to display the current patient. Use the Value property of the scroll bar hsbPNumber as the array subscript to store the patient information into the corresponding text boxes and labels on the form. The names of the objects correspond to the columns, as follows:

lblPatientNumber	Value of the scroll bar hsbPNumber or Column 1
txtPatientName	Column 2
txtDOB	Column 3
txtDoctorName	Column 4
txtDiagnosis	Column 5
txtDateAdmitted	Time when patient was admitted or Column 6

As the final part of the Form_Load event procedure, call the general procedure you just wrote to display the first patient.

9. Write the code for the Write Data to File command button so when it is clicked it appends the information for the patient shown on the screen to the file **A:\Tutorial.06\Cases\Patient.txt**. *Hint*: Open the file For Append. Write the contents of the six objects to the fields in the file you just opened. Make sure you write them in the same order.

10. Write the code to close the file.

11. Write the code for the scroll bar so when the user changes the value of the scroll bar the current patient information (stored in the two-dimensional array) will be displayed in the text boxes and labels. All you need to do is call the general procedure you already wrote.

12. Program the Exit button.

13. Set the initial focus to **txtPatientName**. Save your form and project.

14. Run the program. The sequential file Patient.txt already includes some sample patient data. Click the scroll bar to advance through the existing patient data to a blank screen. Type in patient data of your choice for five patients. After you type in the information for each patient, click the **Write Data to File** command button. Review the patient data by clicking the scroll bar. Exit the program.

15. Run the program again and observe that by clicking the scroll bar, the data you entered has been appended to the file and loaded into the data array in the program for use by Sundown Hospital's admitting staff.

16. Add a command button to the form with **&Print Data** as the caption. Name the button **cmdPrint**. In the cmdPrint_Click event write a nested For loop using the Print method that will print the two-dimensional patient array to the printer. The external part of the nested For loop first will use an If statement to test for a null string in the first column of the next row of the array.

17. Next, write the external part of the nested For loop that will vary the row of the array from one (1) to the number of records you have in the file (check using the scroll bar if you do not remember how many records you have).

18. Write the internal part of the For loop that will vary the column from one (1) to six (6) and call the Print method of the Printer object to print each element in the array's current row. The Print statement in the nested For Next statement will take the form of **Printer.Print PatientTbl(Row, Column);**. The ";" turns off automatic line feeds.

19. Write a Printer.EndDoc statement after the last Next statement that will send the output to the printer.

20. Run the program. Click the **Print Data** command button and examine your output. There is no line feed after each patient's six fields are printed. Add a line containing the **Printer.Print** statement between the two Next statements, click the command button again, and observe the results.

21. Save the changes. Print the Form Image and Code. Exit Visual Basic.

EXPLORE

3. Super Office Super Office sells small office supplies to the general public. Manny Garcia, customer service manager for Super Office would like a program that will read a sequential data file containing item names and prices. Place the item names in a list box and the prices in a one-dimensional array that can contain up to 10 Single data type items. The program should load a ListBox with the item name (sorted alphabetically) and the matching ItemData property of the ListBox object with an integer subscript that references where in the one-dimensional array the price is stored. Allow the clerk to click a ListBox item, enter the quantity, and calculate the extended price by using the ItemData property as a subscript to retrieve the price from the array. When the Add Purchase button is clicked, copy the name of the selected product from the input list box to the output list box. Copy the quantity ordered to the output list box, and compute the extended price and sales tax. Assume the sales tax rate is 5%. Each time an item is added compute the total. When the Reset button is clicked, clear each of the output list boxes, the total, and input quantity requested. Also make sure that no item is selected. When the Remove Item command button is clicked, check to see that a product in the output list box is selected. If so, delete the product, quantity, price, extended price, and tax from the output list boxes and recompute the order total.

Create a PictureBox object to display a logo using a graphic file of your choice. Use WordPad or any word processing program to create a sequential data file with at least five items and prices, and save the file as **Office.txt** in the **Cases** folder in the **Tutorial.06** folder on your Student Disk. Look at any of the sequential files used in this tutorial to see how records and fields are stored. Run the program and correct any errors. Save the form as **frmSuperOffice** and the project as **Super Office - Prices** in the **Cases** folder in the **Tutorial.06** folder on your Student Disk. Print the Form Image, Form As Text, and Code. Figure 6-28 shows the completed form.

Figure 6-28 ◀

4. Consumers Catalog Sales Consumers Catalog Sales sells specialty items directly to its customers around the world. The company would like to have a program that both displays customer address data (Customer Name, Address 1, Address 2, City, State or Province, Zip Code or Postal Code, and Country) and allows for adding new customer data to the file. The data is stored in a sequential file and is read into a two-dimensional array with 50 rows and 7 columns. The existing customer names should be loaded into a combo box so they can be selected by the user. The ItemData property of the ComboBox object will be used to store the row location of the customer information stored in the array. This is necessary because the combo box will sort the names in the box, and the sorted combo box list will not reflect the sequence of the array information. Your program should have four command buttons. The first should clear the contents of the text boxes and deselect the current item from the combo box. The second command button should add new data to the ASCII-delimited file. Each time a new record is added, it is written to both the array and the sequential file. *Hint:* Use the ListIndex property of the ComboBox object with the ItemData property to directly reference information in the array. Additionally, the program should provide a command button to print out a mailing label for the customer displayed on the screen. The last command button should end the program.

Create the sequential data file with at least five records using addresses of your choice in WordPad or any word processing program. Make sure you have seven fields in each record, separated by the comma-delimiter, and that you press the Enter key after each line. Save the file as **Consumer.txt** in the **Cases** folder in the **Tutorial.06** folder on your Student Disk. Run the program and correct any errors. When finished, save the form as **frmConsumersMailing** and the project as **Consumers Mailing** in the **Cases** folder in the **Tutorial.06** folder on your Student Disk. Print the Form Image, Form As Text, and Code.

Answers to Quick Check Questions

SESSION 1.1

1 Creating a program can be divided into three steps. First you create the interface by drawing the controls on the form. Then you write the necessary Visual Basic statements to accomplish the tasks the program needs to perform. The third and final step is a loop — test the program, correct any errors, and test the program again.

2 The Application Wizard creates a project that is a template for a completed program. That is, it will create the forms, menus, toolbars, and other items for you to perform tasks like opening and closing files. You as the programmer must modify this template to accomplish specific tasks like displaying the graphical files you open. The Application Wizard only can create new programs. It is not possible to use the Application Wizard to modify programs that already have been created.

3 A project contains all the information about the files that make up a Visual Basic program. This information includes the forms used in the program, and other files containing Visual Basic statements. You can change the files used by a project by using the Project window.

4 A form is an object that contains other objects that allow the user to interact with the program. For example, the user can interact with text boxes and see descriptive information in labels on a form. A form has several properties that describe its appearance. These properties include the BackColor and BorderStyle. Just like other objects, a form can respond to events.

5 The Index tab is used to search for information directly using keywords. As you type characters, the subjects matching your characters will display in a window. You can click the desired topic to display help for that item. Using the Contents tab is much like looking through a table of contents.

6 Run the current project. This has the effect of switching Visual Basic from design mode to run mode. End the current project. This has the effect of switching Visual Basic from run mode to design mode. Open an existing project.

SESSION 1.2

1 The Properties window is used to change the properties of the active object while Visual Basic is in design mode. Each object, including forms and controls created from the toolbox, has a fixed set of properties you can set by using the Properties window. Different objects have different properties.

2 The Label control is used to display output from your program. This output is controlled by the Caption property. The property can be set using the Properties window while in design mode or using Visual Basic code while in run mode. A text box allows a user to enter information during run time. It also can be used to display information for the user during run time.

3 You can move an object by clicking the object and holding down the left mouse button while moving the mouse on the screen. An outline of the object will be displayed while it is being moved. To position the object, release the mouse button. To resize an object, click the object. Then, hold down the left mouse button on one of the sizing handles. Move the mouse until the object is of the desired size and release the mouse button. To delete an object, click the object and press the Delete key.

4 The Image control is used to display a picture inside the region of the object. The picture that is displayed is controlled by the Picture property. You can cause the picture to be resized to fill the region of the Image by setting the Stretch property to True.

5 You write all Visual Basic statements in a window called the Code window. It allows you to select the object and procedure for which you want to write statements.

SESSION 2.1

1 The Label control only can display information; it cannot allow a user to enter information into it. While the Label control and the TextBox control have common properties such as font size and font type, only the TextBox control allows the user input during run time.

2 During design time, select a text box to make it the active object, then open the Properties window. Select the Font property to activate the Font dialog box. The Font dialog box allows the programmer to select from a list of available fonts, sizes, and styles for the text box.

3 By using the Windows Clipboard you are able to copy not only the current object, but the properties that you have set for that object. For example, if you create a text box with the font changed to Arial 35 point, then copy that control to the Clipboard and paste it on the form, you will not have to set the font size again because the FontSize property of 35 was copied along with the text box. It is a way to simplify redundant tasks.

4 A command button is used to execute code when the user clicks the button. This event is called the Click event. The user can write statements to perform a specific task in response to a Click event.

5 There is only one control on a form at a time that can be active. This control then is said to have the focus. To change the order in which controls receive focus, use the TabIndex property. Begin with a zero (0) for the first object, a one (1) for the second object, and so forth.

6 The Shape control will allow you to create a shape on a form. This is an easy way to visually group related objects. It makes it easier for the user to understand where objects are and how they relate to one another if they are grouped together. The Line control puts a line on the form. This line can be used to divide the form into logical regions. The top of the form can have input areas while a line will separate the bottom where the output area is.

7 Most visible objects on a form, and the form itself, support different colors. While there are times different colors should be used, remember that strong colors can become distracting. Very bright or unusual colors should be used when you are trying to convey a message such as a warning signal, not when you simply are entering data.

SESSION 2.2

1 The Dim statement is used to declare variables explicitly. Variables have a data type that describes the kind of information the variable can store. If the Dim statement is used inside a procedure, the procedure variable is local and cannot be used by any other procedure in the program. The Private statement is used to declare a variable in the general declarations section of the Form module. Private variables exist while the Form module is activated and can be used by any procedure in the Form module.

2   When a user clicks an object it receives focus. At this time, the GotFocus event occurs for the object. When the user clicks or presses the Tab key to move to another object, the LostFocus event occurs. The Click event occurs when the user clicks an object. This happens after the GotFocus event occurs for an object.

3   Exponentiation (^) is performed first
Multiplication (*) and division (/) are performed next in the order of their appearance in the expression.
Integer division is performed next (\).
Modulo arithmetic is performed next (Mod).
Addition (+) and subtraction (-) are performed in the order of their appearance in the expression.

4   Syntax errors are caused when you incorrectly use Visual Basic statements or write other statements that have no meaning to Visual Basic. The Visual Basic Code window will detect syntax errors for you as you write your program. Run-time errors occur while your program is running and are the result of an error that could not be detected when the code was being written. Run-time errors can be caused by trying to perform arithmetic operations on variables that do not contain numbers or by calling intrinsic functions with incorrect arguments. Logic errors occur when you write Visual Basic statements that are correct, but the statements do not correctly solve the problem.

5   Clicking the Print command on the File menu will activate the Print dialog box. You can print the code in your program using the Code option. If you want to print the different objects created on the form, the properties, and their settings, use the Form As Text option. Finally, the Form As Image option will print an image of the form to the printer.

SESSION 3.1

1   A check box is a control that allows the user to place a check mark in the object.

2   A check box can have three values. It can be checked, unchecked, or dimmed. You can find out the status of a check box by looking at the Value property at run time. If a check box is dimmed, the object neither is checked nor unchecked.

3   The Min and Max properties describe the valid range of values for a scroll bar. The value must be between Min and Max. The LargeChange and SmallChange properties describe how much the value of the scroll bar will be changed. When you click the scroll arrows, the value will be increased or decreased by the value of the SmallChange property. When you click in the region of the scroll bar, the value of the scroll bar will be changed by the value of the LargeChange property. The Value property is an integer that defines the current value of the scroll bar.

4   Boolean values are a Visual Basic data type that only can contain the values of True or False. You cannot store any other value in a Boolean variable.

5
```
If lblTaxes.Visible = True Then
    lblTaxes.Caption = 33
End If

If lblTaxes.Visible <> False Then
    lblTaxes.Caption = 0
End If
```

```
If lblJan.Caption > lblFeb.Caption Then
    lblJan.Caption = Val(lblJan.Caption) + 1
End If

If yesterday < today Then
    End
End If
```

6 The Change event occurs when the contents of an object changes. The Change event applies to scroll bars and text boxes. The Click event occurs when the user clicks the mouse on an object. The Click event is useful with the CommandButton and Image objects.

7 When an event procedure for an object changes the value of another object, a change event will occur for that object. If the changed object changes the value of another object, a Change event will occur for that object.

SESSION 3.2

1 A frame is used to contain other objects, like option buttons, so they will operate as a group. A frame also can be used to visually identify parts of a form.

2 When you create option buttons inside a frame, they are said to be contained by the frame. Thus, only one option button in the frame can be active at any one time. You can create several frames on a form.

3
```
Dim pstrPrompt As String
pstrPrompt = "Do you want to " & vbCrLf & "Continue"
```

4 Both an If statement and Select Case statement are conditional statements. An If statement can test several different conditions, however, while a Select Case statement tests the value of one expression. Then depending on the value of the expression, different statements are executed.

5 A control array allows you to create several objects that have the same name and share the same event procedures. You reference individual elements (objects) in a control array using the Index property in parentheses, followed by the object name.

6 Functions return a value with a specific data type. The value returned by a function usually is assigned to a variable name or a property of an object. Subroutines do not return values. Both functions and subroutines can accept arguments to communicate information to the function or subroutine.

7 Message boxes are useful to confirm a user action like exiting the program. Message boxes are displayed by calling the MsgBox function. A Message Box will be displayed when the MsgBox function is called. The window has a title bar, descriptive text, and buttons the user can click. You can take different actions depending on which button the user clicked.

8 Logical operators define the relationship between different expressions, much like conjunctions define the relationship between the parts of a sentence in English. Logical operators include And, Or, Xor, and Not.

SESSION 4.1

1   Several style guidelines will help you create menus that have a similar look and feel to menus in other Windows 95 programs. A menu item's caption should be short enough to appear on one line, but it can contain multiple words to convey its purpose. When menu items contain multiple words, the first letter of each word should be capitalized and each word should be separated by a space. The first letter of a menu item's caption always should be capitalized. If a menu item displays a dialog box or requires the user to complete other information, the item's name should be followed by an ellipsis (...).

2   A menu title displays a menu item. Menu items in turn execute statements contained in their Click event procedure.

3   A shortcut key is a function key (such as F5) or a key combination (such as Ctrl+A or Ctrl+X) that executes a command. Command buttons and menu items support shortcut keys; you cannot create a shortcut key for a menu title. A hot key is a key you press while holding down the Alt key to open a menu or carry out a command.

4   A separator bar is a horizontal line that visually groups related menu items together to make the interface easier to use. Like all components of a menu, a separator bar must have a unique name or be a member of a control array. You create a separator bar by setting a menu item's Caption property to a hyphen (-).

5   A submenu is a menu item that displays another menu, rather than executing code in an event procedure. You can make a menu item display on a submenu by indenting it another level.

SESSION 4.2

1   The Data control uses the Connect property to determine the type of database to be used. By default, the value of this property is Access. The DatabaseName property is used to identify the actual database that is used. After setting the database name, the RecordSource property is used to specify the individual table that the Data Control will reference. Finally, the RecordsetType property determines the kind of Recordset that will be created by the Data control at run time.

2   When a control is used to display data from a database or save data to a database, it is referred to as a bound control. You can bind controls to a database by setting the DataSource property to the name of an existing Data control and the DataField property to a field in the table identified by the Data control. You always should set these properties after creating and setting the properties for the Data control.

3   A text box that can display multiple lines of text is called a multiline text box. To create a multiline text box you need to set the MultiLine property to True. If the text will not fit in the region of the text box, you should set the ScrollBars property to 1 - Horizontal to display a horizontal scroll bar across the bottom of the text box, or 2 - Vertical to display a vertical scroll bar across the rightmost side of the text box. If you want both horizontal and vertical scroll bars to appear, set the ScrollBars property to 3 - Both.

4   AddNew is a method of the Recordset object. When executed, it will create a new record ready for editing. Update also is a method of the Recordset object. Once a record has been changed, all changes are stored in the copy buffer until the Update method is called. Delete is a method of the Recordset object that will remove the current record from the Recordset. It is important to remember that the record still will be visible until you move to another record, even after it has been deleted. To change an existing record, you need to call the Edit method of the Recordset then make any changes to the record, and then call the Update method.

5   The Enabled property, when set to True, will allow the object to interact with the user at run time. If the Enabled Property is set to False, then the user will not be able to interact with the control. When the Visible property is set to True, the control is visible to the user; if it is set to False the user will not be able to see the control.

SESSION 4.3

1   The FindFirst method of the Recordset object will locate the first record in a Recordset that satisfies some criteria. If a record matching the criteria is located, the current record pointer is positioned to the first record in the Recordset satisfying the criteria. If the Recordset contains more than one record that satisfies the criteria, the FindFirst method locates the first occurrence. The following statement would locate the first occurrence of the name "Smith" in the fldLastName field:

```
datContact.Recordset.FindFirst "fldLastName = " & "'" & _
    "Smith" & "'"
```

2   An input box is a window that is opened when the InputBox function is called. It is used to obtain a text string from the user. An input box has two buttons. If the user clicks the OK button, the text string will be returned from the function. If the user clicks the Cancel button, the text string will be empty.

3   An error handler is used so your program will not end as a result of a run-time error. The On Error statement is used to set up an error handler in a procedure. Usually the statement is followed by a GoTo statement. When an error occurs, the statement after the label will be executed. The Resume Next statement is used inside the error handler to execute the statement following the one that caused the error.

4   Data validation is used when a user enters information that will be used late in the program, because you must be sure the data entered has the appropriate data type, and is within an acceptable range.

5   The Resume Next statement specifies that when a run-time error occurs, the next statement to be executed is the statement following the statement where the error occurred.

6   The Exit Sub statement stops the procedure wherever it is placed. If used in a procedure with an error handler, it will allow the user to exit the procedure, if an error is not detected, without activating the code for an error.

SESSION 5.1

1   The startup object is the first object executed when the program is started. The startup object can be a form of a procedure named Sub Main contained in a standard module.

2   A splash screen is a form that requires no interaction from the user and is displayed at the beginning of an application while the rest of a program is being loaded. It shows information describing the program name and version.

3   When Visual Basic creates the instance of the Form object at run time, the Initialize event occurs first. This event only occurs the first time a form is loaded. The Load event occurs next as Visual Basic begins to make the form the active object. The Activate event occurs for the form after the form is loaded. A startup form is activated automatically after it is loaded. Each time the Show method is called or the form gets focus, the Activate event occurs. After the form is activated, it becomes the active object and the

GotFocus event occurs for the object with the TabIndex property of zero (0). A form can become active by user action, such as clicking the form, or by using the Show or SetFocus methods in code.

4   The Hide method will remove the form from the screen, but it will remain loaded. The Unload statement will remove the form from the screen and the computer's memory. If you hide a form you may still manipulate its controls but you cannot do so if it is unloaded.

5   When a form is displayed as a modal form, the user must close or hide the form before another object in the program can receive focus. The user can interact with other programs, however.

6   The Data Form Wizard is used to generate a form with the Add, Update, and Delete controls already on the form and ready to access a table or query in the database. It reduces time in creating code, and once created, the form can be adjusted to be custom fit to the user's specific needs.

SESSION 5.2

1   The NewPage method advances the paper in the printer to the next page and resets the position of the printer to the upper-left corner of the page. The EndDoc method sends any text remaining in the printer buffer to the printer, and then resets the Page property.

2   The Spc argument is used to print blank spaces counting from where the output begins to print. This will allow the user to line up columns. The Tab argument will insert spaces starting from the left margin. Both are ways to line up data on a report.

3   A Do Until loop executes statements until some condition is True. A Do While loop executes while some condition is True.

4
```
Do While rstPacific.EOF = False
    Debug.Print rstPacific![fldProductID]
    rstPacific.MoveNext
Loop
```

5   An accumulator or a counter most commonly is used in a loop. An accumulator is used to tally values like totals sales while a counter is used to count the number of occurrences of an activity. That is, a counter can be used to count the number of records in a Recordset. An accumulator can be used to tally the sales amount stored in each record, and will store the result in a variable. This then can be used to know how many objects, records, or items there are. This is especially useful when the exact number of objects is not known or can change often.

SESSION 6.1

1   When you are reading and writing information that needs to be kept sorted, or you are working with a large amount of data, you should consider using a database. When the amount of data you are reading is quite small, however, you often can use a text file. While you use the methods of the Recordset object to read, write, and locate records in a Recordset, you use the Visual Basic statements (Open, Close, Input, and Write) to read and write text files. You cannot locate a specific record in a text file without reading all the records before it.

2 The Open statement is used to Open text files. If the For Input clause is used, the file will be opened for reading. If the For Output clause is used, the file will be opened for writing, and any existing contents will be deleted from the file. If the For Append clause is used, data written to the file will be appended to any existing contents. The Input statement is used to read a file. When you are finished reading or writing a file, it should be closed explicitly using the Close statement.

3 The EOF function is used to determine the end of a text file. It returns True when the end of file has been reached and False otherwise.

4 `Dim Prices(1 to 20) As Single`

5 Each of these properties applies to a ListBox object. The List property takes one argument — an Integer index. It will return the text contained in the corresponding list item. The ListCount property is an Integer value that defines how many items are in a list. The ListIndex property is an Integer value that defines the active item in a list. If the value is -1, then no item is selected.

6
```
For pintCount = 20 to 100
    Print pintCount
Next
```

7 The Exit For statement is used to exit a For loop before the counter no longer meets the specified condition. It is useful to exit the loop as a result of some error condition like invalid data.

SESSION 6.2

1 The RemoveItem method takes one argument — the index of the item to remove. When called with a ListBox object, the specified item will be removed. The Clear method is used to Remove all the items from a list box at once. It takes no arguments. Both methods set the ListIndex property to -1 after they are called because there is no longer an active item.

2 A one-dimensional array consists of rows whereas a two-dimensional array is made up of rows and columns. You use one subscript with a one-dimensional array and two subscripts with a two-dimensional array.

3 When you open a file for reading, you use the For Input clause on the Open statement. When you open it for writing, you use the For Output or For Append clause. You use the Input statement to read a file and the Write statement to write a file.

4 The Variant data type can contain data from any of the other Visual Basic data types. In addition to storing the variable, Visual Basic stores the current data type of a variable.

5 The Write # statement is used to create, or append to, an ASCII-delimited file. Files created or appended with the Write # statement can be read with the Input # statement.

Debugging

In this appendix you will:

- Prepare a Visual Basic program for debugging

- Locate and fix run-time errors

- Trace the execution of your program

- Set breakpoints in code

- Set watch expressions in code

- Inspect the value of variables and objects using the Immediate window

- Look at the active procedures in a program

Types of Programming Errors

Programming errors can occur in your program when you are writing code or when you are running the program. A **programming error** is any error in a program that causes it to end abnormally or produce unexpected results. A programming error commonly is called a **bug**.

Programming errors can be categorized into three different types: syntax errors, run-time errors, and logic errors. **Syntax** is the set of rules that specifies the proper way to use the statements that make up a programming language. A **syntax error** occurs when you write a statement that Visual Basic cannot understand. If you misspell a word such as Dim when declaring a variable, Visual Basic will detect a syntax error. Syntax errors are found either when you enter statements in the Code window or when you compile a program. **Compiling** your program is the process of translating the Visual Basic statements you wrote into statements the computer can understand. When you encounter a syntax error, look closely at the Visual Basic Help window that describes the statement or expression, and make sure you have typed it correctly.

A **run-time error** occurs when your program is running and usually results from the following:

- A statement that attempts an invalid operation caused by an unexpected user action. For example, a user may have entered a letter into a text box and you tried to use it in an arithmetic expression without verifying the validity of the data first. These errors can be fixed by writing code to validate data and creating error handlers for procedures.

- Errors in your program that result from trying to divide a number by zero (0) or trying to store too large a number into an Integer variable.

A **logic error** occurs when the program does not perform as intended and produces incorrect results. You generally notice logic errors at run time. For example, if you intend to compute the area of a rectangle, you would multiply the length by the width. If your program added the numbers rather than multiplying them, the program would not generate the right answer and you would have created a logic error.

The distinction between logic and run-time errors is not always clear. You might have coded an expression incorrectly. For example, a logic error would occur if you intended to add two numbers together but wrote statements to multiply them instead. When the program is run, the multiplication could generate a number that is too big for the system to deal with. In this example the logic error, in turn, causes a run-time error.

To find and fix run-time and logic errors in program code, you go through a process called **debugging**. Visual Basic provides built-in tools that help you debug your programs. Using the debugging tools described in this appendix will help you fix run-time and logic errors.

Preparing a Program for Debugging

Visual Basic checks for syntax errors when a program compiles, or translates, the code you write into executable code. How a program is compiled, and how errors are handled, depend on settings in the Options dialog box. These settings are saved to your environment, so you should verify that they are correct before you begin to debug your program.

> *Tip:* You may find it useful to display the Debug toolbar containing the more frequently used debugging commands. To display the Debug toolbar click View, then Toolbars, then Debug.

To set the Compile and Error Trapping settings in the Options dialog box:

1. Start Visual Basic and make sure your Student Disk is in the appropriate disk drive.

2. Click the **Open Project** button 🖼, and then open the project named **RunTime.vbp** located in the **Appendix.A** folder on your Student Disk.

3. Click **Tools** on the menu bar, then click **Options** to open the Options dialog box.

4. Click the **General** tab as shown in Figure A-1.

Figure A-1 ◀
Compile and
Error Trapping
settings

prevents program from entering break mode when inside an error handler

compiles procedures when executed for first time

5. If necessary, change your settings so they are the same as those in Figure A-1.

6. Click the **OK** button to close the Options dialog box and save the settings.

The Compile section of the General tab contains two check boxes:

■ If the **Compile On Demand** check box is checked, Visual Basic will compile the current procedure and analyze it for syntax errors as it is run. For example, a procedure will only be compiled when it is called for the first time. When the Compile On Demand option is selected, Visual Basic will not find all the syntax errors until you execute all the procedures in your program. While you are writing and testing programs, checking this box will cause your programs to start much faster. If the Compile On Demand check box is not checked, the syntax of an entire program is checked before the program begins executing. As you write the programs in this book, you can turn off Compile On Demand and then run your program to check for any syntax errors you might have created in different procedures.

■ If the **Background Compile** check box is checked, a program will be compiled while the computer is idle during run time. Background Compile can improve run-time execution speed the first time procedures are executed. This option is available only when Compile On Demand is checked. Leaving the Background Compile option off will ensure that you get the same results described in this appendix.

As with syntax errors, how Visual Basic handles run-time errors depends on settings in the Options dialog box. The General tab on the Options dialog box contains a section named Error Trapping. The three options in this section control the behavior of Visual Basic when a run-time error occurs:

■ When the **Break on All Errors** option button is selected, any run-time error will cause Visual Basic to enter break mode, open a dialog box allowing you to activate the Code window, and display the line that caused the error.

■ When the **Break in Class Module** option button is selected, errors in class modules that are not handled by an On Error statement cause Visual Basic to enter break mode, allowing you to fix the error. Refer to Visual Basic online Help for more information on the Class modules and the On Error statement.

■ When the **Break on Unhandled Errors** option button is selected, Visual Basic enters break mode when a run-time error occurs that is not handled by an On Error statement. In this appendix you use this setting so your error handlers will execute without generating a run-time error.

When you debug a program, you might have several windows open at a time, which might cause windows to obscure each other. Consider making the Immediate window and the Code window as small as possible so you can see each window on the screen. Also, try to keep windows from obscuring the toolbar. You will use these toolbar buttons often, and they might be hard to find if obscured by another window.

Visual Basic Debugging Tools

The Visual Basic debugging analysis tools consist of commands that allow you to suspend temporarily the execution of your program by entering break mode, and then follow the execution of statements and procedures. You can execute each statement in the program line by line and have your program stop executing when a specific statement is reached or when the value of a variable or object changes.

Whenever you suspend the execution of your program, you do so to try to identify a particular problem. This involves looking at the values of the variables and object properties in your program to see if they contain correct data. You can look at the contents of variables and objects using three windows called Immediate, Watch, and Locals. You use the debugging commands in conjunction with these windows as tools to help you locate and fix run-time and logic errors in your program.

Locating and Fixing Run-time Errors

Run-time errors can occur for many reasons, but unlike syntax errors, they do not occur when a program is being compiled. Rather, these errors occur while a program is running and are caused by performing an operation such as storing data of the incorrect type into a variable or object property, or performing invalid run-time operations on a database object like a Recordset. Because this information is not known until the program is running, the statements actually will not cause an error until they are executed.

When you write programs, you frequently can prevent run-time errors from occurring by carefully validating the correctness of user input before using that input in other parts of your program. Consider the following guidelines when writing code using input from the user.

- Numeric data entered into objects like text boxes should be checked before being used in computations. Use the **IsNumeric** and **IsDate functions** to check for valid numbers and dates, respectively.

- Input that is required, like a first and last name, often must exist before the statements can execute. Compare the variable or object properties with the null string "" to test for existence.

- Perform range checking to prevent overflow and other errors.

When a run-time error cannot be prevented, consider creating an error handler in a procedure that will execute when the error occurs. An **error handler**, or error handling routine, in your code determines whether or not it is reasonable for the program to continue processing. Refer to the OnError statement if you are not familiar with the process of creating an error handler. Inside the error handler, your code first should determine the cause and seriousness of the error. Based on this information, your program must decide what action to take. For example, a calculator program may operate on user input that would cause a number to be divided by zero (0). In this case the error handler should advise the user of the program what happened, the possible causes, and continue to let the user correct the problem.

When a run-time error occurs, one of two dialog boxes can open. One contains an OK button that, when clicked, activates the Code window and highlights the statement that caused the error. You then can edit your code to fix the error. The other dialog box contains two items of information—an error number and a description. Error numbers typically are used by an error handler in your code. A well-designed program should alert the user to the problem, but continue to run, even when the program encounters an error or the user gives the program erroneous input.

For debugging purposes, always read the description of the error carefully to determine the nature of the error. You can choose from four actions in the second type of dialog box:

- Click the **Continue** button to try to run your program from the point where the error occurred. Depending on the nature of the error, this option sometimes is disabled, indicating that you cannot continue execution until the problem is fixed.

- Click the **End** button to end your program. This will cause Visual Basic to return to design mode.

- Click the **Debug** button to attempt to fix the program. The Code window will be activated and the statement causing the error will be highlighted. After fixing the statement or statements that caused the error, click the Start button on the toolbar to continue execution from the statement that caused the error. If the corrections require that you change variable declarations or add new variables or procedures, however, end and restart the program from the beginning.

- Click the **Help** button to get more information about the nature of the problem if you do not understand the meaning of the run-time error.

Run-time errors come from many sources. They can be caused by using incorrectly typed arguments when calling functions, or by trying to store data of the wrong type into a property or variable. The underlying cause of a run-time error might stem from other statements in your program. So, as you analyze the error, look at the preceding statements to help you identify the problem. When you write statements to perform arithmetic operations, you must be careful to use the correct data type for the operation you are trying to perform. If you use an Integer data type, the variable cannot store a number larger than

32767. If you try to store a number larger than that into an Integer, you will get an **overflow error**. Generally, the solution to an overflow error is to use a data type that can store a larger number or to check the user input to make sure it is within a valid range. You also can write an error handler that will advise users of the problem so they can try to correct their input values.

Another error is caused when you try to store a character string in a numeric data type like Integer or Single. This error is called a **type mismatch error**. A type mismatch error can happen when a user enters invalid data into a text box that you intend to use as a number. To prepare for this kind of invalid data entry, you can call the IsNumeric function or the Val function on the user input. If the input is valid then call the function; otherwise you could display a message box.

To find and fix overflow and type mismatch errors:

1. Click the **Start** button ▸ on the toolbar.

2. Enter **.25** for the Interest Rate, **15000** for the Periods, and **1000000** for the Amount, then click the **Numeric Overflow** button. The Microsoft Visual Basic dialog box opens with a run-time error message, as shown in Figure A-2.

Figure A-2 ◀
Microsoft Visual
Basic dialog box
with Run-time
error message

error number ——

error description ——

3. Click the **Debug** button to look at the statement causing the error.

   Note that the line containing the error is the Pmt function. One way to allow the program to continue after it encounters this error is to write an error handler that displays a message box describing the problem to the user. Although the program can continue to run, the results will not be accurate.

4. Read the comments in the event procedure. Follow the instructions in the comments to uncomment the necessary lines that will create an error handler.

5. Click the **End** button on the toolbar to end the program, then repeat Step 2.

   Note that the message box appears and the run-time error is handled by the program rather than causing execution to terminate.

6. Click the **OK** button to return to running the program.

7. Enter the text **abc** in the Interest Rate text box, then click the **Type Mismatch** button. When the run-time error occurs, click the **Debug** button.

   This error is caused by trying to store text into an argument of the Pmt function that can contain only numbers.

8. Read the comments in the command button's Click event procedure and fix the program.

9. End and start the program, then repeat Step 6 to verify that the If statement validates the user input before calling the Pmt function. The error handler detects the type mismatch, prevents any calculations, and nothing changes on the form.

10. End the program.

In some cases the statement that caused the error may be only a symptom of the underlying problem. You found the cause of the previous errors by debugging the statement that caused a run-time error. A program will sometimes produce incorrect results, but will not generate a run-time error, or you may want to look at the statements that led up to the run-time error. For example, if you called the Pmt function and the argument values were incorrect, the function call would generate a run-time error. You would need to first determine the argument that is incorrect, then locate the statement that set the value of the argument.

Tracing Program Execution

Often a program contains logic errors—that is, it produces incorrect results, but does not necessarily generate a run-time error or the actual cause of a run-time error is not apparent. This is when the debugging tools are most useful. When a program is producing incorrect results, but you are not sure why, it often is helpful to step through the statements in a program. There are several commands that allow you to follow the execution of your program.

- The Step Into button allows you to execute one statement at a time. When you use the Step Into button, a single statement is executed then Visual Basic enters break mode. If the statement is a procedure call, the procedure declaration for the procedure that will be executed next is highlighted in the Code window.

- The Step Over button works like the Step Into button. If the statement is a procedure call, however, then all the statements in the procedure are executed, and then Visual Basic will enter break mode just before executing the statement following the procedure call.

- The Step Out button is similar to the Step Over button. When clicked, the Step Out button will execute all the remaining statements in the current procedure.

- You can alter the flow of execution during break mode by clicking a statement in the Code window, then clicking Debug, and then clicking Set Next Statement on the menu bar.

To use the Step Into button to examine statements and procedures:

1. Click the **Start** button ▶ on the toolbar.

2. Click the **Exit** command button on the form. Notice that the word "program" in the message box is misspelled.

3. Click **Yes** in the message box to stop execution and return to design mode.

4. Click **View, Toolbars, Debug** to display the Debug toolbar, if necessary.

5. Because you are not sure where the MsgBox function is called or where the prompt is being set, click the **Step Into** button ▣ on the Debug toolbar to begin execution of your program. The first statement to execute is in the Form_Load event procedure, so the Code window becomes the active window and this procedure is highlighted indicating that the procedure will be executed next. The next time you click the Step Into button the first statement in the procedure will be highlighted.

6. Before executing the procedure, correct the spelling for the word **program**. Add a **?** to the end of the prompt.

7. Click the **Step Into** button ▣ twice to execute the first statement in the procedure.

8. Continue clicking the **Step Into** button ▣ until the form appears. At this time, no procedure is executing. Rather your program is waiting for the user to generate an event.

9. Click the **Exit** command button to generate the cmdExit_Click event. The Code window is activated.

10. Continue to click the **Step Into** button 🔳 until the message box appears.

11. Click the **Yes** button in the message box and continue to click **Step Into** 🔳 until you exit the program and return to break mode.

12. End the program.

In addition to stepping through every statement in every procedure in a program, you can step through parts of a program or pause the program and continue executing statements one at a time. When you are debugging a procedure that calls other procedures, you do not have to trace through the statements in a procedure when you know it works correctly. You can use the Step Over button to execute all the statements in a procedure and suspend execution from the statement following that procedure. Furthermore, you can suspend execution at any time by clicking the Break button at run time.

To suspend the program and step over a general procedure:

1. Click the **Start** button 🔳 on the toolbar. Your program is in run mode and will execute the statements without displaying them in the Code window.

2. Click the **Break** button 🔳 on the Debug toolbar. The Immediate window opens and Visual Basic enters break mode.

3. Click the **Step Into** button 🔳 to begin stepping through each statement in the program.

    At this time, no statement is executing. The form has been loaded and Visual Basic is waiting for an event to occur. When you generate an event, the Code window again will become active and you can continue to click the Step Into button to trace the execution of your program.

4. Activate the form and click the **Exit** command button. The Click event procedure is activated in the Code window.

5. Click 🔳 again. The ExitProgram general procedure is highlighted.

6. Click the **Step Over** button 🔳 on the Debug toolbar. You already have verified that the ExitProgram general procedure is working correctly. Notice the procedure will execute and the message box will appear.

7. Click the **No** button to continue running the program.

8. When the ExitProgram general procedure is finished, Visual Basic will suspend execution and enter break mode from the statement after ExitProgram. You can continue to examine the code statement by statement.

9. Click the **End** button 🔳 on the toolbar.

As you debug your programs, you will find it useful to pause the program and then step through each statement that you suspect is in error. When general procedures appear to be working correctly, you should step over them.

Setting Breakpoints

When you suspect a problem is occurring in a particular procedure or that a particular statement is not correct, you can suspend execution of your program at any executable statement by setting a breakpoint. A **breakpoint** is a program line you specify where the program will stop execution and enter break mode. Setting a breakpoint can be accomplished by locating a statement in the Code window and clicking the Toggle Breakpoint button or pressing the F9 key. The Toggle Breakpoint button is available only when the Code window is active.

When a breakpoint is set on a line, the line will appear in a highlighted color. To clear a breakpoint, click the line in the program where a breakpoint is set and click the Toggle Breakpoint button. When you run the program and the statement containing the breakpoint is reached, Visual Basic will suspend execution of the program and enter break mode just before executing the statement containing the breakpoint. The line will appear highlighted.

Once in break mode, you can use the Immediate window and the Step Into or Step Over buttons to find problems in your code. You also can look at the values of variables and objects in the Immediate window. For example, if you have determined that a function such as Pmt is producing incorrect results, you might want to set a breakpoint just before the function is called, and then look at the values of the arguments to determine which one is not correct.

To set a breakpoint in your program:

1. Be sure the program is in design mode. Activate the Code window for the **ExitProgram** general procedure. Move the cursor to the beginning of the following line:

   ```
   pintReturnValue = MsgBox(mstrPrompt, mintButtons,
       mstrTitle)
   ```

2. Click the **Toggle Breakpoint** button on the Debug toolbar.

   The line appears highlighted in a different color.

3. Click the **Start** button on the toolbar to run the program.

4. Click the **Exit** command button. The program enters break mode just before executing the MsgBox statement where you set the breakpoint. You now can examine the statement.

5. Click **Debug** then **Clear All Breakpoints** to clear the breakpoint you just set.

After you have set a breakpoint, you often will want to look at the values of variables or the properties of objects. You do this using the Immediate window.

Using the Immediate Window

You use the **Immediate** window to look at the values of variables and object properties and to change those values. There are two ways to use the Immediate window:

- You can use the **Debug.Print** method in a program. When this method is called, the values of its arguments are printed in the Immediate window.

- You also can type Print statements directly in the Immediate window to look at values in the program. You can type statements in the Immediate window only while a program is in break mode or design mode. Most statements are valid only in break mode.

You also can execute a procedure simply by typing its name and arguments into the Immediate window.

To look at program values using the Immediate window:

1. Make sure the Immediate window is active and the program is in break mode. You may want to resize or move the Immediate window and the Form window so they do not obscure each other.

2. Type the statements into the Immediate window as shown in Figure A-3.:

Figure A-3 ◀
The Immediate window

enter these statements to display values

enter this statement to call the Sub ExitProgram general procedure

```
Immediate                                          ☒
▶ print mstrPrompt
  Do you really want to exit the program?
▶ print Label1.Visible
  True
▶ ?Label1.Caption
  Infinite Events
▶ ExitProgram
```

Tip: You can use a question mark "?" in place of the Print statement to save typing. In the Immediate window, the ? has the same meaning as print.

In addition to looking at the values of properties and variables, you can use the Immediate window to set properties and the values of variables. When you change the values of variables using the Immediate window, the changes take effect only while the program is running.

To set properties and values from the Immediate window:

1. Be sure Visual Basic is still in break mode.

2. Enter the following statements in the Immediate window. Be sure to press Enter after each statement.

```
Label1.Caption = "New Caption"
MstrPrompt = "New prompt for the MessageBox"
```

3. Click the **Start** button 🔲▶ on the toolbar to run the program.

Notice that the Infinite Events label at the bottom of the form now says "New Caption".

4. Click the **Exit** command button. The message box displays the new prompt.

5. Click the **Yes** button to exit the program.

You now can set breakpoints explicitly at specific statements in your program. You can set as many breakpoints as you want throughout a program. When you close the project or exit Visual Basic, all breakpoints disappear. The Toggle Breakpoint button works like a switch. If you want to remove an existing breakpoint, click the line containing the breakpoint, and then click the Toggle Breakpoint button.

In addition to setting breakpoints, Visual Basic also allows you to stop a program based on the status or value of an object or variable by watching an expression.

Adding Watch Expressions

Watch expressions are similar to breakpoints, but **watch expressions** allow you to suspend execution when a condition is True or when the value of an object or variable changes. Like breakpoints, watch expressions can be created, changed, or deleted while a program is in design mode or break mode. Watch expressions are not preserved after you close a project or exit Visual Basic. The more watch expressions you define, the longer it will take your program to execute, because Visual Basic must check each watch expression for every statement that is executed. When you debug a program, use watch expressions sparingly.

Visual Basic uses the Add Watch dialog box to add a watch expression to the project. Figure A-4 shows the Add Watch dialog box.

Figure A-4 ◀
Add Watch
dialog box

enter expression
to watch

define where
to watch expression

define what to do
when something
happens to
expression

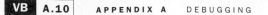

The Add Watch dialog box contains three sections:

■ The **Expression** text box is where you enter the expression you want Visual Basic to evaluate. If you want to watch the value of a variable, enter the variable name. You can copy the expression or variable from the Code window to the Add Watch dialog box using the Copy and Paste commands to avoid typographical errors. The watch expression can be a variable, a property, or procedure call.

■ The **Context** section sets the scope of the expression to watch. This is useful if you have variables of the same name in different procedures. **Module** refers to the form or standard module in your project that should be watched.

■ The **Watch Type** section tells Visual Basic how to respond to the watch expression. If the **Watch Expression** option button is selected, Visual Basic will display the value of the expression in the Watch window but the program will not enter break mode when the expression becomes True or changes. You should consider selecting the Watch Expression option button if you print the value of a variable frequently when you reach a breakpoint. This option also is useful for tracing the value of a variable when you are using the Step Into button to watch the contents of a variable in detail. If the **Break When Value Is True** option button is selected, Visual Basic will enter break mode whenever the expression is True. If the **Break When Value Changes** option button is selected, Visual Basic will enter break mode whenever a statement changes the value of the watch expression.

The watch expressions you create appear in the Watches window. As their values change, the contents of the corresponding variables or expressions also will be shown. Figure A-5 shows the Watches window with the three watch expressions you will create next.

Figure A-5 ◀
The Watches
window

watch expression but
do not suspend
execution

break when
expression is True

break when
expression has
changed

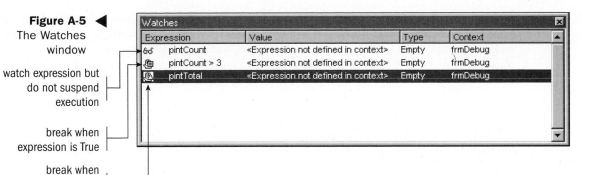

The Watches window contains four columns. The **Expression** column describes the watch expression and its type. The **Value** column displays the current value of the watch expression. Remember that local variables exist only while an event or local procedure is active. When a procedure is not active, the value "Out of context" is displayed. You also will see the Out of context message at design time. The **Type** column identifies the data type of the expression. The **Context** column defines the context of the watch expression—usually, the form name followed by the procedure.

When you create a watch expression, the Add Watch dialog box tries to anticipate the context based on the active procedure in the Code window. If you are watching a variable that is local to a specific procedure on a specific form, activate that procedure before setting the watch expression and Visual Basic will set the context for you.

To set a watch expression:

1. Activate the Code window for the **cmdAddList_Click** event procedure.

2. Click **Debug** on the menu bar, then click **Add Watch**.

3. Type **pintCount** in the Expression box.

4. In the Context section, make sure **frmDebug** is the module and **cmdAddList_Click** is the procedure.

5. In the Watch Type section, make sure the **Watch Expression** option button is selected.

6. Click the **OK** button to add the watch expression.

A more complex expression that causes the program to enter break mode when an expression is True is useful to find why a For loop is not working correctly or an array is exceeding its bounds.

To set a watch expression that will enter break mode when the expression is True:

1. Click **Debug** on the menu bar, then click **Add Watch**.

2. Type **pintCount > 3** in the Expression text box.

3. In the Context section, make sure **frmDebug** is the module and **cmdAddList_Click** is the procedure.

4. In the Watch Type section, click the **Break When Value Is True** option button to select it.

5. Click the **OK** button to add the watch expression.

In some circumstances, you might want to generate a breakpoint when a value changes. For example, if you are working with a payroll program and the gross wages are not being computed correctly, you could write a watch expression to break whenever the value of the variable sngGrossWages changes. This would save time in locating the statement causing the error.

To set a watch expression that will enter break mode when an expression changes:

1. Click **Debug** on the menu bar, then click **Add Watch**.

2. Type **pintTotal** in the Expression text box.

3. Make sure **frmDebug** is the module, and **cmdAddList_Click** is the procedure.

4. In the Watch Type section, click the **Break When Value Changes** option button to select it.

5. Click the **OK** button to add the expression.

Now that you have set the watch expressions, you can look at the values of these expressions as your program runs.

To test the watch expressions:

1. Click the **Start** button ▸ on the toolbar.

2. Click the **Add List** command button. The event procedure begins to execute. Visual Basic enters break mode when one of the watch conditions becomes True. Then the Watches window becomes active and the active watch expression is highlighted. Notice the values of the watch expressions you created.

3. Continue to click ▸ until a run-time error occurs. This error happened because one of the list items contains invalid data. Type the Print statements you used in previous steps in the Immediate window to find the item that contains invalid data. To correct the error you could add the necessary statements to verify the data contains a valid number by using a function like IsNumeric.

4. End the program.

You can edit a watch expression when a program is in design mode or break mode. To edit a watch expression, click an expression in the Watches window, then click Debug, then click Edit watch on the menu bar. This will activate the Edit Watch dialog box, which allows you to change any of the settings in the watch expression.

You can delete a watch expression when a program is in design mode or break mode. To delete a watch expression, click the watch expression in the Watches window, and then press the Delete key.

Tracing the Events in a Program

Another problem with event-driven programs is that improper logic can cause events to trigger each other indefinitely. This problem happens when a statement causes a Change event in one object. That object, in turn, causes a Change event in a second object, and so on. If an object down the line causes a Change event in the first object, this program becomes circular—that is, the events will continue calling themselves indefinitely.

Consider this problem in a simple example with two text boxes. When each text box receives the focus, it sets the focus to the other text box, and focus shifts back and forth between the two text boxes indefinitely. The program seems to lock up, and you cannot click any other object on the form while the text boxes are updating each other. Whenever a program seems to lock up, you should press the Ctrl+Break keys and then check the relationship between the events in your program. Setting breakpoints and watch expressions might be the only way to determine the sequence of events that is happening.

To see events call other events infinitely:

1. Click the **Start** button ▶ on the toolbar.

2. Click the text box containing the text **Text2**. The contents of the text boxes are updated each time a text box receives the focus. You cannot click the End button or the Exit command button to end the program.

3. Press the **Ctrl+Break** keys to stop the program and enter design mode.

4. In the **Text1_GotFocus** and **Text2_GotFocus** events, set a breakpoint in the line that reads **pintTimes = pintTimes + 1**.

5. Click the **Start** button ▶.

6. Click the **Text2** text box. The program breaks and shows you the Code window each time the variable times is updated in the GotFocus events of the text boxes.

7. Continue to click the **Start** button ▶ several times to see the event procedures being called indefinitely.

8. Delete one of the SetFocus statements to end this infinite loop.

9. Click the **End** button ■.

Identifying the exact cause of a problem like this can be difficult. You might need to set breakpoints or use the Step Into button in each event procedure that might be causing the problem, in order to see which events are being called. The best solution to the problem is prevention. Good design and well-written pseudocode and NEADT charts will help avoid such problems.

You should use the Visual Basic debugging tools to diagnose errors interactively in your program. As your programs become larger, be sure to write small pieces of code, and then thoroughly test the code and fix any problems. Then, as you continue developing a program, you can step over those procedures that you know are working.

When you notice that a variable has a value you do not expect it to have, set a watch expression that will cause the program to enter break mode whenever the value of the variable changes. If a procedure seems to be incorrect, set a breakpoint just before the first statement of the procedure executes and then trace each statement in the procedure, if necessary.

Designing Visual Basic Programs

Over the past 30 years, many tools have been developed for planning and documenting both programs and complete applications. One of the first concise development and design tools was NCR's Accurately Defined Systems (ADS) developed in the late 1960s. The more modern common public tools are program flowcharts, data flow diagrams, Gantt charts, Critical Path Method (CPM), Program Evaluation and Review Technique (PERT), structure charts, decision trees, structured walk-throughs, data modeling, query analysis, Computer Aided Software Engineering (CASE), prototyping, and hundreds of proprietary products and methodologies from dozens of vendors. All these tools were, in one way or another, constructed to help the programmer do the following:

■ **Write programs that are correct** — a program that does not accomplish what it is constructed to do functionally is worthless. The program may have some value if it performs most of the things it is required to perform. If a program inadvertently performs unwanted activities like corrupting elements of a database, however, then very serious consequences for both the programmer and the user quickly will appear.

■ **Write programs that are easy to understand** — programs that are impossible for anyone but the original programmer to understand are very dangerous. In any fairly large business, the author of a particular program rarely will be the individual called on to maintain the product. This is true especially in today's Rapid Application Development (RAD) environment where the whole idea is to be able to quickly improve programs and respond quickly to the needs of the users.

■ **Write programs that are easy to change** — programs that can be understood but are impossible or difficult to modify are equally useless. Visual object-oriented languages, especially where the visual interface is concerned, excel at being easy to modify to the demands of the user.

■ **Write programs that are written efficiently** — the language used to construct the program must be powerful enough to remove many of the microtasks that formerly concerned the programmer. Before the advent of object languages, the programmer reinvented the wheel with almost every program. The programmer becomes vastly more productive and efficient by: reusing code; using methods (pre-written named code blocks) that are simple to understand and use, but in reality may be quite complex; and using objects that are provided by the programming language vendor exposed as system objects, or by third parties, that can be configured easily to solve a variety of problems.

■ **Write programs that execute efficiently** — even though the typical program user has tremendous computing power on their desktop, new operating systems (running many programs simultaneously) and the sheer amount of program code that new software requires to provide the vast improvement on capabilities while providing simpler user interfaces, make it imperative that today's programs still must coexist happily and not slow down the user's machine.

(Adapted from Philippakis, A.S., and Leonard J. Kazmier. *Program Design Concepts.* New York: McGraw Hill, 1983.)

RAD Environment Tools Today

Surprisingly, few generalized non-vendor tools have been developed for program construction and documentation for today's Rapid Application Development (RAD) environment. The common tools today consist of pseudocode, an interface drawing, and the Task-Object-Event (TOE) chart.

Pseudocode simply is describing the task(s) that the program should accomplish in standard English. By design, pseudocode should not be written towards any specific programming language, but rather should provide a means for the programmer to think or brainstorm while capturing the essence of the program's requirements.

An interface drawing is a sketch of what the user will see when the program is running. The interface drawing allows the programmer to create a model that describes how the user will interact with the program while suggesting the objects that will be used to perform the tasks and their placement on the screen.

A TOE chart is a simple three-column chart that describes the task the program should perform, the object(s) used to accomplish the task, and the event(s) that will cause the objects and any associated code to execute.

These tools are useful in constructing simple programs and applications. They tend to ignore, however, important sections of the design process like how errors are handled in the program, program construction details like object names, and the flow of various user interface forms during the running of the program or application.

Designing Object-oriented/Event-driven Programs Using NEADT

Like most other program design tools, the Newman-Ekedahl Application Development Tool (NEADT) follows a standard set of steps, known as a methodology, for designing and documenting object-oriented, event-driven programs. This methodology consists of steps in one of five levels that the programmer must accomplish before moving on to the next level. Some steps are required while others are optional depending on the application requirements.

In order to address the shortcomings of existing tools while maintaining simplicity, NEADT was developed as an extension to the TOE chart model tool and to provide a consistent documentation and design format. The NEADT design and documentation tool is being used by the authors in *New Perspectives on Visual Basic 5.0 for Windows—Introductory: An Object-oriented Data-driven Approach* because Visual Basic 5 almost fully supports the pure object model, including classing and inheritance, and integrates advanced system object browsing. NEADT helps solve the serious shortcomings of existing design and documentation tools.

Using the NEADT Tool

First, using any design and documentation tool requires the programmer to completely understand the problem and what data is needed to solve it. In Tutorial 2 the Island Financial company required a calculator program to calculate the future value of an investment at various percentage rates. Using the NEADT methodology, NEADT forms have been created to design and document the program.

The Project IPO Pseudocode Abstract

The conceptual Input-Output-Processing (IPO) model often helps the programmer to visualize the true nature of the problem. After this process has taken place the programmer begins the NEADT methodology by breaking the problem down in English to the macro-task(s) that must be accomplished and any subtasks that also can be broken out of the general problem using the **NEADT Level 1 Project IPO Pseudocode Abstract** form as shown in Figure B-1. Tasks can be listed as simple task groups or modeled into the IPO format.

Figure B-1
NEADT Level 1 Project pseudocode abstract form

Newman-Ekedahl Application Development Tool

NEADT chart   **Level 1 Project IPO pseudocode abstract**

Project Name:	Island Calculator.vbp
Software Version:	Visual Basic 5.0
Developer:	Selena Iniki

General specifications:

Inputs: Initial value of an investment.
            Term of investment in years.
            Annual interest rate.

Processing: Compute two interest rates by adding one percent to the interest rate supplied
            by the user and display the results.

            Compute monthly interest rates based on the annual interest rate.

            Compute the term in months.

            Compute the future value of an investment based on the initial value
            of the investment, term in months, and the monthly interest rate.

            End the program when a stop sign icon is clicked.

            Clear the input and output values, when the Clear Values command button is
            clicked.

Outputs: Three annual interest rates.
            Future value of an investment based on the three interest rates.

Project IPO pseudocode:

Module list:

Legend bas = general bas module, frm = form module, cls = class module

Name	Type	Name	Type
frmIslandCalculator	frm		

Of all the steps in writing a program, or a complete system for that matter, really understanding what you want to accomplish may be the most difficult. This is because most problems are not structured originally or given in the terms that you need to set them up on a computer. Also, some problems may require that you break them down into multiple programs with multiple tasks for each program. For example, Island Financial would like to make a set of tools to help them simplify the work of managing their clients' financial matters. This is an example of a macro (large) problem that must be investigated further and broken down into the actual tasks that Island Financial employees perform for their day-to-day work. These tasks in turn can be ranked from the most to the least time consuming task and the most to the least repetitive task. Then you must determine what tasks can be accomplished by using a computer program(s). Sometimes you will find that simply redoing the tasks on a computer may not be the best way to accomplish the overall goal. In some cases, a complete change in the activity to use the computer to its best advantage may provide the best solution to the actual problem.

The Island Financial problem is rather simple and the NEADT Level 1 Project IPO Pseudocode Abstract form defines the problem in general terms using the IPO model. The task to be performed is to compute the future value of an investment at different interest rates. For clarity, the user interface should change as the user enters information. The data that is required is the initial value of the loan, the term of the loan, and the rate of interest. When the data has been captured the program will calculate the future value of the loan at the interest rate and display the result to the accountant.

The general specifications block in the NEADT Level 1 IPO Pseudocode Abstract form contains the project name (Island Calculator.vbp), the software version (Visual Basic 5.0), and the developer's name (Selena Iniki). Pseudocode specifications for the project are contained in the Project IPO pseudocode block.

User Interface Design

Using the Project IPO pseudocode, the programmer designs the interface screen(s) depicting how the computer's screen(s) should look to the user. This can be accomplished using the **NEADT Level 2 User Interface Design** form shown in Figure B-2, or using the visual programming environment itself to place various objects on the screen that will be used to accomplish the macrotasks and microtasks of the application. This step requires one interface drawing for each form in the project.

Figure B-2 ◀
NEADT Level 2
User Interface
Design form

NEADT chart	Level 2	User interface design

| Project Name: | Island Calculator.vbp |
| Form Name: | frmIslandCalculator.frm |

Screen layout:

Initial value prompt	Input value
Term prompt	Input term
Interest rate prompt	Input interest rate

Interest rate prompt	Future value prompt
Output rate 1	Future Value 1
Output rate 2	Future Value 2
Output rate 3	Future Value 3

| command button Clear Values | command button Compute Future Value | stop sign icon |

The NEADT Level 2 Interface Design form starts with an identification block noting the project name, particular form name, and form shape. The screen layout for the Island Financial calculator contains 11 labels used to display prompts and values, and three text boxes (Input value, Input term, and Input interest rate) for user input. The form also contains a command button to clear the input values, another command button for calculating the future value, and an image of a stop sign icon to end the program. The form therefore contains 17 objects, not counting the form itself. Additional NEADT Level 2 Interface Design forms would be used for each additional form in the project.

Object Event Analysis

The **NEADT Level 3 Object Event Analysis** form shown in Figure B-3, documents each interface form event in the Island Financial calculator project, task description, and whether any error handling is required. It also details task types like calls to other procedures with references and property settings for the Form object. The Event column includes the actual name of the event procedure to be coded. The interface documentation continues with the same details for all interface objects contained by the form including any exposed objects that are used in the application. There also is a notation for other variables and properties that may be affected by revisions to this code.

Figure B-3
NEADT Level 3
Object Event
Analysis form

NEADT chart   Level 3   **Object Event analysis**

| Project Name: | Island Calculator.vbp |
| Form Name: | frmIslandCalculator.frm |

Task analysis and breakdown:

Legend:
Task types: P = Property setting, C = Call procedure, M = Call method

Form Object Name			Design Time Property Settings		
frmIslandCalculator.frm			None		
Event	Task Description		Error Hand.	Task Type	References
None					

Object Name(s) / Type			Design Time Property Settings		
txtInitialValue			Text = ""		
Event	Task Description		Error Hand.	Task Type	References
GotFocus	Set the foreground color to blue. Set the font to bold.			P P	
LostFocus	Set the foreground color to black. Set the font to normal.			P P	

Object Name(s) / Type			Design Time Property Settings		
txtTermYears			Text = ""		
Event	Task Description		Error Hand.	Task Type	References
GotFocus	Set the foreground color to blue. Set the font to bold.			P P	
LostFocus	Set the foreground color to black. Set the font to normal.			P P	

The NEADT Level 3 Object Event Analysis form contains a project identification block. The main block contains the Task analysis and breakdown section. In the Island Financial project there are four tasks that need to be performed on two objects. The first object, txtInitialValue, performs two tasks. When the object gets focus, the appearance of the characters change, and when the object loses focus, the appearance of the characters change again. The second object performs the exact same two tasks. Event code will need to be generated for the LostFocus and GotFocus events for each text box.

Shared Module Analysis

Using the **NEADT Level 4 Shared Module Analysis** form shown in Figure B-4, shared general modules of code are documented as objects and events as they were in Level 3. This form includes the module name, procedure name, and a description of the tasks that should be performed. In addition, there is a reference to the error handler, if any, the task type, and any variables or other objects that are referenced by the task.

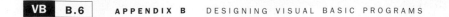

Figure B-4
NEADT Level 4
Shared Module
Analysis form

NEADT chart   **Level 4**   **Shared Module analysis (bas)**

Project Name:	Island Calculator.vbp
Module Name:	Island.bas

Task analysis and breakdown:

Legend:
Task types: P = Property setting, C = Call procedure, M = Call method

General Procedure Tasks

Name	Task Description	Error Hand.	Task Type	References
ValidateInput	Validate each input field.			

Data Validation/Error Response

Finally, the **NEADT Level 5 Data Validation/Error Response** form shown in Figure B-5 details any object or procedure that will require code for data validation or error handling, the actual validation requirements, and the response to be generated due to those errors.

In Tutorial 4 the Atlantic Marketing company required a client tracking system with the capability to search for clients and add, change, and delete information pertaining to those clients using the NEADT methodology. As shown in Figure B-5 input must be validated when two different event procedures occur.

Figure B-5
NEADT Level 5
Data
Validation/
Error Response
form

NEADT chart   **Level 5**   **Data Validation / Error Response**

Project Name:	Atlantic Contact.vbp
Module Name:	frmAtlanticContact.frm
Module Type:	form

Task analysis and breakdown:

Object / Procedure Name	Input Requirements / Validation Rule	Error(s) Description	Error(s) Response
mnuDelete_Click	Current record must exist.	No current record	Exit procedure.
mnuUpdate_Click	Current record must exist.	No current record	Exit procedure.
	Edit method must have been called.	Update without AddNew or Edit	Exit procedure.

When the mnuDelete_Click event procedure happens, there must be a current record to delete. If there is not, the event procedure should exit. When the mnuUpdate_Click event procedure executes, a current record must exist, and the Edit method already must have been called thereby making the record editable. Otherwise, the event procedure should exit.

As you become a more experienced programmer, you will realize that creating programs involves more than simply sitting down at a computer, designing the interface, and writing the code. To ensure a quality product, you should follow these guidelines, modify them to suit your own work style, and spend an adequate amount of time understanding the problem and finding the best solution before writing the actual program. Adequate time spent in planning will save you many hours of work debugging a program or correcting design flaws. Computer programs look and work better with some forethought to the final product and where that product will fit into other programs.

Database Design

In this appendix you will:

- Design a database

- Create a new database

- Create tables with fields

- Define relationships to describe how different fields are associated with each other

- Create queries based on a single table and many tables

The Purpose of a Database

Before the advent of database technology, programs to manage large amounts of data were more complex to create. These programs used traditional file processing systems. In a **traditional file processing system**, each computer application is designed with its own set of data files. Much of the data contained in these files likely existed in files for other applications as well. Furthermore, computer programmers were forced to sort data manually in several different physical files. If you wanted to create reports based on information in multiple files, your program would have to open each of the different files to obtain the necessary information, then examine and process each record (or entry) manually. The same was true if you wanted to change information in multiple files. The following list illustrates some of the disadvantages of traditional file processing:

- **Data redundancy** — in a traditional file processing system, each application has its own files. This causes disk space to be wasted.

- **Inconsistent data** — when the same data is stored in different files, the data can become inconsistent. That is, a person's name may be changed in one application's file but not in another.

- **Limited data sharing** — when each application uses its own files, there is little opportunity to share data between one application and another.

- **Low programmer productivity** — in a traditional file processing system programmers had to write statements to define each record and additional statements to control the input and output of data.

By using a database, each of the problems listed above either is minimized or eliminated. As a result, use of a database to manage an organization's data is increasingly common.

Designing a Database

Before you create a database, you must design its structure. The structure of a database is known as the schema. The **schema** of a database describes each of the tables, the fields in those tables, and the relationships between the information contained in each table. The schema is the structure in the database in which the information will be stored. Just as planning is an important step in creating a program, properly designing the database schema also is an important process.

The first step in defining a database is to identify each data item. A **data item** is the smallest unit of data that has meaning to the user. A data item is analogous to a field. In the database for Atlantic Marketing in Tutorial 4, fields like Last Name and First Name are both data items. Figure C-1 describes each data item stored in the Atlantic Marketing database.

Figure C-1 ◄
Atlantic
Marketing
data items

Client ID	Notes
Last Name	Salesperson Last Name
First Name	Salesperson First Name
Telephone Number	Sales Date
Date Added	Sales Amount
Estimated Sales	Sales Description

After the data items have been defined, they should be grouped together such that data is stored only once. That is, the last name and first name of a client should only exist once and only in a single table. Data items are grouped together into data aggregates. A **data aggregate** is a collection of data items stored and referenced as a unit. A data aggregate is represented in a database as a table. Figure C-2 shows the different tables in the Atlantic Marketing database.

Figure C-2 ◄
Atlantic
Marketing
data items

Contact table	**Sales table**
Client ID	Client ID
Last Name	Salesperson Last Name
First Name	Salesperson First name
Telephone Number	Sales Date
Date Added	Sales Amount
Estimated Sales	Sales Description
Notes	

Each data aggregate or table can have a primary key, if necessary. A **primary key** uniquely identifies each record. In the case of the Atlantic Marketing database, the table named tblContact uses the Client ID field as the primary key. That is, each client ID stored in the table named tblContact uniquely identifies the record. Note that the Last Name field is not a primary key because a last name is not necessarily unique. For example, it is likely that two people could have the last name of Smith. It is possible to use multiple fields as part of the primary key.

After each table is created, associations can be defined. An **association,** or **query,** is a logical, meaningful connection between data items stored in one or more tables. In the database for Atlantic Marketing, sales records can be associated with client records as shown in Figure C-3.

Figure C-3 ◄
Clients/Sales
association

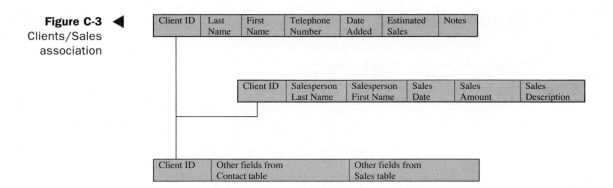

Client ID	Last Name	First Name	Telephone Number	Date Added	Estimated Sales	Notes

Client ID	Salesperson Last Name	Salesperson First Name	Sales Date	Sales Amount	Sales Description

Client ID	Other fields from Contact table	Other fields from Sales table

A common type of association is a **one-to-many association**. That is, for each data item stored in one table, there may be zero (0), one (1), or an arbitrary number of data items in another table. When creating an association, there must be a common data item in each table, like the Client ID field.

Creating a Database

To create a new database for use with the Microsoft Jet database engine, you can use Microsoft Access. While there are other ways to create a database that can be manipulated by the Microsoft Jet database engine, using Access is the simplest. All the information for a database is stored in a single file with the extension .mdb. This file contains all the tables, fields, and other objects related to a database. The example in this appendix uses Access 97. If you are using another version of Access, your screens may differ slightly.

To create a new database:

1. Start **Microsoft Access**. The dialog box shown in Figure C-4 will display asking you whether or not you want to create a new database or open an existing database.

Figure C-4 ◄
Creating a
database

click to create a blank database

2. Click the **Blank Database** option button, then click **OK**.

3. The File New Database dialog box will display asking you the folder and file name of the database.

4. Select the folder named **Appendix.C** on your Student Disk and enter the file name **AM_CMS.mdb**, then click the **Create** button. This will create an empty database.

While you have created an empty database, you have not defined the data items (fields), data aggregates (tables), or the associations (queries) between those data items. The next step in creating the database is to define the tables and the fields in those tables. After the tables are created, the next step is to define how the tables are related to each other, and then define how information in the different tables will be retrieved.

Creating a Table

Each table is made up of fields and each table may have one or more fields. Each field in a table must have a data type just as a variable must have a data type. Figure C-5 lists the data types pertaining to the Microsoft Jet database engine.

Field type	Description
Text	A Text field is a string containing letters, numbers, spaces, and special characters between 1 and 255 characters in length. Names and addresses, for example, are stored in Text fields.
AutoNumber	An AutoNumber field most commonly is used with primary keys. Microsoft Access will assign a new and unique number to each record created. This can be used as the primary key to identify each record uniquely.
Currency	A Currency field is similar to the Number field in that it stores numeric data. A Currency field, however, eliminates the possibility of rounding errors when performing computations on very large or very small floating point numbers.
Date/Time	A Date/Time field can store either dates, times, or both, and is equivalent to the Date data type in Visual Basic. It is possible to perform calculations on Date fields. For example, you can subtract one date from another to find out how many days have elapsed.
Memo	A Memo field is similar to a Text field in that it stores the same type of data, but Memo fields can store up to 64,000 characters.
Number	A Number field stores numbers like integers and floating point numbers. Fields could be totals, amounts, accumulators, age, distance, weights, and size. As in Visual Basic, there are different types of numbers like integers and single.
OLE Object	An OLE Object is used for other applications that can be linked or embedded in a Microsoft Jet database.
Yes/No	A Yes/No field is equivalent to the Visual Basic Boolean data type. It stores True or False values.

Tables store information that does not repeat. For example, the Contact table for Atlantic Marketing contains fields for the Client ID, Last Name, First Name, Telephone Number, Estimated Sales, and Notes. Each of these fields is unique to a single client and is therefore stored in the same table. Just as variable names must adhere to specific requirements, field names also must adhere to certain requirements like the following:

- They can be up to 64 characters long.
- They can have letters, numbers, spaces, and characters except for the following three characters: an exclamation point (!), brackets ([or]), and an apostrophe (').
- They cannot begin with a space.

In addition each field should begin with the "fld" prefix followed by a descriptive name. Each table name should begin with the "tbl" prefix. Each field you create has properties. The term **properties** is used because fields in Access actually are considered objects.

The properties applicable to each field depend on the data type. The following list describes some of the properties supported by fields:

- You can use the **Required** property to specify whether or not a value is required in a field. If this property is set to Yes, you must enter a value in this field when entering a record.

- You can use the **AllowZeroLength** property to specify whether a zero-length string ("") is a valid entry in a field. This property applies only to Text and Memo fields.

- You can use the **Indexed** property to set a single-field index. An index speeds up queries on the indexed fields as well as sorting and grouping operations. For example, if you search for a specific employee name in a Last Name field, you can create an index for this field to improve significantly the performance of the search.

You now are ready to create the tables and the fields stored in those tables for the Atlantic Marketing database.

To create a table:

1. Click the **Tables** tab in the Database window, then click **New**. The New Table dialog box will appear as shown in Figure C-6.

Figure C-6 ◄
Creating a new
table

click Design View

click OK to create
table

2. Select **Design View** from the list box then click **OK**. The table will open in Design view.

3. Enter the name **fldClientID** in the Field Name column, then press the **Tab** key to move to the Data Type column.

4. Select the **Text** data type from the list box. Because the field may store letters and numbers this is the appropriate selection.

5. Click the **Primary Key** button ⛝ on the toolbar to make this field a primary key. Thus, each client ID must be unique. Note the Primary Key icon appears to the left of the field name.

6. Press the **Tab** key twice so the cursor appears in the next row of the Field Name column.

7. Create another field named **fldLastName** with a Data Type of **Text**. Set the Required property to **Yes**. Set the FieldSize property to **25**.

8. Click the Value column of the Required property and set the value to **Yes**. By setting the Required property to Yes, the user will be required to enter data into this field.

9. Set the Field Name to **fldFirstName,** then the Data Type to **Text**. Set the FieldSize property to **25**.

10. Create another field named **fldTelephoneNumber** with a Data Type of **Text**. Set the FieldSize property to **14**. Set the Required property to **No**, then the AllowZeroLength property to **Yes**.

11. Create a field named **fldDateAdded** with a Data Type of **Date/Time**. Set the Required property to **No**.

12. Create a field named **fldEstimatedSales** with a Data Type of **Number**. Set the Required property to **No**, then the FieldSize property to **Single**.

13. Create a field named **fldNotes** with a Data Type of **Memo**. Set the Required property to **No**, then the AllowZeroLength property to **Yes**.

Now that you have created each of the fields, you can proceed to save the table. Until the table is saved, the information about the table's characteristics is not saved on the database.

To save the new table:

1. Click **File** on the menu bar, then click **Save**. The Save As dialog box will display as shown in Figure C-7.

Figure C-7 ◀
Saving a table

enter tblContact in
Table Name text box

click OK to save table

2. Enter the name **tblContact** then click **OK** to save the table. Click the **Close** box ☒ to close the table. Notice the new table name displays on the Tables tab in the Database window.

In addition to the table for the contact information, a table is needed to store the sales information. To do this you must create a second table named tblSales.

To create the second table named tblSales:

1. Click the **Tables** tab in the Database window, then click **New.**

2. Create the following fields:

Field Name	Data Type	Properties
fldClientID	**Text**	Required=**Yes**
fldSalesLastName	**Text**	FieldSize=**25**
fldSalesFirstName	**Text**	FieldSize=**25**
fldSalesDate	**Date/Time**	Required=**Yes**
fldSalesAmount	**Number**	FieldSize=**Single**, Required=**Yes**
fldSalesDescription	**Memo**	Required=**No**

3. Click **File** then **Save** on the menu bar. Enter the name **tblSales** then click **OK**. Close the table.

Creating a Relationship

Microsoft Access is a **relational database**, which means the data stored in multiple tables can be viewed as if it were stored in a single table. Furthermore Access allows you to establish rules defining the relationships between multiple tables. To define these rules, you create a relationship. A **relationship** is used to match data between two tables using a field(s) from each table. For example, in the database for Atlantic Marketing, it does not make sense to create a sales record for a client ID unless there is a corresponding client ID in the Contact table. All relationships in Microsoft Access are created using the Relationships window.

To create a relationship:

1. Click **Tools** then **Relationships** to open the Relationships window.

2. Click the **Show Table** button [icon] on the toolbar if necessary to view the tables in the database. The Show Table dialog box is shown in Figure C-8.

Figure C-8 ◄
Adding tables to
a relationship

select tblContact then
click Add

select tblSales then
click Add

[Show Table dialog box figure]

Show Table

Tables | Queries | Both

tblContact
tblSales

Add
Close

click Close when
complete

3. Click the table named **tblContact,** then click **Add**. When you click Add, the Contact table is added to the Relationships window.

4. Click the table named **tblSales,** then click **Add**. When you click Add, the Sales table is added to the Relationships window.

5. Click **Close** to close the Show Table dialog box.

Once you have added the tables that make up the relationships, you need to create the relationship itself. In this case you need to create a one-to-many relationship between the tblContact and the tblSales tables. That is, for each client ID in tblContact there can be many records with the same client ID in tblSales. A client ID, however, cannot be created in tblSales unless a corresponding client ID exists in tblContact. By creating this relationship, your program does not need to check that these rules are followed. Rather, if you try to add, change, or delete a record that would violate a relationship rule, the Microsoft Jet database engine will generate an error. Your program can trap the error using an error handler. Now that you have defined the two tables in the relationship, you can create the relationship itself.

To create a relationship:

1. Click the field named **fldClientID** in the table named tblContact in the Relationships window.

2. Click and hold down the mouse and drag the cursor to the field named **fldClientID** in the table named tblSales. The Relationships dialog box will display as shown in Figure C-9.

Figure C-9
Defining a
relationship

related by common
field

leftmost side of
relationship is one
side; rightmost is
many side

Notice that the tblContact table is on the one side of the relationship and the
tblSales table is on the many side of the relationship. Also note that the tables
are related using the common field named fldClientID.

When a relationship is being created there is a check box that you can select to enforce
referential integrity. **Referential integrity** is the set of rules that are followed to preserve the
defined relationships between tables as you add, change, or delete records. If you enforce
referential integrity, the Microsoft Jet database engine prohibits you from adding records
to a related table when there is no corresponding record in a primary table. It also prohibits
you from deleting a record in a primary table if there are existing records in a related table.

The primary table in this relationship is tblContact and the related table is tblSales.
You want to be sure that a client ID exists in the primary table for each record in the
related table. Thus, you should enforce referential integrity for this relationship.

When referential integrity is enforced on a relationship, two other check boxes are activated.

- If **Cascade Update Related Fields** is checked, then the corresponding field in the
  related table will be changed automatically when an update is performed on the
  primary table.

- If **Cascade Delete Related Records** is checked, then deleting a record from the primary table will cause all the corresponding records in the related table to be deleted.

The relationship for Atlantic Marketing should enforce referential integrity. Also
updates and deletions should be cascaded.

To enforce referential integrity on a relationship:

1. Click the **Enforce Referential Integrity** check box. Notice that the two check
   boxes below it will be enabled.

2. Click the **Cascade Update Related Fields** and **Cascade Delete Related Records**
   check boxes.

3. Click the **Create** button to finish creating the relationship. The Relationships
   window should look like Figure C-10.

Figure C-10 ◀
Relationships
window

4. Click **File** then **Close** to close the Relationships window. Click **Yes** to save your changes.

The database for Atlantic Marketing has a single relationship. As you create databases with many tables, you most likely will have several relationships.

Creating a Query

Once you have created the relationships, the next step is to define the query. A **query** is a formalized set of instructions to a database either to return a set of records from one or more tables or to perform an action on a set of records. In other words a query is how you ask a question about the data in your database.

The database for Atlantic Marketing needs the following query.

■ One query will view the list of clients so it appears sorted by last name.

In Microsoft Access the most common way to create a query is to use **Query by Example (QBE)**. QBE is a user interface that allows you to select: the tables used in the query; the fields that are to be used; and how the records are to be sorted. You create a query using a procedure similar to the one you used to create a table. First you need to activate the Queries tab in the Database window, and then click New to create a new query. Then you define the characteristics of the query, and finally save it.

To create a new query:

1. Click the **Queries** tab in the Database window, then click **New**. The New Query dialog box will display as shown in Figure C-11.

Figure C-11 ◀
Creating a
query

click Design View ——

click OK to open
QBE window

2. Click **Design View** then click **OK** to open the QBE window.

The next step in creating the query is to define which tables and fields are used in the query. The query you are creating will display each client record and any corresponding sales records so you need to select both tblContact and tblSales.

To add the tables to the query:

1. Click **tblContact** in the Show Table dialog box, then click **Add**.

2. Click **tblSales** in the Show Table dialog box, then click **Add**.

3. Click **Close**. The two tables you added display in the Query1 : Select Query window as shown in Figure C-12.

Figure C-12 ◀
Creating a
query

Now that you have chosen the tables you must select the fields to include in the query. QBE will allow you to select all the fields or just the fields required by the query. The query you will create to join the clients with their corresponding sales data will use all the fields from both tables.

To add the fields to the query:

1. Double-click the field **fldClientID** in the tblContact table. The field will appear in the Query Design grid.

2. Repeat Step 1 for each field in the tblContact table. You may need to use the scroll bars to locate each field.

3. Double-click the field **fldSalesLastName** in the tblSales table.

4. Repeat Step 3 for each field in tblSales. You may need to use the scroll bars to locate each field.

By default, each record in a query will display in a random order. It usually is desirable to sort each record by a field like Last Name. The Sort row in the Query Design grid allows you to control the order of each record. This query for Atlantic Marketing should be sorted by last name. If two records have the same last name then each record with the same last name should be further sorted by first name. You can sort records either in ascending or descending order.

To sort the records in the query:

1. Click the **Sort** row in the fldLastName column in the Query Design grid.

2. Select **Ascending** using the list arrow.

3. Repeat Steps 1 and 2 for the field **fldFirstName**.

The query now is complete. You have selected the fields that make up the query and how the records will be sorted. Now you must save the query.

To save the query:

1. Click **File** then **Save** on the menu bar. The Save As dialog box will display.

2. Enter the name **qryContactSales**, then click **OK**.

This appendix has presented only an introduction to creating a database, its tables, and queries. Most databases you create will have many more tables and relationships but the concepts presented here provide a template for creating more complex databases. It also is possible to create more complex queries that can restrict which records are selected. It also is possible to create queries that create other tables and update data in existing tables.

Microsoft Visual Basic 5.0 Index

If you are using this text as part of our Custom Edition Program, you will find entries in the Index and Task Reference that do not apply to your custom tutorials.

Microsoft Visual Basic 5.0 **Task Reference**

TASK	PAGE #	RECOMMENDED METHOD	NOTES
Accumulators, using	VB 5.33	Declare a variable to be used as an accumulator and set the initial value to 0. Add to the accumulator each time through a Do loop or For loop.	
Arrays, creating	VB 6.13	Use the Dim, Private, or Public statements followed by the array name. Enclose the subscript(s) in parentheses. Finally use the As clause followed by the data type.	**[Dim | Public | Private]** *array-name(lower-bound* **To** *upper-bound)* **As** *datatype*
Arrays, referencing	VB 6.13	Use the array name followed by an integer subscript enclosed in parentheses.	Use 2 subscripts with a 2-dimensional array.
CheckBox control, creating	VB 3.03	Set the Caption property to display a prompt for the object. Use the Value property at run time to determine if the box is checked or not.	See Reference Window, "Adding a CheckBox object to a Form."
Code window, inserting a general procedure	VB 3.30	Verify that the Code window is active for the desired module. Click Tools then click Add Procedure from the menu bar to activate the dialog box. Specify the procedure name. If the procedure returns a value, select the type Function, otherwise select Sub. If the procedure will be used by multiple modules, set the Scope to Public, otherwise make the procedure Private.	When using multiple form or standard modules, be sure the Code window is set to the correct module.
Code window, setting the active procedure	VB 1.38	Click the desired module in the Project Explorer then click the View Code button ▣. Select the desired object then the desired event or general procedure from the object and procedure list boxes at the top of the Code window.	
Code, Printing	VB 2.44	Click File then click Print. Click Code. Use the Range section of the dialog box to print the current module or the Project.	
ComboBox control, creating and programming	VB 6.3	Set the Style property to control the appearance of the object. Set the list property at design time, or call the AddItem method at run time to fill the list with the desired items.	*Object.***AddItem** *"Text"*
CommandButton control, creating and programming	VB 2.12	Set the Caption property to display text in the button. Write statements for the Click event procedure that are executed when the button is clicked at run time.	See Reference Window "Creating a Command Button object."
Comments, creating	VB 2.22	Begin a comment with the apostrophe character ('). All characters on a line after the apostrophe are ignored by Visual Basic.	
Constants, intrinsic	VB 3.17	Use intrinsic constants to improve program readability. Use Help and the Object Browser to find out the constant names that pertain to specific intrinsic functions and object properties.	

Microsoft Visual Basic 5.0 **Task Reference**

TASK	PAGE #	RECOMMENDED METHOD	NOTES
Constants, user-defined	VB 3.21	Create user-defined constants to store information that will not change at run time.	**[Public | Private] Const** *constantname* **[As** *type*] = *expression*
Controls, binding to a Data control	VB 4.18	Set the DataSource property to an existing Data control, then set the DataField property to a field in the table.	Be sure to create the Data control and set its properties before binding other controls like text boxes.
Controls, deleting	VB 1.35	Select the object(s) and press the delete key.	You can use the Edit Undo menu command to undo accidental deletions.
Controls, moving	VB 1.33	Select the object(s) to move. With the cursor inside one of the selected objects, drag the objects to their new position.	
Controls, resizing	VB 1.34	Activate the object to move. Drag one of the sizing handles to resize.	
Controls, selecting a group of	VB 3.14	Hold down the Shift key and click on the controls to select them, or use the mouse and draw a rectangle around the objects you want to select.	Selected controls appear with grayed handles.
Control array, creating	VB 3.11	Activate a control instance. Copy and Paste the object. Respond Yes to the Create a control array dialog. Position the object on the form. Use the Index argument for the event procedure to reference the specific object in a control array.	See Reference Window "Creating a Control Array of Objects."
Counter, using	VB 5.33	Declare a variable to be used as a counter and set the initial value to 0. Add 1 to the counter each time through a Do loop. A For loop will increment a counter automatically.	
Data control, creating and programming	VB 4.13	Set the DatabaseName property to database file, then set the RecordSource property to the name of the Table or Query you want to use. The database and table must already exist.	See Reference Window "Using a Data Control to Connect to an Existing Database."
Data types, choosing	VB 2.30	Create an Integer or Long variable for numbers without a decimal point. Use a Single variable for numbers with a decimal point. Use the Currency data type when performing mathematical operations on data representing dollars and cents. Use Double only for very large or very small numbers. Character strings should have the String data type.	
Debugging, creating watch expressions	VB A.9	Click Debug then click Add Watch to open the Add Watch dialog box. Enter the expression and the context. Depending upon the action you want to take when something happens to the expression, set the Watch Type.	Use watch expressions sparingly in large or long running programs. They can significantly slow down your program.

Microsoft Visual Basic 5.0 **Task Reference**

TASK	PAGE #	RECOMMENDED METHOD	NOTES
Debugging, examining each statement	VB A.6	Click the Step Into button ⬚. The Code window will display each statement with a different color just before it is executed.	
Debugging, looking at variables in break mode	VB A.9	Activate the Immediate window. Type a Print statement followed by the variable or object property you want to look at. You can also move the cursor over a variable or property to display a ToolTip containing the value of a variable or property.	Set Watch expressions for variables you look at frequently.
Debugging, setting breakpoints	VB A.8	Activate the Code window and locate the statement where you want to set a breakpoint. Click the Toggle Breakpoint button ⬚, or click in the left margin of the Code window. The line will appear in a different color.	To remove the breakpoint, click the cursor on the line in the Code window and click the Toggle Breakpoint button ⬚ again.
Debugging, stepping over procedures	VB A.7	Click the Step Over button ⬚. If the statement is a procedure call, the entire procedure and any procedures it calls will execute, then Visual Basic will return to break mode.	Visual Basic will enter break mode if it reaches a breakpoint or watchpoint in the code.

Decision making, using Case a Select statement	VB 3.26	Use Select Case statements with control arrays to determine which object is active and execute the correct statements. When a Select Case statement is used, the *testexpression* is evaluated only once.	**Select Case** *test-expression*
			 Case *expressionlist1*
			   block1-statements
			 Case *expressionlist2*
			   block2-statements
			 Case *expressionlist3*
			   block3-statements
			 [**Case Else**
			   [*else-block-statements*]]
			End Select

Decision making, using an If statement	VB 3.15	Write an If statement to execute one set of statements when one set of circumstances is true, and other statements when another set of circumstances is True. Use the ElseIf statement when the decision has three or more options.	**If** *condition1* **Then**
			   statement-block1
			ElseIf *condition2* **Then**
			   statement-block2
			ElseIf *condition-n* **Then**
			   statement-block-n
			[**Else**
			   [*statements*]]
			End If

Error Handler, creating an	VB 4.37	Prevent run-time errors from causing your program to abort by creating error handlers in an event or general procedure. You can define one error handler per procedure.	**On Error GoTo ErrorHandler**
			   statements
			Exit Sub
			ErrorHandler:
			   statements
			   [**Resume Next**]
			End Sub

Microsoft Visual Basic 5.0 **Task Reference**

TASK	PAGE #	RECOMMENDED METHOD	NOTES
Errors, locating run-time	VB A.3	Click OK or Debug in the RunTime dialog box when displayed. Pay careful attention to the description of the error. Enter Print statements in the Debug window to look at the object and variables involved and correct the statements as necessary. Click the Start button ▶ to continue or end and run the program again.	If necessary, set watch expressions and search through program statements to locate the cause of the error.
Form, activating	VB 5.11	Call the Show method of the form object to display a form and give it focus. Use the vbModal constant to create a modal from.	*Form*.**Show [vbModal]** No other form in the application can receive focus until a modal form is hidden or unloaded.
Form, adding	VB 5.2	Click Project then Add Form to insert a new or existing form into the project. Set the Name and Caption properties as needed.	
Form, repainting	VB 5.10	Use the Refresh method on a form or control to force the object to be redrawn.	*object*.**Refresh**
Form, unloading	VB 5.11	Use the Unload statement followed by the object to unload. Any properties set at run time for the object are lost when the object is reloaded.	**Unload** *formname*
Format function, using	VB 2.37	Use the Fixed format to display data with two decimal places. Use the Currency format to display with a leading dollar sign.	**Format**(expression[, *format*])
Form image, printing	VB 3.39	Call the PrintForm method on a form object.	*form*.**PrintForm**
Frame control, creating	VB 3.9	Set the Caption property to display a prompt in the Frame. Draw option buttons inside the Frame so that they will work as an option group.	See Reference Window "Adding a Frame object to a Form."
HScrollBar control, creating	VB 3.5	Set the Max, Min, LargeChange, and SmallChange properties to define how the object will behave at run time. Use the Change event to check the Value property at run time.	See Reference Window "Adding a Scroll Bar Control to a Form."
Image control, using	VBT 1.37	Set the Stretch property to True to size the picture to the size of the object. Set the Picture property to the file containing the picture. The image can respond to a Click event.	See Reference Window "Adding an Image Control to a Form."
InputBox function, using	VB 4.31	Set the prompt to display a prompt in the box, and set the title to display information in the title bar. Set the default to define which is the default button. If the user presses the Cancel button on the input box, then a null string is returned.	**InputBox**(*prompt*[,*title*] [,*default*])
Label control, creating	VB 1.31	Set the Caption property to display text in the label. Set other properties to justify and change the appearance of the text.	See Reference Window "Adding a Label Control to a Form."

Microsoft Visual Basic 5.0 **Task Reference**

TASK	PAGE #	RECOMMENDED METHOD	NOTES
Line control, creating	VB 2.19	Set the BorderWidth property to change the thickness of the line or the ForeColor property to change the color.	See Reference Window "Creating a Line Object."
ListBox, clearing the contents of	VB 6.24	Use the Clear method on a ListBox object to remove all the items in the object.	The ListIndex property is set to -1 after this method is called since there is no active item.
ListBox control, filling with data	VB 6.11	Set the List property at design time, or call the AddItem method at run time, to fill the list with the items you want.	
ListBox control, referencing items	VB 6.15	Use the List property with an index as an argument to reference the contents of an item in the list. Use the ListCount property to determine the number of items in a list, and the ListIndex property to identify the active item.	The ListIndex property begins at 0 for the first item in the list. If there is no active item this property is set to -1.
ListBox, removing a single item from	VB 6.26	Use the RemoveItem method on a ListBox object to remove an item. The method takes one argument—an index representing the item to remove.	*object*.**RemoveItem** *index*
Looping, fixed number of times	VB 6.19	The *counter* will be initialized to *start*. If it is less than or equal to *end*, the statements in the loop will execute, otherwise, the statement after Next will be executed. Each time through the loop, *counter* is incremented by *increment*.	**For** *counter = start* **To** *end* [**Step** *increment*] [*statement-block*] [**Exit For**] [*statement-block*] **Next** [*counter*]
Looping, until a condition is True	VB 5.26	Create a Do While loop to execute statements while a condition is False or a Do Until loop until a condition is True.	**Do** [[**While** | **Until**] *condition*] *statements* **Loop**
Menu item, creating a shortcut key for	VB 4.8	For a menu item, select the desired shortcut key from the Menu Editor.	You cannot define a shortcut key for a menu title.
Menu, creating	VB 4.5	Open the Menu Editor for a form. Set the Name and Caption properties. The Caption is displayed on the menu. The Name is used to reference the menu item event procedure. Indent the menu to the desired level.	See Reference Window "Creating a Menu System."
Menu, creating a hot key for	VB 4.4	Place an & character before the character to be used as a hot key.	Be careful not to use the same hot key on a menu or menu title.

Microsoft Visual Basic 5.0 **Task Reference**

TASK	PAGE #	RECOMMENDED METHOD	NOTES
MsgBox function, using	VB 3.42	Set the prompt to display a prompt in the box, the title to display information in the title bar, and the buttons to specify the number and caption of the buttons in the message box. MsgBox returns a value indicating which button was clicked. This value can be represented by intrinsic constants.	**MsgBox**(*prompt* [,*buttons*] [, *title*])
Object, defining startup	VB 5.7	Click Project then click Properties. Click on the General tab and select the desired startup object from the list box.	
Object properties, printing	VB 2.44	Click File then click Print. Click Form As Text. The nondefault properties of an object are printed.	
OptionButton control, creating	VB 3.10	Set the Caption property to display a prompt in the option button. Draw buttons inside a Frame so that they will work as an option group.	See Reference Window "Adding an Option Button Control to a Frame."
Program, entering break mode	VB 1.21	Click the Break button ⏸ on the toolbar.	Program will be in break mode. You can type statements into the Immediate window.
Program, ending	VB 1.21	Click the End button ■.	The program will be in design mode after clicking the button.
Program, starting	VB 1.21	Click the Start button ▶.	Program will be in run mode after the button is clicked.
Project, opening	VB 2.5	Click the Open Project button 📂 and select the name of the project from the dialog box.	Project filenames have the extension .vbp. See Reference Window "Opening an Existing Project."
Project, saving	VB 1.17	Click the Save project button 💾 on the toolbar. If you have not saved the project before, the Save File As dialog will prompt you for the form(s) names and the Save Project dialog will prompt you for the project name.	The project file contains the name of the form and other modules in your program.
Properties window, opening	VB 1.21	Click the Properties button 🖼.	
Properties, selecting the active object	VB 1.26	Click on the object to activate it. Click the right mouse button and then click Properties.	

Microsoft Visual Basic 5.0 **Task Reference**

TASK	PAGE #	RECOMMENDED METHOD	NOTES
Recordset, adding records	VB 4.26	Call the AddNew method on an existing Recordset object at run time, change the contents of each field, then call the Update method.	*object*.**AddNew** You cannot call the AddNew method on a query joining multiple tables.
Recordset, deleting records from	VB 4.29	Call the Delete method on an existing Recordset object at run time. After deleting, call the MoveNext method of the Recordset so that the user will not see the record on the screen.	*object*.**Delete** You cannot call the Delete method on a query joining multiple tables.
Recordset, finding records in	VB 4.31	Call the FindFirst method on an existing Recordset object using the necessary criteria to find the first record matching the criteria. Call the FindNext method to locate subsequent matches. Use the NoMatch property to determine if a record was found.	*object*.**FindFirst** *criteria* *object*.**FindNext** *criteria* *object*.**NoMatch**
Recordset, referencing fields in	VB 5.29	Use the name of an existing Recordset object followed by an ! character followed by the field name. If the field contains spaces, put the field name in brackets ([ ]).	*Recordset-name*! *fieldname*
Recordset, updating records	VB 4.27	Call the Update method on an existing recordset, after calling the AddNew or Edit methods, to save the contents of the edit buffer to the database table.	*object*.**Update** You cannot call the Update method on a query joining multiple tables.
Reports, printing	VB 5.23	Use the Printer object to send information to the printer. The Print method will write output, the EndDoc method will send any output in the print buffer to the printer. Use the Tab and Spc arguments of the Print method to format the report. Use the NewPage method to advance to the next page. Use the Page property to determine the current page.	**Printer.Page** **Printer.Print** **Printer.Newpage** **Printer.EndDoc**
Shape control, creating	VB 2.17	Set the BorderWidth property to change the thickness of the line around the shape. Set the BackColor and BackStyle properties to control the background of the Shape. Set the FillStyle and FillColor properties to control the foreground of the Shape.	See Reference Window "Adding a Shape object to a Form."
Standard module, adding	VB 5.4	Click Project then Add Module on the menu bar. The Code window will be opened and set to the new module.	
String, right justifying a fixed length	VB 5.30	Use the Rset statement to right-justify *string* and store the information in the fixed length string *stringvar*.	**Rset** *stringvar* = *string*
Tab order, setting	VB 2.16	Change the TabIndex property of objects that receive focus. The first object to receive focus has a TabIndex of 0, and the second a TabIndex of 1.	

Microsoft Visual Basic 5.0 **Task Reference**

TASK	PAGE #	RECOMMENDED METHOD	NOTES
Text file, closing	VB 6.9	Use the Close statement followed by the filenumber(s) to close. Filenumbers should be separated by commas. If you do not specify a filenumber, all open files will be closed.	**Close** [*filenumberlist*]
Text file, opening	VB 6.7	Use the Open statement followed by the name of the file. Add the For Input, For Output or For Append clause depending upon whether you are reading or writing the file. Add an As clause followed by an unassigned file number.	**Open** *pathname* **For** [**Input** | **Output** | **Append**] **As #**_filenumber_ See Reference Window "Opening a Text File."
Text file, reading	VB 6.8	Use the Input statement followed by the filenumber of a file opened with the Open statement. Append variable names separated by commas that correspond to the fields in the input file.	**Input** #*filenumber*, *variablelist* See Reference Window "Reading a Text File."
Text file, writing	VB 6.35	Use the Write statement followed by the filenumber of a file opened with the Open statement. Append variable names separated by commas as necessary.	**Write** #*filenumber*, *variablelist* See Reference Window, "Writing a Text File."
TextBox control, creating	VB 2.10	Set the Text property to display text in the TextBox. Set other properties to justify and change the appearance of the text.	See Reference Window, "Creating a TextBox Object."
TextBox control, specifying multiple lines in	VB 4.21	Set the MultiLine property to True. Set the MaxLength property to maximum number of characters that will be stored in the object. Set the ScrollBars property to display vertical and/or horizontal scroll bars in the object.	The MultiLine property must be set to True to display scroll bars.
Validating input	VB 4.34	Use the classification functions IsDate and IsNumeric to verify input is correct. When impossible to classify, write an error handler to prevent run-time errors.	**IsDate**(*string*) **IsNumeric**(*string*)
Variables, declaring module level	VB 2.31	In the general declarations section, declare a variable using the Private statement. Variables will be visible anywhere in the form or standard module in which they are declared.	**Private** [*Varname* [**As** *Type*]]
Variables, declaring local	VB 2.32	Write a Dim statement inside of a general or event procedure and specify the data or object type. Local variables are declared inside a procedure. Module level variables are declared in the general declarations section of a module.	See Figure 2-26 for the valid data types. **Dim** [*Varname* [**As** *Type*]]
VScrollBar control, using	VB 3.5	Set the Max, Min, LargeChange, and SmallChange properties to define how the object will behave at run time. Use the Change event to check the Value property at run time.	See Reference Window, "Adding a ScrollBar Control to a Form."

What's On the Student Developer's Kit CD-ROM

Discover more about Visual Basic's capabilities with the New Perspectives Student Developer's Kit CD-ROM. Part of Visual Basic's tremendous success as a programming language can be attributed to the many controls supplied by third-party vendors that can be used in Visual Basic programs. There are hundreds of these additional controls that will perform tasks such as sending faxes, printing bar codes, and performing statistical analysis.

The Student Developer's Kit gives you the opportunity to explore several of these third-party controls from a variety of vendors. Look in the Controls folder on the CD-ROM for folders containing controls from the following vendors.

Vendor	Folder Name	Control Description
AddSoft	AddSoft	Gantt chart and project scheduler
BeCubed Software	BeCubed	OLE tools
Dart Communications	Dart	Internet toolkit
Evergreen Software Tools, Inc.	Visible	Database support tools
Great Lakes Business Solutions	glbs	Installation and software patch software
Larcom and Young	Lyoung	Resize control that will resize forms to fit any monitor
Pegasus Imaging	Pegasus	Graphical and imaging controls
ProtoView Development Corp.	ProtoView	Enhanced bound data controls and development tools
Progress Software	Crescent	Internet and communications controls
Sheridan	Sheridan	Data widgets, calendar widgets, and various enhanced 3D controls

Developer's Reference
Also on the CD-ROM is a complete reference to the standard Visual Basic naming conventions for objects and controls used in this book. This reference chart is in the Naming Conventions folder on the CD-ROM. Templates for the NEADT charts used for design documentation are included in the NEADT folder. All of these files can be viewed and printed from WordPad.

Student Files
All of the student files needed to complete the tutorials and exercises in this book are in the Student files folder on the CD-ROM.

New Perspectives Course Lab
The Visual Programming Course Lab is an interactive tutorial designed to get new programmers started with visual programming. This Course Lab is required for the Lab Assignment at the end of Tutorial 1. Complete installation instructions are included in the Course Lab folder on the CD-ROM.

How to Use the CD-ROM
Refer to the Readme file on the CD-ROM for a complete listing of the contents of each folder on the CD-ROM. Each third-party control, and the Visual Programming Course Lab, has its own Readme file with installation instructions. You can view these Readme files using WordPad.

To use the Student Files on the CD-ROM with the tutorials in this book, refer to "Read This Before You Begin" preceding Tutorial 1.